FORD IDEALS

Being a Selection from
''Mr. Ford's Page''
in
THE DEARBORN INDEPENDENT

Published by
The Dearborn Publishing Company
Dearborn, Michigan
1922

Preface

FROM the first number of The Dearborn Independent under the presidency of Henry Ford, there has been presented weekly a department entitled "Mr. Ford's Page" in which it is sought to offer the ideas of Mr. Ford upon various questions.

This page has enjoyed a very wide reading both at home and abroad and has been frequently reproduced in many languages and in many parts of the world. Its soundness and substantiality, its dependence upon the force of ideas rather than exuberance of statement, no doubt account in large measure for the number of friends it has made.

The present selection for preservation in a volume has been occasioned by the demand of readers of The Dearborn Independent not only for back copies of certain numbers of "Mr. Ford's Page," but also the very wide request for the "page" in book form. This is the sole reason for the present volume's existence. The selection has been made upon the principle of popularity as expressed by our readers, and also upon the principle of diversity, that the reader may have a variety of subjects to consider. A glance at the table of contents will indicate the wide range which the discussions cover.

One characteristic of the page will be immediately apparent to the reader, namely, that independence of thought has not brought with it fantastic angles or impossible counsels. It is not independence that makes for unsoundness; a lack of independence is the fruitful cause of unsoundness because it seeks to square life with what is wrong to begin with. Independence is always giving life a chance to get upon a right basis. It is a constant renewal, a constant liberation from the human tendency to warpedness. Common sense is the most dynamic and independent force on the planet.

The question has often been asked what part Mr. Ford personally takes in the preparation of "Mr.

Ford's Page." Every essential part. He supplies the ideas. Very often he supplies the words in which his ideas are set forth. He does not manipulate the typewriter nor does he occupy himself with the detail of seeing the copy through the press, but the entire inspiration, the point of view, the resistless analysis, the ripeness of judgment, are his. Without him there would be no "Mr. Ford's Page."

This volume is sent out in the confidence that it represents a fair selection of the material that has appeared up to this time.

February, 1922.

Contents

Opposite Views—And
Both Right!

MOST of the things which people say they see, are actually seen. There is no imagination about it. The pessimist who sees things going to pieces, is not deluded; he is correctly reporting what he actually sees. The optimist who sees things soaring up to the height of perfection is an equally good reporter—he is not fooling us or himself—he sees what he says he sees.

But the trouble is, too many people are doing all their seeing within too narrow limits, and while their reports of what they see are true, they are not comprehensive. There is nothing more likely to be misleading than a field of vision so narrow as to leave out part of the points. It is like seeing the elephant so limitedly as to report only his tail or tusks. The animal appears quite differently in a comprehensive view.

Now, all this has an important application to the state of mind in which many people find themselves today. There are perhaps more minds focused on economic problems than ever before, more people thinking, or perhaps it is more truthful to say they are wondering, about the conditions which have befallen human affairs.

It is probably true that though we are all looking and wondering, we do not see very much as yet; but it is still a mighty fact that the minds of the people are focused on their affairs. Formerly we left it all to the government or destiny; but now the governments have failed us, and destiny is not a thing to take without co-operation. And there is a million-fold more chance of seeing when we are looking than when we are not. That is the attitude of people today; they are looking, and presently they will see.

Some people see certain things going to pieces.

They see correctly. Certain established customs, methods, processes, institutions, traditions we have been accustomed to lean upon, are undoubtedly going to pieces, and they are going to pieces irrecoverably too.

It is that last element—the irrecoverability—that strikes fear to many people. They thought that "normalcy" meant the recovery of the old things, the reestablishment of the old way, the restoration of the old habitual leaning-posts. Most people thought of "normalcy" in that way—as yesterday come back. But yesterday is not coming back.

The old world is dead, dead, dead. It is beyond recovery. God himself will not restore it, and Satan cannot.

That is the a b c of the new alphabet, namely, the old world is dead. Not dying, but dead. The things you see going to pieces are its funeral, its decay.

If people would only learn this a b c, it would save them from a great deal of confusion.

But the point is this: those who say that everything they see is going to pieces, are telling the truth, *because their eyes are focused on the things which belonged to the old era.* The old era is dead, and is being buried bit by bit. Every day another fragment of it falls into dust.

Now, if that is *all* that you see—and it will be all that you see if it is all that you look for—no wonder you have the feeling that *everything* is going to pieces.

But if you turn around and see what is coming swiftly up behind your back, as you gaze apprehensively into the past, you will get the other half of the field of vision: you will see the things that are to be.

Perhaps you have seen the oak take color in company with other trees in the autumn. Then came the rains, and the other trees let go their leaves; not so the oak, only a few did he let fall. Then came the winds, and the branches of the other trees were left ragged; but the oak held most of his leafage. Then came the frost, and all the trees were stripped clean and bare of leaves; but the oak leaves shriveled a bit and took on the tone of old Cordovan leather, but for the most part clung to the parent boughs. They are

10

a cheering sight in winter, those shriveled leaves that defied the frosts of autumn; they are a cheering sight as they defy the winter's snow and blast. Then winter begins to wane, and spring is a promise in the air, and green things begin to appear, but still the oak holds tenaciously to last year's foliage. A little later and the leaves begin to fall—in spring. If you had not looked around upon the earth to see what else was transpiring there, if you did not know what compensating work was being done, you might well think that at last every leaf in the world was about to go.

But this is the fact: the leaves that stayed longest, that we had learned to associate with stability—those are the leaves that fall before the new leaves appear.

In the social order, is it not our seemingly most strongly established things that are beginning to flutter down? Are not the most solidly essential services the ones that are now most under doom? Certainly, as anyone who focuses his vision only on the passing things will tell you. It is the collapse of the most dominant methods and institutions that alarms most people. Well, it need not alarm anyone. When the leaves of the strongest tree fall, spring is here. If you will widen your field of vision you will soon see other things springing up to take the place of that which is passing.

So, you have a choice. You can sit and look at the fading out of all that made the old "normalcy" and you can wail about calamity to come; or you can stand up and watch the new era come in, looking for your place in its ranks. If you do the latter, you will see an entirely different state of facts. It will not be imagination, or mental suggestion, or this foolish mysticism of pretending things are all right whether they are or not; it will be fact—the thing is true, the new era IS here.

A business man in a small town said it all very well the other day. Said he: "I just try to accustom myself to the thought that I have waked up in a new world. I don't know just what kind of world it is going to be, but I know it is my duty to keep on the watch to find out so that I may be ready for it. I know there is going to be a new way of salesmanship, and I am trying to find out what it is. I know I shall have to keep wider awake, and I am trying to find out on what lines. I am in a new world and I have got to learn about it all over again. The only things that have carried across from the old world into the new are Service and Honesty—but you can drop the 'Honesty' and save time, for when you say 'Service' you say it all."

That is the attitude! That man was awake to the fact that the new era is here; he wanted to be alert in all his senses when it tried to teach him something. He says he hasn't learned much yet, but he has learned the basic thing—without which he could not learn anything at all—he has learned that the world is new. If that plain fact could be dinned into people's heads and hearts, so that even without understanding it completely, it could become the time-beat of their thinking, a great deal would have been accomplished.

Certainly many things are going to pieces. They ought to! And if you look at them long enough you may get the impression that everything is going to pieces. You should turn around and look the other way, and see the New Era marching up the side of the hill. Then you will see that although the ruin of all our own stupid, inefficient, unjust and unproductive methods is unavoidable and good, the real cause of their disappearance is the New Way which is pushing them out.

While you are looking, be sure and see it all.

"No Help Wanted"—
An Untrue Sign

THERE are good signs and bad signs, but the most unwelcome and untruthful sign of all is that which sometimes hangs in the windows of business places— "No Help Wanted." Or, perhaps, it is not untruthful; perhaps it is stating the exact truth, in which case it is much worse. It is one of those straws which indicate a certain mental current which, followed far enough, tips the voyager over destructive falls and into roaring abysses.

Regard the world from the point of view of the "No Help Wanted" sign and you get a few instructive glimpses for both employers and employes.

Is it not plain fact that in periods when the "No Help Wanted" sign is most frequently displayed, that is just the time when the most "Help Wanted" conditions appear? It is rather strange, but it is true— help is never so much needed as when the signs state that it is not wanted.

What does the man looking for a job want?— he wants help. It is true, of course, to a certain extent, that he wants to *give* help also, but things have become so turned around in this world that it will be generally agreed by everybody that a man seeking a job is seeking help. He is willing to pay for the help with the service he can render, but the main object is to get the help he needs.

Now, in these times, when in so many places the "No Help Wanted" signs are seen, when the pressure of a mismanaged world has dislocated all normal industrial operations, just what does that sign mean? Does it really mean that no help is wanted? Does it mean that no help is needed? Is there any railroad today that can hang out the "No Help Wanted" sign and really intend the deepest significance of that statement? Is there any government that can say "No

Help Wanted"? Is there any condition whatever on the earth today that justifies that sign?

Every one of these is in the direst need of help.

The "No Help Wanted" sign is a limited statement addressed only to the job seeker, and to him it does not mean "No Help Wanted" at all; it means "We Have No Help To Give You."

If you would just abbreviate the sign to read "No Help," as a general description of the slough in which the world finds itself; and then if you would put up another sign—"Have You Any Help to Offer?" as a general description of the need of the world, you would go far toward providing honesty in signs.

"Help Wanted" will always be the normal condition of a world of progressive beings, but the difference between that normal condition and the present would be the fact that the needed help would normally be obtainable. Everything seems to need help now, but it is not obtainable.

There is doubtless a feeling of resentment in some breasts when you say that the man looking for a job is really looking for help. In recent years we have been reared on a feeling that we have certain "rights" which we ought to "demand." Yes, we have rights, but "demanding" doesn't procure them. Our very rights are given us by the help of others. One of our rights is security of life and liberty—never having lived in a society where men are not sure of either of these, we do not vividly appreciate these rights. But we could not enjoy them were it not for the help of others in preserving them for us.

The same way with security of property. Some people sneer at that, too. Well, they wouldn't sneer at it if they knew what the absence of it would mean. Demagogues talked a long time about "putting property rights above human rights," but it is very noticeable that in Russia when they abolished property rights, they abolished human rights also. When you do not respect the things that a man has gathered around him by his own labor for the use of his family, you don't respect his right to life. Robbery (a property crime) and murder (a crime against life) go together, whether in the criminal records of our cities, or in the "social revolutions" overseas. There is a vital link between property and life, just as there is between bread and life: bread is property; and the right to bread is property, also.

So, we all have to have help, even in the most normal times. When the business concern places the sign "Help Wanted" in its doorway, meaning that it needs more employes, it is seeking help just the same as the man who is looking for a job. The employer confesses that he cannot live without help, and the employe confesses the same thing; it is true of all of us. We had better recognize it and cease our profitless flirting with fine-sounding fallacies which have collapsed wherever and whenever the slightest pressure of testing has been put on them.

The so-called government of Russia proclaimed all the rights, real and imaginary, in the category of wild anarchy. It has failed even to procure the right of enough to eat. It was quite natural that Sovietism should be a political failure as at present operated, but why could not the Soviets raise wheat? All that Russia needed was bread. But even the simple laws of seedtime and harvest were ignored by the so-called "makers of the new world." Men who cannot feed themselves are thereby dethroned from the place of leadership.

We need "direct action" of a constructive sort. The thing needed now is not theory, but something that moves.

Suppose you are a man out of a job. You see a shop which says "No Help Wanted" and you know, of course, that the sign means that the shop needs help before it can give any. Have you an idea that will start another wheel turning? Have you any help to give that shop? Can you open any channel for the outflow of its product? Can you serve as an ignition point in its organization?

The man in the front office is tied in a knot by business conditions—can you untie him and set him going again?. He is smothered in his own habit of doing things—can you show him a way to shake loose and get into action again?

The man who brings help with him is always welcome. The world wants help. It needs it. It will reward the man who brings it—whether to a little broom-shop in the alley, or the biggest business in the world.

If you can set the smallest business going, you have done something at which the biggest men often fail.

One point to consider is this: help differs with the need. A year or two ago the world asked only the kind of help which anybody could give, the help of energy and labor to keep it moving in the way it was then going. The kind of help then asked was virtually as easy as pushing business down hill.

But conditions have changed. Business arrived at the foot of the hill in due time. And now it needs a different kind of help.

There are, of course, thousands of theories, millions of ideas. But what counts now is help to get up hill again. As a matter of fact, the world is through with theories. The world has starved on the best theories ever devised. What it asks is an object lesson in something actually going. If a man can start even a wheel-barrow, or dirt cart, he will take rank among the people whom the world is waiting for, the helpers that the world must have.

If a man can start himself going, even; if he can swing out of his rut and so organize his efforts to start going and keep going at something which supports himself and renders an equivalent to others, he has shown himself to be of the quality of world-helpers.

Great hosts are out asking for help. If they could start things for themselves by doing needed things they never thought of before, it would send such an impulse of energetic self-reliance through society, that the tide would turn; for the tide is turnable.

Managers Must Share the Blame

THE government will not be in a position to advocate economy and efficiency in private business
until it has demonstrated these qualities in public
business. And the government will scarcely demonstrate these qualities until it gets the idea that economy
is more than the cut-off of expenditure. Economy
has frequently nothing whatever to do with the amount
of money being spent, but with the wisdom used in
spending it. The expensiveness of government is due
to its inefficiency, and that cannot be cured by "saving
money." It can only be done by reorganization. And,
as reorganization frequently means the cutting out of
useless jobs, it is easy to understand how, in politics,
very little of it is undertaken.

Cutting out jobs has an inhuman sound and it can
be used with immense effect in rousing the prejudices
of thoughtless people. If formerly it required ten men
to do a piece of work, and a reorganization of efficiency enabled that same work to be done by nine
men, resulting in a decrease of one-tenth in the cost
to the public, there is danger of the habitual howlers
setting up a cry:

"Yes, but what about the tenth man who lost his
job? And what about the other nine men who must
work harder to make up the tenth man's work?"

The answers are, of course, quite simple and easily
understood by anyone who will use his mind.

In the first place, the fact that the work is now
being done by nine men does not imply that the tenth
man is unemployed. He is merely not employed on
that work, and the public is not unnecessarily carrying
the burden of his support by paying more than it ought
on that work—for after all, it is the public that pays!

An industrial concern that is wide enough awake
to reorganize for efficiency, and honest enough with

the public to charge it necessary costs and no more, is usually such an enterprising concern that it has plenty of jobs at which to employ the tenth man. It is bound to grow, and growth means more jobs. A well-managed concern that is always seeking to relieve the labor cost to the public is certain to employ more men than the concern that loafs along and makes the public pay the cost of its mismanagement.

That, then, is a point worth remembering; the tenth man was an unnecessary cost on that certain commodity. The ultimate consumer was paying him. But, the fact that he was unnecessary on that particular job does not mean that he is unnecessary in the work of the world, or even in the work of his particular shop. It is a matter of seeing that production costs no more than it should, and that the public is not loaded with costs which good management can avoid.

The public pays for all mismanagement. More than half the trouble with the world today is the "soldiering" and dilution and cheapness and inefficiency for which the people are paying their good money. Wherever two men are being paid for what one can do, the people are paying double what they ought.

This should be understood. There is a feeling that employers use efficiency to increase their personal profits. The surplus of an industrial enterprise is what insures it, keeps it going. Efficiency is not the act of taking a man's wages from him and putting it in the money box; efficiency is seeing that the public is not being charged two prices for one service.

Human sympathy is a fine and potent power. But if the public knew how much of its burden is due to the unnecessarily heaped-up cost on some of its daily commodities, they would be able to view this question in another light. The tenth man, and the ninth man, and the eighth man too, if possible, should be lifted off the load which the people bear. As to the feeling that in such efficiency those who are left must work beyond what they ought, this should be considered: the test of good management is that it makes work easier, not harder. Efficiency that is obtained by

18

loading an extra burden on men already doing a full day's work, is not efficiency. The difference must be made up out of the brains of the managers. It is not a question of eight men, or nine men doing ten men's work; it is a question of good management finding ways of doing the same work with the lesser number, the difference being in the improvement of the method used. One man now moves a casting which twenty men formerly strained. themselves to lift. The one man now only presses a button. The difference is in the methods used, not in the greater burden heaped on the one man. In doing the work of 20 men he now does less than any one of the 20 formerly did.

There is far too much shortsightedness and false feeling about it. This is the result of ignorance and thoughtlessness. People don't realize that the industrial system has no magic about it, and that they themselves sustain it. When its wastefulness and carelessness and laziness pile up, then everything stops, and the people wonder why!

This readjustment should not be the task of the managers of industry alone; the workingman himself ought to bear a part in it. The workingman who has intelligence and foresight would be showing great efficiency in the management of his private affairs if he would shun the job where he felt he was a sort of "fifth wheel to the coach."

Labor can do half of this job of readjustment by simply realizing that a day's work means more than merely being "on duty" at the shop for the required number of hours. It means giving an equivalent in service for the wage drawn. And when that equivalent is tampered with either way—when the man gives more than he receives, or receives more than he gives —it is not long before serious dislocation will be manifest. Extend that condition throughout the country, and you have a complete upset of business. All that industrial difficulty means is the destruction of basic equivalents in the shop.

Management must share the blame with labor. Management was lazy too; management found it easier to hire an additional 500 men than so to improve its methods that 100 men of the old force could be released to other work. The public was paying, and business was booming, and management didn't care a pin. It was no different in the office than it was in the shop. The law of equivalents was broken just as much by managers as by workmen.

And the process of reduction should go on among managers just as much as elsewhere. There are too many jobs up in the front office—and that is where the real trouble starts. Reorganization for efficiency really begins where all the inefficiency came from, in the front office.

As a matter of abstract fact, everybody agrees with the principle here stated. If we have 100 men tied up on jobs that can be done by 75, it is not only an inefficient use of human effort, it is also an unfair charge against the public which must pay for the extra 25. The public has been doing this on every commodity it has used, and it has swamped the public. Everybody grants that.

The matter of jobs is easily taken care of. There are thousands of things waiting to be done in the world. There is productive work waiting for more man-power than the world possesses. Jobs that are unnecessary to production are not jobs. They are cancers eating into the body of the people's earnings. Cutting them out is curative.

We need more of it. It is the only way we can insure everybody going back to work.

On Taking Sides

THE human race is not a brotherhood as yet. It may become so at some future time, but it is not so now. For one thing, there is no sentiment of brotherhood throughout the world. For another thing, there is a very strong and well-established sentiment of strangerhood, which education, civilization, contact and understanding have been powerless, to diminish.

We so commonly accept as possible facts, the things that we wish to be true, that it was once our habit to say that if the peoples of the world only understood each other, the reign of perfect amity would arrive. But there is no lack of suggestion that, in some cases, the better some of the peoples understand each other, the more they dislike each other.

It is not so very different in individual matters: we accept the majority of people because we do not know them; the majority of those we avoid are the ones whom we know.

If it be true that there are in the world two or more opposite and antagonistic elements which can never be reconciled without doing violence to the very nature of things, then it follows that until the superior element arrives at mastery and the inferior element is disposed of, such a thing as unity is not to be thought of.

Our present times are times of break-up. Many people stand aghast at the opening seams which appear throughout society. There are rips and fissures where apparently all was cemented into a solid whole. "What does it all mean?" the people cry in their anxiety. It simply means that where we thought there was unity, there was no unity at all—it was all veneer; society has been "kidding" itself into believing that it could ignore the profounder principles and secure a superficial sort of unity by the process of back-slapping and

21

glad-handing and general meaningless chatter about human unity.

A suspicion of this is always with mankind. "Let sleeping dogs lie," is a common proverb, but it does not describe a secure state of things. If security depends upon our keeping certain dogs asleep, then it is not security. For sleeping dogs will wake, and then security will be gone. If dogs awake are dangerous, the only possible security is in taming them so that asleep or awake they may be friendly, else remove them from any possibility of doing harm.

Anyway, no matter what may appeal to us in the form of theory, the fact is present and indisputable, that there is in the world a new consciousness of differences between groups, and that this consciousness is most felt and is most manifested in countries which most profess democracy. It is a popular manifestation, that is, it appears among the people, growing up out of them, not imposed upon them from above or from without.

It must be very clear to anyone who thinks about it that the present situation could not have arisen if the previous situation had been what we supposed it to be. That is, if everything had been as lovely as we supposed it to be, if the "sleeping dogs" were really not dangerous, then what has happened within the last year could not have occurred. There were sores left unhealed, there were differences left unsettled, there were rival claims left undecided. And there never will be peace until the sores are healed and until the differences are settled and until the rival claims are finally and rightly adjudged.

Now, what does this mean, practically? It means this: there will be division and strife until the naturally and eternally superior thing is acknowledged in its superiority.

"The survival of the fittest" is more than a term of science, it is more than a statement reeking with the sense of universal struggle, it is the declaration of the method of history and the objective of destiny —only the fit do survive.

The main difference in human thinking arises with reference to what constitutes the fitness of the fit.

22

One side says that might makes right, and the other side says that right makes might. One side says that the brute will reign, the other side says that the angel will reign. To common sight it looks as if power would win, and money, and influence, and force, and majorities. That is the way flesh-minded men figure it. But faith-minded men see it differently and more truly. They see that there is an essential element of superiority without which money, majorities, force, influence and prestige are failures already. The flesh-minded men are always saying that the swiftest wins the race and the strongest wins the battle. But history is sufficiently long for us to confirm the truthfulness of the faith-minded man's declaration that "the race is not to the swift, nor the battle to the strong."

But we must not be misled by this term "the survival of the fittest" into the delusion that the fit survive by struggle. Not so. If there is a "struggle for life" it is on the part of those elements which are already passing away; they struggle to retain their place. The superior elements of life do not have to struggle to maintain their place nor to retain their superiority. Not at all; their whole strength is to be what they are; "he that believeth shall not make haste"; struggle belongs to the defeated.

All of which has a side light on tolerance. Some people do not like the word. Nevertheless it stands for a real elemental fact in our civilization. Tolerance is possible only to the superior; the lower elements are always intolerant. The nearer right a man is, the more tolerant he is; his tolerance is in ratio to his immersion in error. Good grows and multiplies of itself and crowds wrong to the corners; it is wrong that struggles and fights; the good does not have to.

What is occurring in the world today is this: under a false notion that vital differences could be patched up by a specious attempt at "good fellowship," the world has gone along for many years trying to pretend that nothing mattered much so long as nothing interfered with our fun or our pursuit of money. It has been mostly pretense, a rosy cloud of words without meaning.

Well, reality has overtaken us again, as it always will. There are strains of blood that will not mix, there are great group ideas and ideals that will never agree, there are great contrary claims that will never be reconciled. We have been pretending that it doesn't matter, but life is teaching us that it does matter; the differences are rolled back upon the consciousness of humanity once more, to be dealt with more wisely than we dealt with it during the miscalled "era of good feeling," which was only an era of camouflage.

A great deal of mushy sentimentalism has gone by the board. Some people, mistaking the matter, say that it is "idealism" that has disappeared. No, only sentimentalism. Sentimentalism is mushy, and soft, and polite, and likes a nice book in a cozy corner. Idealism is willing to fight, and be unpopular, and rouse nasty language and get its head cracked, if need be, for the honor of the idea.

In the meantime, let every man be true to his own position, if he is honestly convinced it is the true one. And let us give room and liberty for everyone to profess his own loyalty. The world is breaking up into its component parts. Every man must line up with the group to which his inmost soul gives its vote. It is a time of taking sides, and a man must take his own side. Afterward, when once again the position is made clear, we may find a better plan of working and living together in spite of our differences, and yet without denying them.

Wrong Ripens and Rots—a
Fact Worth Considering

THERE are many good people in the world who are in great mental distress because they see very clearly the evils which exist, and because they are impatient to do away with them. This combination of clear seeing and impatient spirit is very destructive of interior peace, and many are running around with the impression that the rest of the world is wrong because it takes the matter less anxiously.

Every man who is doing something, knows that there are thousands of people who have each chosen another thing that they think he can do. And most of these thousands are people who are troubled with the disease just mentioned—clear seeing, complicated with an impatient spirit. Their home-made prescription by which they hope to cure themselves seems to be a very simple one, namely, to get some one else started on the line of action which their impatient spirits dictate.

There is a surprising number of people in the world who would be immensely relieved if you—"you are the one person in this world to do it"—would simply do the thing they want done, and which they are sure is the only proper thing to do.

It is a rather difficult matter to deal with, because most of the activities proposed are good, with a promise of being useful. But most of them will never be realized at all, because they will never be done by one person for all the rest, but rather by all the people for themselves. And another reason is: the people to whom the work is given have the habit of looking around for someone else to do it.

What we overlook is that only people can do things. It seems simple enough to say, and yet it is hardly simple enough to understand. Any number of individuals are buzzing around the world today under the delusion that people are the last element to be selected, on the theory that you can always get the people if you can get the money.

Indeed, that is the new process of beginning a "good work"—induce somebody to give money, and then, after the money is given, the person who receives it will undertake to find people to do the human side of the work; the consequence being that in a short time you discover that "the work" never had any human element at all, and that the money which it certainly had is gone.

One would say offhand: If you see a thing to be done, go and do it. If you cannot do it all, do what you can; you cannot take the fifth step until you have taken the first four. If you cannot do anything at all, consider whether the time has come to do anything. Times grow ripe, like everything else; yet many people think they can pick ripe events off green years; which cannot be done any more than ripe apples can be picked in months when they are green. Many reforms are picked green; many progressive plantings are done, not in mellow soil, but in the frozen ground. People don't observe the times and the seasons.

Now, take the evils in the world. They are many, and perhaps the weightiest burden we have to carry is the wonderment that they are allowed to exist. But there they are. Everybody doesn't see them; but you, let us say, can see them clearly. Everybody doesn't realize how these evils are eating into the life of the people; but you, let us say, see it so clearly that it is a pain to you.

Now, you can spoil your own life, sour your friends and bring your very vision into question by insisting that everyone sees exactly what you see. They will see it when the time is ripe, but not until then, and you are very foolish if you fret about it.

There are men working day and night on the problem of cancer; but as for you, you don't think much of cancer because it has not come within your life. And you would possibly resent it very much if a cancer researcher should continually insist that you take up an interest in cancer. You would say, "I don't want to. I am not called to consider cancer. That is your field, not mine." Very well, you would be right.

Don't you see that with everyone working in his field, not insisting that the whole world come in also, much is being done? Every little while reports come from this field or that of achievements, and you had not even heard that men were working in those fields. Yet they are, each doing his work, and when the time is ripe, up goes the flag and the job is completed.

There are sentries along the frontiers of all our problems, men and women here and there who are sometimes lonely, who wonder why they must pace their beat alone; but we know that where sentries walk now, the whole army will march soon. Some people are sentries, to whom it is given to be on watch, this one on the frontiers of cancer, this one on the frontiers of financial diseases, this one on the new boundaries of statesmanship, this one on the limits of a new order of social life. Sentries all, but never so foolish as when they insist on calling the whole army out before the day dawns.

If it is given to a man to see that a certain condition exists, he is sentry at that point to give the alarm. Presently at the right time, the time set by the director of destiny, his work will bear fruit.

"Well, but," the impatient spirit cries, "what about the evil done in the meantime? We must do something to prevent that!"

Well, do it!

"But," says the impatient spirit, "I can't do it." Rightly said; you cannot, neither can anyone else. You cannot ripen an apple faster than it will ripen, and you cannot rot it faster than it will rot. These things appear to be under the law.

The people have the evils they deserve, no more, no less. By "deserve" one does not mean the judgment which any human being can pass as to desert: one means that all of us together have the sort of life that we have made, and we will continue to have it until we are fit to remake it in better quality.

When people begin to feel the evil; when there runs through society a new consciousness of the stupidity and the wrong of certain things; when the false notes begin to irritate us; when the heat of indignant resentment begins to break out in thought and speech —these are the first streaks of the new day, or, to change the figure, these are the first flushes of color which begin to show that the fruit is ripening for the autumn.

What is needed by people who see the evil is a still clearer sight; they need to see that the evil will collapse, utterly collapse. And what people of impatient spirit need to learn is that they must detach themselves from the system they despise and turn their efforts against it.

All of us want to slay the giant with one dramatic stroke of our sword. As a matter of fact, the giant usually dies from self-generated poisons.

Whatever the moral judgment of the morally sensitive people is against, that thing is inevitably doomed. Though it become the social rage and sweep all the people within the circle of its viciousness, it is nevertheless doomed. Indeed, when you see evil at the height of its popularity and power, when you see all who speak against it ridiculed and despised, you may be very glad—for from that apex the fall is swift and sure. Never forget that. That is the ripeness of the times for the fall of the fruit. It falls, it rots, its pulp fertilizes more wholesome growths.

Poisons That Creep Into Industry

I T IS a pathetic illusion of the people that perfection can be found in government or industrial organizations. Ceasing to believe in the eternal verities they transfer their worship to little gods of temporary fashion, bowing down before each one of them in turn as if at last the answer to all questions had come.

We have learned a great many things of recent years, one of which is that there is no perfect wisdom, foresight or ability. Governments get things done because they have the power to command power, they have unlimited means to ride over all mistakes; some of their mechanical achievements are at a cost that would be ruinous to even the largest privately controlled means. It is not dishonesty, it is not wilful waste, it is mere human frailty which even connection with a government does not cure.

Likewise a great industrial institution. At first it was a very wonderful thing that large production could be secured. The very bigness of growing business impressed the mind, and the increasing flow of goods made people believe that the apex of human daring and ingenuity had been reached. But new developments proved that mere bigness was not all. Big production sometimes spelled big waste. And so,. a new element entered industry—the element which took the name of "efficiency": the saving of time, labor, material, money: producing as good an article at a lower cost, or perhaps a much better article at a lower cost, and thus permitting the buyer to profit, too.

That was merely the addition of brain to brawn, the mixing of mind with machinery.

Then came something more: the element of humanity began to thrust itself up through industrial development, and forward-looking manufacturers and managers began to consider *men*. It was natural that

29

the product should usurp the center of the stage in its time, but it was also natural that the producer should arrive to share the attention given the product.

This was the beginning of the era of good will in industry. Employers who were fit for their jobs began to see that while it was an excellent thing that the buyers of their products were treated honestly, there were other people to consider, too—the men in the shop.

Of course, a great deal of nonsense accompanied the eruption of this new idea. New ideas always have that handicap. Professional "welfare workers" saw their opportunity. A great deal of impertinent paternalism was indulged in. Attempts were made to model men on office-made standards and to regulate home life on professional theories, and it did not work out very well, although it did accomplish some good and was a hopeful omen. The object of all welfare work ought to be to make itself unnecessary; to establish men in their sense of dependency is most harmful.

But this arrival of the idea of humanity in industry has always had to reckon with the parasitic nature of men. It is amazing how many men would like to regard industries as perennial Christmas trees which hang with free fruits. No industry has anything but what is put into it by the men who are in it. What "the company ought to do" is only what work and management permit it to do.

It has followed, therefore, that those who looked for the complete purification of industry by the humanitarian idea, have been disappointed. In the very best intentioned industry, if it be of great size, there are undoubted injustices and perhaps even occasional brutalities, which do not grow out of the policy of the industry, but out of the nature of the men engaged in it. It is a matter of observation, and worthy of much thought, that the treatment accorded the workers between themselves, the cruelty of man to man, is beyond that which the least humane management would attempt.

A great industry is like a human body. If you analyze it closely you will find all sorts of disease germs in it. If you specialize on the individual injustices that may occur within it, you will appear to have gathered such a mass as spells death to any organism or organization. Yet, the industry goes on. Its product is of service to the world. It provides the means of livelihood to thousands of families. It fills its place in the world and, in the main, has the respect and good will of men.

It is undeniable that the disease germs are there. There are men whose sense of human relations may be blunted. There are perhaps general methods which could be improved. There is always the tendency of men and managers to break up into cliques—"office politics," "shop politics," as it is called. There are men who like to gain and keep personal power. There are men whose very ideas circulate as a poison through the organization.

And when you segregate these men, these ideas, these tendencies, you wonder how in the name of decency the organization survives!

Well, it is just like isolating a disease germ in the body. There is nothing to be said in favor of the disease germ. But we have learned that every healthy body contains disease germs. There is enough disease in any body to kill it, if resistance should fall below the requirement of health. The reason that the body remains healthy even while carrying disease germs is that the health germs are in the majority. You could make a very startling report on any body by merely finding and counting the disease germs within it. But it would not be a complete report.

An industrial organization is like a human body in that respect. The poison creeps into it. There are methods of elimination, of course, but a certain amount of poison manages to lurk around. And the only reason for the organization retaining its health and activity is the existence of the health germs which always resist the poison. When resistance lags or ceases, death comes.

This is an idea which should occupy the mind of every worker in any industrial concern which has this antagonism between good ideals and only partial achievements. In such a case, men tend to one of two extremes. Either they condemn the whole business as one immense hypocrisy living on false estimates, or they totally deny that there is any evil in the business whatever.

Both are wrong. The evil is there. But evil is to be resisted, it is to be overcome with good, the poison is to be drained off. That is the part of all who see where the wrong is. It is a big mistake so to focus your eyes that you can see nothing but the wrong; it is an equally big mistake to close your eyes so that you cannot see the wrong at all. The evil, if it is there, is to be recognized and resisted.

And this also is true: unless this warfare against the poison is kept up, it soon exerts its toxic power to such an extent as to paralyze all possible resistance. Some of this poison is in the management; some of it is in the shop. It looks much worse when it is found in men of authority, than when it is found in the rank and file of the workers. But even officials are not immune from penalty. Usually they go quickest of all when they become poison to the organization.

Nobody ought to assume for a moment that because something is wrong it has got to stay wrong, or that it is going to stay wrong. They have got to assume that, like a gum boil, when it comes to a head it is going to burst. When poison becomes so manifest in an organization that the men begin to notice it and those who really desire the health of the institution are beginning to feel it keenly, then is the time when it is just about ready to break.

The only power any wrong can exert over us is to make us believe that it is here to stay. Expose its transient character and its sting is drawn.

Be Very Careful of Success

S UCCESS is the enemy. It is the only enemy that can overcome men who are invincible to failure. Men who cannot be beaten though they fail a score of times, men who cannot be discouraged by an army of difficulties, sometimes go tumbling down as the result of a little success. More men are failures on account of success, than on account of failure.

It is very easy to show how this comes to be.

Here is a railroad that has suddenly come to its senses. It has not done anything very wonderful, it has merely roused itself out of its loafing. It has not introduced a single new plan, it has not practiced a single magical formula, it has simply taken the old, time-worn system and tightened up the bolts, put in some grease and compelled it to go! It has done only the simplest and most common-sense things. It has cut out the slack and the loafing and the senseless waste. It has made cars and locomotives and men do what they were created for—move!

Now, it is a commentary on the slough into which we had fallen that when one railroad did that very simple thing, it made a sensation. That really is a point to think of. When the simple, common-sense thing is so unusual as to cause a sensation, it is proof that common sense is not being used very extensively, else people would be more familiar with it.

But with all the buzz and talk, there comes another element, that most people would not look for. Every man down the line knows that the railroad is doing its work better than ever before, that a new spirit and a new alertness have come into the work, that clumsy duplication and the necessity for loafing have been cut out. And every man naturally feels better about it. Anyone who tells you that a man prefers the dog's life of loafing to the real life of going after something and getting it done, does not know men.

Besides that, the common-sense thing is so unusual

33

that it causes a great deal of outside talk. Common sense in business administration appears to be so unusual that it is "news." And thus the men on the railroad know that the world is talking about the big improvement they have made in railroad operation.

They make clippings of the papers and magazines. They take a personal satisfaction (which is right and proper) in all the praise that is given. They enjoy it thoroughly.

But all the time they are unconscious of what this praise, and all this credit for success, is doing to them. The most common mistake of all is the belief that when people begin to buzz, it is a sign that something has been definitely and finally accomplished, that success has been won. We are such simple creatures that we imagine the race is run the moment the cheers are heard.

Now, in the illustrative case of the railroad which we are using, it is very easy to see how praise and the sense of success works upon the minds and energies of men.

If the manager has kept his head at all, he knows that though much has been done in lifting the old system out of its rut, it is not to be compared with what is yet to be done. And just there is one of the differences that mark men: you find one type of men standing still, complacently enjoying the little good work they have already done, smiling over it, receiving congratulations upon it, simply sucking it dry of all that can minister to their sense of pride and personal satisfaction.

If the manager is of that type, he has reached the end of his achievement; he is through, so far as making progress is concerned. The man who thinks he has done something, hasn't many more things to do.

But there is the other type of manager who is so busy with the things yet to be done that he cannot stop to enthuse over what has already been done. His is a long-range program. What he has done he regards as a beginning—maybe a mighty good beginning, but only a beginning after all. His eye is far ahead on plans yet to be realized, new ideas yet to be introduced. He spends no time congratulating himself. Of course, he misses a lot of the soft enjoyment of the other type; he misses a lot of that enervation which comes from basking in praise and adulation; he seems rather callous to public opinion—but all that is because he has not yet done the thing for which he will perhaps deserve praise.

Now, this man sees defects that the satisfied crowd of men don't see. He sends for his railroaders, and points out what is wrong. He brings them to book on this dereliction of duty or that failure of alertness. He talks to them in a tone which reveals none of the self-satisfaction which they supposed was the constant atmosphere of the inside office—satisfaction with all the praise and buzzing which was going around.

"Why, boss," they seem to say, "what difference does a little thing like that make? See how well we are doing. Why, here is a newspaper clipping which says . . . .," and they go down into their pocketbooks for the cherished bit of paper.

Don't you see what the air of success does? Don't you see how it has seduced these men? Don't you see that after fighting failure through, they are now ready to surrender to a little success?

Success is the enemy. It brings those elements with it that minister to our softness. There are more people desiring to enjoy life than to contribute something to life. A man wants recognition and reward; we say these are natural desires, and so they are. But when a man gains recognition, the temptation is very great to stop and enjoy the recognition. And when he gains reward the temptation is to think that he has "arrived." Who can count the number of the men who have been halted and beaten by recognition and reward!

Make your program so long and so hard that the people who praise you will always seem to you to be talking about something very trivial in comparison with what you are really trying to do.

If success comes you will have to work twice as hard to keep on top of it; once it gets on top of you, then success becomes your failure.

People at large will never be convinced of this, of

course, and it is not necessary that théy should. It is only when they approach the perilous place of popular approval that they must be sternly warned.

The people transfer their own feelings to the successful person, and then think of his success under those terms. They see the statesmen carried aloft, the ruler exalted, the man of achievement moving along to the plaudits of the people. And they think how lovely, how enjoyable, how perfectly satisfactory such a position must be. And so the attainment of that loveliness and enjoyableness and satisfaction becomes their idea of success. If they only knew it, the man so honored was probably fuming because he was wasting his time to make a public holiday—he wanted to get back to his work.

This much is certain: had the man who was thus honored behaved himself so unseemly as to indicate that he thought he deserved all that adulation, had he shown that success was to him what the people thought it was, they would have dethroned him.

It is all a very strange game, and the man who is deceived thereby is lost. Better have a job too big for popular praise, so big that you can get a good start on it before the cheer-squad can get its first intelligent glimmerings of what you are trying to do. Then you will be free to work. And being free to work you will have achieved the truest success and satisfaction.

Who Is the Real "Owner"?

THE question of ownership is not so acute as it was. Not long ago there was a theory abroad that if so-called "private ownership" could be abolished and "public ownership" set up, then all our troubles would cease. It has been tried in various ways, on a huge scale as in Russia, on a small scale as in some American cities. The net result so far is this: if you propound a theory that the cook should be driven out of the kitchen and that the whole boarding house personnel should be brought into the kitchen to superintend the cooking of the steak, you might be fortunate enough to find a boarding house that would try out your theory. But from the standpoint of a well-cooked steak it is only a matter of time when you are going to call the cook back.

The question of ownership will be settled when it ceases to be acute; that is, it will settle itself. What the world is restless about is the recognition of certain ideas, not the general position of the people. Ideas have a hard time being born, and restlessness is part of the general operation. Once born, however, the effect is rather greater easiness of mind than a strong overturning of the fundamentals of life.

A man owns what is given him in his personality and what he earns by his labor—that, and nothing else. If a man has character, he owns it; no one can claim a share in it. If he owns self-respect and the respect of his neighbors, it is his, absolutely his. If he has the gift of foresight, if he has the faculty of insight, if he has the power to plan and to manage and execute, if he has the qualities of a leader—these are all his own. They are his in a personal, private sense. The mind and the eye are greater reapers, and what they reap cannot be taken from them.

But what else is his? What can he absolutely own in the physical realm? By common consent he can own all that he needs for the living of his life—if he

37

earns it. Civilized mankind recognizes the investment of a man's soul and body into his home and all the material requirements of his life. That is what we mean by "the sacred right of property"—property is sacred by reason of the thought and sweat and blood that human beings have put into it. When you take that from a man, you take his life. Where property is not respected, life is not respected.

But what about all this other wealth—this great expansion of industrial wealth that we see all around us? This is what people mean when they talk about "ownership."

Well, take any big concern you may happen to think about. Who made it what it is? Everybody who had a hand in it. The man whose idea inspired it. The men he called in to help him. The public whose patronage supported the business. They all made it. They are the only ones who own it because they are using it.

Well, but what about the "millions" that the business has made? Let us see where those millions are. There are "millions" in the buildings, "millions" in the machinery, "millions" in the outlying sources of supply, "millions" in railroads and tank cars, "millions" in material, "millions" in goods on the market.

Now, no one can put those "millions" in his pocket when he goes home at night. No one "owns" those "millions." They are out in use by hundreds of thousands of people all the time. If tomorrow the world should be turned upside down and another "class" should take control of business, it would have to leave the "millions" right where they are—else there would be no service nor business.

That was the crude, childish thing that occurred in Russia. They rushed in and took those "millions" out and then wondered why they could no longer pro-
. duce their daily bread.

There is a great deal of misunderstanding about wealth. Wealth is not money. Wealth is in things of use. That is where all the wealth of the big industrial institutions is—in things of use. All of it lies out-of-doors. It cannot be locked up in safes. If, however, it were all divided equally, so that everyone

38

now participating in its operative benefits could participate in its dead value as material, what would it amount to?—this one would have a few bricks, that one half a wheel, another a pile of junk.

In fact, it was only because all this material and all this effort were successfully taken out of the field of absolute private ownership and piled together into one well-planned whole, that the public could be served as well as it is. Redistribute it all back to its private ownership, and the public is left gasping for everything that it needs.

But what people usually have in mind when they talk about "ownership" is not the question of who ought to own the bricks and the mortar and the furnaces and the mills, but rather the question "who ought to be boss?" That is really the big question in most minds. "Who set this man over us?" is the often unspoken challenge.

Well, this is very much like asking, "Who ought to be the tenor in the quartette?" Obviously, the man who can sing tenor. You could not depose Caruso. Let any theory of musical democracy come, depose Caruso to the musical "proletariat"; very well, there is no substitute; Caruso's gifts are still his own.

Who will be the leader of the army? The man who can lead. Who will be the pilot of the ship? The man who knows the way. Who will be the leader of the country in a moral emergency: men say this one or that one, but God said "Lincoln."

In lesser things it is the same. The man who can, is the man who does. No one chose the real leaders of today; they came forward because they could lead, and men followed them because they knew a leader. They came up from the ranks, all of them. The new leaders are in the ranks now.

Some young men, poisoned by the cynicism of a false social philosophy, do not believe this. They feel sore within, they are straining and stressing. That is good. That is the way leaders are born. There is a great deal of that kind of feeling before a man is forty. Don't interpret it as rebellion, it is growing pains. The old principles still hold true. Modern industrial development hasn't changed a single rule

39

of life—and cannot! Go back to your grandfather's copy books, and what the maxims said then is true now. Men rise today, just as they have always done, by backing their native gifts with their acquired energy.

This much is certain: no one will long remain "boss" who was not called to that work by nature and development. It would be an extremely simple matter to displace all the "bosses" and leaders today, but it would be an extremely difficult matter to replace them. That was the trouble in Russia.

But say that by force you do replace the natural bosses with artificially created ones, what happens? Why, shortly there is nothing left to "boss," the whole thing has just crumbled away into uselessness.

So, there are correctives. In the natural course of events the incapable man cannot get into positions of power, but if through an unnatural, artificial course of "pull" or "favor" or "relationship" an incapable man does rise to that position, natural law soon begins to operate: he fails and his failure is apparent to all.

If there is a great industry which has ceased to serve the people; if there is a great industry whose leader has ceased to care for it and has begun to exploit it; if there is a great industry whose leader has been poisoned with the thought, "This is mine and exists for my benefit alone"—you will not long be puzzled about the problem of ownership. Nature will soon settle it.

"Swelled Head" in Business

THERE is a disease known as "swelled head"
which may be contracted in any line of activity,
but which is particularly dangerous in business. Because of the inelegance of its name and the common-
ness of its occurrence among light and giddy youth,
it is regarded not as a dangerous disease, but as something light, like the ailments of childhood. We know,
however, how serious the ailments of childhood can
be when they attack grown persons.

If we were to be very strict about words, we
should perhaps say that the term "swelled head" was
hardly descriptive. If the head of the patient actually should enlarge and his brain power increase,
the disease would not exist. It is the feeling of enlargement in heads that have not enlarged nor expanded at all, that constitutes the abnormal condition.

That is to say, the condition described as "swelled
head" is a delusion—the patient thinks he has expanded when he has not. The only element in him
that has increased is his self-esteem, and when that
increases out of proportion to everything else, there
comes an unbalanced condition which is just as dangerous to his affairs as insanity is to society.

This ailment is not confined to men in small and
unimportant positions, although it is found there too;
but it is frequently found among men whom the world
thinks to be "big men" because they wear big titles
and *deal in big things*. There would seem to be little
reason for much swelled-headedness among the "big
men" of today, for it is precisely in their fields that
all the big failures and all the big humiliations have
come.

There is, of course, such a thing as a sense of self-
satisfaction in one's work, a sense of being able to do
the thing required, a sense of mastery, and a plain
knowledge of having accomplished something when a
good job has been done—these are the wholesome

41

flavors and reactions of honest work. They are not to be confused with the disease of "swelled head." The difference between them is this: the former has the work for its center; the latter has one's self for its center. And self-centered persons (not necessarily selfish persons) are in great danger of letting themselves get in the way of their work. They are in great danger of the delusion that their work exists for their glory.

The sign of a little man is so various that it is next to impossible for an ordinarily observant person to mistake him. He never forgets himself. He is afraid to surround himself with bigger men than himself, with men who know more, or who can give him help. Thus the little man is a fool; if he knew where his interest lay, he would surround himself with the biggest and best men, and by his just treatment of them retain their services. But the little man lives in daily dread that somebody will show up more meritoriously than he, and he strives to keep a false preeminence by seeing to it that, little as he himself may be, those who surround him are smaller still. This is often true because the little man is usually himself a subordinate who fears displacement. But even a subordinate who can surround himself with superior and efficient assistants is not in nearly so much danger of displacement as one who deliberately hammers down the standard of his organization.

The disease of "swelled head" has its preliminary symptom in shortsightedness. No one who can see very far ahead or very far around, is ever troubled with it. The world is so big and there is so much to be done that a man can contract "swelled head" only *by comparing himself with himself.*

Is not that the trouble? The process is usually something like this: a man goes to work earnestly and intelligently, and as a consequence his work attracts attention. Any man who works this way is bound to make an impression. In course of time this man is advanced, and the recognition thus accorded has the effect of making him still more earnest and intelligent, and therefore more useful and desirable. So

42

another advancement inevitably comes; and perhaps another, and another.

Then one day, the man stops to consider what has befallen him and the idea creeps into his mind that he must be quite a fellow. Look what he was *then*, and look what he is *now!* Comparing himself with himself, you see. It is the first whisper of the tempting serpent.

The man receives his last advancement—and usually it is his *last*—with the feeling that at length he has arrived. He has ceased to regard every new step as a new challenge to his ability; he has come to regard it as a decoration pinned on him for what he has done some time in the past. As a result, he sits down to enjoy his new place and his new title—and his degeneration begins right there. He has caught "swelled head" and the treatment needed to cure that is often very drastic and severe.

Where did the disease begin? In the man's thought that advancements are decorations instead of new challenges. Nobody has "arrived" until he has filled his post and is leaving it—only then can a judgment be rendered on his work.

Can you imagine a newly elected President of the United States entering the White House with a smug smile and saying to himself, "Well, at last I have attained success—I have arrived—I have become President"—can you imagine that? Oh, no, for just at that moment there would come thundering through the corridors of his soul the cutting challenge—"What kind of a President?" Ah!—that is a question to be answered after four or eight years of service.

The President does not arrive until he leaves; it is then his record is made; it is then his measure is recorded on history's page. The exalted position is sometimes only a loftier stage upon which to enact a tragedy of failure.

It is true everywhere. If you are promoted, it is only another burden, another demand laid on you, with the questions: "Can you carry that? Can you fulfill that?" The reward for good work done is always more work. Not decorations, nor titles, nor "soft snaps"; these are the snares which have wrecked many a career.

It is better to remain a good bookkeeper and to be known as such, than to be promoted because you are a good bookkeeper and think that you can dispense with the qualities that made you a good bookkeeper. Unless you take those qualities with you, enlarged and intensified, you are only ascending the scale to a more spectacular failure. Promotion that is not regarded as a challenge to greater and better performance may easily become a snare.

We want to write the word "success" too soon. It should be kept for the epitaph. Any man who thinks he is a success, has come to his terminal. He is about ready to get off. He is running under the momentum of past steam. He is coming down with a form of "swelled head."

One fact about this disease should be noted: it does not always take an offensive form. It does not always show itself in bumptiousness. A man may be a victim of it and yet never suspect it. When a man settles back as if he had done all he ought to do, when he begins to have the deliciously drowsy feeling that, after all, he has done pretty well—it is time to be on guard. The disease is not unpleasant to the victim and therein lies its danger. He should distrust such thoughts and go on a hunt for something hard and difficult and "impossible" to do—something that will bring back a normal sense of proportion.

Regarding Charity, Welfare
Work and Other Matters

THE world doesn't owe anybody a living, but everybody owes it to the world that he get a living
and in getting it leave a margin of service for the
others. Nothing is more productive of a sour spirit
than the mistaken belief that we are here to be waited
on, and nothing is more productive of breadth and
prosperity of life than the belief that we are here to
do something beyond that which necessity compels us
to do for ourselves.

It is hard to get such an idea clearly accepted today, because there are so many words that have lost
their meaning through overuse. It is next to impossible to talk about "service" in these days without
having the very word lose itself in a tangle of pre-
conceived ideas—ideas which were born in the wishy-
washy period of romantic idealism out of which we
are happily passing.

It is hard for another reason, namely that this
whole period of sentimental idealism to which we have
just referred had the effect of giving a namby-pamby
surfacing to any number of people. The idea went
abroad that "service" was something that we should
expect to be done for us. Untold numbers of people
became the recipients of the well-meant but over-done
"social service" of others. Whole sections of our
population were coddled into the habit of expecting
something, as children do. There grew up a regular
profession of doing things for people, which gave an
outlet for a laudable desire for service, but which
contributed nothing whatever to the self-reliance of
the people nor to the correction of the conditions out
of which the supposed need for such service grew.

Worse than this encouragement of childish ex-
pectancy, instead of training for self-reliance and self-
sufficiency, was the creation of a feeling of resentment

45

which nearly always overtakes the objects of charity. People often complain of the "ingratitude" of those whom they help. Nothing is more natural. In the first place, precious little of our so-called charity is ever real charity, offered out of a heart full of interest and sympathy. In the second place, no person ever relishes being in a position where he is forced to take favors from anyone.

This situation creates a strained relation: the recipient of another's bounty feels that he has been belittled in the taking of it, and it is just a question whether the giver should not also feel that he has been belittled in the giving of it. Service is objected to by no one, appreciated by all; but who would designate charity as "service"?

Charity never led to a settled state of affairs. The charitable system that does not aim to make itself unnecessary is not performing service: It is simply making a job for itself and is an added item to the record of non-production.

Factory welfare work that does not educate the factory personnel to a point beyond the need of chaperonage, is not doing its duty. The work of every welfare worker is similar to that of the physician, namely, to perform the work so well that it will soon be unnecessary. Welfare work is not a crutch for a permanent injury, it is an educational program which justifies itself only by placing its beneficiaries beyond need of it. Whatever is permanently necessary is just plain decency and justice and should not be decked out with names which suggest that somebody deserves credit for being just a little bit more human than he was expected to be.

It may sometimes seem that an advance step is charity, but it need not be stigmatized by that word—it would better be called vision. A man sees the proper thing to do for those who have not the facilities as yet to do it for themselves, and he does it—it only means that he uses the power at his command to bring in the New Era in that particular matter. The New Era has been "inching along" for some time in this manner.

This was really the way in which "human rights"

came in. They first began as "privilege." Those who could get "privileges" got them. But the fact that "privileges" could be had by one group led the way to their being had by all groups. Every inalienable right we now possess was once a "class privilege." We scold a great deal about "privilege" these days, and it is right to do so, for what we nowadays call "privilege" is mostly daylight robbery; but at the same time it is well to remember that there are instances where the privilege of the few is really a prophecy of the coming rights of the many.

Humanitarianism is splendid when it is not professionalized. But it is not a good word. Suppose there comes a time when everyone will be self-sufficient, so far as the material assistance we can render each other is concerned, where then will be the field for "humanitarianism"? That is, the kind of humanitarianism that really gives you the feeling of veterinarianism.

There is only human helpfulness, and directly that is systematized, organized, commercialized and professionalized, the heart of it is extinguished, and it becomes a cold and clammy thing.

Human helpfulness which is never card catalogued nor advertised is the most helpful agency in the world today. There are more orphan children being cared for in the private homes of people who love them, than in the institutions. There are more old people being sheltered among friends, without money and without price, and with no thought of either, than you can find in the Old People's Homes. There is more aid by loans and other assistance between family and family than all the loan societies or banks are doing. That is, human society on a humane basis, looks out for itself. It is a grave question how far we ought to countenance the commercialization of this instinct. We certainly ought to subject it to the severest scrutiny to find, if possible, by what interests and for what interests it is being commercialized.

Above all, however, we should devote ourselves to the cultivation of the old-fashioned virtue of self-reliance in our people. Americans were formerly self-reliant; Americans in blood and spirit doubtless form the self-reliant part of our population now. But we have received large admixtures from other countries where an obsequious attitude is counted necessary before one can even receive one's rights. That was carried to America by a sufficient number of people to have its effect, especially on the officers of municipal government. Foreigners thought an alderman was a great personage and a policeman a power to be placated. It wasn't good for the alderman or the policeman to be thus exalted. Good old-fashioned American self-reliance is a much better attitude to adopt before all political powers. We need more of it in the country right now.

One of the common sayings which came out of the dawn of common sense on this whole question was this: "Help a man to help himself." But how have we been doing it? We have been starting too far this side of the root of the matter. The way to help a man to help himself is to get the idea firmly rooted in his understanding that his help is in himself. That is the entire basis of our much boasted self-government. Only a self-reliant people can be self-governing, and if we have found the government slipping away from ourselves, we may take it as a sign that we are losing our national virtue of self-reliance. There is something tragically comic in lazily relying on a government that relies on us. And if a government ceases to rely on the people, and the people cease to rely on themselves, that is the beginning of dissolution. We do not, however, think of dissolution for this nation or government; it is made of the principles that forever endure.

Let every American become self-protective from coddling. Americans ought to resent coddling like a drug. Stand up and stand out; let weaklings take charity; we will have Rights because we will simply go to work and make them; create them, and then enjoy them.

Where High Wages Begin

HIGH wages sounds mighty good. That is, to most people. It is true that a few men seem to think that high wages will ruin business. But the majority of people know better than that. The grocer, the clothier, the furniture maker, the boot and shoe man, the banker—all know better.

There are short-sighted men who cannot see that Business is a bigger thing than any one man's interests. Business is a process of give and take, live and let live. It is co-operation between many forces and interests.

Whenever you find a man who believes that Business is a river whose beneficial flow ought to stop as soon as it reaches him, and go no farther to refresh and enrich other men's fields, you find a man who thinks he can keep Business alive by stopping its circulation.

There are some men who, if they got all they wanted, would get everything, and so destroy the very thing they seek. This is lack of vision.

What do we mean by high wages, anyway?

We mean a higher wage than was paid ten months or ten years ago. We do not mean a higher wage than ought to be paid. Our high wages of today may be low wages ten years from now.

If it is right for the manager of a business to try to make it pay larger dividends, it is just as right that he should try to make it pay higher wages. For wages are the chief dividend—on the money side at least—. and more people are dependent on them.

But where the commonest mistake is made is here: We sometimes imagine that it is the manager of the business who pays the high wages. Of course, if he can and will not, then the blame is his. But if he can, it is not himself alone that makes it possible.

When you trace it all down to its source, it is really the workmen who earn the wages. Their labor is the productive factor. It is not the only productive factor, of course, for poor management can waste labor just as it can waste material and make it unproductive.

But in a partnership of good management and good labor, it is the workman who makes good wages possible. He invests his energy and skill, and if he makes an honest, whole-hearted investment, good wages ought to be his reward. Not only has he earned them, but he has had a big part in creating them.

The employer who, in fairness, is paying good wages is not, therefore, to be applauded as an angel. It is not all his doing. If his men did not do their part in making the business productive and profitable, he would not have the big wage to pay. So that the credit is not all his. He is only sharing justly, or nearly so, with the men who were his active partners in the business.

It is not a question of the employer showing his generosity, or playing My Lord Bountiful, or anything like that. It is simply the square deal. And it is the only practical way of keeping a business productive and profitable.

A business whose benefits come to a halt in the company's office is not a healthy business. The benefit has got to circulate so that every man who had a part in creating and running it has also a part in enjoying it. It is simple fairness.

Paying good wages is not charity at all—it is the best kind of business.

The kind of workman who gives the business the best that is in him is the best kind of workman a business can have. But he cannot be expected to do this indefinitely without proper recognition.

Good wages help keep the good workmen a good workman for the sake of the business.

The man who comes to the day's job feeling that no matter how much he may give, it will not yield him enough of a return to keep him beyond the margin of want, is not in shape to do his day's work. He is anxious and worried and it all reacts to the detriment of his work.

But if a man feels that his day's work is not only supplying his basic need, but is also giving him a margin of comfort, and enabling him to give his boys and girls their opportunity and his wife some pleasure in life, then his job looks good to him and he is free to give it his very best.

This is a good thing for him and a good thing for the business. The man who does not get a certain satisfaction out of his day's work is losing the best part of his pay.

Do you know, the day's work is a great thing—a very great thing! It is at the very foundation of our economic place in the world; it is the basis of our self-respect; it is the only way to reach out and touch the whole world of activity.

All of us are workingmen these days. If we are not, we are parasites. No amount of money excuses any man from working. He is either producer or parasite—take your choice.

All of us don't do the same things, our jobs are different. But all of us are working for the same end, and that end is bigger than any of us.

The employer who is seriously trying to do his duty in the world must be a hard worker. It is useless for him to say, "I have so many thousand men working for me." The fact of the matter is that so many thousand men have him working for them— and the better they work the busier they keep him disposing of their products.

Wages and salaries are in fixed amounts, and this must be so in order to have a basis to figure on. But where the profits exceed these there ought to be profit-sharing. Wages and salaries are a sort of fixed profit-sharing, but it often happens that when the business of the year is closed up it is discovered that more can be done, and then more ought to be done. Where we are all in the business working together, we all ought to have some share in the profits, either a good wage or salary, or added compensation.

The business man's ambition ought to be to pay the best wages the business can carry, and the workman's ambition should be to respond to make the best wages possible.

A business man sometimes does not know just how to say this. There are men in all shops who seem

51

to believe that when they are urged to do their best,
it is for their employer's benefit and not their own.
It is a pity that such a feeling should exist. But perhaps there have been enough abuses in the past to
justify it in many instances.

If an employer urges men to do their best, and
the men learn after a while that their best does not
mean any reward for them, then they simply go back
into the rut and all the urging is wasted.

But if men follow the urging and do their best,
and then see the fruits of it in their pay envelope, it
is proof to them that they are an essential part of that
business, and that its success largely depends on them.
They feel also that there is justice in that business
and that their efforts will not be ignored.

It ought to be clear, however, that the higher wage
begins down in the shop. If it is not created there it
cannot get into the pay envelopes. It must begin there,
and it ought to keep on circulating until a just proportion of it gets back there, and when profit-sharing
time comes the men who helped to make the profits
should not be forgotten.

So when the workman is urged to do his best, it
ought not to be a game that is playing on him. His
best ought to mean the best for him as well as for the
business. And unless it does mean this his best is
going to be hard to get.

It is a sense of fellowship in work that we need.
And fair dealing will give it to us. Why do we have
these classes of "capital" and "labor" set apart as
enemies? Simply because fair dealing has not been
the rule. What is "capital" without "labor"? And
what is "labor" but "capital"? And what earthly use
is "capital" unless it labors and produces the things
which life requires?

We must get together on these matters, and the
only way we can get together is to begin with fair
dealing.

One ounce of fair dealing is worth a ton of fair
speeches.

Every business that employs more than one man
is a partnership. This is so whether the man at the
head of the business acknowledges it or not.

Suppose a man invents an article which is capable of wide use by the people. With his own two hands he cannot make enough of them to satisfy the demand. He might work hard all his life and make only a few.

So he gets other men to give their labor that his creation may gain currency in the world. It is still his idea, but they help him to spread it. Without his idea there would not be so many jobs in the world. Without their labor there would not be so many articles of commerce.

You see, the man at the head can no longer say MY business, but all of them together can say OUR business, and when this is the spirit, and it is practiced all the way through, the very best kind of partnership exists.

There is too much of the "my" and too little of "our," both in the shops and the head office. The workman has got to assume that it is "our" business. It is the only way he can feel that it is "his" business, too.

The source of every productive result is the day's work. That is the seed from which every fruitful crop springs. The farmer gets no more out of the ground than he puts into it by his labor. And it is what the worker puts into the business that makes it pay.

What would any of us be without work? Who is so pitiable as the man without an occupation that contributes something to the life of the race?

And just as pitiable is the man who drags himself through the day's work as if he were a slave, doing as little as possible, and that little badly.

He is a brake on the wheels of industry. He is lowering its wage-paying power. He is like a faulty machine that costs more than it produces. Multiply him by a sufficient number and the business is ruined —it loses its power to support anybody connected with it.

There will never be a system invented which will do away with the necessity of work. Nature has seen to that. Idle hands and minds were never intended for any one of us. Work is our sanity, our self-respect, our salvation. So far from being a curse, work

53

is the greatest blessing. It is only when it is mixed with indolence or injustice that it becomes a curse.

Take it from a man who has worked from his earliest years, and who is a workingman now, and proud to be one, that no one can get any more out of his job than he puts into it.

Not because any man says so, buf because it is the real nature of things.

The Army Is Never "Laid Off"

WE HEAR a great deal these days about getting back to a peace basis. Some countries seem to be finding it a hard thing to do. But this is probably because they hesitate to face the other charges that must come with the new peace.

Our own problem is not simple, but it is not impossible. We went on a war footing in double-quick time. We broke all records, even the records of nations which were more accustomed to the war-thought than we were.

Now we ought to get back as quickly as we made the first change. We ought not to wait to be pushed back by the pressure of business—we ought to go back under our own will.

That seems to be the point where some plans failed; it was expected that we would be pushed back into the old channels by a strong rush of business.

The rush has not come. A sort of "between acts" period is upon us. The world is readjusting its mind after nearly five years of strange experience. The new beginning has not been as brisk in certain lines as some people expected.

But it is coming. There can be no doubt of that. The war is over in a way, and still it is not over. The iron hand is still on the world, stopping up many avenues of action. So that we have not really arrived at the "after the war" period as yet. Peace has not been signed. Blockades have not been removed. The nations have not settled down to the work of rebuilding. When they do, you will see things begin to move in a hurry.

America is in good condition to begin. We were a peace people clean through. Our industries were organized for peace. For that reason it was a bigger job for us than for others to go on a war footing. We had everything to get ready and to make. And we did it very well, considering the time we had. We did it very well indeed. The Kaiser would agree with that.

This will make it easier for us to go back where we were. Our peace machinery is all intact. It only needs to be set up and started. In many places it was not even taken down, but was set at once doing war work. We are ready for business.

But suppose business isn't here. Are we to sit down and wait? Is there nothing for us to do?

It is not the American way to sit down and wait. If not enough is doing, we must start something.

When a man has not work enough for the moment to keep his circulation up, what does he do? He begins to exercise for the sake of stimulating his circulation. He runs; he swings his arm. He starts doing something in order that he may not stagnate.

Now, business is simply circulation. Usually there is enough of it to keep us going. That is, we have enough regular business to keep us warm. But if it slows up, the sensible thing is to refuse to slow up with it. If we cannot do a certain thing we have been accustomed to do, we must do something else.

For the cost of a month of war we could make such public improvements in this land as would be worth most of the territory involved in the war. We could make a new Eden of the Mississippi Valley, turning it into the great garden and powerhouse of the country. We could build the canals and establish the waterpower we have been talking about and have never seen our way clear to do. We could develop a greater agricultural area and make the produce of former years look like a handful.

There are any number of things waiting to be done which will bring fabulous benefits to our country if we would only turn out to do them. And they are the very things which must be done if American business is not to burst its already tight bounds.

Somebody may ask where the money would come from. That is easiest of all. If it were a shortage of men or food that confronted us, it would be serious; but money is the cheapest thing there is.

All the money we spent on the war is here now. It is only the material that is gone. The war is paid for, so far as money for its support is concerned. Every man who contributed a bushel of grain, a ton of material, or a day of labor to that great enterprise has been paid. All the borrowing we did, we borrowed from ourselves, and we spent it among ourselves. All the money we lent, or the larger part of it, was spent here among us. When the borrowed money is paid back, it will be paid to the citizens who lent it. It will still be here.

There never was such an outpouring of money as during the war. Everybody had money to lend to the Government, and everybody got part of the benefit of the money he lent. It made big things possible. It made large central management possible. It kept up the circulation at a critical time.

Now, if it were necessary, why could not such a collective enterprise be undertaken for the purposes of peace? The Government is only ourselves. It is our central office. When the Government undertakes anything it is really ourselves doing it, whether it be fighting a war or building a canal.

Lack of employment ought to be as rare in the United States as snow is in the tropics. And so it would be if we thought more of the collective welfare and less of individual profit.

There is no denying that we gain or lose together. When everybody is busy, everything moves, and we all profit thereby.

And what makes everybody busy? Well, the first motive power is the necessity of three meals a day. If everyone stopped eating, very little business would be done. We must feed ourselves, and the work of doing that breeds a lot of related work, and so it goes on, broadening into what we know as modern business.

When business slows up, is it a sign that the people have slowed up on food? No. Usually it is a sign that those who handle the money are afraid to set things going. With no pressure on their gainful nature from without, they refuse to start a motive power within.

The basis of business is always with us, in the primary needs of life. The medium of business is

57

always with us in the form of money. It is only a question of starting the thing going.

We don't have to wait for China or Germany to give us the sign to get busy; we can get busy right here among ourselves, on our own concerns.

This brings it straight down to the individual who has capital, and who hangs on to it because he cannot see more of it rolling in. He ought to start something. Every man of money has in his money the surplus push which will start the wheels turning again.

The time to push is when the momentum from without has ceased.

Now is the time for the man of the future to invest in the future. If he has any building to do, let him do it now. If he has a stock to create, let him make it now.

Nobody is taking any chances when he gets busy meeting the future beforehand.

This little breathing spell is a good thing to take advantage of. Now is the time to spend money and prepare for tomorrow's business, because it is going to come rolling in fast.

And then there is the human side of it. Let us take a lesson from the Government in this. The Government has a great army to provide for. The business of that army is to fight. But suppose there comes a lull of months when there is no fighting to do. During this war it has happened, as it sometimes does in industry, that there is nothing for an army to do in the task it was organized for.

We have seen whole winters pass with nothing special for the armies to do.

Did the Government lay the men off and stop their pay, saying, "Come back when the fighting opens up again and we'll put you on the payroll"?

No. The Government felt itself under obligation to keep that army intact and in good trim.

Where is the difference between our fighting armies and the armies of peace—our great industrial army?

There are about twenty millions of men engaged in the industrial maintenance of the United States. They are our great standing army of production. They are necessary to our existence as a self-supporting people.

58

No calamity could overtake the country that would equal the removal of this great force from agriculture, manufacturing and transportation.

Yet what is done with these men in slack times? They are turned out at their own charges, and expected to be on hand when they are needed again.

It isn't good management. It isn't the kind of treatment to which loyalty responds. It breaks us up into separate interests, when really we are but one interest and ought to be united for the general welfare.

This is one point where we are wrong.

It is easy enough to place the blame, but it is hard to prove the blame. If any one man could remedy it, that man could be blamed for not doing so. But it is too big for any man or group of men to cure by their own efforts, and therefore it is too big for them to bear the blame for it.

It is something we must all try to do together, and do on a system. We must so adjust matters that the slack in employment will be automatically taken up. Dullness in one line must be offset by brisk effort in another.

If we set about it intelligently we could find profitable productive work for twice the number of our present industrial army. America teems with work waiting to be done. America will never be oversupplied with labor if we develop our resources as we ought. It is the duty of men of vision, men of resource to lay out the new channels for the industry of new millions of men. There is enough to be done in America to engage our largest man-power to the farthest generation.

Individually, it is our duty to endeavor as far as we possibly can to regard our own men as our own regiments in the struggle for industrial civilization, and to feel a responsibility for them in slack times. We do not allow our shop machinery to rust in times of dull business; why should we allow our men to deteriorate? The cost of tiding over enforced stoppages ought to be figured in as a cost of the business itself.

If we undertook to do this, we would be surprised at the speed we would make in looking for large public undertakings to be started in order to fill up times of slack employment. In fact, we would soon have matters arranged so that slack times would be impossible. When one line slowed up, we would simply switch on another, and so keep things going.

It is our duty to do each of us our bit in solving this problem, and we may be sure that when American business men try to straighten out the industrial situation and make it square all round, they are going to succeed. Nothing but selfishness can hinder, for selfishness is blind.

This talk of the returned soldier being a problem hardly squares with the facts. He is only two millions of our twenty millions. He ought to fit back into business life as readily as he fitted into the army.

To hear some men talk you would think that the returning soldier would double our dependent population. He is bringing up the reserve force that will put the country over the top.

They talk of putting him to work building roads, booming worn-out real estate schemes, and so forth. It is a wonder they would not ask him about it first!

No doubt, after the outdoor life of the army, thousands of young men will have no desire to enter the office and store again. They would prefer the farm. But why plan to settle them 3,000 miles from the chief markets? There are hundreds of thousands of unused acres of farm land at the very back doors of our large eastern markets.

Leave the big unsettled tracts of the West for wholesale reclamation and power projects. It would be splendid if we could enlist an army of men to make the desert bloom and make every mile of our streams and every foot of our land productive. That would be an Army of the United States indeed! And it would appeal to heroism and constructive generalship. And it would bring a service record of which any man might be proud.

There are big days coming to us. We must get ready for them. We must act as if we had the orders in our hands now. We must begin to organize our forces and processes so as to achieve the most and the best we can.

Prevention Is Better Than
Sympathy

PAINTING the blotch on the skin, and leaving the blood unpurified, is poor medical practice and poor business. Unless we go to the root of our wrongs and grub them out, it is of no use to try to doctor the branches. Pruning the thorn will not change it into a potato plant.

You can fight a symptom until the patient dies on your hands, but unless you get at the cause of his distemper you are only wasting your time and giving the disease a stronger hold.

Take the life of our people, for example. We know that something is wrong with it. It would be extreme folly for us to deny that.

The man who does deny it is usually the man who is profiting by the things that are wrong. Because his nest is soft, he coddles himself into believing that every nest is soft. He does not want to be disturbed by any other view of it.

This is one of the strong marks by which you may distinguish sympathy from selfishness.

Granting that something is wrong in our method of life, the wise course to take is not to go about tinkering and doctoring the effects, but to dig straight in toward the causes.

You will find, for one part, that something is wrong with the people themselves. There is a great deal of shiftlessness in the world, a great deal of waste, a great deal of drifting.

You will find men who want to be carried through on the shoulders of others. You will find men who believe that the world OWES them a living, by which they seem to mean that their employer owes them a living. They don't seem to see that we must all lift together and pull together, or nobody will have any living whatever.

It is one of the most harmful thoughts a man can harbor—that he is at the mercy of any other man. We are all units of power. We are all parts of the social order. Wherever one of us holds back or falls down, there is a gap, and the whole line suffers by that much.

All this is true enough, but to stop here is to miss half the truth. Many people stop here. They lay the whole blame for poverty and failure and suffering and waste upon individuals.

But our scheme of society is at fault, too. We do many things badly. We permit too many practices that take advantage of the weak. We open too wide a field to the grabber. After we have charged up all we can to individual fault, there is a big social fault that must be accounted for.

And one of our most glaring mistakes is to try to cover up the results of social faults by charity, instead of striking at the causes which make charity seem necessary.

Charity at its best is only a makeshift. It is an endless patching of a garment that ought to be thrown away and a new one made. Charity lowers the self-respect of the person who receives it and it deadens the conscience of the person who gives it. It offers far too easy an escape from a harder job.

We say we are sorry for the hungry man. How sorry are we? We are sorry enough to give him a little food. But are we sorry enough to go out and tackle the conditions that make hunger possible?

We say we are sorry for the unemployed. But how sorry are we? Are we sorry enough to shoulder the job of abolishing unemployment from the land by a new and daring system of industrial advance?

It is easy enough to be sorry, and to ease our own sorrow by a trifling gift. For that is really what we do in most of our makeshift charity—we simply ease our own pain at the sight of suffering. Whether we really ease the suffering of the other man, or improve his condition, is quite another matter.

We were sorry for the man wounded in battle, and so we supported the Red Cross and other humane agencies. But how many of us were sorry enough to

62

undertake to abolish war altogether? To aid the wounded was easier than to tackle the big blunder that has been wounding men for centuries.

We can go on to the end of time patching up the wounded who ought never to have been wounded, feeding the hungry who ought never to have been hungry, helping the poor who ought never to have been poor—and at the end of all our efforts we shall still have war and poverty as much as before.

Regarded from the standpoint of efficiency our charity system fails; no matter how hard we try we are never able to cover the ground. We are always missing someone. From whatever angle you study it, charity is a poor substitute for reform.

We must go deeper if we are ever to accomplish anything worth while.

And we must quit being satisfied with our charity if we are ever to see the real job that awaits us. And it is no easy job, either; it is not for bunglers, nor for hasty people, nor for any one who believes in anything but sound construction.

The doctors are ahead of us on this line. Their great word now is, Prevention. When typhoid breaks out, they do not content themselves with giving their best service to the afflicted individuals; they know that typhoid is a disease that no man ever ought to have, and so they search out its source. They abolish it there.

The progress of medicine does not consist merely in discovering cures for disease, but in abolishing it so utterly that it will cease to be a problem.

We need that word in our efforts toward a better kind of social and industrial life—Prevention.

Instead of organizing great machinery and making great appeals for money to camouflage the effects of our social system, we ought to be at work preventing the effects.

The very best charity we know anything about is to help a man to the place where he will never need it.

Nothing seems more useless than the trouble we take to ease the effects, when half the trouble would serve to destroy the cause.

We get up fancy dances, we give theatricals, we

63

make budgets and take up collections, we sell tickets for this and that from one year's end to the other—we undertake great expense to grant a little temporary benefit, and when we get through we haven't touched the real problem.

Surely the futility of it ought to get through our minds very soon!

It is not the charitable mind that one objects to. Heaven forbid that we should ever grow cold toward a fellow-creature in need. Human sympathy is a great motive power, and no cool, calculating attitude will take the place of it. One can name very few of the great advances which were not due to human sympathy. It is in order to do something for people that every notable service is undertaken.

The trouble is that we have been using this great motive force for too small ends. If human sympathy prompts us to feed the hungry, why should it not give a much greater prompting toward making hunger impossible?

If we have sympathy enough for people to help them IN their trouble, surely we ought to have feeling enough to help them OUT OF their trouble.

The difficulty is that the latter is a different sort of task. This kind of help costs more than common charity.

We must look beyond the individual to the causes of his misery, not hesitating to relieve him in the meantime, of course, but not stopping with that.

It is a pity that we have to confess that more people can be moved to help a poor family than can be moved to give their minds toward the removal of poverty altogether.

We have a human conscience all right; cannot we develop it into a social conscience?

But people say, "What can I do?" And men in positions of leadership say, "What can we do?" Well, this is certain—whatever is done will have to be done by all of us together, so that it is time for all of us to get busy.

And this is certain—we cannot improve conditions by kicking over the methods which make our conditions as good as they are.

64

Grant that something is wrong; still we cannot say that everything is wrong. If it were, there would be much more suffering in the world than we now see.

Comparing the present with the past, there is far less poverty than ever before; our material life is on a much higher level than it has ever been.

So far, so good. But comparing the present with what ought to be, and what could be, we cannot fail to see that much is yet to be done.

What can we do to create what ought to be?

Our first duty is our own duty. We must do our best where we are. We must be fair where we are. We must do honest work where we are.

No one who throws down his tools is helping to abolish poverty.

Whatever we may agree to do in the future, we may be sure of this: we shall never be able to make any program go without work.

If work is to be necessary in the better order of things, work is a good quality to develop now.

Every man who works is helping to drive poverty out of the world—first his own, and then that of his fellow-beings.

The man who does better and more productive work today than he did yesterday is a social reformer of the highest type. He is doing something genuine. He is squaring his own account with the world, and helping others to square theirs.

Every time a man stops work, he throws that much extra burden on others; he creates that much more poverty for the world.

It is not the men who are doing the talking who are solving our problems, but the men who are at work. When they talk, they know what it is about.

And after work, the next duty is to think. No-body can think straight who does not work. Idleness warps the mind. It is a wonder we do not hear more about that fact—that the practiced hand gives balance to the brain.

Thinking which does not connect with constructive action becomes a disease; the man who has it sees crooked; his views are lopsided.

No one man can think out our great problems for

65

us. We believe in democracy because we believe that the collective mind is better than any single mind.

It is the people thinking together, and planning together, and acting together, that make the great advances possible.

In the long run the people are cool-headed.

That is one of the reasons why changes seem to come so slowly: the people do not risk the big mistakes which end in the big tragedies. Every age teems with theories which only require to stand awhile, and then their falsity is revealed.

We don't have to test every theory that is offered. Let it stand. If it is right, it will endure. If it is wrong, the public mind simply outgrows it.

No one can imagine how much worse off we should be if we followed every theory and every leader that promised us the Golden Age.

So, if our progress seems slow, it is only the people's carefulness not to make a mis-step.

But there is progress being made all the time, now in this direction, now in that, and then all along the line. And such progress is a social creation. It is the people moving up.

And that is the only kind of progress there is.

If we have not always gone forward rapidly, there is a very great fact to set against that fact: the race has not had to retrace many steps because of false moves.

Success Plays No Favorites

SOMEONE has said that "imitation is the sincerest flattery," but that is only a hint to those who wish to flatter. Imitation is a confession that the thing which is imitated is better than one can do himself; it is also a confession that one is content to be an imitator.

The truth about imitation is found in another saying—"Imitation is suicide."

Certainly it is the end of initiative and independence; it is the farewell of originality; it is the deliberate abandonment of individuality, and the enemy of genius.

This has a direct bearing on a subject in which everybody is interested—Success.

Too often we hear Success spoken of as if it can be imitated. Successful men are held up as examples to young people who are advised, "Do as this man did it." Methods of success are held up for imitation with the counsel, "Follow this course and it will lead to success."

But success does not come by imitation. An imitation may be quite successful in its own way, but imitation can never be Success.

Success is a first-hand creation. Take a thousand successful men, and each man's story will be different. It will be original. His grasp of opportunity, his methods, his plan of meeting and overcoming obstacles, all of these things will be different.

The most dangerous notion a young man can acquire is that there is no more room for originality. There is no large room for anything else.

Let us put to one side the usual arguments against imitation in the search for Success. Everybody knows what they are, so that we need not recount them here.

But it is not always so clear why much of our Success advice is dangerous.

It is very unwise to look too long at the successful person. It is most unwise to copy after him.

Because the things which you will first see, the qualities which will stand out as marking him, are probably not the ones to which he owes his success. And yet, because they are most prominent, it will appear that they hold the secret of his power. Very often they are blemishes, and had they not been over-balanced by other qualities which are not so easily perceived they might have caused his failure.

You see a man who is very successful and who is at the same time very unfeeling. His heart is hard. He regards other men as so many bricks to build with. His conscience seems to be asleep. He rides over every human instinct and crushes every human consideration that would oppose him. Looking at such a man, it is easy to say, "To succeed, you must be like that; you must harden your heart and go rough-shod over everything."

Or you may see another successful man who appears to be very daring. He seems to do everything thoughtlessly, on the spur of the moment, in a brilliant dare-devil spirit. He does not appear to trust to anything but luck. But matters turn out fortunately for him, and therefore it is easy to draw the conclusion, "The way to be successful is to fling ahead regardless, gamble with chance, and trust affairs to come out all right."

These appearances may be very misleading. Dishonest men do sometimes achieve great financial success—American financial history shows that. Unfeeling, cruel-hearted men sometimes win great fortunes in industry—we don't have to look far to see it.

But the question is: Is their success due to dishonesty and hardness, or to qualities that are not so prominent?

We must declare that dishonesty is not sufficient to win success. A man must have something beside a hard heart to win success.

He may have these undesirable qualities—he may have them in large measure—but has he other qualities beside?

If you look closely at these men you will see that they do have other qualities. They have strength, foresight, knowledge, skill, experience, endurance, application, determination, gifts of management, judgment.

But these are not surface qualities. They do not stand out. They are seen only on close examination of the man and his business.

Take a group of successful men, sort out the ones who have undesirable traits of character—men who have broken the laws of the land and the laws of humanity, men who have wrung their money out of other men's labor and out of the public's necessity—and you can easily make out an argument that Success is the sign of a bad character.

But the law of Success is impartial. So long as you have the qualities necessary for success, it is to be won, even if you have other qualities which alone would spell failure.

You may have a character which is perfect in every other respect, and yet if you lack the qualities necessary to success, you will never win it.

Success, then, is a matter of certain qualities coming into play.

Now you cannot imitate a quality. You must create it, develop it. If you are fooled into thinking that hardness and dishonesty are qualities of Success, and you develop these, you will find that they will not make you a successful man at all. Hardness will make you a bully and dishonesty will make you a crook. You must develop other characteristics if you would be successful.

We are not considering genius here at all. Genius is a gift. It comes to very few. We are discussing the normal man who enters life endowed with physical health, his five senses, and the average degree of intelligence.

The genius walks into his success. The rest of us must work for ours.

Now, what is Success?

Some say that Success is not money. Well, it is doubtless true that money is not the whole of Suc-

69

cess, and yet in these days you never see any kind of Success that does not have money somewhere around it. Certainly money is not the end of life, but it is a sign. Since everyone needs money to live as he ought, to develop himself, to give scope to his powers, money has become not only a necessary part of living, but the ambition to command enough of it to do these things has become a commendable ambition.

Success is each man finding the work he can do best, doing it to his highest satisfaction, and getting the proof of his service in a suitable reward.

If he is the kind of man who has still greater visions of service which need still more money to realize, Success is his getting enough money to fulfill his service. There is no harm in large sums of money if they are kept at work opening up lines of opportunity and service. The only harmful money is the money which lies idle, or is used to block progress.

Money for money's sake is a perfectly stupid motto. Money would be as useless as a heap of brass checks if it were not used for development. So that it is true that money itself is not the whole of Success.

And then there are certain lines of service whose Success does not require money for their enlargement, and therefore money is not the sign of their worth. Take a successful surgeon, for example. His skill is his capital. He will make money, of course, and he deserves to make it. But often he will do service that makes him no money at all, and still it will be highly successful, because it accomplishes its object. But the surgeon does not need millions in order to extend his skill. That skill is in his hand, controlled by his brain. He cannot multiply it. He cannot standardize operations and do them by machine. Therefore, though his financial success is deservedly satisfactory, he has not the same need of capital as another would have.

But in the industrial line it is indispensable that financial success be won, else there is no way to keep going, there is no way to open up new lines and create new jobs for men, there is no way of paying better wages and so contributing to the general human welfare.

So that it is true again; money is not the only standard of success, though in some lines of service it is.

But in every Success, whether it be professional or industrial, the same qualities are necessary. And these cannot be imitated. They must be real. They must live in the man himself and grow out of his nature. Few of them are natural growth, however. They must be developed, trained, kept under discipline.

No man wins success without paying for it.

No man fails without good reason.

The law of success is no respecter of persons.

If a man whom we feel to be bad turns out to be a success, it is because he has fulfilled the law of success. If a man whom we feel to be a very good man is a failure, it is because he has failed to fulfill the law of success.

There is no favoritism.

The law of success is a fair law. It gives all a chance. It doesn't choose the extraordinary man and favor him. Most successful men you meet are really ordinary men who have applied themselves to one thing and paid the price to win.

And the law of failure is just and fair. We dislike to think this sometimes, but unless it also is true, then there is nothing but confusion, no guide-posts to direct us.

We know there are failures just as we know there are successes. Honest men fail and dishonest men fail. Hard-hearted men fail and kind, humane men fail. Why?

To find the reason we must examine failure as carefully as we examine success. And, as in the case of success, the truth is not on the surface.

There is always a reason for failure, just as there is always a reason for Success, and it is found in disobedience to one part of the law of Success.

If failures did not fail, there would be no law. All would be chance. The fact that failures fail is not a discouraging fact; it is just the other side of the law by which those who have fulfilled the law of Success, succeed.

71

There is always a good reason, one which impresses us as entirely fair when we understand it.

To state the law of Success is a pretty big task. We may try to state part of it at another time. But certain elements of it are clear at once.

There is no Success without Application. This means concentration of mind, labor of hand and brain, and a complete surrender of one's powers to what one wishes to do.

There must be Confidence in one's plan, not because it is one's own plan, but because, after surveying the whole field, the needs of the people, the fitness of the service one intends to give, one knows that he is on the right track.

There must be Courage. Unless you have tried to do something for yourself, you have no idea how often your courage will be tested, how often you will stare bleak failure full in the face, how many almost crushing obstacles will arise to fall on you and block the way. The road to Success is hard, and often the feet bleed and the heart nearly fails. People only see the end of it, and even the end is not all sunshine. So unless you have courage, a courage within your own heart that keeps you going, always going, no matter what happens, there is no certainty of Success. It is really an endurance race. It is a test in holding out. The untried venture has no friends anywhere. It must make every friend it gets.

You must have Knowledge of what you are doing. Now, this is within every man's reach. There is no favoritism here. You must know all there is to know of your particular field, and keep on the alert for new knowledge. The least difference in knowledge between you and another man may spell his success and your failure. Guessing does not go. Trusting to luck is folly. Going it blind is taking a chance that may prove disastrous. You must KNOW. And this, of course, means that you must be a sincere searcher all the time. Yes, even when you have become what the world calls a success. For the world moves swiftly, and it is as bad not to keep up with it as never to have caught up with it. Today's success is no security for tomorrow's success. Your knowledge must be the up-to-the-minute kind.

As to the moral qualities, the more you have the better. Dishonest men, by obeying the other laws of Success, may have won a place. But it is becoming harder and harder to do that. They may have been dishonest in dealing, but they cannot be dishonest with materials. They must build their brick wall true, or it falls down. They must honestly obey the law of strain, or their bridge collapses. They may cheat their customer once, they cannot cheat nature even once. Better not try to cheat either, for dishonesty is a dry-rot that creeps in everywhere. Other things being equal, the honest man has the better chance of winning. The same is true of human kindliness. All other qualifications being equal the humane man has the edge on the hard man.

Personal Relations—Their Importance for Life

IF YOU trace down the troubles which afflict us all, the big disturbing troubles and the little nagging ones, you will discover that a large proportion of them have their roots in personal relations.

Trace them and see. See what an amazingly large influence is exerted on your life by what you think of other people, and by what you think other people think about you.

Wrong personal relations are the greatest obstruction that a man can meet. Almost any other kind of obstacle he can face with a high heart; but broken relations between himself and his fellows afflict his nature like a wound.

We were meant to get along one with another. We were meant to be in harmony. And no other proof of this is needed than the fact that the better we know each other the more we trust each other; and the larger the number of people who work in harmony the greater the results of their work.

People always think better, work better, see more clearly when they are in harmony with the people whom they know. But their minds are clouded, their hands are heavy and their foresight is blinded when they carry within them the feeling that they are at odds with their kind.

It is like a strain in one's body; it is painful and hindering. Humanity-at-large seems to be one body; our immediate circle of associates, friends and kin make a sort of inner body, and any break or strain that occurs with them hurts and hinders us.

If a man leaves the house in the morning after an angry word with his wife he has practically ruined his day and hers, too. He ought to go back and fix up the strained relations. Husband and wife simply cannot live their best or do their best under strained conditions.

You can pretty nearly identify the man who left home in a sulk—probably you could identify the wife, too, if you saw her. The signs of moral accident and mental injury are about them. They are cripples so far as human harmony is concerned.

Railroad managers long ago learned how dangerous it was for an engineer to climb into his cab and take charge of a train, after he had left home in a tantrum. It would be safer to hold up the train while the engineer went back home and made up with his wife—far safer.

If you cannot identify these injured minds by the faces they carry, you can usually do so by the work they turn out. It is crippled work. None of us can work unless our minds are free.

There is a hint for employers in this. It is just as possible to injure human relations by wrong shop methods as by wrong home conditions.

The workman can be made to feel that he is under a driver or under a leader. If he feels that he is under a driver you have simply pinched up his initiative and good-will to such an extent that he cannot, at least does not, do his best.

If he feels that he is under a leader, whom he respects and trusts, then his initiative and strength are released, and his day's work is free and full.

Nervous strain operates on people to their disadvantage. Fill a child with the feeling of constraint, and he will appear to you a most stupid youngster, although he may in reality be a bright child. Chill a performer by criticism and antagonism in advance, and you simply freeze up the stream of his skill.

Now, if you simply want the people who help you in your shop to know who is boss, you can let them know it all right—know it in such a way that they will never forget it nor forgive you.

The cheapest and easiest thing in the world is to show your authority. You can show your authority till doomsday and make people fear it too; but you will never make them respect it.

The authority which men respect is the authority of superior knowledge and good-will.

75

When you fill a shop with fear, making men slaves who bend to their tasks when the overseer's eyes are upon them and slacken when the "boss" passes on— you haven't a free industry at all. You are running a sort of prison.

It is not the DRIVE of the boss that makes production; it is the loyal good-will of the workers.

You see, this directly concerns personal relations in industry. Handling men, giving them leave to act upon their own good-will and not under constant compulsion, emancipating them from all fear and anxiety and insecurity in their thoughts of the shop and the job—this is the secret of good-will in production.

You cannot secure all this by good wages alone. High wages help to relieve anxiety about living conditions at home. But if in order to keep those high wages a man is kept on tiptoe of anxiety while he is at the shop, the very purpose of high wages is perverted.

That is all we have to go on—personal relations. And personal relations mean that we know one another, that we acknowledge one another to be men, that we deal squarely with one another, that we have confidence in one another, and that we feel good-will toward each other.

The day is coming when good-will shall be the most valuable asset a man can have.

Now just to enlarge this circle of thought a little, take the so-called question of "labor and capital." When you boil it down, what do you get?—a lot of broken human relations.

The capitalist is just a man. The laborer is just a man. They are born, grow, marry, live and die in the same way. Their joys are pretty much alike, and so are their troubles. They are plain human beings. Circumstances have placed one in one job, the other in another job. But in the end it is always the same job.

Well, what has driven them apart? What makes them say hard things against one another?

They have gotten out of touch with each other, broken the human relation, that's all—and often through no fault of their own.

76

Take certain capitalist papers and read them. You will be amazed by some of the statements they make about the laboring class, as they call it. We who have been and still are a part of the laboring class know that the statements are untrue. We feel that if the writers only knew the people of whom they write, their views would be changed.

And then take certain of the labor papers and read them. You are equally amazed by some of the statements they make about "capitalists," so-called. Some of us who know that capitalists are just men, many of them working harder than they ever did years ago when they were classed "laboring" men, know how unjust some of these statements are.

And yet on both sides there is truth, of course. The man who is a capitalist and nothing else, who gambles with money in the fruits of other men's labors, deserves all that is said against him. He is in precisely the same class as the cheap gambler who cheats workingmen out of their wages. There is no difference.

Now, if you look close you will see that in the capitalistic and the labor press there is a sort of middle-class who pander to the prejudices of the class they serve. The statements we read about the laboring class in the capitalistic press are seldom written by managers of great industries, but by a middle-class of writers who are writing what they think will please their capitalistic leaders. They write what they imagine will please; they have no desire to correct or instruct.

Examine the labor press and you will find, in some parts of it, another middle-class of writers who seek to tickle the prejudices which they conceive the laboring man to have.

And what is the result? Why, one class reads material that inflames it against the other, and the other does the same. The result is that we have two great necessary and complementary classes in contempt of each other without even knowing each other —taking the word of middlemen-writers for it.

Now, this will never do. This is inhuman, unreasonable. You can no more indict a class than you can indict a nation. Good and bad are mixed up in all classes. The only class line any sound-minded man ought to recognize is the line drawn by decency and morality.

Because one man is at the machine end of an industry and another man is at the management end, that is no reason why human relations should be broken between them. That is no basis for class distinctions. If the manager thinks it is, he is wrong. If the machinist thinks it is, he is wrong too.

Men are not divided by the kind of work they do, but by the kind of men they are.

Men who are doing their own work as well as they can, who are working out methods which will bring more justice into industry and more comfort to mankind, who are on the side of progress and order and humanity and right—these men belong to one class, no matter what their financial rating may be.

And men who are shirking work whenever they can, who are inventing new tricks to steal the fruits of others' labor, who oppose better conditions and who are standpatters on all the privilege and injustice and semi-slavery that exist—these men belong to another class, and some of them are capitalists and some of them are laborers.

It is the first class that is going to make the world a better place to live in and the lot of humanity more desirable. It is the class to which every man of goodwill should belong—does belong by his very nature.

Nothing is more perilous to right human relations than to take your views of any man through a third man's eyes.

Every one of us has had the experience of being made suspicious and unfriendly toward a person on another person's say-so, and having to revise our opinions as soon as we came to know the man himself.

Something like this is going on all the time. It makes for disorder in all our relations, industrial, social and domestic. You see it in almost every shop —two men at loggerheads, simply because they have received their views of each other from unfriendly second-hand sources.

The cure of all this is to come together, know each other, see the man as he is, know him in his natural feeling and intention—and when we can do this, there are very, very few human beings in whom we cannot find a basis of fellowship.

And until we can do this, the wiser way is to suspend judgment altogether.

Half the disharmony in human relations today is founded on assumption, guesses, misinformation.

One of the regrettable and yet inevitable results of our modern industrial development is that it places us so far apart. We all remember the time when we knew every person in the shop; it was a kind of family. We knew about good luck and bad luck at home; we knew about new babies and about the sicknesses and deaths; we had a fellow-feeling for one another.

Human beings have not changed. Human relations are just as necessary now as they ever were. And men have not become machines in the meantime. We must contrive some way of retaining the human touch in industry. We shall need it as long as we need the human element and that will be until the end of time.

One way to do this is to maintain the superiority of men over machines. You can drive a machine until it breaks—you must not drive men that way.

Another way is to retain human initiative in industry. A shop that is organized in fear may be apparently a smoothly working organization, but it has not the willing "shove" of the shop that works from loyalty. Even the driver cannot drive all the time. And the shop personnel that works all day in the feeling of fear or anxiety is always on the look-out to get another job. It doesn't pay to be changing men.

Old employes, like old friends, are best.

Satisfied employes, men who are on their honor, men who feel that it is to their own interest to do their best—that is the best organization any business can have. But you cannot get it through friction. You must get it through real human relations.

When we all feel that we can trust one another,

that we do not have to be continually on guard against each other, that our loyalty and interest are not going to be taken a mean advantage of, then how freely the work flows, how freely a man gives his best to his job!

We need better personal relations everywhere. It is the great need of the world just now. All that looks dark on the horizon of modern life is really the result of bad personal relations. And it can be cleared up by a new growth of genuine friendship among us.

That, after all is said and done, is what the brotherhood of man means—we trust each other, we wish well to each other, we help each other.

Cultivate Your Own Market

THERE was a time when the wise men assured us that Commerce would be a world preventive of war. Trade was valuable, we were told, and only a fool would want to kill off his customers. Much was said also about the better acquaintance which would grow out of international business; we would like the Chinese better because we bought tea from them; we would understand and appreciate the German because we bought goods from him; and every nation which did business with Americans would learn to love and respect them.

Well, at the apex of the greatest commercial age the greatest war broke out. And if there is any truth at all in the mass of explanation that has been made, our business relations with each other had a great deal to do with it. Some of the greater business men of Germany have told how the war was figured in advance on a profit basis, and there are enough facts at hand to indicate that business had more to do with the outbreak than politics had.

At the same time, and in spite of the commercial element in the causes of the war, there ought to be an enlightening and binding quality in the commercial relations between nations, and there would be if business were only what it ought to be and can be.

The signs of the times are that the world is ready to go back to the same old business basis as before, and if it does we are only laying the basis for new misunderstandings.

If the nations are to become business competitors again, the old spirit of antagonism will be revived.

Two men or two firms may be competitors and live together without rupturing their relations with each other, without departing from the law of decency; but that is next to impossible for two nations to do.

When the political power of a government puts itself behind the competitive commercial ambitions of its money magnates, acts are likely to be committed of which no private competitor would dream. It is to the credit of the United States that our Government refused to allow American business to take unfair advantage of the stricken nations of Eurupe in stealing their markets from them; and one òf the very great moral acts of the war was the assurance given by America that we were above making a grand grab for the very living of those nations for whose help we raised armies.

And yet, in spite of this, there is every indication that the world is going to slip back into the old system of one nation cutting under another for the sake of trade.

It isn't the amount of trade that makes a nation great, for if you will study the more recently industrialized countries you will discover that the change consists mostly in taking the people off the land, away from agriculture, and running them through a factory system whose sole aim and object is the creation of great private fortunes.

The creation of private fortunes, like the creation of an autocracy, does not make any country great; nor does the mere change of an agricultural population into a factory population.

What accomplishes the desired end is the wise development of its natural resources combined with a high development of the skill of its people, and a general diffusion among all classes of the prosperity thus gained.

Foreign trade is full of delusions. The ultimatè basis of foreign trade is going to be the supply of those commodities which cannot be raised or manufactured in the places to which we send them.

If every nation were fully developed so that it could supply itself with the articles' it now imports, foreign trade would be diminished just that much.

We ought to wish for every nation as large a degree of self-support as possible. Instead of wishing to keep them dependent on us for what we manufacture, we should wish them to learn the arts themselves, to clothe and feed and house themselves and build up a solidly founded civilization.

When every nation learns to produce the things which every nation can produce, then we will be able to get down to a basis of serving each other along those special lines in which there can be no competition.

The north temperate zone will never be able to compete with the tropics in the special products of the tropics. Our country will never be a competitor with the Orient in the production of tea, nor with the South in the production of rubber.

A very large proportion of our foreign trade is based on the backwardness of our foreign customers. Selfishness is a motive that would preserve that backwardness. Humanity is a motive that would help the backward nations to a self-supporting basis.

Better than shooting the African native to make him buy your cotton and your beads, is his development so that he can supply his own needs and build up a business in the commodities of which Nature has given his country a monopoly.

Take Mexico, for example. We have heard a great deal about the "development" of Mexico. Exploitation is the word that ought to be used instead. When its rich natural resources are exploited for the increase of the private fortunes of foreign capitalists, it is not development, it is ravishment.

You can never develop Mexico until you develop the Mexican. And yet how much of the "development" of Mexico by foreign exploiters ever took account of the development of its people? The Mexican peon has been regarded as mere fuel for the foreign money-makers, that's all. Foreign trade has been his degradation.

Yet think what Mexico could be, with its people trained to use the resources of the land, and supplying the world with those commodities in which she most abounds. She would then become a different kind of a customer, it is true, but also a better kind.

Start Mexico working. Teach her people how to erect and manage their own industries. Give them

83

the benefit of our experience and guidance. And then you have done something for the peace and prosperity of the world.

Short-sighted people are afraid of such counsel, for they say, "Where would our foreign trade be then?".

When the natives of Africa begin raising their own cotton and the natives of Russia begin making their own farming implements and the natives of China begin supplying their own wants, it will make a difference to be sure, but does any thoughtful man imagine that the world can long continue on the present basis of a few nations supplying the entire world? We must think in terms of what the world will be when civilization becomes general, when all the peoples have learned to help themselves.

Take Germany for example. The United States formerly depended on her for dye-stuffs. Now we are making our own. Isn't it right that we should make our own? Had Germany any ground for believing that we should always remain dependent on her when our own initiative could make us independent? Is Germany doomed because foreign trade is cut off?

Not at all. Germany has the land with which to feed herself and in the absence of foreign trade she is left free to develop herself.

When a country grows mad about foreign trade it usually depends on other countries for its raw material, turns its population into factory fodder, creates a private rich class, and lets its own immediate interests lie neglected.

Here in the United States we have enough work to do developing our own country to relieve us of the necessity of looking for foreign trade for a long time. We have agriculture enough to feed us while we are doing it; and money enough to carry the job through without a jolt.

If there is anything more stupid than the United States standing idle because Japan or France or any other country hasn't sent us an order, when there is a hundred-year job awaiting us in developing our own country, it would be difficult to discover it.

Every nation's country is its farm, so to speak.

It can live on it. There are always chores to do to keep up the farm. There are always improvements to be made—and there's the farmer to do it and food in his granary to support him while he is doing it.

Commerce in its purity is a great fact. But commerce began in service. Men carried of their surplus to people who had none. The country that raised corn carried it to the country that could raise no corn. The lumber country brought wood to the treeless plain. The vine country brought fruit to cold northern climes. The pasture country brought meat to the grassless region. It was all service.

When all the peoples of the world become developed in the art of self-support, commerce will get back to that basis. Business will once more become service. There will be no competition, because the basis of competition will have vanished. The tropics have a monopoly of sunshine. The temperate zones have a monopoly of the hardy grains. The great pampas have a monopoly of pasturage for cattle raising. The mineral regions and the oil depositories have a natural monopoly of these things.

And the peoples will develop skill which will be in the nature of monopoly and not competitive. We already see evidence of these national gifts in the arts. From the beginning the races have exhibited distinct strains of genius: this one for government; another for colonization; another for the sea; another for art and music; another for agriculture; another for business, and so on.

Lincoln said that this nation could not survive half-slave and half-free. The human race cannot forever exist half exploiter and half exploited. Until we become buyers and sellers alike, producers and consumers alike, keeping the balance not for profit but for service, we are going to have a topsy-turvy condition.

Until society in its relations balances, the account is going to be wrong. And the best way to balance it is to make every nation as nearly self-supporting in the common necessities as is possible. Then commerce may be built up on those articles which do not depend on competitive throat-cutting for their advancement, but on sheer need and supply.

France has something to give the world of which no competition can cheat her. So has Italy. So has Russia. So have the countries of South America. So has Japan. So has Britain. So has the United States.

Everyone knows, also, that our present system of foreign exploitation is a menace to our own peace. President Wilson saw that most clearly in the Mexican situation. Fortunately for our country, both President and people saw what the trouble was down there. It was nothing more nor less than the demand of exploiters that we protect them while they skimmed the cream of Mexican natural wealth.

There is no backward country in the world but would welcome any foreign producer who comes in with a view to developing the country. Because, whenever you undertake to develop a country you must develop the people, too. Whenever any people raises the cry, "Our country for ourselves," as Mexico said, "Mexico for the Mexicans," it is a sure sign that they have been exploited by outsiders. Nobody objects to true development because everybody sees the good and shares in the benefit of it. But human nature, even in the black savages of Africa, who are exploited in the rubber trade and the diamond mines, objects to being regarded as mere human fuel for foreign forge fires.

Men who are kept busy at home do not start wars for foreign markets. And foreign markets that are won through service and not through commercial trickery are never the breeding cause of wars.

A nation, like a man, should be self-supporting. Having squared his own account, the man becomes a good citizen, a good customer, and a peaceable factor in the general prosperity. So also the nation.

But, if after the battle of guns, we are going back to the battle of goods again, in the same old spirit of injury and deceit, we are only preparing for the day when, as in 1914, we drop our order-books and seize weapons.

It is the part of wisdom to abolish war everywhere and first of all in Commerce.

"Labor and Capital" Are
False Terms

A MONG the tools we work with are words. Words stand for ideas, but ideas are often held back for lack of words, as freight is held up for lack of cars. Many men who possess ideas are hindered because they do not possess enough words to deliver them. You may notice this in current discussions of our social problems. It sometimes happens that people who indulge in these discussions exhibit a lack of word-tools with which to complete their mental work.

For example: you may hear the whole human race summed up under two heads, Labor and Capital; and you may hear serious discussions proceed on the assumption that these two "classes" comprise all the elements of the social problem.

When you take the man who works with his hands and set him on one side, and the capitalist-idler on the other side, you have not divided the human world. There are hosts of people in between. But because we are tied to the terms Labor and Capital, we go along under the notion that we have included everybody.

The figure 4 will not serve if 7 is meant; neither will the word "capitalist" serve when it is only "manufacturer" that is intended.

The trouble is that under the terms Labor and Capital we include elements we do not intend.

We ought to be absolutely merciless in our intellectual isolation of capitalists, so that we may see them clearly by themselves and not mixed up with other elements that do not belong there.

To speak only of Labor and Capital is to permit too much good company to surround the mere capitalist who produces nothing and who skims the cream off other men's product.

Under that formula which divides the world into

two classes, the dangerous capitalist is allowed to escape in the crowd, or take to himself the credit of other people who happen to be mistaken for members of his class. He claims the credit due the manufacturer, banker, legitimate financier—for it must always be borne in mind that a man may be a manufacturer, a banker or a gifted financier without being within a thousand miles of the status of a mere capitalist.

There is a tendency in some circles to recognize the poverty of these word-tools "labor" and "capital," and to help enrich them by adding another—"public opinion."

The idea is that somewhere between "labor" on the one hand and "capital" on the other, there stands a neutral body of humanity which is neither "labor" nor "capital," but the Public.

This idea is erroneous. It is applicable only in the most narrowly local way. If a small group like the street railway employes or the milkmen—any small group that serves the larger group—has an industrial disagreement which prevents its giving service, thus causing public loss or danger, then this entity which we call Public Opinion asserts itself, because the Public is larger than the group that disturbs its functions.

But in the larger social sense, when you have marshaled all the people who are involved in the social problem, you have none left to classify as the Public —there are no neutrals. Public Opinion, as it is commonly meant, can exist only when the majority is not directly concerned in a disagreement but only affected by its results.

. If there were "labor" and "capital" only, as two camps, with Public Opinion between, and if this Public Opinion were definitely decided as to the difference between the two camps, then the difficulty would be as good as settled.

If Public Opinion were some great Court of the Human Conscience to which, on a set day, Labor and Capital could both go to plead their cause and get a verdict in agreement with the will of the Public, it would be very simple. But in the larger social problem, when you have drawn up your litigants, there is no one left to man the bench.

Better than Public Opinion is the Social Conscience; this exists over and in and through all social divisions. We know, some of us vividly and some of us vaguely, that something is wrong with the social system. And we know that we scarcely know enough about the trouble to set it right. But the world and his wife, of all classes and interests, are mulling the matter over in their minds. By and by they will decide that the trouble is here, and here, and there, and having decided this, the Social Conscience, which is far more effective than Public Opinion, will step in and set right the wrong.

We are always doing that. The difficulty is that no individual life is long enough to see how steadily social progress has been made, how relentlessly the Social Conscience has kept on the job. We can hardly visualize the progress that has been made in our own lifetime. Certainly we are leaving a better system to our children than our fathers left to us. And it is certain that those who come after us will build upon our work where it is good, and tear it down where it is bad. Our work is bad wherever we have allowed selfish or class interest to rule it. It is good wherever we have looked to justice and humanity to guide us.

But what we were saying is that in adding the word-tool "Public Opinion" we have not helped very much our poverty of word-symbols for the things we are trying to think intelligently about.

If we must divide the world into two camps, why not label them Producers and Non-Producers? That rules out the idlers of every class—and we must isolate the idlers first. When we find the producers and classify them according to their value to the productive process, then we are in a position to go on to the question of distributing the rewards of production.

It is in industry as in the recent war: the war could not have been carried on only by the men who bore rifles in the front trenches. The engineers, the transport men, the commissary, the managing officers, the financial geniuses, the planners and managers both military and civil—these also had a part in the war.

89

It required six men to maintain one soldier in the field. So, when you say Labor or Producers, whom do you mean? Not only the infantrymen of industry at the machines in the shops, but all who in any way are essential to the making of the product.

The man whose idea gave birth to the machine, the draughtsman whose skill determined the relation of part with part, the trained machine maker whose ability and experience brought the machine into existence, all these have their part as well as the workman who operates the machine after it is built and installed.

The manager who may not soil his hands at all, whose workbench may be a desk, whose job is to make the shop a harmonious whole so that neither time, effort nor material is wasted, also has a part in the product. Management is an essential part of industry, it is a trade in itself.

Then there is the financial end of the business, whose part is to see that enough money is brought in to pay the workman and to carry the business over slack periods or periods of expansion—this also is productive work. Everyone knows what a tragedy it is when a business fails through mismanagement or bad financiering. It simply destroys jobs, throws men out of work, renders their earning ability a total loss for the time being, and often makes a sad difference in the condition of families.

So, when you have begun with the workman who is the infantryman of industry and gone on through all the departments which co-operate with the workman to render his work effective and his job profitable and secure, you reach the man who is sometimes called "the big boss." And yet because he is "the big boss" it does not follow that he is a mere capitalist.

In the division of humanity into "Labor" and "Capital" you may not fairly include the manufacturer with "capitalists."

A manufacturer works. He has a part in the production of useful commodities. He earns his bread.

But a capitalist doesn't work at all. In a false phrase, "his money works for him." Having control of capital which he did nothing to acquire he uses it to

90

skim a heavy tax off other men's product. When you get to these idlers who gamble in money, you have reached the "capitalist," but in all fairness we ought to be careful upon whom we place that name.

Someone asked recently who came first, the workman or the capitalist? The questioner meant who came first, the workman or the manager, the laborer or the inventor?

In the simple work of the early man which consisted entirely in self-support all were equal, but the world was not the comfortable civilized sphere which we have today.

In the work of industry, that is, the creation of work for others by which articles of use might be made for all, the man with the idea came first. Industry did not begin spontaneously. Someone first had an idea. Most of the men who had the idea which set others to work, did not have the money. They were not "capitalists" in the modern sense. Their capital was in their idea. If they gained money afterward, they gained it by what people paid for the use of their idea in usable form. Mere capitalists, men who possess money and nothing else, men who use their control of money to escape useful work—this class of "capitalists" never has ideas that help the world. It schemes to fatten on other men's ideas.

Sometimes the man with an idea makes money, sometimes he doesn't. Our history is full of the tales of men who really discovered the idea and failed to profit by it. They were not managers. Some "capitalist" took it and made money out of it.

But when the man with an idea combines managing ability with it, and his idea fills a felt want in the world, he makes money. He doesn't make it alone, of course; everyone who works with him helps him.

The question then comes: Does he make too much? Does he take too large a share for himself? Is he overpaid for what he has contributed?

Well, he usually begins in a very small way. A business that now employs over 50,000 men began less than fifteen years ago with 20 men. The idea proved useful and acceptable to the public, and busi-

ness grew. If whatever that idea made in money had
been equally distributed every Saturday night between
the proprietor and the 20 men then employed, do you
suppose the business would ever have had a surplus
on which to grow to its present dimensions, giving
employment under far better conditions and better
pay to 50,000 men than the first 20 men enjoyed?
No. Things being as they are, the business might
have lived and supported 20 men. But the chances
are it would have died, and the idea would have been
seizĕd and exploited by others whose sole object would
have been profits and not service and industrial improvement.

Capital that a business makes for itself, that is
employed to expand the workman's opportunity and
increase his comfort and prosperity, and that is used
to give more and more, and ever more men work, at
the same time reducing the cost of service to the public—that sort of capital, even though it be under single
control, is not a menace to humanity. It is a working
surplus held in trust and daily use for the benefit of
all.

To regard such surplus as a personal reward is
hardly possible to the intelligent and honest possessor
or controller of it. One big reason stands in the way
of any man regarding such surplus as his own, namely,
that he himself did not make it all. It is the joint
product of his whole organization. The manufacturer's idea may have released all the energy and directed it, but certainly it did not supply it. Every
workman, whatever his part, was a partner in the
creation of it.

And yet no business can possibly be considered
only with reference to today and to the individuals
engaged in it. To liquidate every day or every week ˉ
or every year would be the death of business; it would
prevent expansion, it would subject the business to
the mercy of every up or down of conditions. This
means, of course, that it would constantly jeopardize
every job involved in the business.

The best wages ought to be paid. A proper living
ought to be assured every participant in the business,

92

no matter what his part. But for the sake of that business' ability to support those who work in it, a surplus ought to be held somewhere for the business' benefit. And that is the only relation the honest manufacturer has with the surplus profits which his idea made possible.

Ultimately it does not matter where this surplus is held nor who controls it; it is its use that matters.

Capital that is not constantly creating more and better jobs is more useless than sand.

Capital that is not constantly making the conditions of daily labor better and the reward of daily labor more just, is not fulfilling its highest function.

The highest use of capital is not to make more money, but to make money do more service for the betterment of life. Unless we in our industries are helping to solve the social problem, we are not doing our principal work.

The Right of a Man to His Work

THE Rights of Man! It has been the battle cry of progress for generations. But what are the rights of man? What determines them? And who guarantees them? We talk quite glibly about human rights without stopping to consider whether they are really rights or not, and if they are, how they came to be.

It is one thing to *claim* a certain right. It is another thing to have the community *recognize* your claim as a right. And it is still quite another thing to have that recognized claim *acknowledged* in such a way that you can avail yourself of it.

Human rights were not always what they are today.

With the organization of society, the number of human rights tends to increase.

The reason for this doubtless is found in the fact that when you organize human society you do it by regulating everybody connected with it. You cut off certain elements of freedom here and there. You do this, of course, for the purpose of preventing trespass on the freedom of all the people. Civilization is restraint.

But in doing this work of restraining the wild and reckless tendencies of men, you balance it by defining certain Rights which they keep. You cannot define your own rights without defining the other man's, too.

When government is set up, taxation goes with it. But the right of taxation on the part of the government involves the right of representation on the part of the man who pays the taxes.

That in turn involves his equal participation in the benefits which the tax money purchases.

Thus Civil Rights grow. They become by demand "equal rights," for the only way to keep one man's right from trespassing on another's, is to keep both rights equal. And that is the essence of democracy.

Here in America we have long been proud to say that we believe in "equal rights before the law" for all men. Whether we really achieve that desirable condition is another question.

But Civil Rights do not exhaust human rights. Our rights as citizens are a small part of our real rights as human beings.

To sum up the list of Rights claimed for people today would make a list longer than this page. It runs all the way from the right to be well born, to the right to be fairly judged when life is done, and it includes all that goes between. If we were only as keen about our duties as we are about our rights, this would be a fine old world.

The Rights of which we hear most today are those which concern men's life in Industry.

Now when men lived on the land and got their living by farming, that mode of industry gave rise to certain rights—land rights, riparian rights, road rights and the rest.

And so when men began to organize themselves in modern industrial work, the new form of life brought its rights along with it too—they grew out of the circumstances; they grew out of the human conscience as it considered the balance of equity between man and man.

Some of these rights we have discussed in this column at one time or another, but there is one which is paramount, which precedes and conditions all the rest.

It is The Right To Work.

Years ago, when anyone could get a plot of land and support himself, besides adding a little to the surplus of the world, they used to preach The Duty of Working.

There is not much chance for that kind of preaching nowadays. We are more accustomed to the sight of men hunting for work than to the spectacle of men trying to escape work.

Among the new industrial rights, then, is this— The Right of The Man to A Job.

As long as we have reorganized society on an industrial basis, we have got to see that our industries offer a place to every worker to earn his living.

That is primary humanity. You may thresh around it for a hundred years, but it will still be facing you in the end.

It would not do much good to discuss the theory of this. It is very simple. Every human being has the Right to live in self-respect. It is the collective duty to acknowledge that right by providing for it. In a natural state of society it would take care of itself. As matters are now, it must be deliberately provided for.

Now, assuming that there are more men than there is work, what are we to do in order to protect men in The Right To A Job.

A number of ways suggest themselves at once. We shall do scarcely more than name them.

The work day might be shortened, thus curtailing the output of a worker and forcing the hiring of another man to keep up the output. The disadvantage of this plan, of course, is that it cannot be extended indefinitely. Let us agree that good management could reduce the work day to a point where the physical health of the worker would be benefited and the strength of the business not injured—yet, even so, it is doubtful if this alone would guarantee anyone a job.

Again: child labor might be diminished and its place supplied with adults. Without doubt the employment of children has had the effect of keeping many men out of work. We have seen in our own country—although it is quite common in other countries—mere children in competition with their own parents for jobs. That is a most shameful condition.

So that if there are those employed who by right ought to be in school or in the home, the placing of them in their proper spheres would release a large number of jobs for men to take.

But it ought to be evident that these methods, including farm and labor colonies and other suggested remedies, only touch the problem in spots.

The need is for something bigger and more dependable. These other improvements ought to be made also, of course, but in themselves they are not sufficient to cure the whole evil. They ought to be undertaken on grounds of simple human justice, regardless of whether they really help to solve the problem of unemployment or not.

We have to begin to guarantee our national prosperity where it begins—with the mass of workers.

We have got to be just at the bottom of the ladder first, trusting that a policy of justice at the bottom will result in justice at the top too. But we ought not stop to speculate: we ought to begin to be just at the beginning of things, regardless.

This is not asking charity for Labor. It is only asking for Labor what has already been done for Banks and Business—a Method to realize on its assets.

A man awakes in the morning. His chief asset is his ability to perform a day's work. He ought to be assured of a chance to realize on that asset, just as the business man was assisted to realize on a stock of goods, or a bank on a stock of perfectly good notes.

Neither would this involve a policy of "making work"—giving the men something to do for the sake of keeping them busy.

With the advance of inventive genius and with the perfection of human methods of business management, more and more jobs are going to be created and the conditions of labor are going to be increasingly improved. Here and there we see private employers who are doing their full part to reduce the problem of unemployment, and they are not doing it as a charity, but because a busy world is a good world to do business in—it is a buying and selling world.

But the Government, which has the whole country to oversee, has mountains of work that it ought to do too. The United States in many places resembles an unkempt, undeveloped farm.

There are great campaigns of work needed before our country can compare with any European country in the utilization of its advantages and resources.

We have arid lands to irrigate, deserts to fertilize, water power to develop, national road systems to build, railroad and other transportation systems to double and triple to take care of our needs; we have canals to build and reforestation projects to undertake—indeed, there is no end to the NECESSARY and URGENT work to be done.

If the United States undertook to do all that ought to be done, it would drain private industry of its manpower.

A Federal Industrial Reserve, established to take up the slack in employment would be a great step toward protecting in this country the Right of A Man To A Job.

There are those who claim that a certain proportion of unemployed men is desirable from the industrial standpoint. A crowd of men clamoring around the factory gates for jobs helps keep the men inside steady and helps keep wages down, they say.

That is a detestable philosophy. It is cold speculation in flesh and blood and anxiety and hunger. We don't want any condition that is dependent on unemployment for its steadiness.

What we want are enough jobs to go around. And just as there was enough wealth to do business, though not enough money until the Federal Reserve System got to work, so there is enough work for all, though it is not as yet divided into jobs, but will be when we tackle it in a big national way. When the People, through the Government, become an employer on great public projects, unemployment will become a thing of the past.

The Fear of Change

VOICES on every side are counseling us to fill ourselves with fear. Wherever you go, whatever you
read, the tones of calamity are strongly emphasized.
The proper aftermath of war does not seem to be a
sense of relief at all, nor a spirit of gratitude for the
deliverance, nor yet a hopeful view of the future.
Our loudest advisers would have us believe that the
only proper feeling is one of dread for the dire events
that are expected to follow.

All this is very strange when you stop to consider
it, because it is not so many months ago when anyone who forecasted the future in other than rosy hues
was denounced as a "calamity howler."

Today, however, Jeremiah is chief among the
prophets.

And when this occurs, it is a sign.

No stronger sign could be given that something has
been wrong and still is wrong in America than the
readiness of a certain class to accept this counsel of
fear.

The man whom you can reduce to a state of fear
by threats of retribution, is not reduced to such a
state by your words, but by the corroboration of a
guilty conscience within him.

One is justified by human experience in gauging
the degree of guilt by the readiness of the fear. When
a spokesman arises and says, "Yes, we have a great
deal to fear," it is probably true that he and those
he represents really have much to fear. But it does
not follow that everyone has.

Those whose conscience is clear, who know that
they have done their duty and have not denied their
obligations to humanity, who have not thought themselves better or more deserving than their fellow-
creatures—these do not have to take refuge in fears.
They are free to scan the future and to greet whatever it may have in store.

The accusing conscience, the life that knows it has ignored the rights of others, is Fear's ally. Well, what about the mysterious future? What are its portents? What is the outlook? False prophets always prophesy peace, and the reason their prophecy is false is that there never is peace in the way they mean it.

So, if this page were to begin on the note of "Peace, peace," you could at once set it down as false. As long as there is life there is Change. The peace of stagnation is an attribute of death.

That, therefore, is one element we may expect in the future—the element of Change.

Whatever we may regret about it, the old world as we knew it can never come back. It can never be the same again. Even if every human being on the globe devoted himself to reconstructing the old world as it was, it could not be done.

And the reason for this is that we ourselves have changed. We are not what we were. We can never be the same again. Something has passed over us and upon us that has rendered us different. We have changed our angle of view. That which formerly seemed all-important now occupies a lower place, and that of which we seldom thought has been made the chief interest of life. The world has really been turned upside down as far as its thinking is concerned.

Of course, this is nothing new. It has always happened, though not always so suddenly and inclusively as it has happened now. We are continually changing and life is always changing for us and the world is changing beneath and around us—so why fear Change?

And yet there are people who really do fear it. These are the people who are falling victims to the propaganda of Fear today.

To shrink from a new situation is, in ordinary times, a sign of weakness. When a man feels that he is afraid to tackle anything out of the ordinary routine, when circumstance throws an obstruction in his way and it cows him instead of rousing him, then he has lost his zest for real life.

Life is just one unexpected thing after another,

and if a man fails to appreciate the glory of the unexpected, his pulse is slowing up. It is Change that
keeps men alive, just as it is the flow that keeps water
pure.

But aside from the fear which is a sign of weakness, there is another fear which is a sign of selfishness. It is that fear which has clutched a whole class
in America today.

We have been pretty calm and easy-going in
America. We have left a great many leaks which
shrewd men use to exploit for their personal gain.
We have unregulated power which unscrupulous men
use to entrench themselves at the expense of others.

And the whole posse of get-rich-quick thieves, and
the whole clique of get-richer-still blunders, and the
whole class of those who fatten on the productive
thought and labor of others, are the ones who fear
the specter of Change as it were an accusing spirit.

And in their case impending Change is an accusing spirit. For what can be changed to anyone's
hurt is wrong to begin with. The right system cannot
be changed. Even an improvement of the right system injures no one, but helps all. But if Change
strikes the grafts of the idle rich class and hurts
them, it is a proof that their system is wrong and
harmful to others.

Anyone who has been living by his productive
thought and labor, who has been mindful to bring
his fellow-men along with him, who has never thought
in terms of his own wealth and glory but always in
terms of the general good and prosperity, such a one
has nothing to fear from Change. He usually foresees it and meets it half way. It is his friend and ally.

Why should it be so hard to get this thought into
men's minds, that Change can only hit those matters
which ought to be changed for the better?

If our rich idlers are made to work for their bread
and contribute something beside their ornamental
presence to the general good, will that be a disastrous
change?

If those who live by dickering instead of by laboring are made to get down to business and earn their
living, will that be a change to be feared?

If the whole mass of human spiders, financial, professional and social, are hindered from spinning their webs to catch hard-working human flies and their earnings, is that a change to be dreaded?

If the dishonest, shrewd, scheming, gambling, double-crossing tribe of shirkers are put out of their feathered nests and made to pay their labor for their living, will such a thing mean "the end of civilization" as some of the fear-peddlers tell us?·

Instead of bringing "the end of civilization," they will constitute a very promising beginning along sadly neglected lines.

It is a pretty safe method to follow, when you hear a man raving about the danger there is to Civilization at the present moment, to ask him, "Which of your grafts is in danger?"

You don't see people who do their daily work honestly and well going about and spreading this fear.

You don't hear of the farmers calling mass-meetings and warning each other to look out, that something is going to happen!

Why? Because these people are doing their duty to mankind. They are producing their living. They are not living off other people. Their conscience doesn't accuse them.

This is very significant. It is so significant that you had better consider it a moment.

The fear-peddlers of the present hour are the privileged class, the big grafter class, and its servants—and these servants are the reactionary politicians, and the newspapers which seem to believe that all Change and improvement is of the devil.

Observe and see if this is not true. Watch the "voices of warning" and see if they do not issue from those classes where the Guilty Conscience would naturally become most active in times of threatened Change.   ·

Surveying the disorder in Europe, its cause would appear to be the determination of the privileged classes that the world shall go on in the old way, and the utter impossibility of the world going on in the old way. For we must remember that when kings were dethroned, Private Privilege was not dethroned.

Kingship was always built upon the foundation of class privilege, and it was possible for the head to abdicate without breaking up the system. Kings were useful to private privilege because they helped keep the people's respect for high graft. But Privilege can get along without kings if it can only control the people by other means. Here in the United States we have never had a king, yet we have a privileged aristocracy which can be as sharply defined as the nobility of England or the Junkers of Germany.

So, unless these privileged classes of yesterday can start again on yesterday's plan, they will not start at all, and that is at the bottom of the disorder of Europe. They are trying to hold back the tide of progress, which is impossible.

Europe has been the scene of endless war simply because it has distrusted and feared Change.

The danger of Europe today is not that Progress is knocking at her door, but that she will fear to open the door, and will come to her senses only when the door is broken down. Progress will pass, even though it must batter down the barricades of selfishness and prejudice. But it would rather pass peacefully through the doorways of those who trust and welcome it.

Two thousand years of civilization have not taught certain parts of Europe the primary lesson that no nation or system is stronger than the strength and privilege of its humblest member.

Things were coming to an end in Europe even if the war had not intervened. When men deliberately invent a philosophy, print it in books and teach it in schools, which pretends to prove that certain classes are the destined slaves of other classes, the question of privilege being a matter of caste or birth, it was significant that the end was near. For no sooner do you formulate an erroneous philosophy than you inform the world where to strike, and it strikes.

The teaching that any class is good enough to rule another class is the old theory of the divine right of kings revamped and applied to a privileged aristocracy.

Who is so foolish as to believe that the people of Europe, having rid themselves of autocrats, are going to turn around and submit to the same misuse from aristocrats?

"But," say some of those aristocrats with an ex-pression that would be comical were it not so pitiable, "But, if this new thing comes, then my privileges and my vast wealth and lands disappear!"

And why not? Why should not land be put ,to productive use? Why should not wealth minister to the good of all the people instead of the luxurious tastes of the few?

The land cannot be destroyed, neither can the wealth. It is just a taking of the useless thing and making it useful. Surely that is civilized and right!

There are two evils we want to abolish from our world: one of them is Poverty, the other is Privilege. Now, how can we abolish Poverty? You do not ac-complish it by destroying the poor. You accomplish it by destroying the causes of Poverty.

Then how can we abolish Privilege? You do not do it by standing the privileged class against stone walls. You accomplish it by abolishing the causes of Privilege. Privilege has just as definite causes as Poverty, and they are just as easily controlled—just as easily.

No one will be hurt in the good Changes that may be in store for this world. Not at all.

Even the idle nobleman who loses his luxury is not going to be hurt—he will be a better man with-out his idleness, his useless luxury and his expensive vices.

They say that some of the princes of Europe are going into business, becoming clerks and salesmen and farmers. Well, have they been harmed? Not at all. They are more princely now than they ever were with the baubles of rank dangling from their narrow chests.

Get the gambling aristocrats and the selfish capi-talists to work for a year, and they would never go back to the old life. They will come round and thank the influences that made them get out and hustle and become of some use.

If the poor will thank you for abolishing Poverty,

the useless rich will thank you for abolishing Privilege. Because a good Change works good all round.

That is why a man with a clear conscience need never fear a Progressive Change. If he is a worker now, he will be needed in the world whatever happens.

Nothing will ever happen that will dethrone the worker. He is the one class whose place is secure throughout all time. The man who produces by his thought or his labor will always be in request and in favor. He constitutes the continuing class—he is the hold-over through every change.

That is why the workers are not afraid.

If a moral were needed, this might do: to escape fear and a guilty conscience, become a worker. And this applies very directly to the wealthy idler whose fears are very lively just now.

How Much Domestic Trouble Is Preventable?

IT IS impossible to state the exact proportion of the world's trouble which is preventable, but we are well within the limit when we say that it approximates 75 per cent. We shall never be in a position accurately to appraise mankind's earthly life until we have exhausted our last experiment for that life's betterment.

Most of the trouble that man is heir to, except old age and death, is preventable; a vast amount of it is curable even after it occurs; and, taking life on its practical side, it could be made much smoother than it is.

In excepting old age and death as troubles which are incurable, it is not intended to adopt a hopeless attitude toward them. Old age is not a trouble, rightly speaking. It ought to be in many respects a man's happiest period of life—its golden sunset. And it would be this if only other conditions were right. It is when old age comes before its time as the result of hard conditions or wrong methods of living, or when it comes without any sunset glow, that it becomes a burden and a trouble.

As for death—in the economy of nature it is one of the arrangements that make for progress. It lets the generations come on. It allows new ideas to sweep up on the shores of the world. Perhaps it also gives great assistance to the human personality in its own development.

But even as inevitable as death now is, inevitable as perhaps it may remain throughout human history, there is no need of its being the trouble we experience. Ripe deaths are not grievous; it is only the untimely ones that leave scars upon our lives. When the young man dies with his future unfulfilled; when the young father dies leaving his wife and brood of children;

when the strong men of the world drop off long before their natural time and from causes that were clearly preventable, then death becomes unnatural—it becomes a great trouble.

So that even when we are compelled to make exceptions of old age and death from the list of preventable troubles, there is a sense in which the injury they do is also preventable. When old age comes in its time, when death comes as the harvest comes, at the ripe end of a fruitful life, it is natural, often it is even beautiful, and the wounds thus made are not the unnatural ones which are made by untimely passings and breakdowns.

Now, if these two great experiences can be so regulated as to lose their terror and hurt, what is there which we cannot say about the lesser troubles which harass us?

Take domestic trouble, for example—perhaps one of the bitterest of troubles which afflict mankind today.

It is impossible for the man who is wrapped up in his own happiness and who has no means of knowing what is the exact condition among his fellow men, to realize just how much domestic trouble exists in the world. Get a few thousand men together and the bulk of such trouble, past or present, which they represent is really appalling.

And yet it is mostly preventable. Perhaps it is fair to say that it is all preventable. A little wisdom exercised beforehand, a little forbearance afterward, would be the cure of most domestic difficulties.

Most people marry in the delusion that they are marrying Perfection. Of course they are not. But at least they are marrying a possibility of happiness.

When two people believe that they think enough of each other to marry, they possess therein a possible foundation for future happiness no matter how little romance they may have in their lives.

Domestic happiness is not so much a matter of Love as of Good Sense. Many people who claim to love each other, are unhappy together. Many people who smile at the mention of love are very happy together, simply because they have good common sense.

107

Those who say it is impossible to base domestic happiness on good sense, mutual forbearance and mutual respect are drawing their conclusions from novels instead of life.

Many domestic disasters could be prevented by a knowledge of the course which domestic life often takes. Two young people marry—as it is right they should, and, other circumstances being favorable and equal, they can hardly marry too young—and they fancy they will never, never change. Sometimes they even swear to each other that they will never change.

But, they do. They cannot help it. They change because they grow. He becomes more of a man, and she more of a woman. He becomes more critical—not necessarily in his manner, but in his insight; she opens her eyes also. If the truth were told it is probably the woman who comes to the balanced view of' matters first.

Dreams cannot last forever, and it would be a pity if they should. For the realities are better.

But the passing of the dream is a dangerous period, for it tends to make one or the other, sometimes both, to feel that they have been tricked.

However, they have not been tricked. A hundred to one they have not married unwisely. They are simply going through a normal experience—a moulting period, as it were.

But there is the first danger, the suspicion that they have married unwisely.

The second danger is more to be feared, namely, the false belief that the first part of the married life is the best, and that if that part disappoints, there is nothing but misery waiting in the future.

Now the fact is that the first part of marriage is not the best. It seems to be so at the time; even outside beholders are betrayed into thinking it so; but it is not. It may be more ecstatic, more spring-like, more ruled by the stormier emotions of joy.

But after all, there is no happiness like that of Darby and Joan at their own firesides many, many years after—she not a bit deluded about him but knowing him to be a true man, and he not a bit deluded about her but knowing her to be a true woman, and both loving each other more deeply than they ever did before, but perhaps not saying so.

It should be incorporated into our marriage ceremonies, so that young folks would not be deluded when it arrives, that a time of change will come when the fresh young affection will begin to make room for something deeper and more enduring.

It should be impressed upon young men and women that it is this latter time that they are really playing for, that all sorts of inconveniences and disappointments in the readjustment period should be borne wisely for the sake of the better understanding and the better loyalty which is to come in later years.

In business, in education, in every other line of life men play for the distant prize. In marriage the prize is to be loyally understood 25 years from the wedding day. It is worth everything to achieve that.

If this second danger, the danger of thinking the first part the best, can be avoided, the course of domestic life is usually safe.

All this, however, takes no account of those far too many homes which have snagged on both rocks. Because husband and wife think that the fading of the early glamour is proof of their having made a mistake, and because they mistakenly think that the end must necessarily be grayer and gloomier than the beginning, there is very, very much bitterness in the world.

There is hardly any bitterness one can conceive that approaches the bitterness of a married couple who fancy they have made a mistake.

That is why our divorce courts are so busy.

But observe this: *There are more mistaken divorces than there are mistaken marriages.*

We don't need divorce courts in this country half so much as we need Courts of Explanation and Courts of Reconciliation and Courts of Understanding.

When you have divorced two people you have simply turned two soured souls into society to exercise a souring influence on others.

The most powerful argument in favor of the divorce grist is that divorce is in the interest of the happiness of the parties concerned and not society;

and that argument is completely neutralized by the fact that the happiness of those parties more often consists in saving their marriage than in destroying it. A certain lawyer, who once did a large divorce business, reformed, and for the purpose of making an experiment for his own satisfaction began to be the friendly adviser of all who applied to him to obtain divorces for them. Their application opened the door for his inquiries, and he found himself able in all but a negligible percentage of cases to be able to effect a good understanding and reconciliation.

Our more progressive communities also are waking up to the folly of grinding out divorces wholesale. They are now establishing intermediary courts where the applicants for divorce may be reasoned with.

It is not to be expected that this official intervention for the sake of preventing divorce is going to be fully successful. In the first place, the relation of adviser in such matters should not be official at all, but friendly. In the second place, the official adviser is seldom the type of person who knows the profounder phases of the problem with which he deals. In the third place, the people whose domestic life is most worth saving are the very people with whom even these intermediary institutions would hesitate to deal.

Yet it is true that husband and wife, in circumstances of domestic bitterness, seldom possess the means of coming to an understanding by themselves. It is one of the strange aspects of this difficulty that people who, of all the people in the world, are closest to each other, should in their own most intimate and important concerns be farthest apart. But so it is—and it is far from being the only paradox that human nature presents.

There must be some outside influence from somewhere to enable two such unfortunate people to see their true condition. And even this influence cannot be effective unless the man and woman themselves adopt a spirit of simplicity and regard themselves as a grown boy and a grown girl who have simply lost their way in one of life's most intricate forests. Only in this spirit can they profit by that which the heart

110

of friendliness and the wisdom of experience would offer them.

If it could be made clear as a matter of education or public information that changes of temperature in the married life are not abnormal but perfectly natural; if it could be made clear that the day of dreams comes to an end and the day of grown-up reality begins; if it could be very strongly insisted that team-work, team-work and again team-work is the chief rule of domestic success—absolute confidence, loyalty and exchange of views—many domestic sorrows would be avoided.

And then if it could be made clear to everybody that the idea of divorce being an escape is not true—that instead of being an escape, divorce is more likely to be a leap into the fire—that would be of vast assistance also.

If the testimony of divorcees could be taken on this point, the revelation would be startling.

Marriage may be repaired; it is broken, at great peril.

Domestic happiness is not only of private importance. It is the world's business, the future's business, how our domestic life goes. A great many undesirable conditions in the present day can be traced by the untoward domestic conditions.

Take a shop which is manned by men of unhappy home life and compare it with a shop manned by men whose home life is happy, and you will see a vast difference in the quality and quantity of the output. Moreover, you will see a vast difference in the wisdom and reasonableness with which the men manage their private and industrial affairs.

The business man who is in domestic difficulty, and who is not doing anything to clear it up, is up against the strongest kind of competition in the business man whose home affairs are well adjusted. It would be an interesting sociological investigation to compute how many business failures have been connected with domestic failures.

A man's first success ought to be in his home.

There are no two men and women on the face of the globe, no matter how much they may prate about "affinity," difference of temperament and "incompatibility," who could not together make a most excellent home, one that would attract the widest and worthiest circle of friends, if they only wanted to.

And it would be worth doing. It would be the strongest asset either of them could have.

There is a baneful connection between domestic failure and every other kind of failure.

But cheating the domestic bogie means team-work. It means talking it out together. It means compromise here and there. It means experiments, now with her way of managing matters, now with his. It means "bear and forbear" and the old-fashioned rule that only one shall be grouchy at a time. It means a sense of humor, too, for the oldest and wisest of us are only boys and girls.

But perhaps it means first and deepest of all the solid fact that domestic difficulty is absolutely preventable. It is not fated. It is not necessary. It is not inevitable. It is preventable. And if through ignorance or ill-will it is not prevented, then it is very far from the necessity of going through to a break-up, for it is curable.

Farming—the Food-Raising Industry

NOW that the planting time has come, it is the duty of everyone who can to get out of the factories and into the fields to raise food. Our all-year factory life is a mistake. It is a physical as well as an economic mistake. We somehow got started on the wrong track when the industrial system was established in America. Factory and farm should have been organized as adjuncts one of the other, and not as competitors. Men were never meant to stay within walls while Nature is waking the Earth to her annual labor and clothing the visible creation with beauty and fertility.

If we adopted the practice of going outdoors to work when outdoor work was the seasonable and natural thing to do, and came back to indoor work when the food-producing processes of Nature were complete, we should be a happier, healthier people and many of our economic problems would be solved.

It is the nature of men, when the spring-time comes, to wish to work in the soil. They take a delight in the wholesome odor of the freshly upturned earth in their back yards. There is a deep instinct for the soil in every one of us. Where is the man who has not wished scores of times that he might live and work in the country among growing things? Our natures crave direct contact with Nature herself.

The pity is that life is not organized so that this perfectly wholesome instinct might be gratified. If we could all leave the factories when the time comes to plant corn, and return to the factories after the harvest, not only would we be better men physically and mentally, but the effect on the social situation would be most beneficial.

We are engaged in something like that in our factories. We are encouraging the men who can do so to go back to their land, raise a crop, and come back to us when the crop is harvested.

A man who works on the land in the proper season, and returns to work in the factory when the land is resting, is living a very wise program. He is living his life in rhythm with Nature. He is maintaining his health. He is keeping his mind in fine tone. And he is doing a service to society.

We may talk as much as we please about industrialism, but the fact remains that Agriculture is the first of the arts—it is basic. No wheels turn, no invention thrives, no commerce is carried on, no business is done if the furrows remain unturned. The farmer heads the van. When he stops the whole world-procession comes to a standstill.

Everyone knows this. That is to say, everyone assents to the truth when such a statement is made. But very few realize it. Fewer still ever think of it as imposing a personal obligation on themselves.

If we had the complete figures, showing to how great an extent the farm had been abandoned for the factory, they would be startling. They are startling enough for a single large concern.

In one factory it was found that 10 per cent of the men had come directly from the farm to work in the factory, and half of these were owners of farms.

Bear in mind, it is not the exodus of farmers' children we are considering now—that exodus which has been going on since the city lights first attracted boys from paternal acres—but the exodus of the farmers themselves, the mature generation upon whom the weight of agricultural responsibility rests.

These men have come in by hundreds and thousands to take advantage of the high wages paid in modern industry. They are a good class of workman. They are, for the most part, sober, steady, thrifty and intelligent. It is easy to understand why any employer should wish to keep them.

But if the employer will check up his classification lists showing from what previous occupations his employes have come, he will very directly be met by the question whether he is not party to a serious dislocation of effort by inducing to stay with him men who would be better employed raising food.

These farmers should be helped to see that any financial benefit they may seem to derive from farm-abandonment is only apparent and temporary. That is, in ceasing to raise food they are creating a condition which nullifies the benefits of high wages. The price of food today is one of the reasons why our high wages possess less purchasing power than they should, and the high price of food is due to a decrease in the food supply, which in turn is caused by the movement from farm to factory.

The man who comes from the farm to the factory for the sake of high wages may seem to profit for a time, but he is making it harder for everyone else, and eventually for himself also—for when he ceases to be a producer of food, becoming merely a consumer, he is caught in the jaws of the very situation he has helped to create.

If a factory worker's land is lying idle, he should go and work it—always with the understanding that he can come back to the shop, if he wishes, when the crop is harvested.

If he has rented his farm, he should go back at this season and see that it is being properly planted and maintained.

The knowledge of farming is so precious that everyone who possesses it has a sacred duty to use it. Experienced farmers ought to be as unwilling to leave the land to inexperienced hands as are engineers to leave valuable machinery in the hands of amateurs.

It is not always possible to send back the man who did hired work on the farm, for often that would mean turning him out of one job to seek another which he might fail to find.

But if we were living under a plan where it was understood that the Spring and Summer months were the months of outdoor work, these matters would be more easily adjusted.

Turn aside from the farming question for a moment and look at the building question. In the upset of conditions that followed upon war, the various factory industries absorbed thousands of trained builders—carpenters, bricklayers, stone masons, plasterers, etc.

Now, building is largely a seasonal trade. That is, it is best pursued in the "outdoor months." What a waste of power it has been to allow builders to hibernate through the winter, waiting for the building season to come round.

And what an equal waste of skill it has been when experienced building mechanics have been forced into factories to escape the losses of the winter season, and, in order to hold their jobs in the factories, have been forced to stay there all through the building season when they might have been outdoors helping to build homes for the people or shops for industry.

What a waste this all-year system has been, anyway! If the farmer could get away from the shop to till his farm in the planting, growing and harvesting season (it is only a small part of the year, after all), and if the builder could get away from the shop to ply his useful trade in its season, how much better they would be, and how much smoother the world would proceed.

Suppose we all moved outdoors every Spring and Summer—the whole nation with its wife and family—and lived the wholesome life of outdoor work for three or four months! Wouldn't that be very much better than an insipid vacation at some inane summering place?

And after that we would all move back to the city for the Fall and Winter work in the mechanical and manufacturing field. But how much better we would be in every way upon our return! How invigorated! How tuned up! How balanced we would feel!

Well, it is not at all impossible.

What is desirable and right is never impossible.

It would only mean a little team-work, a little less attention to greedy ambition and a little more attention to life.

Those who are rich find it desirable to go away for three or four months a year and dawdle in idleness around some fancy winter or summer resort. The rank and file of the American people would not waste their time that way even if they could. But

116

they would provide the team-work necessary to this outdoor seasonal employment, and they would be quick to see how much more evenly Nature's contribution and Humanity's contribution to Life would be balanced.

It is hardly possible to doubt that much of the unrest we see about us is the result of an unnatural mode of life. Men who do the same thing continuously the year round, in the midst of the same scenes, and shut away from the health of the sun and the spaciousness of the great out-of-doors, are hardly to be blamed if they begin to see matters in a gloomy or distorted light.

The physical strain consequent upon unnatural modes of life has a great deal to do with the causation of social irritability and general discontent.

Why should a change of scene always be in the nature of a vacation, or upon the doctor's orders?

Why should we not have it as a part of the normal workaday affairs of life?

What is there in life that should hamper normal and wholesome modes of living? And what is there in industry incompatible with all the arts receiving in their turn the attention of those qualified to serve in them?

It may be objected that if the forces of industry were withdrawn from the shops every summer it would impede production. But we must look at the matter from the most universal point of view.

We must consider the increased energy of the industrial forces that should spend three or four months every year in outdoor work.

We must also consider the effect on the cost of living which would result from this general return to the fields.

Besides this, we must consider the great and steady increase of general needs which such a program would stimulate, and the prevention of "slack times" everywhere.

The farm has its "slack times." That is the time for the farmer to come into the factory and help produce the things he needs to till the farm.

The factory also has its "slack times." That is

the time for the workman to go out to the land to help produce the food which is the ultimate factor in all human activity.

Thus, by taking the "slack" out of every line of work through the application of this seasonal disposal of industry, we should be restoring the balance between the artificial and the natural.

But not the least, perhaps by far the greatest benefit would be the more balanced view of life we should thus obtain. The mixing of the arts is not only beneficial in a material way, but it makes for breadth of mind and fairness of judgment. A great deal of our unrest today is the result of narrowness of mind and prejudiced judgment. If our work were more diversified, if we saw more sides of life, if we saw how necessary was one factor to another, we should be more balanced.

Every man is better for a period of work under the open sky. It clears his mind of cobwebs. It draws away the ill-humors of the blood. It puts us in touch with the ancient harmony of night and day, sun and shower, seedtime and harvest. We can live so closely with one thing and fill our minds so completely with one aspect of life as to become unbalanced as far as any fair and practicable judgment upon the whole of life is concerned.

Let us never be afraid of these ideals of better things. The very fact that they come to us is a prophecy that one day the reality will come, too. And where an ideal is social enough to include all of us in a new and beneficial plan, it is pretty certain to be a true ideal, destined to realization.

"A Few Strong Instincts and a Few Plain Rules"

ALL that the world needs for the guidance of its life could be written on two pages of a child's copy book. "A few strong instincts and a few plain rules" would set the world singing on its way, instead of tying it up in the periodical blunders which hinder progress and give a sense of infinite and irremediable confusion.

Learning may need large space, thousands of volumes, vast experiment and failure and progress; but, strange to say, Wisdom carries very little of such baggage.

There are a few truths all of us know when we have reached the more mature years, and we see them to be the very foundation wisdom of life—plain, enduring, true. But when we happen to mention them in conversation we are met, if not with the words, then with the spirit which says, "Old stuff! Give us something new."

A curious illusion persists among us that because we have *heard* a thing, we therefore *know* it. Repetition is not desired. We begin to refer contemptuously to "platitudes."

Well, it is very evident to the observer that a "platitude" is a truth of which everybody has *heard*, but which few really *know*.

The world has heard everything that is necessary to the re-establishment of life in universal peace, universal prosperity, and universal progress. It has heard every essential principle any number of times. And yet there is no sign that it fully knows them.

If you saw a man continually making sums on paper in which 2 plus 2 equaled 5, you would say, "But 2 plus 2 equals 4."

"Yes, yes," the man would reply, "every school

child knows that. Tell me something new," and go on making the same mistake.

He would be behaving very much like the human race today.

"Yes, yes," says the world impatiently, when a simple principle of life is uttered, "we know that. We heard it when we were children. Everybody knows that. Give us something new," and goes on in the same way as before.

What does it mean? Simply that we do not know anything until, convinced of its truth, we act upon it.

The truth of things escapes us, mostly because truth is so simple. If it came only in the scholar's vesture, in a dead and learned language, behind a barrier of books which a lifetime would not suffice to master, it would be hardly possible that the world should miss being wise.

But Wisdom comes in such simple guise that more often she is received by the peasant than by the prince.

All the personal and social morality known to the race is summed up in the brief Ten Commandments, and all the higher and finer principles of life are summed up in the Sermon on the Mount, and both of them together are not enough to fill a penny pamphlet.

Whatever may be the form in which the World Covenant of the Nations is written, you will find every true assertion in it harking back to the Decalogue; and whatever may be the finer service attained by the choicer spirits among mankind, it will never exceed the Words Spoken on the Mount.

And yet, these would be among the things of which lovers of newness would say, "It is old and stale. Give us something new."

Now, as a matter of fact, there isn't anything new; and if there were it could only be attained through a complete use and absorption of what is old and true.

At the core of everything is The Principle, and principles are from eternity and to eternity.

All of our apparent going forward is simply a progress farther into the heart of Principle. It is not a learning of new things, but a new learning of the old.

It has always been wrong to steal; it always will

120

be wrong to steal, whether it affects the potatoes a farmer has planted, the child's affection which the parent possesses, or the territory which forms an integral part of a nation's sovereignty.

If you take this single matter of stealing, and trace it through all the operations of the political, financial, industrial, social and moral worlds, you will find that—shall we say more than half?—of the world's trouble is caused by plain stealing.

If the entire story of the recent war—including the quarter century of preparation for it—is studied along the line of this single clue of stealing, the discoveries would be amazing.

It is not too much to say that if the world were to learn no more in the next century than to live by the truths it already knows, the year 2,000 would dawn upon an Earth without a single sore problem. So, much of our progress consists in going back and starting over again on another plan, when it might consist in going from one complete conquest to another!

Yet, if you insist on these simple, fundamental principles without which no substantial achievement is possible anywhere, the ready retort is that "everybody knows them."

Everybody does not know them, although everybody may have heard of them.

You don't know that a lie is wrong until you know that when lies are circulated in the human interchange of speech, it is like flooding monetary currency with bogus coins.

Speech is the currency of thought among men. We depend more on the genuineness of men's words than we do on the genuineness of the coins that circulate among us. Let the suspicion get abroad that men's words are bogus and not the coinage of truth, and the whole system of human exchange breaks down.

Until we know that, until we act upon the knowledge that falsehoods injure the most delicate nerves in the social body, we cannot be said to know the simple principle of truth-telling. And until we *do* know it, it doesn't matter how many new-fangled matters may be presented to please our fancy. Truth-telling is mighty old-fashioned, but it will still be a vital principle a million years hence, wherever confidence between man and man is the basis of fellowship or co-operation.

If a censor should go through the world today, cleaning out everything that needs a lie to bolster it up, abolishing everything that has the taint of deceit upon it, forbidding everything that needs to be concealed or dissembled, there would be such a housecleaning in governments, banking houses, industries, societies and combinations as would leave the world unrecognizably clean.

Why, it is the very lack of confidence in the ability of high-placed persons to tell the truth and stand by it that has led to all the difficulty at the Conference of Paris! The nations have no confidence in each other's fair professions. Why? Simply because they feel that this "old stuff," this "platitude" about the basic importance of truth has not yet been learned by the world.

Why demand novelties for a world that has yet to learn the A B C of common man-to-man honesty?

The impatience of the world goes even deeper than that. There is not only a tendency to thrust aside these old-fashioned basic principles, but there is a still more dangerous tendency to believe that morality of mind and body has no place in big affairs at all.

"Yes, yes," is a common remark, "we take these things for granted without mentioning them."

The trouble is that we do not take them for granted unless we insist upon them. This world is built on morality—and morality is simply honest thinking and honest doing. There is nothing that endures without this morality.

There will never be any system of government, or society, or business, or progress—no possible living together at all, except on a basis of this morality.

Yet we see one great group of men contending that all we need for the millennium is a new system of distribution, and another great group is insisting that all we need is a system that will forever guarantee to the inheritor of a dollar the right to collect

6 to 10 per cent from the man who did not inherit the dollar.

No. It doesn't matter how mechanically perfect a social system may be devised—the better it is the more miserably it will fail without a fundamental morality to infuse and sustain it. It is like making a hoe. The style may be fine, the proportions right, the pattern perfect; but if you make it of soft tin, it will not be a good hoe.

The world teems with social plans and programs, but you will never get a just and happy society until there is a high degree of common morality to pour into the molds.

It is one of the fallacies of modern thought, this notion that we may sidetrack this vital element which distinguishes man from the brute and raises society above the herd.

In olden times the teachers of Wisdom refused to admit to their instruction any man who was not clean within and without, a man well grounded in the moralities. For the old masters reasoned that he who had not learned the fundamentals could not learn the other things. Wisdom presupposed morality.

The old masters were right. They grasped a truth which is beginning to emerge again in our day, namely, that men who are in wrong relations with the moral universe are not to be trusted with the secrets which make for progress.

We have seen what use was made by man of his command over the forces of nature in the recent war.

We may shudderingly imagine what would have happened if man's knowledge of nature's mysteries had been greater than it is.

All of which impresses us strongly with the thought that if still more power is to be won by human beings, it must be kept under the restraint of conscience and used according to the dictates of morality. Else knowledge becomes our destruction instead of, as it was intended to be, our great good.

The Farmer—Nature's Partner

THIS is the time of year when city people think of
Nature as a big showroom, filled with bloom, per-
fume and song. A sunnier season has come, liberating
us from the protection of confining walls and the necessity of stoking fires. Multitudes of people have no
other conception of Spring than as a delightful change
in the weather.

There is one man, however, who knows better. He
knows that the first songs of the returning birds are
but the whistles announcing the turning of wheels in
Nature's great food factory. The increased warmth
of the earth is turning on the power which moves the
processes of that first industry. Spring freshets, wood-
land flowers, balmy breezes, cordial sunshine—all
these are to him much more than themes for poetry;
they are signs that for him his day's work has begun,
a day which lasts from seedtime. to harvest.

Of course we know, even when we do not fully
realize, that if the Farmers should let the birds whistle
unheeded, and decide to let this year pass without
labor, the wheels of nature could grind as they pleased,
the sun could furnish heat and the clouds drop moisture, and it would not avail mankind. Without the
labor of man—and in this relation, "man" means the
Farmer—the whole produce of the earth would
amount to no more than matted weeds.

We are living and working today by virtue of the
food which men planted in the Spring of 1918 and
harvested in the Autumn of 1918. And we shall be living and working in 1920 as a result of the food which
is even now in process of production in this year, 1919.

Farming is the First Industry. Without it there
could be no other industry. The complete absence of
steam or electric power from the earth would not result in so absolute a tie-up of effort as would the ces-
sation of farming.

All this seems hardly worth the saying, it is so

elementary, so widely known. And yet if there is any division of human labor upon which the inhabitants of large cities expend little if any thought, it is the work of Farming. For all that multitudes of people know, their food is made in factories and purveyed in the stores. That the loaves of the bakeries were once brown fields of grain, the meats of the markets once grazing herds, the canned goods on the grocers' shelves once laboriously cultivated crops, is all too little considered.

The purpose in calling attention to this is not to enlarge the consideration of the unintentionally inconsiderate, but to throw a sidelight on the general neglect which has been visited on the most fundamental industry.

Because the Farmer's work was done at a distance from the cities, thus preventing him from acquiring that "veneer of civilization" which goes with starched collars and polished shoes, it became a superior fancy with city people that the man who trod the furrows was their inferior. The list of nicknames applied to the Farmer is ample proof of this.

Of course, the Farmer had the better of this situation all the time. He could see the joke. He knew wherein his position had advantages of which city dwellers were ignorant. The healthfulness, independence, sterling honesty of the work in which he was engaged made it incomparably more desirable than the work by which many city people lived.

Nevertheless, it reacted on the Farmer to this extent: for a long time the inventive genius of the world was almost exclusively exercised in behalf of the city dweller and his industries.

Machinery for city industries, conveniences for city homes, opportunities for city people, all of these commanded the attention and services of progressive leaders, to the almost total exclusion of interest in the Farmer, his needs and his situation. He was remembered chiefly at election time—and then it was to get something out of him, not to do something for him.

Only a few persons were engaged in trying to make the farmer's business more efficient, and of these fewer still did anything with an undivided purpose to aid him.

How the Farmer has been held up by trusts when he bought; beaten down by trusts when he sold; derided by ignorance when he appeared in the city.; ignored when he would send his representatives to legislature—all these injustices form some of the best known chapters in the history of American agriculture.

The effect of this soon began to appear. Young people are sensitive, not so ready to weigh certain attitudes in the balances of an impartial judgment; thus there began a decrease in the number of Farmers' sons following the ancient profession of agriculture.

This in turn had its effect on the life of cities, on the cost of living, until there was never a time in the history of the world when the value and virtue of Farming was more profoundly appreciated than it is today. We ought no longer to rest under any doubt as to where the credit is due for the great changes which have come not only in Farming itself but also in the public attitude toward it.

The Farmer himself has furnished the initial stimulus for the vast improvements which have come or are coming into his business. He agitated for schools in which his boys could be taught scientific agriculture. The numerous agricultural colleges scattered throughout the land have made Farming a profession and given it the dignity of an art. It was only when medical knowledge was systematized, so that it could be tested by wide experience and communicated to inquiring minds in an authoritative way, that medicine rose from the darkness of superstition into the clear light of practical science; and so with Farming.

The science of the soil, the romance of rotation of crops, the creative improvement of strains of cattle, the organization of dairy production, the efficient planning of farm work and the business-like marketing of crops and produce—all of these have not only given the Farmer and his son the inner sense of belonging to the great world of business, but have also placed in their purse the world's certificate of service in the form of handsome payments.

More than that, inventive genius has placed itself

at the Farmer's service, and it will be found that this inventive ability did not originate in cities, but on farms. One who has gone from the Farm to the machine shop, or who all his life has worked at intervals in both, has a better idea of the Farmer's needs and a more ardent desire to meet them, than the engineer who simply seeks to design a new kind of implement or machine to catch the farm trade.

Man-power and horse-power are rapidly receding before machine-power and water-power.

The effect of this is to decrease the number of days work required to produce a crop, to decrease the strain upon the Farmer's strength, to decrease the demands upon his financial resources; while, on the other hand, it increases the time he has for planning his work, increases the reserve of energy he can give to the mental side of his job, and makes for a larger, broader life for him generally.

Farming need not be an all-year job. The Farmer, his crop harvested and his field work done, should be free to devote himself to other lines of work and so broaden his experience and improve his point of view.

The tendency to give credit for these betterments to conventions of city people is dying out, for it is becoming more and more evident that only the Farmer could have done as much for the Farmer as recent years have seen done.

We have greatly overestimated the cities—most people will agree with that. When we all stand up and sing, "My Country 'Tis of Thee," we seldom think of the cities. Indeed, in that old national hymn there are no references to the city at all. It sings of rocks and rivers and hills—the great American Out-of-Doors.

And that is really The Country. That is, the country is THE Country. The real United States lies outside the cities.

The food that sustains us, the raw material that feeds our factories, the broad waterways on which our commerce floats—all of these have their sources outside the cities.

The wealth with which people speculate has its origin in scenes far different, and if you want to see

127

the true foundations of the Treasury of the United States, look at the soil beneath your feet.

The fresh moist earth is the greatest of all gold mines, and the wealth it produces does only good and never harm.

We are going back to this ideal of the land some day. Both as an economic measure and as a plan whereby each man may get the most pleasure and profit out of life, all of us are going to be proud to be known as tillers of the soil.

Some one has humorously said that the dream of the Farmer is to occupy an office in a city skyscraper, while the office man in the skyscraper has one great desire, which is to raise chickens on a farm.

Both desires are natural. The Farmer wants to have his share in the busy life of the world of industry, exchange or professionalism. The worker, business man and thinker want to have a share in the processes of nature, to bury their hands in the soil and see growing things come to maturity beneath their care.

Some day we are going to be sensible enough to see that the best thing that can happen to both classes will be such a seasonal interchange of work. City people grow narrow, too. Working in the soil would give them more wholesome views. And the modern improvements of farm conditions are doing more to prepare for this new mode of life than any amount of economic argument to the contrary.

Limitations Are Guide Posts, Not Barriers

I T IS better to be "narrow" and to know a few things with certainty, than to be "broad" and be doubtful and hesitant about everything. Take, for example, the fact of limitation. Everybody has his limitations. Everywhere there are limitations. There are certain things some of us will never be able to do, and there are definite boundaries set up around every force and principle known to man.

Limitation is not only a personal fact; it is a universal fact.

But to establish such a fact is not the end of the matter. There still remains the manner in which men react to it. Facts are facts, but to one man they may mean discouragement and defeat; to another man, guidance, inspiration and success.

It is curious to contemplate, that we need to modify very, very few natural facts; but we need greatly to modify certain attitudes which men adopt toward the facts.

Now, in the matter of personal limitations, this difference in the attitude of men is very marked: One man regards his limitations as a big "Forbidden" sign set squarely across his path, another man regards his limitations as a very useful signpost set up at the side of the road—"This Way To Achievement."

We must not overlook the fact that both of these men may be right and still be contradictory of each other. If a man is headed straight forward on the road that he should go, his limitations serve as a guidepost. But if a man is determined to angle off and not keep the road that leads to his destination, then his limitations will confront him as prohibitions.

It is all a question of whether a man regards his limitations as Nature's friendly hint, or as her hostile hindrance.

We hear a great deal about the power of the human will, and he would be bold indeed who should set limits to what any man can do. If the most unlikely man should set himself with all his strength and will and spirit to achieve the most unlikely success, he would be likely to win to an amazing degree. The full exertion of the Will carries one far.

But it goes without saying that such a man could not possibly win so full a measure of success as the man who was naturally equipped and applied himself just as diligently.

The man who exerted all his powers in an unlikely field, that is, a field for which he was not intended, may have the satisfaction of overcoming difficulty, but it is quite apparent that had he applied the same energy to a likely field, a field for which his bent and ability fitted him, his success would have been very much greater.

You see, in bucking his limitations he consumed so much of his power in negative effort that less of it was available for positive effort. If he had worked within his limitations, making them serve him, instead of fighting them and so losing their co-operative value, he would have had the stream of natural tendency with him instead of against him.

Limitations are not to be condemned until they are understood. We misunderstand them when we regard them as wholly negative. We often think of limitations as the "Thou Shalt Nots" of life. You shall not be a poet. You shall not be a statesman. You shall not be a surgeon. You shall not be a scholar. You shall not be a society pet. You shall not be a merchant.—That is how we thing of limitations.

But limitations are positive. Instead of insisting on what you cannot do, they indicate what you can do. When the stream of your energy runs strongly toward one career, that is a positive indication; it is the limitation of your energy to the career in which your best chance of success may be found.

Limitations in this sense are signboards guiding you into the right path, warning you against the by-paths which open on this side and that.

That which throws up limits against your being a poet, is the very strength which equips you to be an engineer, or whatever your special bent may be.

Follow the direction in which your limitations point. \

A man carries his own directions inside himself, in the nature of his tastes and capacities.

Every thing he cannot do is a finger pointing to the thing he can do.

Every failure he makes is an indication of the line in which his success may be found.

Limitations exist; no one can deny the testimony of experience on that point; but they exist as friendly hints to man, not as hindrances across his path.

It is like this: you are driving along a highway across country, and the highway is fenced on both sides, preventing your driving out of the path and losing your direction. The fence is there, it is true, but it defines your path; it does not obstruct it. That is what our limitations do; they define our path. But try to turn out of the path, and they obstruct us. We were meant to go forward. When we turn aside from the path of our nature and capabilities, our limitations become obstructions.

That is the fundamental truth of limitations:— their principal function is not to tell you what you cannot do, but what you can do. Their service is positive. A man who takes counsel of his irremovable limitations will find the work he was meant for. Certainly he cannot succeed in a work he was not meant for, and just here is where his limitations serve his interests. ✎

The principle might be extended to include other phases of life. It is not only in the choice of our vocations that we find limitations, but in all other undertakings too.

Society is as much hedged about as the individual. We know there are certain courses which society cannot countenance, because they are the antithesis of social integrity. All the laws of conduct relative to property, health, demeanor, traffic, industry, marriage, are simply signs of limitation which we set up because we have learned that outside certain limitations there are no such desirable conditions as peace and security and progress.

But you will notice that these limitations which society sets up are not for the discouragement of any proper activity; they only declass those conditions which make for disruption and ruin.

Well-disposed people find these limitations to be a guide of conduct. Self-seeking persons find them to be a check. That is, those who are headed right find the law to be their friend, while those who are headed wrong find the law to be their foe. It is chiefly a matter of attitude.

And then, ranging still farther afield, there are those wider and yet not less defined limitations which inhere in our humanity.

Man is a creature whose vision excels his power, so that he is always apprehending with his imagination many, many matters which are far outside the reach of his hands. Mystery hedges him on every side. But here again the positive side of limitations comes into view, for the surrounding mystery has had as definite an effect on man's mind as the light has had on his skin.

And here too the same impulse to ignore the limitation comes into view, and leads to many grotesque notions. But the impulse, here as elsewhere, springs from the same misconception as to why the boundary lines exist.

Nothing seems more unreasonable than that, of two babes born in the same home and reared under the same conditions, one will exhibit an almost miraculous aptitude for a given line of work and the other none at all. It would seem that if one man can do it, any man can. And in the same way, the limitations which surround our humanity seem unreasonable too. Man, we know, is the heir of all the Past and, we assume, the heir of all the Future too. Then why, we ask, cannot he penetrate this mystery or that? Why cannot he unlock all Nature's secrets with one turn of the key? Why cannot he disclose the invisible world with one effort of his will? Why is he limited to a small planet as far as his corporeal self is concerned, and to a little space in time as far as his consciousness is concerned? Why these limitations, which in moments of swelling impatience he would thrust aside and enter boldly the long locked chambers of mystery?

Well, we may reasonably expect that the frontiers of mystery will recede little by little as man becomes able to occupy the new territory and use it for good instead of ill. But even with this expectation in view, it remains none-the-less true that our limitation with regard to those profounder matters is not a hindrance to our evolution.

Always the price of man's advance is his faithful use of what he has. And it is only as mankind learns how to perfect and purify life on the simpler outlines now vouchsafed to him that he can expect new revelations of purpose and power. In becoming trustworthy in what the race now has, it will become fit to receive more.

So all through the sphere, from the matter of personal vocation to that of racial status, the fact of limitation appears as a friendly one, capable of wearing a frowning face only when we view it from a rebellious angle.

Some Power has marked the path of individual destiny as well as the path of world destiny. It is all good destiny insofar as the super-hint, which we call limitation, is followed. Otherwise destiny becomes delayed and confused, until in a good hour we find the secret of limitation again, and follow it to achievement.

All Men Are Created Needful

IT WAS once the custom of men who posed as thinkers to do acrobatic stunts with that proposition of our Declaration of Independence which asserts that "all men are created equal," and to spend weary and profitless hours discussing what "equality" meant and whether the proposition expressed a fact or merely an ideal with which the Fathers of the Republic pleased themselves.

We have been caught in the wake of that discussion many times and have heard it declared with monotonous persistency that men were *not* created equal, that they never could be equal, that equality would be a most tragical condition on the earth.

Then, descending spirally from the tip of the ideal to the stump of the fact, we have heard it demonstrated over and over again that physical equality did not exist, that mental equality did not exist, that moral equality did not exist; and so on through all the possible classifications of human divergences.

So far as the meaning of the statement in the Declaration is concerned there is no room for wide difference of opinion. The doctrine is that men are equally endowed with certain fundamental *rights*, not that they are equally endowed with certain *qualities*.

Indeed, the very fact of the inequality of men in respect of their qualities, is the reason their equality of rights had to be declared and decreed.

The minute you declare equality of human rights you imply inequality of human quality. It is one way of warning the highly endowed individual that his higher possessions do not give him any right to interfere with the fundamental rights of others. The most inferior individual has rights which even the most superior dare not violate.

Of course, as long as we remain safely on the high plane of general principles we move along peacefully without disturbing challenges. But when we

134

try to apply the principles, we find ourselves confronted with all the aspects of human nature. Within the limits of the Declaration of Independence we are safe enough, for the Fathers were thinking mostly about the fundamentals of political rights. But when we approach the newer ideals of rights and equality we find ourselves floundering in a waste of conflicting theories.

Someone has said that it makes all the difference in the world whether your attitude says, "I am as good as anybody else," or "Everybody else is as good as I am." And so it does. Likewise when a man preaches the equal division of property, it makes all the difference between selfishness and sincerity whether he means that he should divide with his neighbor, or his neighbor with him. And as to equality, no matter in what we may agree that it consists, it makes a world of difference whether the plan is to equalize everybody on a low standard or on a high one—levelling up, or levelling down.

Some extremists seem to believe that a levelling down will result in a levelling up. But they have not looked long enough at the figures.

Certainly we ought to be agreed—it is probably time to say that we all are agreed—that certain indispensable necessities to self-respect and independence must be put within the reach of all.

The physical basis of life must be made secure, not on the narrowest margin on which life can be maintained, but on a margin sufficient to permit soul-room, so to speak—room for the individual to grow, to show what is in him.

To say that these ought to be made inalienable, that is, put beyond the possibility of loss, is to go further than common sense would warrant. To guarantee a man a living simply because he took the trouble to be born into the world would be to create a larger race of idlers than we now have. No; justice is served, humanity is honored and equality is established when we put the indispensable within the reach of all, even of those whose ability is not equalled by their willingness to do.

The minimum rights of human beings are life, liberty, the opportunity to express in service all the power that is in them, and in every emergency beyond their control a livelihood that is honorable to their manhood. These rights are based on our *equality of need*. All of us, regardless of our individual endowments of mind or heart, need food, shelter, clothing and the satisfaction of the social sense which is "a sense of belonging." The great man never becomes so great as to rise beyond the need of these; the small man never becomes so unimportant as to sink beyond the need of them. They are the equal necessities of our common humanity.

With this equality established, even if no more were permitted, there would still be a firm foundation —a place to start from—which would in time see the inequalities of endowment appear in human life. Natural gifts are never equal. Where we have erred is in lavishly rewarding the possession of great gifts as if they were the creation of the man possessing them, and penalizing the man who has no great gifts, as if the lack of them were his fault.

To possess a great gift is in itself a great reward. To have power and insight, a stored-up energy and an intuitive knowledge as if in some mystic laboratory of the past all the drudgery of learning had been finished—this is indeed a great reward, as also is the sense of usefulness in putting that gift at the service of others.

We cannot pay the big mind that comes to earth with great visions to unfold and realize, and we should not penalize the little mind which comes only with two willing hands to help work out slowly and laboriously the other's glowing vision. The bodies of both inhabit the same environment under the same conditions, and the self-respect and honor of one requires as careful safeguarding as those of the other.

And yet equality can be so conceived and regulated as to destroy liberty. That would appear to be the difficulty in Russia. Taking a low standard which owes its existence in the first place to a denial of fundamental human equality, and making that the standard to which the newer practice of equality must conform, the result is that equality is made a cage instead of an opportunity.

The only inequalities within our power to remedy are those which have to do with the material side. Much is being said about so manipulating the conditions of human existence as to produce a super-race, but that is so far in the future, even should it be possible at all, that it cannot serve as a substitute for what we ought to do today.

It is sometimes said that if we were only economically adjusted to a true and practical kind of equality, then would genius begin to blossom among us. We are told that it is our economic conditions which make for a scarcity of great leaders and seers and developers of new powers.

Well, that sounds hopeful enough, and yet when one looks abroad on those classes which have never been "hampered by the necessity of working for their living," is the percentage of genius very large among them?

Hardly. Outside of the new dances and new methods of flimflamming the producing public, we owe scarcely anything to them—certainly not enough to justify their position as idlers and meddlers and a sort of semi-royalty in this nation of ours.

One is not even sure that an increase of economic equality will make us a morally better people. Look at those same classes which have been "emancipated from labor" and you don't find high morality in excessive degree, do you? Why, those people are part of our inferior classes!

That is to say, it is easy to prophesy too much from our efforts to straighten out the imperfect practices of our society. But even that ought not to deter us from the effort. For this must always be true: that upon those who see the wrong the duty devolves to right it, and they at least are better for the attempt. We must do right because it is right and not from delusive expectations of what results will be.

Opportunity is equal now. If anything remains unequal it is the power to use it. You cannot make opportunity anything but equal. If a person cannot measure up to his opportunity, you cannot make him

137

measure up. The question of justice enters only in the event of that person having been subjected to such conditions as prevented him from having a fair chance to measure up. If he was deprived of early training; if compelled to work in early youth he ruined his health; if constantly borne down under the burden of injustice he lost his spirit and ambition—these inequalities, of course, are chargeable to society and are social sins.

No one will deny that we have made progress along these lines, and if anyone points to the prevailing talk of disturbance, one may simply reply that it is one of the proofs that we have made progress.

As our intelligence increases, our needs increase; and as our needs increase, our demands increase; and as our demands increase, the greater the readjustment necessary in industrial, social and political practices.

We ought to welcome change for the better. No one wants the world to remain what it was even a few months ago.

If there is one point on which counsel is required today it is this: Change is not the main thing, for mere Change may be Change For The Worse. We must keep our eye on the constructive and forward-looking effort, so that our changes may be toward a better and greater civilization.

Can You Make Your Job Bigger?

THERE are many ways of forging ahead, some of which are mere spurts soon succeeded by retreats; but the best way, the way that involves least doubt and yields most satisfaction, is the method of getting ahead with one's job.

There are men who get themselves ahead regardless of whether their job goes ahead or not—self-boosters; but these men are soon looking for other things.

There are men who get way ahead of their jobs, in which case they must be given more and greater opportunities to progress.

But the man who goes ahead *with* the job and *on* the job and by reason of the job, is the man who makes the most substantial progress.

This may sound very much like some of the advice that was given us when we were young, but there is one quality about most of the advice we got then which we ought not to overlook—it was good and true; and much of it is just as true today as it was then.

Everywhere there are men who think they could do something else much better than they are doing their present work. It is customary to make light of such men and their dreams, and even to doubt that they would be a bit better in another job than they are in their present one.

But, taking for granted that their view of the situation is the true one, what is the answer? Simply this: either they must themselves act on their faith in themselves and find the other thing which they think they can do better; or they must do so well the thing they are now doing that with this accumulated experience their desire for something different will command confidence and respect in those who may be able to help them make the change. You see, it all comes back to the job.

The job is the barometer of the man. No matter what it is, you can always tell how much of industry, judgment and carefulness a man brings to his work by watching how he does what he is doing.

You can always tell a slouch by his work, whether his work be in finance or farming, in professional or in industrial life.

It doesn't matter what it is, there is no job so menial that it cannot tell as much about a man as the presidency could.

Just now there are more menial jobs than there will be in the future; and as long as there are menial jobs, someone will have to do them; but there is no reason why a man should be penalized because his job is "menial."

There is one thing that can be said about "menial" jobs that cannot be said about a great many so-called more responsible jobs, and that is, they are useful and they are respectable and they are honest.

Did you ever see dishonest callouses on a man's hand? Hardly. When men's hands are calloused and women's hands are worn, you may be sure that Honesty is there. And that's more than you can say about many soft, white hands!

But even so, the time is coming when the hand will not be subjected to so much hard work as falls to it today. Steel fingers and arms will do many things that fleshly arms and fingers now do, and a part of at least the physical burden will be lifted off our race.

It is very natural for a man who is alive in his mind and vigorous in his ambition to desire a job that is fit for him. But does he ever stop to think of this:
—What is to hinder any job being made fit for any man?

There is not so much difference between men as we sometimes think. We like to classify men by races or intelligence or business success, and thus reach the conclusion that there are "superior" and "inferior" people.

But any man who knows his own heart and his fellow men, knows there is scarcely any fundamental

140

difference between human beings. There is more real difference between two breeds of dogs than there is between the most highly cultivated man in the world and the most unfortunate mortal. Our likeness to one another is astonishing. It ought to keep us more balanced in our judgments of our fellow men.

People classify men according to false standards, and are quite satisfied to do so—why? Because by that means they can always contrive to make themselves appear "superior" to someone. No matter how many people may be superior to them, if they can only be superior to men inferior still, that fully satisfies those who hanker after human gradations—our American snobs.

One of the reasons the man who is engaged in hand-work wants some other kind of work is this: he fancies that somehow hand-work is a little lower than head-work. Well, that formerly was the theory. But it isn't so any longer. Thank heaven! the hand-worker has at last come into his own, and even measured by the financial rewards he is on a higher plane than many a so-called "head-worker." Many a man wears a white collar who isn't earning what a grimy handed worker is paid today.

It is a terrible thing that we ever allowed this false idea to belittle the nobility of hand-work! Why, hand-work keeps the world going. When next you ride home on the street car at the rush hour, note the hands of the men who ride with you. They are not soft and pink and manicured; they are big and rough and smeared with oil and smudge. Look well at those hands, for they turn the very world on its axis, making it a planet of power by day and a glory of light by night, and really give our country the industrial reputation it has gained.

Hand-work! All the arts engage the hand. The balanced work-ration includes both head and hand. When the creative hand is denied its place in the world's work, life becomes unbalanced.

But perhaps there is another and deeper reason why men sometimes grow discontented and seek a change: they want a career, and the job they have may not seem to promise a career. Again the question comes:

Could that job be made so as to afford a man his career?

The time has come, as already stated, when drudgery must be abolished out of labor. It is not work that men object to, but the element of drudgery in work. We must drive out drudgery wherever we find it and set men physically free. We shall never be wholly civilized until we remove the tread-mill from the daily job.

Of course, invention is doing this in some degree now. We have succeeded to a very great extent in relieving men of the heavier and more onerous jobs that used to sap their strength, but even when lightening the heavier labor we have not yet succeeded in removing monotony. That is another field that beckons us—the abolition of monotony, and in trying to accomplish that we shall doubtless discover other changes that have to be made in our system.

But here is the point: If invention must do these things for your job, why don't you search for the invention?

Your job is your field. If you say you are too good for your present job, have you ever given any thought to methods by which your present job could be made good enough, or even too good, for you?

You say you want a job on which you can look forward to a life's career: Have you ever studied your own job from the standpoint of making it a worthy life career?

You know, if these things are to be done, somebody must do them. If all of us leave the job that doesn't fit us without doing something to make it fit men like us, we are not making progress very fast. If we simply desert our jobs, leaving them to whomsoever happens along, we are not making the world much better for our fellow men. If the man who follows you on the job is going to be up against the same conditions that you were, the world has not moved forward one step so far as that particular job is concerned.

Then, if someone is destined to do these things, why not you? Who knows the job better than you do? It is quite possible that men do not always find their career in the first job they get, nor always in the second. But this much is true: Every job is destined to become in some sense some man's career, and if that is true it ought to be so adjusted as to make a worthy career for him.

Now, there is no worldly success greater than leaving more jobs and better jobs where we found new jobs and less desirable ones. The trend of progress will never be toward a decrease in the number or quality of jobs—always in an increase. Every new idea brings new jobs. Every time a job is improved, it breeds more of them, and by its influence makes better the jobs around it.

This is just a suggestion toward finding a career and finding success: How do you know that the career you seek and the success you desire is not right there in the job you have? How do you know you cannot make it a career, and turn it into a success? There's a field for your invention. There's a chance to serve humanity down to the last working day of Time.

And be sure of this: in thus moving, not ahead of your job, nor in despite of your job, but in moving ahead with the job and on the job and by the impetus you give the job, the other rewards of labor, too, will be yours in abundance.

A Nation of Pioneer Blood

ONE of the great things about the American people is that they are pioneers. They are of pioneer blood. Even though most of the world has been trodden by man, and the farthest frontiers have been linked together by the intrepid inquiring spirit of the pioneer, the blood of high adventure has not thinned nor cooled, and where we lack lands and seas to explore we are making up by conquering new continents of life.

Ask anyone you meet what his origin is, and you will discover that his family roots are overseas. If not a pioneer himself, he is a pioneer's descendant.

The "forty-niners" are practically all gone, and those equally audacious men who visioned cities on the prairies; but in any shop in any city you can find men who came half way round the world in search, not of a new country, but of a new life. Pioneers!

In a near-by neighborhood whose residents had long prided themselves on being completely American, the school-teachers inaugurated a letter-writing contest about the advantages of life in the United States, and when the little essays were published in the local paper the neighbors were astonished to learn that 50 per cent of the children wrote as travelers, as pioneers —they had not been long over from foreign lands where they were born.

Astonished, too, by the testimony of their own eyes, that the little foreign-born children could write better essays on Americanism than the American-born children could, because the little immigrants had a background of contrast. They had the outlook of the pioneer.

It is perfectly clear, when we think of it, that a man who has spirit enough to pull up his roots and betake himself to a strange land and a strange people from a motive of bettering his condition, is a superior sort of man.

He could have remained overseas. He could have settled down into the conditions which satisfied his forbears, and which still satisfy many of his fellows. It is natural for men to do this, unless they have an urge within which drives them to seek the better thing.

And so he comes to us, by way of the great seaports. He comes down the gang-plank a bit bewildered. His dress is not as ours; his speech is not as ours; all his habits stamp him as a stranger.

To the ignorant he brings amusement. To the exploiter of human labor, he brings a temptation. But to the man who sees and understands, he brings a prophetic vision.

Who is this man with his bundle? He is a pioneer. Make way for him.

Now, wherever we go in this country we find pioneers or the sons of pioneers. Not the pioneers of Mayflower nor yet of Revolutionary days—pioneers of five and ten years ago.

It makes little difference if your forefathers did come over in the Mayflower—they were immigrants, strangers in a strange land, pioneers—and we are their sons.

So that the spirit of initiative, the very bloodstream of high daring, the vital urge to rest nowhere until Opportunity is attained, are bred in the very fibers of our bodies.

Of no other people can it be said in the same sense as it is said of the people of the United States—"They are the pioneers of every people under heaven."

It is only natural, therefore, that the pioneer spirit, denied further exercise in exploration of new seas and conquest of new continents, now turns itself to other exploits, different, yet calling for the same old daring of the pioneer.

It was natural at the outset that the first comers should pioneer upon a new venture into freedom. Had they been no more than colonists, set down in a certain place to build up an imitation of the land they left, the history of the world would have been very different.

Colonists they were at first, but colonists of their own free will, and that made them pioneers.

145

Therefore they were not imitators but creators, and it was not long before the attempted imitations of government and social conditions were banished in a great ebullition of the creative spirit. They called it "revolution" then, but it was creation. It depends upon your point of view which one of these words you use. Creation is always an uncomfortable, even a reprehensible process in the view of the old, outworn but exceedingly profitable forms which it removes.

It was just as natural that within this newly created form of opportunity new freedom of effort should reveal itself. Invention, enterprise, commerce, wealth, power followed quickly, as they always follow where men breathe free air.

If the late war may be said to have expanded the limits of human freedom everywhere, especially where freedom was not complete before, it may also be said, as a consequence, that we are on the eve of a new era of inventiveness, a new influx of epoch-making ideas.

Just as rain cannot fall in some regions, so ideas cannot be born and developed in an atmosphere of oppression. But the temperature of the world has become more favorable of late, and we may expect to see a great downpour of ideas which will further liberate man and make him free of the world in which he finds himself.

All this is just another way of saying that we are a pioneering people. We seek the conditions of freedom, and all else follows as day follows night.

Our latest great pioneering effort was directed toward opening a new route through world war to world peace. We pioneered the thought of a war being fought to end all war. We pioneered the thought of a war being waged in utter scorn of material profit from it. We pioneered the thought of actually compelling the peace terms which settled a single war to serve also as the machinery which should prevent all future wars.

In doing these things we are exhibiting our pioneer blood in its best strains. We are striking out upon new paths as truly as did Columbus when he set sail toward the mysterious west.

The prominent feature of the American pioneering spirit is that it is constructive. We do not always realize that there is a perversion of the pioneering urge which it behooves us to watch.

Illustrations of this lower sort of adventure are numerous in history. There are pioneers who rush to a land upon first reports of its richness, to strip it bare and carry away its wealth. There are other pioneers who move in to occupy the land, develop and conserve it, and enhance its value and usefulness.

Where we have known exactly what to do in our pioneering work, we have done it with directness and speed. But where we have not known exactly what to do, we have gone carefully, with true pioneer caution, in order not to cause injury through our ignorance.

That, perhaps, is a fair description of our social attitude these days. There can be no doubt whatever that we feel the surge of pioneer blood in us once more as we contemplate social conditions in our country. We feel the impulse once again to strike out new highways, new roads through the social wilderness, which the thronging feet of happy people may wear into great world paths by which all people may come to peace and prosperity.

Just remember that we are a race of pioneers; that there is no active blood in our nation that is not descended from the pioneers; and then examine the tendencies of today in the light of that thought, and see if our people are not feeling the unrest to be on the pioneer path once more and discover newer and better regions of life and its pursuits for all men.

That, undoubtedly, is the direction in which we are going to explore next—the direction of social advance.

But we are cautious about it. We know that everything we have achieved in the 300 years of our occupancy of this continent is not bad. We know perfectly well that we could not have worked and thought and sacrificed without accomplishing something worthy to be built into the noblest temple of social justice our breed could ever rear. So we are cautious about

147

it: in trying to get rid of what is faulty and wrong, we do not desire to injure what is useful and good.

It was not the pioneer who destroyed the wealth of game and forest and soil; it was the thoughtless hordes that followed—those who stayed at home until hardy men had struck out the paths and subdued the dangers. And the true pioneer will not bring disaster to what is good in the new regions which he seeks to subdue to justice and righteousness.

No one can contemplate the nation to which we belong without realizing the distinctive prophetic character of its obvious mission to the world.

We are pioneers. We are the pathfinders. We are the road-builders. We are the guides, the vanguards of Humanity.

The American people represent the human extract of that which was the best in all other countries, the pioneers of all pioneers, and we are therefore destined to lead the plain peoples of the world in any path we lay out; they are confident that we will lead them into no slough, no miry swamp of disaster.

Is not that a most solemn responsibility for us to bear? Ought it not to guarantee that such confidence will not be misplaced?

When the American Pioneer strikes out the path, the world may know that it will be safe for all the fathers and mothers, young men and maidens, and all the little children of humanity—a safe road for mankind.

Human Nature and the
Social System

THERE are two positions from which one may consider the economic conditions under which we live, and the one you chose will determine the attitude and emphasis of any thought or action taken with reference to those conditions.

You may say that it is the economic condition which makes mankind what it is; or you may say that it is mankind that makes the economic condition what it is.

It is worthy of notice that wherever a situation is desirable, mankind usually claims the credit of creating it. But wherever a situation is faulty and self-destructive and full of injustice and pain, mankind has a tendency to charge that up to "nature." So you will find a large proportion of partisans claiming that it is the economic system which makes men what they are. They blame the faults of our industrial system for all the faults which we behold in mankind generally.

And you will find other men who say that man creates his own conditions; that if the economic, industrial or social system is bad, it is but a reflection of what Man himself is; his social conditions being determined by his own nature.

It may be true, of course, that these things interact; it probably *is* true. But it would be hard to gainsay that the point of beginning, the casual motive power, is in man himself.

What is wrong in our industrial system, for example, is a reflection of what is wrong in man himself. But there is no doubt that after he has created this wrong system, it begins to react upon him in punitive or other influential ways. That is, character acts upon conditions, and conditions upon character—an endless interaction.

It ought not to be hard to admit this. In fact, it seldom is hard when we remove the matter far enough from our own concerns. Teachers dislike to admit that the faults of the educational system are their own faults writ large. Physicians dislike to admit that the faults of the present systems of medicine are their own deficiencies organized. Manufacturers hesitate to admit that the mistakes of the present industrial methods are, in part at least, their own mistakes systematized and extended. But take the question outside of a man's immediate concerns, and he sees the point readily enough.

The workman has no trouble whatever in seeing that the faults of modern business systems are not and cannot be anything other than the faults of business men themselves; because business men make business systems. The business man sees just as readily that the faults of labor organizations are the faults of workingmen themselves.

And all of us together—the whole of human society—make the social system.

Now, if you allow relentless logic to take its course with this form of statement, and begin to speak of reforming the social system, then you find yourself confronted at once with the problem of making a profound and complete change in human nature. And that is a pretty big job. It has never been accomplished wholesale.

It is just at this point that simon-pure idealists mount their cloud-horses and soar into regions where we cannot follow them. And it is also at this point that our so-called "practical" men propose programs that fairly clank with materialism.

Why is it that so many fine idealists lose all contact with reality? And why is it that so many hard-headed practical men lose so completely their contact with idealism?

If some method could be devised by which idealists could be anchored to an anvil and a sledge hammer, and hard-headed practical men enlightened and refined by a dash of Vision and an infusion of a venturesome and divine belief in the supremacy of

150

righteousness, then we should see both these types yield more useful service to their kind.

We should be slow about drawing conclusions before we have all our data.

No doubt, with a less faulty human nature than ours is, a less faulty social system would have grown up. Or, if human nature were worse than it is, a worse system would have grown up; though probably a worse system would not have lasted so long as the present one has. It is only its good points that have kept ours in force so long.

But, things being as they are, there are very few who will claim that mankind deliberately set out to create a faulty social system. Granting without re-serve that all the faults of the social system are in Man himself, it does not follow that he deliberately organized his imperfections and established them. We shall have to charge a great deal up to ignorance, shall we not? We shall have to charge a great deal up to a certain innocence as well. Take the beginnings of our present industrial system, for example. There was then no indication as to how it would grow, nor as to the points in which it would show its greatest imperfection. Everyone was glad to see it begin. Every new advance was hailed with joy. No one ever thought of "capital" and "labor" as hostile in-terests. No one ever dreamed that the very fact of success would bring insidious dangers with it.

And yet with growth every imperfection latent in the system came to light. A man's business grew to such proportions that he had to have more helpers than he knew by their first names; but that fact was not regretted, it was rather hailed with joy. And yet see what it has since led to!—an impersonal system wherein the workman has become something less than flesh and blood, a mere part of a system.

No one believes, of course, that this dehumanizing process was deliberately invented. It just grew. It was latent in the whole early system, but no one saw it and no one could foresee it. Only prodigious and unheard of development could bring it to light.

But there is yet another consideration which the first set of facts does not include. Take the industrial idea; what is it? The true industrial idea is not to make money. The industrial idea is to express a serviceable idea, duplicate a useful idea, by as many thousands as there are people who need it. To produce, produce; to get a system that will reduce production to a fine art; to put production on such a basis as will provide means for expansion and the building of still more shops, the production of still more thousands of useful things—that is the real industrial idea.

"Yes, but what about the workingmen?" Ah, that brings us to the point. When the system grows by its own momentum to such proportions that it begins to press upon fundamental human rights or to violate fundamental human instincts, the social question arises.

And what is the social question? Simply the question of how this industrial system can be so adjusted as to recognize human rights.

The industrial idea did not start out with the intention of violating human rights. Nevertheless that is what its extreme development tended to do. Therefore the clash, which is called the social question.

Here again we approach the problem: Which is first, human nature or its social and industrial environment? It becomes clear that once a system and human nature come into conflict, human nature and human rights represent the stronger force. Mankind is still creative enough to change the system to conform with human imperatives of Right.

This also has a bearing on the changeability of human nature. Those who are sometimes discouraged by reflecting upon the impossibility of changing human nature wholesale and for the better, thus changing the social system for the better also, should carry their reflections a little further. They should reflect on the impossibility of any system, no matter how important, changing human nature enough to make it content with violations of its needs and rights. Let any system of government, industry or business curtail or contravene fundamental human rights, and it is not human nature that changes—it is that system!

So that, after all, the inflexibility of human nature may be our most hopeful fact.

152

We all know, we all feel, that the only way by which human nature at large could be influenced to condone or support a bad system of any kind, would be to render that bad system profitable to humanity at large.

Now, we know that no bad system can be profitable to humanity at large. A system universally and unexceptionally bad would simply collapse. It would be like trying to maintain a sound currency system in a nation of counterfeiters; it would simply be impossible. The counterfeit has its fleeting value simply because the mass of money is sound. And unfair, greedy, inhuman, wicked systems last as long as they do only because the opposite majority qualities give them room for profitable play.

No doubt the faultiness of human nature is the cause of the faultiness of our social system. But equally without doubt the faultiness of our social system is not the *intention* of humanity, else the faults would not be so universally denounced and opposed.

Our ignorance is responsible for the faults being there, but it is our incorrigible desire for public and social righteousness that makes it impossible for the faults to remain there forever.

Mankind is not perfect by any means. But mankind has not yet given its collective vote to the Devil.

The Modern City—
A Pestiferous Growth

THE modern City, with its suppression of all that
is sweet in its natural environment, its enforcement of artificial modes of living, its startling dis-
parities of leisure and employment, its hideous extremes of self-conscious wealth and abject poverty, is
probably the most unlovely sight this planet can offer; certainly it represents the most unwholesome condition that challenges our thought today.

For the City concentrates within its limits the és-
sence of all that is wrong, artificial, wayward and
unjust in our social life. It is, as it were, the spot
where the internal social impurities break out in a
festering sore.

Much discussion has been devoted to "the problem of the City," but for the most part it has shuttled
back and forth between a liking for community life and
a liking for the companionship of nature, between
the City lover and the country lover—and, of course,
that is not the question at all.

A City is a camp that has become stagnant and
which grows by' accretion. A City is a camp that
has ceased to march, a community that has called a
halt.

There will be no argument in this page against the
desirability of a settled life. Nor will there be any
assertion of the superiority of that phase of society
where the people followed their flocks as their flocks
moved hither and thither seeking pasture.

It was doubtless a milestone of progress when men
began to plant vineyards, for vineyards have to be
tended, and tending them keeps the vine-dresser resi-
dent in one place.

But to recognize the advantage of settled community life is not to put in a plea for the modern
City, for it is doubtful if the modern City can be

considered as in any sense a community. Oh, we call it a community, of course; we talk a great deal about community spirit, and the like; but anyone who knows the modern City knows that it is not a community—it is any number of communities, few of them sympathetic one to another.

The modern City is broken into as many communities as there are interests in it, and the modern City is the great meeting place of all our social antagonisms, both those that are engendered by differences in taste and culture and those which grow out of economic causes. The result is that such communities as we have are antagonistic, competitive, mutually exclusive.

The modern City is a classic illustration of what ensues when we fail to mix the arts.

The three great arts are Agriculture, Manufacture and Transportation.

The City automatically excludes agriculture as one of the arts possible to its inhabitants; it does this because the land whereon it stands is too crowded for the soil to exercise its natural function, and where it is not occupied by buildings it is overlaid with pavement.

Manufacture was the center around which the City grew. It may have been a very simple form of manufacture at first, like the making of flour out of grain, or the making of shoes out of hides, or the making of cloth out of wool.

But wherever a productive machine is set up with a roof over it and operatives around it, there the City begins.

There are two bases for the community, one a necessity of nature, the other a necessity of progress. Man was not made for solitude. He is gregarious. Not only "hath he set the solitary in families," as the Scripture has it, but families also group with other families, and as the individual finds his fulfillment in the family, so the family finds its fulfillment in the community.

Then, again, progress is not solitary. We can do few things alone. Directly we undertake to achieve worth-while results in the physical world, we dis-

155

cover that we need help. We discover also that men delight to work together, that they are formed for creative co-operation.

So that it is a far different thing to condemn the City than to condemn the community. The community is natural. The City is not.

It is the one-sided, lopsided development of industry, as industry is represented by the manufacture of articles of use and commerce, that is primarily responsible for the modern City—that, and the neglect of the other two arts, agriculture and transportation.

In our day,-however, transportation is beginning to catch up. It is still far from what it ought to be, but it is immeasurably better than once it was. And as a result, the City is beginning to feel the influence of an art that will be one of the chief forces in its undoing.

At first it seemed as if transportation would have the effect of further augmenting the City, but now it is effecting a spreading out of cities and populations. The suburban car and the automobile have rendered confinement within the City unnecessary for large numbers of people. And one of the most hopeful facts is that, whereas only the well-to-do once found it possible to get away from the city, now the workingman finds it not only possible but advantageous to live in the country, and thousands of them are doing it even while they work in the City.

And as transportation facilities become better and more numerous, this movement to the country will be increased.

The "problem of the City" is a bundle of the most baffling problems we know. It not only includes problems of health, morals, administration and economics, but problems which go deep into the very nature of man.

The solution of this problem has eluded our best minds for decades and decades. In spite of all the expenditure of money and thought, all the sacrifice of labor and spirit, "the problem of the City" grows more acute instead of easier.

And what is the answer to this?

Plainly, so it seems to some of us, that the ulti-

156

mate solution will be the abolition of the City, its abandonment as a blunder.

There are a number of movements all converging to this end—some of them in utter unconsciousness of this end—and not the least of them is a certain theory of taxation which has seized upon the minds and imaginations of the people. Nothing will finally work more effectively to undo the fateful grip which the City habit has taken upon the people, than the destruction of the fictitious land values which the City traditions have set up and maintained.

We shall solve the City Problem by leaving the City.

Get the people into the country, get them into communities where a man knows his neighbor, where there is a commonality of interest, where life is not artificial, and you have solved the City Problem. You have solved it by eliminating the City. City life was always artificial and cannot be made anything else. An artificial form of life breeds its own disorders, and these cannot be "solved." There is nothing to do but abandon the course that gives rise to them.

There is nothing impossible or unusual in this. We have seen in our own day cities spring up in a month. Well, if our people should be made free of the soil in their own country, you would see whole cities shrink to nothing in the same length of time.

Nothing can long exist that is not self-sustaining. The City is not self-sustaining. No American City— and we are the best fortified in the world in this respect—could survive, without suffering, a single week's interruption in the traffic in supplies from the farm.

The farm is self-sustaining. The City can serve the farm with regard to conveniences, but not with essentials. Essentially, the farm is complete within itself.

The City has exercised its illicit charm to draw to itself the very people on whose devotion to the art of agriculture it depended for its livelihood. As a result of this overgrowth of the City at the expense of the farm, the City is now finding it hard to live. When the City is driven out to get food, it must go to the farm. And that is where it is going now.

157

The balance of life—in all its aspects—can only be preserved by a natural balance in the attention given to all three major arts—Agriculture, Manufacture and Transportation—without which, or in the neglect of any of which, nothing goes very far.

And the best way to obtain this balance, as we are beginning to learn, is to have the same people practice more than one of them.

As has been previously stated in these pages, there is no sound reason whatever why one immense group of men should be confined within factory walls all the year round simply because they happen to live in the City, and there is just as little reason why another large group of persons should be confined to their farm-acres all the year round just because they happen to be farmers.

Agriculture would be better served if the man-power of the manufacturing interests were devoted to it a part of the time every year, and manufacturing would be better served if the man-power of the farms could change occupation during the season when the ground is resting. And the life of everybody, the physical and economic life, would be benefited. Besides which, small manufacturing centers would dot all our countrysides, and wide farming areas would encircle our present dense communities, relieving them of congested abnormality, and the country of its unnatural loneliness and separateness.

The mingling of the arts will help restore us to economic balance and racial sanity.

Catching the Boss's Eye

IT IS most unfortunate that we are so strongly under the influence of the idea that to catch somebody's eye, to attract admiring attention, to get full credit for what we do, is the one element which we must not omit from any effort we make; that to do a piece of work and not get the credit for it is little less than a calamity.

Not very long ago it was urged in an article intended to stimulate the ambition of young men, that they should endeavor strenuously to do something that would catch their boss's eye.

The surprising point about this advice is that it was given by an employer himself. Had it been written by an aspiring young workman, it would be easy to account for; but how a boss could utter such counsel is beyond ordinary power to explain.

If all our productive operations were manned by men who were straining to catch the boss's eye, industry would become a sort of vaudeville, a game of catch-as-catch-can, a race for recognition.

Of course, there are certain factors in this desire for recognition which must be reckoned with before we can deal intelligently with it.

It is beyond dispute that our modern industrial system has warped this desire terribly out of shape and rendered it almost an obsession. There was a time when a man's personal advancement depended entirely and immediately upon his work, and not upon anyone's favor; but nowadays it depends far too much, as we all know, upon the individual's good fortune in catching some influential eye.

It is perfectly clear that as long as this situation exists, 'men will strive to meet it; that is, men will work with the idea of catching somebody's eye; they will work with the idea that if they fail to get credit for what they do, they might as well have done it badly or not have done it at all.

One result of this, as far as the work itself is concerned, is that it becomes a secondary consideration. The job we are doing, the article we are producing, the special kind of service we are rendering, turns out to be not our principal work at all. No. Our main work is our personal advancement. This thing we are doing now is not being done for its own sake, this service we are doing is not being done because it is a service, but because it is a platform from which we may practice the art of catching somebody's eye, the art of skillfully attracting credit-bringing attention to ourselves.

Now, we submit, this habit of making the work secondary and the recognition primary, is unfair to the work. It makes recognition and credit our real job, while the job we are paid to do is used merely as a kicking-off place.

And it also has an unfortunate effect on the worker. It encourages a peculiar kind of ambition which is neither lovely nor productive. It produces the kind who imagine that by "standing in with the boss" they will get ahead. Every shop knows this kind of man. And the worst of it is there are some things in our present industrial system which make it appear that this kind of game really pays. Foremen are only human, and it is natural that they should be flattered by being made to believe that they hold the weal or woe of workmen in their hands. It is natural also, that being open to flattery, their self-seeking subordinates should flatter them still more to obtain and profit by their favor.

The trend of industry is and ought to be farther and farther away from a condition which gives any individual the power of life and death—for that is virtually what bread-and-butter power is—over another. We don't want a race of overseers who fancy they control human destiny; and we don't want a race of workmen who think they have to cringe and cajole to get recognition of their merits.

The desire for recognition is natural. But it is far from being the highest desire. The real workman knows that his work is his unanswerable witness. Far higher than the desire for recognition is the cre-

160

ative desire, which finds its satisfaction in work well done whether anyone sees that it is well done or not.

But of course, some modern industrial conditions tend to smother that kind of workmanship. Wherever the emphasis is on quantity at the expense of quality, wherever the emphasis is on profits at the expense of service, wherever the commercial side of production is emphasized at the cost of the human and serviceable side, then the workman finds himself in a sort of scramble for selfish benefits whether of money, rank or job, and he can hardly help becoming infected with the regenerate tendency.

Now, everyone will agree that the person who is over-anxious about getting credit for what he does is not an impressive person, to say the least. But he may not be entirely blamable, either.

He may be a product of that false philosophy of life which teaches that a man is successful only insofar as he gets credit for being so; and believing that, he may perhaps also have the experience of credit unjustly withheld from him, and so he grows over-anxious. One false extreme has simply worked another false extreme in him. He is to be pitied and led out of his obsession. Certainly, he is not to be dealt with in a way that would deepen his sense of injustice. The sense of personal injustice is one of the most painful burdens a man can bear about with him.

Just where to draw the line between a laudable desire for recognition and an overwhelming thirst for credit is not easy to do; the one is normal and the other is abnormal. But we should say that the line of demarcation exists somewhere in the individual's attitude toward the work he is doing.

If his inclination is to do his work well whether he foresees special credit or not; that is, if he has a pride in his work quite apart from its possible relation to other men's opinions, then it would be probably safe to say that his desire for recognition would be normal.

But if his work means no more to him than an emblem with which to attract attention, if when without any hope of recognition for the particular job on which he is engaged, he slurs it over and neglects it, then it is apparent that his desire for recognition is not born of high workmanly pride, but of selfish personal interest of a rather small caliber.

It would be pleasant to declare that good work always is seen and recognized, but it would scarcely be true. There is far too much work produced for all of it to be judged accurately. But it would be absolutely true to declare that a good workman is always seen and recognized. His work may escape observation; he himself cannot well do so. All the carefulness, dependability, honest pride and power he builds into his work is somehow built back into himself. It is reflected back upon him. And, of course, that kind of shining cannot long be hidden. For it is a matter of character then, not merely of articles of manufacture.

The matter of personal advancement is one which is not considered as carefully as it ought to be. And much of the misconception concerning one's credit for one's work grows out of the kind of idea of advancement which he may hold.

A great evil was begun when the sphere of advancement was placed outside of the job instead of within it.

Nowadays advancement means getting out of one's job into another job, if one can. It doesn't mean becoming a better workman at what you are doing; it means becoming a workman at something else, at another rate of pay, and with another degree of respect attaching to your rank.

Of course, when this kind of advancement means also more of the means and comforts of life, more of the opportunities which one would give to one's family, nothing short of cosmic suppression could prevent men from striving for it.

Thus the competitive element is injected into life. And we are strongly of the opinion that when these things, the means and comforts of life, the desirable opportunities which one would give to one's family— when these things are left at the peril of the breadwinner's success or failure in a mad competitive scramble for this favor called "advancement," then our system of life is sadly in need of humanizing readjustment.

Under the present strife and strain men are not free to consider their work alone, they are driven to consider the methods—fair and unfair—by which they may attract attention, win favor and gain advancement.

If men were assured that their livelihood and respect as members of society were assured from the beginning, then we should have a sounder foundation on which to appeal to them to make their advancement within the limits of their work.

But this subject of advancement deserves attention by itself. Suffice it now to say that if a man has faith to trust his future to the quality of his work, the chances are very high that his faith will be rewarded. The strength of faith is that it does not look for the reward; it does not demand what one deserves, it only asks that one be deserving.

By doing the thing for which you know you may get no credit, you are doing something which will never be lost to you—you are building certain qualities which cannot be hidden.

One of the commonest faults observable in men is that they overreach for credit. And, of course, where one overreaches one does not receive. After all, we must leave a little of our lives to Destiny.

Patriotism an Inclusive
Emotion

L OVE of country is a sentiment inherent in men.
There is a sacred element in the spirit of patriotism for this reason. No matter how hard the land
may have been to the dwellers thereon, no matter how
harsh the governmental conditions imposed, no matter
how bitter the memories which thoughts of native
land evoke, no matter how unfavorably the place of
our nativity may compare with the land of our adop-
tion, there is still an ineradicable love of country which
is a vital part of us from the earliest dawn of our
consciousness until the last shadows begin to close
in upon us.

It is inconceivable that there could exist, outside
the pages of fiction, a man who, regardless of grievances, was without a special love for some branch
of the human race, some division of the earth's surface, some city, state or bit of homestead.

All our love of the earth begins in love for our
own land. All our love for Humanity begins in love
for our own people. All our love for Freedom begins
in love for our own institutions.

As an illustration of the depth of the patriotic
sentiment, look at the Irish. With their memories of
their native land deeply colored by suffering, how
they cling to Erin still! How they laud her as the
fairest ,among the isles!

Or take the Jew. He has been without a flag and
a country these twenty centuries, yet how his heart-
strings twine about old Jerusalem, the glories of her
past and the greater glories prophesied for her future!

It is not merely because the land feeds us and
caresses us and gives us pleasant lives that we love it.
Men have most deeply loved the lands where they have
suffered most. Patriotism in its purity is not a selfish
sordid sentiment.

Of course, every virtue has its counterfeit, every noble principle has its superficial imitation. The more sacred the principle the more readily is it seized upon by designing persons to lend an air of genuineness to their questionable purposes. This needs no proof. We see it with reference to every lofty sentiment, not patriotism only.

The principal fallacy to which—not real patriotism, mark you—false patriotism succumbs is the fallacy of exclusiveness. Because we love one country we must suspect the motives and defeat the purposes of all other countries—that is the fallacy.

It is commonly reported, of course, that those who remember that they are members of the Human Race as well as of their own nationality, are promoting the doctrine that a man ought to love all countries, his own no more than another.

Aside from this being merely theoretical, it is impossible. No man ever has or ever can love another people as he loves his own, another land as he loves his own, or other institutions as he loves his own.

He may wisely acknowledge the worth and beauty of the other land, the greatness and usefulness of the other people, the wisdom and character of the other institutions—but this is not patriotic love. He may even see that the other land is more desirable from many points of view, that the other people are more highly developed and more efficient, that the other institutions are more advanced; yet he will but love his own the more and covet for them the good characteristics of the others. We cannot get away from these facts. They are written in our very hearts.

All love is given us for purposes of inclusion, not exclusion, because love is an expansive emotion. This is a truth which everyone will readily acknowledge. We have a respect for the women of other races because we respect the mothers, wives and daughters of our own. We have a heart for the welfare of all children because we have a heart for the welfare of our own. And so on. We are able to understand, sympathize, respect, solely because we know from our own experience what the situation is. That is why we respect an alien's patriotic love for his own country. We know that sentiment in ourselves; therefore, we respect it in him.

But reasoning from the analogy of the social affections a distinction should be made: there is a love of attachment and a love of respect. Our domestic affections form personal attachments. But there are people on the other side of the city, in another city, or in another country, with whom we should be very loth to form personal attachments—with whom, indeed, nature would prevent us forming personal attachments—yet whose rights as men we cherish as strongly as we cherish our own. Isn't that true?

You don't have to be willing to live in the same house with a man in order to cherish his rights as a man and citizen. By virtue of his membership in the human race you are "for" him in the protection of certain fundamental rights which as a human being he possesses, and which neither a difference in speech nor allegiance can change. We know men as men, not as nationals. We know them as human beings. That is our primary knowledge of men, as members of our kind.

There is a profoundly natural element in patriotism. But something tragically artificial marks all national antagonisms. It is natural that a man should love his own people and his own spot of earth; it is unnatural that he should hate another people or another spot of earth simply because it is not his. Love of our own country does not involve hatred of other countries. The man who tries to prove his patriotism by the extent of his hatred is a suspicious patriot.

In other words, patriotism is not an exclusive emotion—it does not shut out; it lets in. And though we cannot love others as our own, we can still love the rights of others, their peace, their prosperity and the security of their children. The moment patriotism takes wings and enters the spiritual realm, that moment it blesses all people.

If there is any one quality in the Genius of America to whose existence we can point with confidence, it is the quality of heightened regard in which we hold the rights of all peoples on the earth—an internationalism of sympathy and understanding and good wishes.

The United States never has and never will become productive soil for the seeds of international hatred. We will never rise against lands or peoples to do them harm; we will only rise against the aggressive Errors of which lands and peoples have become the self-deluded servants; and we will even minimize the chances of having to do that, by being in the world the friend of Light and Freedom.

The United States was never more avowedly the Servant Nation of the world than now. And never did the Servant status hold nobler honor.

The nations whose histories are embalmed in ancient books, whose ruins dot the desolation of desert lands, fell before the subtlest temptation that can ever lure a nation—the temptation to Mastery. To bear world rule, to make vassals, to be world conqueror—this is the rock on which nations have made shipwrecks of themselves. They forgot the eternal Wisdom which taught: "He that would be greatest among you, let him be as one that serveth."

The United States has never wanted to master any nation. The utmost expenditure of money and eloquence and influence and false incentives of every kind, has utterly failed to inoculate our people even slightly with the virus of imperialistic ambition.

Even after our part in the Great War, with results that must be grateful to every lover of Liberty and Order, we find ourselves strangely untainted by the animus of militarism. We did what we had to do, we did it as well as we could, but it was not such business as we would care to be doing all the time.

There is one source of pride to every American and that is, though we broke all our records of militaristic preparation and achievement, though we gained a name for courage and initiative, yet with the spoils of the world laid down before us we have kept faith with our traditions and have refused one iota of reward. The nation paid in blood and sweat and sorrow—for what? For the privilege of serving the world without recompense.

We ought to think more of our own United States

as the Servant Nation of Mankind, the great, strong, trustworthy, righteous nation whose joy is to serve all the peoples in the things which pertain to peace and progress.

In proportion to our population, our area, our wealth, and the extent of our history, there are fewer of the means of destruction to be found within the boundaries or under the control of the United States than of any other nation. Why? Because we would rather serve than enslave, we would rather help than hurt, we would rather live in a family of nations than in an imperialistic system where the strongest desperado among the nations ruled.

Love the United States! Why, even if the United States were but an ideal, but a dream, but an Utopia written in books, but not yet realized by man, we would love it! Unrealized, it would be like heaven. How much more, then, does every human heart on the earth love the real United States? And if we are distrusted and disliked anywhere it is because some among us, forgetting who and what they are, have said or done things which made us appear in a light less than our own.

We shall keep our people in prosperity and our neighbors in peace and the world in sanity and equipoise by going quietly about our mission of serving all mankind in the things which endure.

False "Success Philosophy"

THIRTY years ago every boy in the United States was educated in the idea that it was possible for him to become President of the United States, that he ought to aspire to that position, that to achieve it would represent his success; and, of course, there was a great waste of human energy; we only needed four or five men for that job. It would be interesting to know how many of our Presidents were told in their boyhood that they might attain that office.

We do not waste so very much time on that sort of prospect for our boys nowadays.

One reason may be our increase in regard for the Presidency. We think of it now as a place of Destiny. We judge any man a fool who would seek it as a personal distinction. We have seen too much of the responsibility it involves to make it the sign and symbol of any man's individual success.

But perhaps another reason is that our idea of Success is also changing.

There has been a great falling off in the "Success philosophy" recently, as you may have noticed. It was rather overdone for a long while. Its foundations were false; its motives were false; its emphasis was false. Moreover, it is doubtful if all the "pep" and "ginger" and "hustle" which it prescribed has increased the Success total of the nation one degree.

No doubt we were in error in much of our "Success" teaching; not in insisting that everyone ought to be a Success, but in defining what it was.

It goes without saying that any kind of Success which would put us all in administrative offices, and leave none of us out on the farm or out in the shop, would be rash.

It is wrong to advocate anything which, if universally applied, would ruin the world. That is the difficulty about militarism: it says that a stiff bit of war now and then is a mighty fine idea; but immedi-

169

ately you apply that principle universally, what have you? A universal shambles! On the other hand, when you apply pacifism universally, what have you? Universal peace! A universal shambles would soon totally destroy all life. But universal peace interferes with nothing that does good.

What would be the result if this thing which we are advocating were to be applied everywhere in everything and to everybody?—that is the question we ought to ask ourselves.

And if we are advocating something which, if universally adopted, would prove destructive; or something which depends for its Success on a large section of the people being excluded from its benefits, then we may be sure it is a fallacy.

The great universals—those things which if applied everywhere to everybody would be beneficial— are religion in the moral world, order in the social world, and fundamental industry in the physical world. These things never turn destructive, no matter how widely nor how thoroughly applied.

The trouble with much of our "Success" doctrine, then, was this: if everybody had become successful in the way it advocated, this would have been very far from a successful world. It would be a most tragically unbalanced world. Not that failure is needed to balance Success—that is not the idea at all; but Success must have certain universal qualities, or it is not Success at all.

Several weeks ago we discussed the mistaken idea that one had to catch the boss's eye in order to obtain advancement. This matter of advancement is related to what we are discussing now.

The principal reason the majority of men wish to advance is that it means more material reward for them, more creature comforts, more opportunities for themselves and their families.

When you put down in cold print that here in this human society of ours there is a majority of jobs which do not yield men these desirable things, and that there is a smaller number of jobs which do yield them, and for this smaller number the whole mass of men is scrambling, it doesn't seem right, does it?

When a man gives all of his day and an equal proportion of his strength and ability to his work, and still does not receive as many of the comforts of life as another man who also gives his day and his strength and ability to his job, it seems that something is out of order.

Of course, it is easy to say, "Well, let him get more skill and get into a job that pays more! Yes, but suppose he does. Suppose everybody does. Make your theory of advancement universal, and you have a few "good jobs" crowded and a host of necessary jobs empty! That kind of Success would be suicidal even for those who attained it, not to mention the general life of society. There are just two questions to settle in this relation: Is a man who contributes the same proportion, time, strength and skill as another entitled to the same proportion of the good and necessary things of life? That is, should the rule be, "From each according to his ability; to each according to his need"? There is a great deal to be said for that view.

And the second question is: Are those jobs which do not reward men with the good and necessary things of life, good and necessary jobs? Must we always have sections of human duty which stigmatize men with a diminished reward? Or is every honest employment of equal dignity and usefulness in the general scheme of things and therefore entitled to a dignified reward? These are questions which ought to receive close attention. The opinion of the sponsor of this page is that every job should be a necessary and useful job, and on that ground should reward its performer—no matter what its nature may be—with the good and necessary things of life.

That is to say, it is a great pity that advancement has come to mean advancing out of the job. If all the able men, men able to advance, should advance out of their jobs, the useful production of the world would stop. We need miners. What a fallacy it is to say that when the miner becomes a lawyer he becomes a "Success." If every miner capable of being a lawyer should "advance" to that profession, what would become of mining?

We must get over the snobbery of thinking that the men in the professions are the only men who could get there. We must cease the injustice of thinking that the men who remain in agriculture, mechanics and manual labor, remain there because they haven't the ability to get out of them! We owe a great debt of gratitude to the men who stay in these callings because they like them, because the work satisfies their natures.

It is due to our ignorance that we have been deluded by a false "Success" philosophy into believing that if these men had possessed any "brains" they would have got out of productive employment into unproductive work.

Too many people believe that Success consists in getting your bread and butter by dickering or talking instead of by producing.

There are two kinds of advancement: one inner, . the other outer. The inner advancement consists in improving the quality of the man himself, his character, his experience, his skill. This ought to be the first concern of every ambitious young man. Instead of being keenly on the lookout for another job, he should be keenly on the task of learning how to put out better work.

As to the outer advancement, it is comparatively easy in this busy, restless, changing country of ours to get a chance at a better job. The test is in filling it. It is a pitiable mistake to think that all you have to do is to get the title, get the office, get the authority, and you are made. No. Attaining this outer court of Success is merely approaching the examination rooms where so many are found wanting and are turned back.

It is no trick at all to get a chance at a more responsible job than you have now; the trick will come in holding it. And then the advantage of interior advancement will become apparent. You know, the directors of great enterprises are not simply in search of good-looking young men who can adorn a title and imitate the air of business men. A title is never a bit bigger than the man who holds it—and some mighty big titles shrink to mighty little proportions through the lack of ability of those who hold them.

What a young man wants is a sure investment—and merely getting a chance at another job is just a *chance,* that's all.

But when advancement begins within the man himself; when he advances from half interest to strength of purpose; when he advances from hesitancy of decision to decisive directness; when he advances from immaturity to maturity of judgment; when he advances from apprenticeship to mastery in the line of work he has chosen; when he advances from a mere dilettante at labor to a worker who finds a genuine joy in work; when he advances from an eye-server to one who can be entrusted to do his work without oversight and without prodding—why, there is no use making any question about that man's advancement; he is advancing; he is advancing himself and his work, and that is all there is to it. He is making himself irresistibly worth while advancing. And the consequence is that the boss who does not advance him outwardly to the limit of his inward advancement is a fool who has no conception of his own interest.

After all, about the only doctrine of the old "Success" philosophy that is true forever is that, in all essential things, a man's destiny is within his own control. His outer world corresponds pretty accurately to his inner world.

Competition and Co-operation

THERE was a time when we heard a great deal
about the comparative merits of competition and
co-operation, but somehow the interest has seemed
to die away from such discussions during the last few
years; we have had something definite to do, something which we all had to unite to do, and in the
practical requirements of the times we forgot mere
academic talk.

It is possible, of course, to say a great deal in
favor of competition as a principle; possible also to
say a good deal in condemnation of it as we see it in
practice.

We may mean one thing when we use the term
"competition," and then be vastly surprised to see
that the thing which really passes for competition in
the world is not what we meant at all.

Ordinarily, the competition which we have in
mind during our discussions is a much higher grade
activity than the actual competition of the work-a-day
business world.

There is a vast difference between the competition
of our philosophical moods, and the unprincipled
throat-cutting and jabbing which actually goes on.

Our generation has lived to see the most competitive lines of business become closely organized
trusts, simply because competition—ruthless and con-
scienceless competition—became the death of competition. The most powerful and relentless competitor
simply killed competition altogether. He did it by
destroying the power of his competitor to compete.

It is when competition is destroyed through that
fashion that we begin to realize how beneficial it has
been. We frequently make laws by means of which
we try to bring back the old-time competitive conditions. And directly we get them back into practice,
we begin to see that even they were not altogether
desirable.

We know enough now to say that the competition which ends in the powerlessness of the majority of competitors and in the kingship of one, is not the kind of competition that anyone with insight or foresight could commend as the rule for society as a whole.

That is to say, the kind of competition which, raised to its highest power, results in the defeat of the many and the overlordship of a ruthless few, is thereby proved to be fallacious. For when you get a principle which cannot be universally applied without doing infinite damage, you simply do not have a universal principle, that's all. This destructive kind of competition is not capable of universal application.

If you will examine the kind of competition which merits this description, you will find that it lacks many of the qualities which must be found in that generous form of rivalry out of which progress comes.

In the first place, it is personal. It hinges on the aggrandizement of some individual or group. It is a sort of warfare. It is inspired by a desire to "get" someone, which is what "getting the better of him" usually means.

It is wholly selfish. That is to say, its motive is not pride in the product, nor a desire to excel in service, nor yet a wholesome ambition to approach to scientific methods of production, but simply a desire to crowd out all others and monopolize the market for the sake of the money returns, and substitute a product of inferior quality.

That is the competition which has strewn the path of life with ruined hopes, broken hearts and stained names—the competition which burned with fierce fires of lust for power and gain and prestige.

It always ends in tragedy—the tragedy of winning under such conditions, and the tragedy of losing. No success can be called a true success which is bought at the cost of another's undeserved pain. It is open to the man who strives after success to make himself sweat and suffer as much as he dares in order to reach his honest goal, but to get there at the cost of other men's chances in life is far too large a price to pay. And it is a price which will one day be exacted of him who compels it.

175

That is the test:—extend your form of competition out to its last success, and what does it do? Does it draw hosts of men to you in glad co-operation? Or does it drive hosts of men into the darkness as despairing wrecks?

It will do no harm for the ambitious young man to measure his plans by this test. Young men ought to be planning, not according to the lower sort of rules which exist on certain planes of business today, but according to the higher rules which are bound to become operative when Business becomes Service and not mere selfish rivalry.

To compete for money or markets, for themselves alone, and not with reference to a superiority of product or service, is to take the downward track in business.

Now, there is a form of competition, which is really deserving of a better word to describe it, and which is an honest rivalry to improve conditions generally by improving the articles of commerce and the conditions under which they are produced and marketed.

When a man succeeds in this, he discovers that he has not played a shut-out game at all. He discovers that he has not ruined anyone in the process. He can go to sleep at night without a troubling conscience.

For his success has not spelled defeat for anybody; it has spelled opportunity for everybody around him. And instead of exalting him at the expense of other men's lives, it simply opens the door for the widest co-operation between himself and his fellowmen.

He has not worked for personal glory. He has not worked for mere riches. He has worked to achieve the highest quality of product and service, and in his cup of success there are no bitter dregs at all—at least none of those dregs which come of taking unfair advantage or causing the ruin of other men.

So there you have two forms of competition and their ends. One ends in a monopoly of the most autocratic and dangerous sort—all our great trusts were built by means of the financial bludgeon. The

176

other ends in greatly increased opportunity and wonderfully extended forms of practical co-operation.

The trend of everything which is lasting and good in the economic world is toward the co-operative principle, not necessarily along the express lines advocated by certain theoretical sociologists, but in harmony with the principle that we are all fellow-workmen on the same essential task.

If cut-throat, personal, selfish competition were the natural and practical method of working, why is it that it cannot be applied *within the group*, instead of only between great groups?

That is, why is it that the workman within the shop is not encouraged to compete against the shop, to beat the interest of the industry in which he is engaged, to count his organization his enemy? That would be competition brought right down to the individual workman—why isn't it done?

Because such competition would ruin all production in a very short time. Competition made universal would be universally destructive. It would be like the soldiers of two armies turning each man on his comrade—it would be fighting, but it would get nowhere.

No. In order for the destructive competition of the larger groups of interest to continue, the men within each group must be co-operative; they must give up competition among themselves and work for the good of the whole.

Well, then, if this wide substratum of co-operation is necessary to the competition of the higher financial and speculative groups; and if the competition of the higher groups, when introduced to all the industrial groups that make production possible, would simply destroy all productive processes, it must be perfectly clear that the basis of our progress is co-operation and not combative competition at all.

The principle that you cannot apply all round is a pretty doubtful one to follow at any time.

The cause of the curse of competition, whether we view it as the strife of powerful financial groups which are gambling in the products of honest labor, or as the strife of the obscure individual to benefit

177

himself at the expense of the man who works next to him, is our false standard of reward. We have made that standard to be Money or Recognition.

Rich man and working man both compete in the same hurtful spirit when they are under this wrong view of matters. We want to catch somebody's eye or the world's eye. We want first of all the money which this brings, when, if men only knew it, the quickest way to both recognition and reward is just the way of service and no other.

If the world saw among all classes more competition for excellence, many of the evils of the time would disappear.

For the conditions from which we suffer and of which we complain are not the fault of the Creator, nor of the earth, nor of nature, nor of the round of the seasons; they are just the result of twists in human nature which has not yet learned the art of living, of so handling and distributing and using the wealth of the earth as that all shall be supplied.

Modern competition is more like the mad scramble to get out of a theater at the cry of "Fire!" than like anything else one can think of. If we would all be ready to do the best thing for every one as a whole, we should all come through safely and with rightfully earned wealth. We need to do the universal thing, and keep doing it. And the greatest and most inexhaustible of all the universals is—Excellence! He who strives to excel never fails, and in his success he never hurts a single soul.

Land Is the Basic Fact

IF LAND is the bottom economic fact, it is not because land gives us a place to stand in the sun,
but because it is the source of our physical sustenance.
It is not room that is valuable, but productive power.
Having room upon the earth is the privilege of every
homeless wanderer, but having food is another matter.
No human skill can produce food. It is the function of utilizing the natural forces to do that. And
as these forces do not function apart from the earth
itself, land becomes the fundamental of property, and
food the fundamental of wealth.

It is one of the significant facts of human history,
though one never sees it referred to, that the earth
has always proved equal to its task of providing the
entire living creation with the faculties to obtain its
food.

There has never been such a calamity as a world-
wide famine. Local famines have sometimes occurred,
and in the days before commerce and transportation
such local famines had all the awfulness of a universal famine. But it has always been the case that
if one section failed from natural or other causes,
other sections were plentifully able to fill up the lack.

The fertility of the earth is such that certain sections of it could feed the whole if necessary.

A genuinely universal scarcity of food has never
afflicted the earth. Nature has never failed.

But we appear to be entering an era when human
manipulation is seeking to produce the same results
which, were they produced by Nature, would be
deemed the height of human misfortune.

It is an astonishing fact, this. Simple-minded
people would think that men would not dare to produce artificially the phenomena of widespread famine,
and do it for gain. There is something terribly de-
fiant of all retributive forces in the universe, in such
a course.

We are now learning that so abundant is the yield

179

of Earth that even during the great war, when it seemed that four-fifths of the world had been drawn into the work of destruction, there was still enough food for all and to spare.

True, we felt a scarcity at times, but it was not a scarcity due to insufficient production; it was a scarcity due to emergency diversion.

Great quantities of food were diverted, not because there was much actual lack, but to reassure those who feared a future lack and whose morale was being broken by that fear.

This diversion began at the home. The American wife and daughter began to save here and there, and the aggregate was enormous.

As long as we were "doing without" of our own free will, as long as we knew that our deprivation was not caused by the greedy injustice of others, but by a humane program for helping the world, we did without gladly. The American housewife joked over her makeshifts and substitutes. They were not forced upon her by profiteers, but by dictates of humanity.

It makes a very great difference *why* you do a thing. If you fast for three days on account of your health, doing it willingly, it is a very interesting experience and costs you very little suffering. You are really eager throughout the time, interested in the experiment.

But let a man miss one or two meals because of his poverty, and the deprivation is very, very bitter. It isn't only the loss of the food, but the loss of the sense of self-support, and this pulls him down far more quickly than mere physical fasting could do.

Yes, it makes a great difference, *why* we do a thing.

It turns out upon investigation that much of the food we saved during the war period has accumulated into very large surplusage of war and other stores; so much so, indeed, that a fear has been expressed that the loosing upon the general market of these quantities of foodstuffs would result in a calamitous reduction of food prices.

This very fear is evidence enough of the huge stores of accumulated food.

But the fear is evidence of something else.

There was a time when the whole food situation was regarded from the point of view of the consumer. Men grew rich out of many things, but not out of food. The farmer did not grow rich, nor did the miller, nor did the baker. Food was free of the shackles of greed.

But insensibly all that has changed. Within our own generation we have seen the beginnings of the financial exploitation of the food of the people.

It began in wheat "corners" and "pools," which used to be so public and spectacular that the newspapers gave all details. So full and free was the information concerning these market coups that the people protested against gambling in their very bread.

Well, the protest only had the effect of stopping the individual daring of exploiters and the publication of their acts. Nowadays the same thing is accomplished, but far more disastrously to the country, and no one hears anything about it. All the food is cornered all the year round by all the exploiting interests, so that it is impossible for the poorest man to point to an edible on his table that is not taxed to the limit by a gigantic trust.

Sometimes our attention is riveted to this or that commodity, such as wheat or meat; but it doesn't matter as to details; the fact is the whole Food Supply of the people has been placed under an exploiter's tax.

When you find that meat is too expensive because it has increased 100 per cent in two years, you take to some perfectly adequate substitute like rice.

And when you look into the channels through which the rice comes to you, you find it under the control of the same forces that made meat impossible to you. You find, moreover, that due to these "modern methods of merchandising," of which so much untruth is told, your rice costs you 75 per cent more than it did a year ago.

It is certainly a great game that drives people to substitutes, and then corners the substitutes. The same forces that made butter impossible in hundreds of thousands of homes, has control of the oleomargarine supply.

Now, if there were not enough food, human nature would accept the fact with a certain degree of
equanimity.

But there is enough. There is more than enough
right now. And there is very much more than enough
in sight.

But there's the "market"—ah, the delicate, high-
strung, sensitive market!—that must be protected.
And, pray, what is the "market"? Why, it is the exploiters! Just the food gamblers!

It is amazing how much nearer the truth we get
when we strip away the verbiage and state matters as
they are.

If you want to see how far we have come from
considering the people as having the first interest in
the food supply, all you have to do is to observe the
fear which is felt everywhere about giving the people
a chance at the surplus food stocks. It would hurt
the "market"!

Maybe it would; but would it help the people?
That is a side of the matter which the exploiters never
consider.

The Food Question is the chief public economic
question. It doesn't much matter if our ballot is free,
if our bread is at the mercy of profiteers.

We can chant about Liberty and Equality all we
please, but it will not mean much if an invisible government of food gamblers is able to levy extortionate
tribute on our dinner tables.

Fortunately this matter has attracted the attention of Congress; unfortunately the whole emphasis
has been on the food "business."

The only Food Business that can ever justify itself
to the human race is the Business that raises Food
in sufficient quantity and distributes it under such
conditions as will enable every family to have enough
of all that it needs.

It may be that one way we shall take to break the
food trust will be to raise such overwhelming quantities of all kinds of food as shall make manipulation
and exploitation impossible. We shall probably do
that by means of the new modes of power-farming

which are coming into vogue with such rapidity in all parts of the United States, and elsewhere in the world.

And then, perhaps, we shall witness a revival of the small flour-milling business in our communities. It was an evil day when the village flour mill disappeared. Co-operative farming will yet become so developed and perfected that we shall see associations of farmers with their own packing houses in which their own hogs will be turned into ham and bacon, with their own flour mills in which their grain will be turned into commercial foodstuffs.

Why a steer raised in Texas should be brought to Chicago and then served in Boston is a question that cannot be answered on good business principles so long as there could be raised near Boston all the steers that city needs. This centralization of food manufacturing industries, entailing as it does enormous costs for transportation and organization, is one very serious cause of the era of prohibitive prices in which we find ourselves.

Ideals Versus Ideas

A MERICANS are the most idealistic people in the
world, yet of all human beings they are the most
impatient of being called idealists because they fancy
that somehow the name involves frills and fads with
which practical people have nothing to do. They
fancy that idealism is emotion and sentiment. They
are under the impression that it is feminine.

Well, the rose by any other name would smell
just as sweet, and idealism may exist without the
name. We may as well call it progressiveness, or
wide-awakeness, or foresight. Idealism does not necessarily involve emotion or sentimentality. It takes
its color, of course, from the temper and experience
of the person who possesses it, but so do politics, religion and business.

To be an idealist is simply to be able to see what
does not yet exist in the minds of others.

Things have two existences, an ideal existence and
an objective existence. Or, to say it more simply,
things are ideas before they are things; the idea is
before the thing itself, and the thing itself cannot exist
apart from its idea.

The busy world around us existed in ideal before
it existed in material.

Someone thought of everything you see, before it
really appeared.

There never was a rubber eraser on the end of a
lead pencil, until someone saw with the eye of his
mind a rubber-tipped pencil. After seeing it in the
ideal world, he proceeded to make a copy in the so-
called "real" world.

And that is the history of everything with which
mankind has had to do.

If you go back still further, it may be that this is
also the history of the world and the stars; the creative power first saw them as ideas, and then realized
them in matter.

184

Every inventor is an idealist, because he is working on something that has not yet appeared.

Every prophet is an idealist, because he is living in a world or in a social condition which has not yet come into existence.

And, in a way, every one who looks backward and lives in memory, every aged person who lives in a world of people long since vanished and amid activities long since ceased, is an idealist. That is, the idea occupies a larger place than the "real."

Except for idealists, there would have been no United States of America. Our government and institutions and liberties were spun out of the invisible essence of men's minds just as literally as the spider spins its web out of the substances of its body. The Fathers of the Republic had no pattern to go by, save the pattern of the ideal government which existed in their minds. They transferred that pattern out of their ideals and put it into constitutions and laws; the people began to mould their lives in accordance with these; and, lo! the new political entity was born.

Take the League of Nations; it is nothing but an ideal. It does not function yet. It only lives in men's minds and ideas. Yet how real it is! By watching the growth of that absolutely new appearance on earth, we can observe the method by which things that never existed before are born out of the world of ideality into the world of reality.

Therefore an idealist is nothing strange.

The human mind is a channel through which things-to-be are coming into the realm of things-that-are. Were it not for ideas and idealists, the race would still be wandering around in the eastern deserts.

But there is a difference in idealists, and perhaps this gives us a clue as to the disfavor with which some of them are regarded.

There is, for example, the idealist who has no ideas. There are many such.

The difference between ideals and ideas may be hard to define in theory, but it is clear in practice.

An idea is a gangplank thrown across the gap between the ideal and the real.

The air is full of many magnificent ideals that

185

cannot step ashore into the real world because there are no ideas for them to walk upon.

If you have an ideal, that is good. If you have an ideal, and also ideas as to how to work it out, that is better.

Idealists without ideas are often made the butt of jokes. That is wrong. The very existence of the ideals, even in a hazy form, shows the pressure that is being exerted from the invisible side of life for the bringing of better ways. Every ideal, particularly every moral and social ideal, indicates the pressure of better conditions which are trying to break through and become the rule of our life. But they cannot break through until roads are built for them, and these roads are the ideas which will work them out into practical use.

As far as actual life-pressure is concerned, the idealist who has vision without ideas is living on a far higher plane than the practical man whose ideas were never enlightened by a single ideal. The mind of the idealist at least has wings. And then, again, there is the idealist whose vision is so distant from what we have or can have now, that he is derided as a deluded dreamer. Still, he may not be. Some minds have longer-sight than others, and it behooves the short-sighted mind to be modest in the presence of the other.

The vision may seem the height of foolish impossibility today; half a century hence it may be the commonplace of every day.

There are idealists who see the things which will appear next year or ten years hence. They are the more practical kind, because their ideals are accompanied with workable ideas. And then there are idealists who see further than the best of us can sense; but this is no reason for declaring that they do not see truly.

The American is a practical idealist. That is, he is gifted with ideals which can be readily realized. He respects ideals that can be immediately brought down to reality.

It must be confessed that the progress of our idealists is not evenly balanced.

We easily conceive new and better methods in mechanics and business; we teem with a practical idealism which can be harnessed to the interests of the workaday world; and yet it must be said that we are not so successful when the ideal happens to be social or political.

That is to say, our social and political progress has not equalled our mechanical and commercial progress.

Why? Is it because we have fewer social and political ideals? Or is it because we are not so capable of translating social ideals into practical ideas, and political ideals into practical political ideas?

Is it the American genius to work in iron and steel, and not in the substances which determine the social structure?

We would be loath to admit this. And yet the facts stare us in the face.

Let us not be like England. For centuries, she has been mistress of the seas. She has organized and ruled an empire so vast that the sun never sets upon her domain. She has reaped the harvest of commerce from every quarter of the globe. She has influenced the literature of the world. She has given many of the pattern laws of the world's liberty.

You would think that a country which could so organize the greater part of the world would have the most perfect home social conditions to show for it.

Yet, England's social fabric threatens to fall to pieces. Few countries are as upset as she is today. Few populations have such a list of injustices and oppressions to show.

Thus it becomes clear that a nation may be very capable in many ways and yet neglect the greatest of tasks, the making of a happy, prosperous life for her own people.

What will the United States gain even if she wins the commerce of the world, and cannot create just social conditions at home?

What glory is it to any nation that one class rises in wealth and power, while all the other classes are made to feel an increasing burden of costs and uncertainty?

There is plenty of social idealism in the world.

Indeed, sometimes it would appear that that is the only kind of idealism which exists.

Yet there is a great dearth of practical ideas of social betterment. There are hosts of theories. In some parts of the earth those theories are being tried by earnest believers in them, yet they are not proving successful.

The need of the time is a social idealism which will also provide ideas by which the ideals may be worked out; not only hazy desires for a better world, but practical plans for the building of a better world out of the one we now have. The world we now live in is the world we must transform; we cannot destroy it; we must live with it until we leave it better; and practical ideals are our only hope of making it better.

What Is Education—Cargo or Motive Power?

SOME people are proud of their good looks. Others are proud of their social standing. Still others are proud of their wealth. Most people are proud of their ancestry, because it was good and honest. But it would be very easy to find a large class of people who are proud of what they know, proud of the knowledge that they have gathered; and they would not be confined to the so-called educated classes either.

Knowledge is such a vague term that it is well to understand just what may be meant by it.

The fact that certain fluids will take stains out of a tablecloth, is knowledge. If the housewife knows that, it may come handy to her. But you may search through thousands of books in the big library and never find that special part of knowledge mentioned.

The farmer's boy knows at which pool the trout is to be found, and that is knowledge, but it would never win him praise from a college.

The weather-beaten land-looker can tell by a glance at the sky what the weather will be, but he could not qualify among the scientists who are wise in these things.

There are many kinds of knowledge, and it depends on what crowd you happen to be in, or how the fashions of the day happen to run, which kind of knowledge is most respected at the moment. There are fashions in knowledge, just as there are in everything else.

When some of us were lads, knowledge used to be limited to Bible knowledge. There were certain men in the neighborhood who knew the Book thoroughly, and they were looked up to and respected for it. Biblical knowledge was highly valued then.

But nowadays it is doubtful whether deep acquaintance with the Bible would be sufficient to win

a man a name for learning. Although it must be
said that knowledge of that Book would indicate a
well-stored mind, it would not win much respect
among the wiseacres of the day, because fashions in
knowledge have changed.

Knowledge is something that somebody once knew
and left in a form which enabled anyone else, who
wanted to, to know it.

If a man is born with normal human faculties, if
he is equipped with enough ability to use the tools
which we call "letters" in reading or writing, there
is no knowledge within the possession of the race that
he cannot have—if he wants it!

The only reason every man does not know everything that the human mind has ever learned is that no
one has ever yet found it worth while to know that
much.

Men satisfy their minds more by finding out things
for themselves, than by heaping together the things
which somebody else has found out.

You can go out and gather knowledge all your life,
and with all your gathering you will not-catch up
even with your own times.

You may fill your head with all the "facts" of all
the ages, and your head may be just an overloaded
fact-box when you get through.

The point is this: Great piles of knowledge in the
head are not the same as mental activity. A man
may be very learned and very useless. Any college
professor will tell you that. And then again, a man
may be unlearned and very useful, very wide-awake
in his mind—and any professor of psychology will
tell you that, too.

The object of education is not to fill a man's mind
with facts; it is to teach him how to use his mind
in thinking.

And it often happens that a man can think better
if he is not hampered by the knowledge of the past.

If Columbus had paid attention to "facts," if he
had held them in reverence, if he had believed that
all knowledge was in the books and there was none
to be had outside the books, he would never have set

190

sail. Columbus did not study geography; he made it. It is a very human tendency to think that what mankind does not yet know, no one can learn. And yet it must be perfectly clear to every one that the past learning of mankind cannot be allowed to hinder our future learning. There is almost everything to learn yet. Mankind has not gone so very far, when you measure its progress against the knowledge that is yet to be gained, the secrets that are yet to be learned.

One good way to hinder progress is to fill a man's head with all the learning of the past; it makes him feel that because *his* head is full, there is nothing more to learn. Why, you could take a thousand men, fill each man's head full of knowledge—so full that he could learn no more—and even then no two of those men would be learned in the same things. Each would be calling the other ignorant. Merely gathering knowledge that other men have acquired may become the most useless work a man can do. The only fair standard by which accumulated knowledge may be judged is this: Here is a lot of knowledge. Are you capable of learning it? If you are capable, you are an intelligent person. If you are not capable, you are not. If this or that subject were submitted to you to be learned, you could learn it. Left to yourself, perhaps, you would not learn it, not because you are incapable of learning it, but simply because it is not the kind of knowledge that your life or genius requires.

Here is a man who knows a great deal about sea-shells. There is a whole science of sea-shells. This learned man is so interested in sea-shells, and has gathered so much knowledge about them, that he has written large volumes on the subject. But how many even of our learned men know anything about sea-shells? How many want to know? And yet—here is the point—they are capable of knowing, they would learn mighty quickly if a knowledge of sea-shells were of any use to them.

All of us learn quickly the things we are interested in, the things which we need in order to do our work in the world.

Everybody is a specialist. The baker is a specialist

in doughs and yeasts and ovens. The molder is a specialist in sands and molds and iron "heats." The horseshoer is a specialist in hoofs and bellows and welding compounds. Our mothers used to learn more from the "feel" of cloth than could be written in many pages. Everybody is a specialist.

Now, just how much knowledge must be held in common by everybody, is also a matter of fashion. It is largely a matter of the class of people you want to associate with. If you trot in one class you will discover that you are expected to be able to talk about art, and music, and poetry and similar subjects. Thousands of people are chattering about those things who don't know anything about them at all, but they have learned the phrases, and they pass for "educated." A scholar of wide fame said just a little while ago— "It is now possible in our best society to express opinions about a book without having read it, or to gabble about art without knowing a single fundamental principle."

People do this because it is expected of them and because it is the fashion. Most of the fads of society are intellectual fads, which change like the style of hats.

Of course, if you want to gather knowledge like pebbles and exhibit it, all right. There is one form of human vanity. But to flatter yourself that you are learned, while the man who does not follow your fad is unlearned, is to add a vicious flavor to your self-flattery.

There is a young fellow, standing before you. His skin is clear, his eyes are bright, he understands what he sees, and his mind is awake. He doesn't know everything. As educational fashions go nowadays he may "know" comparatively little. That is, his head may yet be unburdened by a load of facts out of books.

No, he doesn't know everything. But as you look at him, as you note his comprehending gaze, as you mark the cool glance of his eyes, this thought comes to you: "He doesn't know everything, but there is nothing he could not know if he wanted to; and when he chooses his work in life, he will learn it clear through to the end and beyond."

He doesn't have much knowledge, but he has a lot of brains.

And, listen!—if you are ever given a choice between brains and knowledge, choose brains.

With brains you can get any form of knowledge you need. But, better than that—with brains you can use any kind of knowledge that you have. Without brains, no amount of gathered knowledge will ever amount to a straw.

The best thing a book does for a man is to make him think. All that a school can do for a man is to teach him how to think.

It isn't what you get out of a book, but what a book pulls out of you, that makes books useful.

A man is like a well. There is a lot in him, if he can only get it out. Sometimes a book, or a conversation, or a course of instruction, acts on him like priming on a pump—it brings out of him what is in him. And that is all that Education means.

A man is like wood or stone. Some kinds of stones you can bring to a high degree of polish. Some kinds of wood, too. But many indispensable stones are rough and cannot be brought to a polish. So with some kinds of wood. All men do not take a polish. Webster did; but Lincoln didn't. And it is a big mistake to say that the polish counts for all. It is the texture that counts. And the texture of a man is his vitality, his energy, his character, his courage and his rock-bottom brain power.

When in Doubt—Raise Wages!

THE first step to take in a situation like the present is to raise wages where necessary. Simply raise wages. There may be other steps necessary to make, there may be other improvements to be instituted, but this is the thing that ought to be done at once and widely—raise wages. Nothing that anyone can do in the time at our disposal can meet the situation so thoroughly, nothing will go so far to restore confidence and establish a sense of the justice of our social intention, as just to raise wages.

But this is the one step which the speculative and profiteering world seems determined not to do.

"Why not do something else?" they say. And so we begin to see all sorts of substitutes offered for the simple solution of raising wages.

There can be little or no doubt that many of the "investigations" which come up like mushrooms in times of great public complaint, are mere substitutes for the real and practical remedy, which is the increase of wages.

If investigations had ever proved of practical assistance to the producing class, if they had ever really corrected the basic abuses, we might view them with more hopefulness. But what have they ever accomplished? Have they ever made any appreciable difference in the life problem of the working man?

Investigations have, as a rule, been substitutes for the direct cure. When public impatience approaches the breaking point, then someone seeks to allay it with an "investigation." The result usually is that the point of the investigation is changed, and before the work is over it has been cleverly maneuvered into a political boom for or against somebody. It develops a "hero" or a "goat," and the real problem is left just where it was before.

There is just now a "food investigation" gathering force in all parts of the country. No one can say

194

aught against it. It is high time we knew all the details of profiteering in food. It is high time someone discovered and exposed the faults in our system which permit even the people's bread to be put at the mercy of gamblers.

But, does anyone honestly expect that the investigation will have more than a nominal and temporary effect? · Does anyone believe that prices will ever again be what they were ten years ago? No.

We have been on the upgrade on food prices for ten years. If memories were not so short, if there were some sort of accounting in the household, it would be shown that food began to advance a decade ago and that we were in the pinch of high prices even before the European war began. Did anybody offer to investigate then? No. We saw to it that certain wage advances were made to meet the rising costs.

Then, fortunately for the speculators, the war came on and proved a handy alibi for the next four years. But two months after the war had ended, the price of food in the United States had advanced 25 per cent over war prices.

The country began to murmur, then to protest, then to threaten. There was but one obvious thing to do—raise wages. When a man is overboard, he needs a life preserver. You can investigate the accident afterward. When a nation is actually in distress over the food problem, when a people have to omit the other requirements of life in order to concentrate their attention upon the matter of getting food, the first need is to relieve that situation, relieve it immediately. You can investigate afterward.

Any difficulty with the food supply of a people, especially where the difficulty is a money difficulty, is equal to an emergency—a war emergency, if you will—and should be met by provisions for the people's safety. "Public safety" includes a safe margin of food obtainable without dangerous anxiety on the part of the people.

The concealed logic of most "food investigations" would run somewhat on this line: "We must do something. If we raise wages, that will enable the people to buy food, but it will reduce our profits. If

195

we force a reduction of prices, that will hit our profits, too. The best way to do is to have an "investigation" and this will educate the people as to the reasons for high prices; if skillfully conducted it will frighten out the little profiteers, and the big profiteers will be whitewashed and, in effect, licensed to continue."

Now, it makes all the difference in the world from whose standpoint you view the matter. The only safe point of view for any lover of the security and prosperity of his country to take is the point of view of the consumer, of the workman's wife who goes to the store with a greatly shrunken dollar, of the workman himself who finds that his utmost labor will scarcely provide a living. These, in the last analysis, constitute the food problem and it must be investigated from their standpoint and relieved in a way that will relieve them.

Obviously the man with a family is not going to worry about potatoes being $2.50 a bushel, if he has the $2.50. Obviously he is not going to be anxious about the high cost of living if, after paying for his living, he has the same proportionate amount of money left over to put aside against a rainy day.

To come down to the human side of the question as it affects our producers, the problem never has been the high cost of living but the inadequate rate of wages. They pay willingly if they have it. But they don't have it. Wages have not kept pace with cost increases. The result is very serious in our most vital interests. You cannot pinch the American home without injuring the heart and efficiency of the nation.

Raise the wages first so that the people may live without anxiety during the period of your investigation, and then proceed with your examination of the whole food system. But do not, as you value your country's security and happiness—do not substitute an "investigation" for definite first aid.

Everybody knows what the result of an investigation will be. There will be, first, a great uproar concerning hoarded food. This will not touch the great hoards of the chief food makers, but only the local stocks. Already there have been seizures in some of the large cities of the country, and the figures

196

that have been given out look very imposing in the newspapers, but they shrink to triviality when divided by the population of the city in which the stocks were found. The discovery of a million dozens of eggs in a city of 1,200,000 population simply means that that city is one dozen eggs ahead per person—a week's supply.

Then it will be discovered that the little local retailers have profiteered a cent or two on trust products, and they will be severely criticised for it, although it will never be published that the little local retailers are making less under the high price regime than before. That is a curious fact: the fortunes and dividends of the big profiteers show upward curves of increase; the little fellows are barely scraping along. But punish the little fellows!

And then it will be discovered that the cost of producing, preparing and marketing food has really increased. It will be possible to show that the farmer has received a well-merited, though not extravagant, share of the increase, and that certain material costs help to account for part of it; but there will still be the fact that at the top an increased profit arises, and that no one engaged in the food business has really suffered.

Everybody "got theirs," as the expression is, but they have gotten it from the man whose family eats the food. And that man too commonly has not kept even within economizing distance of the rise in food costs.

The figures make it clear. Wages have increased in this country about 50 per cent. This increase is practically eaten up by the increase in rents alone, not to mention clothing, medical attendance and fuel. But when you measure a food increase running all the way from 75 to 200 per cent, it becomes apparent whether wages have kept pace or not.

If it were planned to produce a peasant class here in America, if there were a conspiracy among the money-kings to force the American people down from the standard of living to which they have lifted themselves and create a race inured to poverty and deprivation, it could not be better attempted than just

197

the way we are going now. No wonder the preachers of discontent and violence are seizing upon the occasion to say that now that the war is over, the American people are being beaten down to the level of the lower class British workman or the French and German peasant.

The emergency remedy—regardless of what the ultimate cure may be—is just this: some profits must be turned into wages. We are learning that it is no longer possible for one man to keep the profits. A profit-making business is the creation of profit-making men, and the only way the obligation of the business to the men can be recognized and met is by a scheme of profit-sharing. Whatever form this may take, it means higher wages.

There is food here. There are people needing it. There is money enough to transfer the food from those who have it to those who need it. We shall have to see that the money reaches the points which this food transaction has stinted.

Having done this, you may then investigate with all the thoroughness possible, without the suspicion of making it a substitute for the right and needful thing.

Humanity Is Our Basic Wealth

THE principal interest in this country is not business, markets nor profits; it is not agriculture, manufacturing nor transportation; it is not science, education nor any form of material progress: the commodity of principal importance in this country is just —People. Without people the other interests would have no meaning. Without people they would not exist. It ought, therefore, to be plain to any mind that in relative importance People come first, and these others second.

We pause here for a moment to permit the wiseacres to cry, "Platitude!" Any truth that is inconveniently plain, too plain to be relished and yet too true to be ignored, is shelved by the cry of "platitude." But somehow it doesn't stay shelved.

People sometimes say, "Yes, yes, we know all about that. Don't keep repeating it. Everyone agrees, but don't make the truth a nuisance by insisting upon it."

But does everyone know, and does everyone agree? Certainly there is little evidence of it in the situation which confronts us today.

Here we are faced by a condition of affairs which may hold for the world greater danger than even the war held; we are at a time when the mistaken policy of greedy economic powers may set loose tendencies from which humanity might never recover—start lesions in the social organism that could never be healed. And yet do we ever hear that the place to begin our cure of the illness is with the People?

No, we hear plenty of wise talk about protecting the market, protecting the expectations of those who bought low to sell high (how remarkably tender this country has become of the gambling game of the speculative profiteer!), protecting this or that bad business condition due to mistaken theories that ought to be destroyed so thoroughly that they shall never deceive the business world again—we hear anything and everything except what can and should be done for the relief and protection of the People!

Our wise men seem to believe that the People are like the earth, a foundation that cannot be moved, a platform on which any kind of business or market program may be safely staged. But, the constant danger of surprise is just here—the people are not a stable mass on which anything whatever can be built; they are not the unchangeable quantity that the soil of the earth is; they are subject to change, to independent action.

Decrease of confidence is worse than decrease of profits.

And worse even than the lowering of the climax of business records is the lowering of the *morale* of the People.

We can recover from almost any deterioration in this country except a deterioration of the People.

Why, look at it a minute. What have we been doing the past 10 years? We have been trying to get a better class of people. American business saw very clearly a few years ago that its success depended on the elevation of the human standard in every industry. We started educational and Americanization work. We supplied higher living standards. We encouraged an increase of intelligence and self-respect and a higher level of material needs. And we supplied the increased wages necessary to maintain these desirable human qualities.

What has happened to that clear vision? Surely something has happened to it. In the present condition of national affairs we have scarcely thought of the People at all. We have thought of Things, Things, Things. We can afford to make a big sacrifice in Things if that will prevent a deterioration of the American standard of human values.

Take the housing condition, for example. Isn't it true that we hear more of the need of the landlords to charge more rent than we do of the need of the people to be housed? The financial element is discussed to the almost entire exclusion of the human element.

There is a very, very serious lack of housing facilities in all our industrial centers and it is working
social deterioration to an observable degree. There
is too much crowding for health and morals. There
are too many "come downs" from decent living quarters to unbearable ones—quite too many for the self-
respect of thousands of families who were just beginning to taste the delights of clean, roomy, modern,
wholesome living conditions. There is too much
crowding among unmarried work-people, thus doing
away with the moral and physical hygienic value of
personal privacy and freedom.

In fact, if there were a deliberate conspiracy to
lower the whole line of American standards of living, it could not be accomplished more surely than by
just bringing about such a lack of housing accommo-
dations as we are now suffering.

Of course, it will be asked, "Why are there fewer
houses? Are there so many more people in the
world?" There are fewer people in the world. The
lack of housing can be traced directly to the greatly
increased appeal of industrialism to the people during
the past five years. There are fewer people in the
world but they have suddenly become newly distributed; there are more people in the cities. The housing
problem is a problem of cities and of such smaller
towns as have industrial interests.

Industrialism happens to be the cause, in this way:
first, the war rate of wages enabled many families to
move into better houses—which is very desirable, of
course, though it is a reflection on the conditions
which existed before the war when families lived in
unfit conditions. Second, the families who formerly
occupied a house between them, were enabled by war
wages to take a whole house; and this tended to decrease the number of available houses. And third,
there was a great influx from the agricultural districts to the city factories. This was a movement so
vast in its proportions as to constitute a migration—
hundreds of thousands moving from the country into
the city lured by the prospect of high wages for war
work.

In one city of the United States which before the

war always had a comfortable housing margin, there are now 25,000 families wondering where they can live. There are no houses to rent. Such houses as may be rented are held at rentals which in themselves constitute a serious hardship upon needy people.

Out of this condition has arisen a great volume of complaint and discussion. Here and there an individual employer has adopted the role of house-builder for the sake of his own employes, but in the main the condition remains unchanged.

There is vast complaint against rent profiteers and some attempts have been made to regulate the rapacity of their greed, but none has been successful. Again there is a great defense made of landlords. And so it goes on and on, everything discussed and nothing done, every interest protected and the People left to get along the best way they can.

That is the danger. After all, it is not a question of houses. It is not a question of rent. It is a question of People.

Transfer your interest to the food question and the same rule applies. It is not a question of profits. It is not a question of saving speculative values in storage house stocks. It is not a question of steadying the market. It is a question of People.

Simply change the complexion of the emergency. Suppose it were a disease sweeping the land. Everybody would then see that it is a question of People. No one would stop to consider anything else. Of course, the element of social fear is more active in great plagues; we do what we can for the victims in order to save ourselves from contagion. With houseless families, it is different; we do not fear we will "catch" their homelessness. With hungry People it is different, too; we do not fear we will "catch" their hunger. Yet in permitting these conditions to exist we are encouraging an epidemic of low morale and discontent which may breed social dangers from which none of us can escape. If our sense of social safety were as well developed as our sense of physical safety, our concern for affairs today would be greatly increased.

If this were a war emergency, what would we do?

Why, we would think of nothing but meeting it. All through the war everyone said, "Money doesn't matter. Money is of no use whatever unless we use it to clear up this intolerable condition." Well, the case is not different now. Money is of no more use now than it was then, unless it be used to prevent the slump in American living ideals which the present food and housing conditions will bring about.

The great fact is this: This is a situation which can be met, an emergency which can be relieved by money. The food is here. The material for housing is here. Money will make both available. After the emergency is met it will be time enough to take steps to prevent its recurrence. In the meantime infinite damage is being done to our first wealth, our most precious wealth, the one element which gives our national resources any value at all—the People. If money can prevent a blow being delivered to their ideals and confidence, money must be used to do it.

Not as a dole. In higher wages first, so that each family can meet its own needs and prevent any deterioration of health, or courage or self-respect. And in investment next—each man of means building houses by the hundred until the last homeless family shall be under its own ample roof.

There will be just as much money in the country afterward as before. It will simply have been used to meet an emergency, that's all. But what is better than money, there will be a strong American People, maintained in their strength, in their initiative and in their respect for themselves and reverence for our country.

Managers and Men Are Partners

WHEN a man has a business the responsibilities of which he cannot carry alone, he looks for a suitable partner. He realizes without any special thought or argument that if he is to secure certain desirable qualities in his partner he must be ready to give assurance that those same qualities will be present in himself. That is to say, expecting loyalty, he will stand ready to be loyal. He recognizes that partnership in business, to be most successful, must be something more than a mere financial arrangement; he recognizes that it involves certain co-operative relations, and that if these are not properly adjusted the partnership will be a failure.

A partner is not one who takes part of the proceeds of the business, but one who contributes part to the success of a business. Partnership is a positive relation.

Now, sometimes the partner contributes capital; sometimes skill and experience; most commonly he contributes only his labor. It is the latter form of partnership, commonly called "employment," which concerns us now.

It is not usual to speak of an employe as a "partner," and yet what else is he? Whenever a man finds the management of a business too much for his own time or strength, he calls in assistants who take part, or partnership, in the management with him. Why, then, when a man finds the production part of a business too much for his own two hands should he deny the title of "partner" to those who come into the factory and help him to produce?

Every business that employs more than one man is a partnership, whether it is legally so termed or not. We may deny it as much as we please, we may resent what it implies, but nevertheless it is a fact. The moment a man calls in assistance in his business, even though the assistant be but a boy, that moment he has taken a partner. He may himself be sole owner of the resources of the business, sole director of its operations, but only as he remains sole manager and sole producer can he retain the title of "independent."

No man is independent as long as he has to depend on another man to help him.

The employer is not independent; he cannot go down into his factory and with his own two hands produce sufficient to maintain the business. He is dependent on other men coming in and helping him.

The employe is not independent; with his meager facilities he cannot produce articles up to modern requirements. He is dependent on other men who have created improved means and methods of production, who have cultivated the market, who have the gift of organization and administration which enable him to use his acquired skill.

As our present social life is organized, the one without the other is helpless, as is proved by every dispute that stops the wheels of production.

It is useless for one group or the other to take airs to itself as if it were the one indispensable unit. Both are indispensable, and one can unduly assert its importance not only at the expense of the other but at its own expense as well. It is utterly foolish for the groups to think of themselves as groups at all—they are partners; and when they pull and haul against each other, they simply injure the organization in which they are partners and from which they draw their support.

Now, so much for foundation truth. Not everyone, of course, will agree with this view of the relation between so-called "capital and labor." But it is very significant that in these times no responsible man will openly disagree. This question: if the employe is not a partner, what is he?—is a hard question to evade. It is a much harder question to answer if you desire to regard the employe as not belonging to the business.

The fact is, we are up against the problem of hu-

205

man relations today, and we are up against it in a serious way.
- Not that the problem of human relations is a hard one, but it has been neglected so long that it seems more difficult than it really is. Human relations, especially in industry, have become the subject of first importance today not because of any fundamental change in life, but because they always were of first importance only heretofore we failed to recognize it.

Yet we had many warnings. It was always easy to settle the material part of any undertaking. Wood, iron, sand, brick, machinery—these were never a problem. A brick was used in a conspicuous place or in an obscure place as the user desired, to be cut or broken or crushed without compunction, as the necessities of the case required. Bricks were always bricks. Many times the material part of an undertaking was arranged beautifully, but just as it seemed that the whole business was to start off smoothly, something went wrong with the human equation.

That is the only difficulty in the country today. The material world is just what it was, but something has happened in the human world.

Now, if anything went wrong with machinery or the mechanical processes of production, we would immediately know what to do. We would deal with machinery according to the law of machinery, with production according to the laws of efficient production. We would not expect machinery to exhibit qualities that belonged to the animal world, nor would we regard production from any standpoint but its own.

Well, if we are to establish human relations on a dependable basis we shall have to recognize that these working partners of the business are human. If you confuse them with the machinery, you will discover they have the power of will. If you try to confuse them with material processes of any character whatever, you will find that men live by mental and spiritual values.

American business could well afford to devote the next six months to a thorough overhauling of the standard of human relations throughout every line of activity.

You may talk about material and efficiency and profits from now until the end of the world, but if you omit the human equation, all your plans are due for a fall some day.

There is coal and ore aplenty in our mines; our fields supply us with the best and yield an immense surplus; business awaits us in overwhelming volume both at home and abroad; if we are held up anywhere, it is in a lack of a spirit of partnership between those who plan and those who execute the work of a great business.

You don't use force against machinery when it does not work; you adjust it. What folly it is to think that force will take the place of righteous adjustment in human relations!

The difficulty has been that in the swift and enthusiastic development of American industrial enterprise, the first and only thought of both employers and employes was given to the business. Perhaps it is to that fact that American business owes its present standing in the world, that Americans of every degree have given it their undivided effort and attention.

But now that the material side of business has reached a growth that makes description impossible and dwarfs all the records of human achievement, it is becoming painfully apparent even to the dullest vision that we shall now have to catch up on the human side.

Some of us saw this before others did. But it is evident now in the general condition of society. There is a definite demand that the human side be elevated to a position of equal importance with the material side. And it is going to be done. It is just a question whether it is going to be done wisely, in a way that will conserve the material side which now sustains us, or unwisely and in such a way as shall take from us all the benefit of the work of the past 50 years. Business represents our national livelihood, it reflects our economic progress, and gives us our place among other nations. We do not want to jeopardize that. What we want is a better recognition of the human element in that business. And surely that can

207

be achieved without dislocation, without loss to anyone, indeed with an increase of benefit to every human
being.

And the secret of it all is in a recognition of human partnership. -Until each man is absolutely self-
sufficient unto himself, needing the services of no
other human being in any capacity whatever, we shall
never get beyond the need of partnership.

We have always been partners whether we acknowledged it or not, and it has been our refusal to
acknowledge it which has created an atmosphere of
antagonism instead of one of harmony among us. It
is unnatural to deny what already is, and the denial
brings other evils with it.

Partnership means a unity of endeavor, a loyalty
of effort, a sense of belonging and being necessary,—a
freedom of suggestion and initiative in the business,
and a sharing in the profits according to one's contribution toward making these profits. If the employer
wants his men to be his partners, he must stand ready
to be their partner. If he expects them to contribute
to his business achievements, he must expect to contribute to their success, too. Partnership means contributing to, as well as taking shares from.

The fact is that we would not need complex and
confusing systems if we only had the proper spirit.
The very essence of right human relations is in having the right spirit. Nothing is impossible of satisfactory solution and adjustment when men confer in
the right spirit, and the right spirit is simply this—
the spirit of willingness to do the right thing.

New Paths to Fame

IT ALL depends on what you are made of and your point of view, whether such times as the present appear to you as the end of all opportunity or the beginning of the new years of surpassing openings for invention, initiative or just plain productive industry. There never was a better time to be young than just now. In spite of all the apparent upset and unrest and change, these times are richer in material for new combinations of grit and power than any which this country has seen during the past 50 years.

It is when humanity is solidified, and every process is hardened by custom, and ways of doing things become set and fixed, that it is difficult for the young man to create something of his own and get a new idea started on its way.

But in times like these, when nearly everything seems ready to take new forms, when so many problems are pressing for solution, everybody is hospitable to new ideas, the times are kind to new enterprises, and people look with hopefulness upon anything that promises relief and benefit.

The pity is that there are not more good ideas to take advantage of these favorable circumstances.

It may not at once be clear to the young man why the times should be so propitious. But it can be made clear by a simple illustration. It is a common remark that opportunities were many "when the country was new." It means that before the life of the nation became limited to certain channels there was a certain freedom of initiative, there was a clear field to be laid out any way desired.

Well, in a better sense than ever before, the country is again "new."

In pioneer days the man with initiative had almost nothing to work with. There were few people, little available material, limited fields for development. But what a difference nowadays! Here are over 100,000,000 people. Here are rich stores of materials and inexhaustible resources, and there is no limit to expansion.

The country is "new" again with every advantage ready to the hand of the man with vision enough and courage enough to go in and mould plastic conditions to his idea.

There never was more to be done; there never was a warmer welcome for the Doer; there never was so much backing ready waiting for the man with a serviceable idea. The future of America is being made right now, and the shining names of the next half century will be names which today are wholly obscure.

This does not mean that we are predicting the appearance of great men of genius in the country. The need is not so much for genius as for vision and courage.

There is a good deal of misunderstanding about "great men," anyway. Great men are only men who do great things, and it frequently occurs that they themselves are only ordinary men who have shown extraordinary devotion to their own idea and their own job.

It isn't genius we want so much as ordinary ability used for all it is worth. Ordinary ability is all the world needs; the concentration of ordinary ability on the problems awaiting solution.

As to great men in the special sense, they are usually in waiting before a national or world emergency. The emergency reveals them. The recent war created no great men, it only revealed them, called them forth.

But with successful, useful men the case is different. They are the result of the reconstruction period that follows an emergency. They are the men who take advantage of the new combinations of circumstances. With conditions to be rebuilt, they take the opportunity of getting in on the ground floor. And the ground floor was never so large, opportunities were never so numerous as they are now.

This is not the time to preach success; this is the time to put into practice all the success doctrine you have ever heard. The present moment is supremely the moment of action.

We need a revival of old-fashioned American ambition to get ahead.

The gouging and gambling, the profiteering and plunging which characterize some of the business of today, do not spring from the American spirit of "getting ahead." They are destructive, illegitimate, false.

American ambition is first to DO something, achieve some great and useful service, and then to reap the reward.

We ought to return to the old-fashioned system of encouraging boys to go out and make their mark, and to deserve well of their fellow-men. In other days boys were instilled with the confidence that nothing was too high for an American boy to aspire toward. And it is just as true today as it was then, indeed, if one may say so, it is truer, for where there was one path upward in those days there are a hundred paths now. The young man of today is so much better off that it may be worth while to indicate it in detail. There was a time when the path to distinction and service in this country was almost exclusively a professional path. A boy could study law and graduate into politics. Indeed, to wear one's hair a little longer than other men's, and to make speeches in the legislature was once considered the height of success. And then through politics, he could branch into whatever business happened to open up.

There was little or no emphasis laid on the industrial path. Few people ever thought of Work—plain work—as a path upward. No. It must be professional, genteel, dealing with the abstract ideas of politics and government, or with some other science.

Today, however, all that is changed. The first thing the majority of American boys think of as a successful career is not some statesman making a speech, but some artisan making a useful commodity, and making it so well and in such quantities that everyone buys and uses it.

Some people are inclined to say that this is a descent to "materialism"—this emphasis on making things.

But anyone with his eyes open can see very clearly that the major part of our trouble today is just a lack of this kind of "materialism." If we had more houses for people to live in, if we had more railroad cars to carry them what they need, if we had more means of enabling the farmer to farm more land with less help, if we had better and more productive systems of mining coal and other raw materials—why, that would pretty nearly solve all the troubles that afflict us now.

The world is full of ideas as to what ought to be done—but of what use are these ideas until a man comes along who will actually do the things and set it going?

You don't have to be a statesman to help the world nor a philosopher, nor a poet; you have only to think out something, perform something which will make it easier for the world to live.

To take an illustration from the problem of the day:—the man who could multiply houses with rapidity would be a world blessing just now. We make everything quickly but houses. We manufacture machinery in a new way, we fabricate ships differently than was ever done before, but we build houses in practically the way they have always been built.

If, for example, someone should discover an art which would enable us to build a house out of the earth excavated for its cellar, what a boon to humanity that would be! Nor is the idea so far-fetched as it may seem. One reason why the war-torn portions of France are being restored to the people so quickly is that the French dwelling is usually constructed out of materials found on the premises. The French family's house is literally dug out of the earth.

Go to the root of all the so-called "capital and labor difficulty" today and what do you find? Simply the lack of houses for people to live in, and the consequent high prices of such houses as there are. Or a lack of food, and high prices of such food as there is.

All the difficulty, you will observe, is due to the lack of production of such articles as mankind can produce. Houses are a product, so is food, so is every other article man needs in his living.

Well, then, the way to serve the world at this stage of its trouble is not to enunciate new laws, nor give it a new art or literature, but simply give it the things it is suffering for—houses, food and the various articles of use.

We don't need statesmen to solve the difficulties of our country at this time: we need workers. We need men who will tell us new and better ways to produce what we lack. We need fresh eyes to examine our old methods and cut them down where they are cumbersome and wasteful. We need men who are young enough and free enough to cut loose from the old and settled ways, and break new paths for the world's energy to use.

This is the call that awaits ambitious young America. Time was when the utmost encouragement you could give a boy was to say, "You may be President some day." But now we can say to him, "You may be the man who is to discover the new way of housing the people." "You may be the man who is to revolutionize the methods by which food is produced." "You may be the man who will teach us how to make a pound of coal do the work of ten and still retain all of the coal for heating purposes."

Let Every Man Think
for Himself

CONFERENCES are often good and sometimes useful, providing the right people confer. Even when conferences do not end in agreement, they at least end in a clearer understanding of what the parties claim. But a clearer understanding does not necessarily make for agreement, because where there is no desire to agree, an understanding of your opponent's claim simply enables you to attack it with straighter aim. This was illustrated in the recent Senate investigation of the steel strike; each side claimed that its contention was proved by the other side's statement. The better they understood each other, the further they were apart. So that a good deal more than mere conference is needed in important disagreements. Conference is simply the bringing together of the several elements of the dispute. If the elements be like oil and water, they will not mix. If they be like fire and powder, there will be a blow-up. Conference may issue in conflict as well as in cooperation. It all depends on the things involved, and on the spirit which the conferees bring.

The difficulty with most conferences is that they are too small. An individual or a small group wants to be taken as the embodiment of the grievances, aspirations, wisdom and determination of a whole class, yet everyone knows how difficult it is for another to act for him in vital matters. We select a little hall holding 200, and we try to pack into it the men who claim to represent every phase of opinion in the United States upon a certain emergency question, and the result is we make speeches and debate and resolve and pledge—and leave the mass of the interested parties unenlightened and unbound in any way.

It may be argued that everybody cannot go to the great national conferences. But maybe there would not be so much need of the big conferences if there were more little ones—informal, casual ones between man and man.

Industrially, there should be such an intimate knowledge of all the conditions by both parties, and the spirit of fair adjustment should be so constantly operative, that a stoppage of work for the purpose of fighting each other by argument should be as unnecessary as a stoppage of work to keep the roof from leaking.

A whole lot of conferring is made necessary because a whole lot of conferring has been neglected.

Things have come to a pretty pass when workmen can only speak to their employer through the medium of a government committee, and when employers can only speak to their men through the medium of agents whose entire interest—financial, professional and social—is bound up in the continuance of a quarrel and the fomenting of misunderstanding.

The blame for it is to be found in the day-by-day neglect of daily communication between employer and employe.

The employer who knows his job never lets a bad condition come to a head any more than an engineer who knows his job allows his engine to break down before he repairs it.

The employer who knows his job does not permit bad conditions to remain a day after they are discovered, any more than an aviator would allow a leak in his gas tank to run longer than was required to fix it.

When an improving eye is kept constantly on the business, when an employer knows all that his men know about the business, when a spirit of partnership reigns so that both parties feel free to communicate one with the other, then the matters which tend to grow big and demand big conferences to settle them, are nipped in the bud and never allowed to work harm either to the conditions of the business or the relations between the men engaged in it.

There is always great satisfaction expressed when a conference goes ahead to settle something. But there will be more ground for satisfaction when conditions become such that no conferences are needed.

Conference indicates that the parties have grown so far apart that something extraordinary is required to bring them together. Absence of conferences will indicate that the parties are in communication and agreement all the time, which should be their normal state. There are, however, certain naturally opposed interests which cannot be exclusively identified with any class, which ought to be more or less in sincere conference all the time.

First, there is the conflict between Individual Interest and Collective Interest.

We are learning that, even though we may possess the power to satisfy our utmost desire, it may be very unwise to use it, because individual interest sometimes gets into the way of collective good. We can live together in society only as we recognize the balance that should exist between rights and duties. What we call "rights" are usually our individual rights; what we call "duties" are usually the rights of others.

Men sometimes say they are "claiming their rights" when what they are really doing is infringing on the rights of others.

There should be a subconscious conference always in session within a man's heart, and its subject should be the maintenance of a balance between the individual and the collective good.

Sometimes individual good is collective harm; in which case it must be modified. For it cannot be individually good in an enduring way if it is collectively harmful, since the individual, too, is part of the collective interest and will suffer in this degree from his own wrong-doing.

Neither should the collective good be pushed to the extent of harming the individual. That is the trouble with most robust theories of the state—they make the collective interest everything and the individual little or nothing.

Freedom and progress depend on keeping the balance between these two, making each contribute to the best interests of the other.

Many of the problems which vex our life today could be boiled down into the simple statement that individual good is trying to increase itself at the expense of the collective good. It cannot be done. For a time it may seem to be possible, but it cannot be done. The moment one or the other interest becomes selfishly dominant, the law of compensation is disturbed and that moment the source of both begins to dry up, and both suffer.

Again: there should be constant conference between the Present and the Future. We sometimes forget that there is a tomorrow coming. In some respects our forefathers forgot that generations were to follow them; their inability to foresee the future led to much waste of energy and material.

The tendency is to use up today and all its stores recklessly, heedless of the generations to follow. Here is where individual and collective interests appear again in conflicting attitudes. Individual desire is to conserve something for the next generation; the father tries to prepare the future for his son, just as he tries to prepare his son for the future. But collectively we are almost entirely indifferent to the future. It is with the utmost effort that any legislation can be secured, which conserves the natural resources of the country against criminal wastage, and saved for the future.

So that where there are opposing tendencies, there ought to be continuous balancing of ends, that there may be no destructive overreaching.

To revert to the industrial situation again: where there is a distinct difference between the individual and the collective good, there ought to be a balancing of their claims in each man's mind.

The best kind of conference takes place in the mind of the man who calmly balances both interests and judicially assigns to each its share. If one interest absorbs all, then the reaction that comes from the other interest is fatal. Never did any interest go up at the sore cost of another legitimate interest but it came down again in loss and sorrow.

We are swayed too much by the speeches of others who are paid to speak, by the writings of others who are paid to write; we are swayed too little by the judicial thought of our own and other sincere minds.

There is a danger of outside conferences taking the place of our own thought.

Let every man think for himself. Let every man call a conference of his own powers, his Common Sense in the chair, his desires and his knowledge of things as they are pleading the case before him. Let every man be his own judge. There is safety in the quiet thought of the people, safety and constructive progress.

It is a patriotic duty—patriotic not only to the Country, but to all Humanity—in these days when to demand is to have, to consider carefully what the end of any course must be. All of us have common sense enough to know that a system of "everything coming in and nothing going out" is just as disastrous as the opposite course.

Every man must seek the solid footing on which he can stand secure for life, and that footing is the same for every one of us; a decent return to the world for our living, and a decent return from the world for our labor.

Universal Training—
Yes, for Usefulness

IT MAY be said once for all that there can be no
objection whatever to "universal training." The
sooner we recognize that fact and get down to constructive details, the better it will be for the country
and the people of the country. If there is anything
of which our nation shows an increasing daily need it
is "universal training," and enough energy is wasted in
debates upon the point to start the whole program
and give it a strong push toward success.

We have a sort of "universal training" now. Our
system of elementary education is that. We require
that every child shall be trained in the use of figures
and letters. We do this in order that the native intelligence of the people may be developed and then
liberated into usefulness. Education is mostly the
giving of the "know how" to minds that are capable
of doing, once they know.

We are insisting on that in our industries, too.
Ability to read and write is an important factor in
obtaining safety in our industrial operations. Safety
can be taught; much of it can be taught by print;
but if the factory personnel cannot read, of what use
is the print? So we establish schools in our factories
in order that men may be taught to read and write,
and thus be brought into contact with printed information. A mind without command over figures
and letters is like a country without postal or tele-
graph service: communication is very slow and difficult.

We have entered upon campaigns in which we
try to bring "universal training" to a city or state
with regard to health. There are certain diseases, like
tuberculosis and typhoid, which may be as totally exterminated as rattlesnakes have been. But it cannot
be done until all the people co-operate. And in order

to co-operate they must be instructed. And so we enter upon campaigns of instruction, and we can measure the results very accurately. When we mobilize public co-operation for any of these activities, we see the success of it almost immediately.

The principle of "universal training," then, is quite firmly established in our common life.

The difficulty and dissension arises when we try to determine just what foᴦm that universal training shall take.

Some men say, "We ought to train everybody to shoot," and so they make the slogan read thus: "universal military training."

Shooting is admittedly not a productive art. We don't use it in our daily business. Millions of people get along very nicely without ever firing or even owning a gun. Indeed, there have been great campaigns of education against the use of guns. We teach boys that to use guns on birds is a very destructive sport, which costs the nation dearly in loss of bird service to our crops. We have laws prohibiting the use of guns on birds whose plumage attracts the milliner. If you fire a gun in your village street, the village marshal will apprehend you and the village justice of the peace will fine you. The skillful use of firearms may be an admirable accomplishment, but the consensus of public opinion in our families, in our neighborhoods, in our cities, in our states, is that the fewer guns there are, the safer it is. Indeed, our social sense is so much against guns that if you are caught carrying one without a special permit the authorities will consider you a questionable character.

But without further arguing that—it has been threshed out quite fully on both sides—the way to determine what form our "universal training" should take is to ascertain in what particulars our people most need to be trained. That we all need to be trained in the use of our faculties goes without saying; and we have the schools for that. That we need to be trained in respect for law is also agreed; and we have public opinion and the laws for that.

But there are other needs for training which most people are always talking about, but which they seldom consider as proper subjects for "universal training."

We Americans are too individualistic. That is a rather smooth and inoffensive way of saying we are selfish. The selfish man is always an individualist. If the individualist isn't always personally selfish, the effect of his attitude is the same.

We need universal training in teamwork. That is one of the arguments the militarists put forth, that military training teaches teamwork. True. But any work which engages large numbers of men in a common object will train them in teamwork. Militarism is teamwork with a destructive object. Isn't it possible to get the same degree, yes, even a higher degree of teamwork with a constructive object?

It would be a splendid thing if young men could be drafted into the public service for a year, for discipline in serving the general good—"soldiers of the common good," is a phrase someone used. Service for someone beside ourselves is the most broadening experience we can have. It surrounds our natural individualism with a wide circle of "otherism." When a man lives only for himself, thinks only of himself, he is in danger of human dry-rot. So, then, imagine that we had a system of conscription by which young men should be drafted for a year of training and service.

Their training would consist in all the things a young man ought to know. The authorities had to do all that when they called the army in 1917, but they had not time to do it thoroughly. They were calling those young men for another purpose than to make them more valuable to their country. But under real "universal training" for constructive national service, these young fellows, taken at an age when they can either be bent for life or straightened up for life, would be trained to be fine bodies. And then they would be trained to be fine, alert, steady minds. And then they would be trained to be useful, willing servants of society at large.

-The nation is suffering from a house famine. Suppose we had an army of 500,000 or a million men who could do for the homeless of the United States what

221

small detachments of our army are doing for the homeless of France and Belgium.

Sometimes the health of the nation suffers, and thousands of deaths and measureless sorrow could be prevented if only we had an army of public servants who could go in and do the things necessary to halt the plague and abolish it from the stricken section forever. Most of the work of this kind that is being done now is dependent on the volunteers of science and the volunteers of humanitarian sympathy. Why could it not be done by conscripts of the nation whose conscription would be a noble and ennobling initiation into the greatness of public service?

We leave for greed and private interest to do many of the things which we ought to do for ourselves as a collective interest. If we did them we should not only have, as a nation, the profit of them when accomplished, but we should also have the training and experience of having performed a constructive act as a public service.

More than that, we need "universal training" in economic facts. The over-reaching ambitions of speculative capital as well as the unreasonable demands of irresponsible labor are both due to ignorance of the economic basis of business. Nobody can get more out of a business than the business can produce, and yet nearly everybody thinks he can. Speculative capital wants more; labor wants more; the source of raw material wants more and the purchasing public wants more—and the poor business that tries to satisfy them all succeeds in satisfying none, and in the end destroys itself.

The family has to be trained that it cannot live beyond its father's income, and presently even the children know that; but the public never seems to learn that it cannot have more than it produces.

If we had "universal training" in the facts of economic balances, we should keep our affairs on a more even keel most of the time. There would be none of this utterly false belief that only a state of war can keep the balance between the various parties to production. That theory is nothing but militarism without a uniform; it is introducing into economic life all

222

the destructive fallacies which make war the colossal stupidity which it is.

There are dangerous interests in our country which are very active in trying to propagate a "universal training" in economic untruth. The world has just been treated to the spectacle of one whole nation practically ruined so far as its economic organization is concerned, because the forces of unrest and ignorance had actually succeeded in getting a real "universal training" of the people in wrong notions of things. No doubt the people were sincere, but even sincerity does not change the facts. And in this country the same danger threatens, that the people will be trained in a theory of economic life which is false, and which they may not discover to be false until they work it and suffer ruin from it—unless, of course, a better "universal training" intervenes to prevent that.

Our whole "Americanization" work ought to go deeper than proficiency in English, knowledge of our governmental structure and loyalty to the Flag; it ought to deal with the deep foundations of moral, social and economic soundness. Well-grounded in the nature-of-things-as-they-are, the American people would be so "universally trained" in the truth that they would be defended against the attractive half-truths which are current everywhere today.

Strike Profiteers Are the Cause of Strikes

WHEN two unreasonable parties refuse to reach an agreement, their quarrel should be confined to themselves alone; it should be prevented from doing harm to others. But when two reasonable parties cannot come to agreement, it is time to look behind the scenes for a third party whose interest is to keep them quarrelling. This applies to labor disputes as well as other disputes. Sometimes both employer and employe are unreasonable and do not seek agreement but conquest: in which case their unreasonableness ought not to be permitted to cause inconvenience or loss to the public. But there have been occasions when both employers and employes were reasonable enough to be able to reach an agreement, and were prevented by hidden influences.

It should not be forgotten for a single minute that though a strike may mean loss of money, time and peace of mind to all directly concerned—to workingman, manufacturer and public—it does not necessarily mean the same loss to everyone.

There are interests that make money out of certain kinds of strikes. If these strikes did not pay somebody, there would be fewer of them.

An analysis of the matter shows that there are three kinds of industrial disputes.

First, there is the justifiable strike—the strike for those proper conditions and just rewards to which the workingman is in all fairness entitled.

The pity is that men should be compelled to use the strike to get what is theirs by right. No American ought to be compelled to strike for his rights. He ought to receive them naturally, easily, as a matter of course.

These justifiable strikes are usually the employer's fault. Some employers are not fit for their job. Em-

224

ployment of men, direction of their energies, arranging that their reward shall be in honest ratio to their production and to the prosperity of the business—that is no small job.

An employer may be unfit for his job, just as a man at the lathe may be incompetent. The lathe man gets into trouble with his work, and so does the incompetent employer with his. Justifiable strikes are a sign that the boss needs another job—one that he can handle.

The unfit employer causes more trouble than the unfit employe. You can change the latter to a more suitable job. But the former must usually be left to the law of compensation.

The justified strike, then, is one that need never have been called if the employer had done his work as he ought.

But there is a second kind of strike—the strike which may be named The Strike With a Concealed Design. In this kind of strike the workingmen are made the tools of some hidden manipulator who seeks his own ends through them. Whoever this manipulator may be, his designs will not stand the light.

To illustrate this kind of strike: Here is a great industry whose success is due to having met a public need, to its efficient and skillful methods of production, and to its known record for just treatment of its workingmen. Such an industry presents a great temptation to speculators. If they can only gain control of it they can reap rich benefit from all the honest effort that has been put into it. They can destroy its beneficiary wage and profit-sharing, squeeze every last dollar out of the public, the product and the workingmen, and reduce it to the plight of other business concerns which are run on these low principles.

Their motive may be the personal greed of the speculator, or they may wish to change the policy of a business whose example is embarrassing to employers who do not want to do what is right by their employes.

But how gain control?—that is the speculator's problem. One of the simplest ways is The Strike With a Concealed Design.

It works this way: The industry to be attacked cannot be touched from within, because its men·have no reason to strike. So another method is adopted. The business in question may keep many outside shops busy supplying it with parts or material. If these outside shops can be tied up then the great industry may be crippled, and that is what the speculators want.

So strikes are fomented in the outside industries. Every attempt is made to curtail the factory's source of supplies. It is a simple game when once understood, and the public has no idea how often it is played.

Now, if the workingmen of the outside shops knew what the game is, they would refuse to play it, but they don't know; they serve as the tools of designing capitalists without knowing it. There is one point, however, that ought to rouse the suspicions of workingmen engaged in this kind of strike. If the strike cannot get itself settled no matter what either side offers to do, it is almost positive proof that there is a third party, a hidden hand, interested in having the strike continue. That hidden influence does not want a settlement on any terms. Its whole profit is in the trouble and in the continuance of the trouble.

If such a strike is won by the strikers, is the lot of the workingmen improved? After throwing the industry into the hands of outside speculators, are the workmen given any better treatment or wages? Who is most likely to work with the workingman along lines of progress and prosperity: the manufacturer whose home is where his plant is, whose reputation among his neighbors is dear to him, whose interest in his employes is born of acquaintance and daily fellowship?—or the outsider, the speculator, the profiteer, who does not know his men from iron spikes and whose only interest in the industry is to squeeze dollars out of it until it is dry?

That is the pity of some strikes which linger on and on after settlements are possible—the deluded strikers are fighting the battles of cunning speculators and do not know it.

Then there is a third kind of strike—the strike that

is provoked by the Money Interests for the purpose
of giving Labor a bad name. The American Workman has always had a reputation for sound judgment. He has not allowed himself to be led away
by every shouter who promised to create the millennium out of thin air. He has had a mind of his own
and has used it. He has always recognized the fundamental truth that the absence of reason was never
made good by the presence of violence.

In this way the American Workingman has won
a certain prestige with his own people and throughout
the world. Public Opinion has been inclined to regard with respect his opinions and desires.

But there seems to be a determined effort now
being made to fasten the Bolshevik stain on American Labor, by inciting it to such impossible attitudes
and such wholly unheard of actions as shall change
public sentiment from respect to criticism.

It is quite in keeping with the higher disorderly
elements that they should employ the lower disorderly
elements for the purpose of destroying the morale and
reputation of the American Workingman. All the disorder does not originate with the workingman. Much
of it comes from higher up.

The American Workingman's most valued asset
is his reputation for cool-headed, balanced judgment
and respect for law and order. If he loses that, what
does he gain?

But—and here is the point—if he does lose that,
the powers that would exploit him and reduce him
to the lowest form of wage-slavery, would be the gainers. Losing his good name, the American Workingman loses all; his enemies are the gainers.

It is time for us to ask some questions: If the
workingman does not make money out of strikes, who
does?

It is time for every striker to ask himself: Who
stand to make money out of this strike? Who will get
the chief benefit if we break down this industry?
Whose game are we playing, anyway?

The man who makes profit out of strikes, be he
billionaire manipulator or self-seeking labor leader, is
a menace to the nation, a traitor to the well-being of

humanity, and the personal assailant of every workingman.

In the second and third kinds of disorder which ' have been described here, the concealed speculator orders the strike; the dishonest labor leader plans it; the rowdy element fans it into violence—and the honest misled workingman pays for it, and continues to pay!

Anyone who knows the American Workingman as he really and naturally is, must be convinced that he does not want to be the tool of evil designers who are not his friends, and who cannot build prosperity. Some people make prosperity; other people sap it'; the latter devitalize and destroy it.

There ought to be high wages everywhere—as high as the business will warrant; and any business that is serving the world and is efficiently managed will warrant it. There ought to be profit-sharing too, that each man may be a partner and not merely a "hand."

But it is not the boss who makes high wages; it is the men. If the boss stands in the way of men getting what they earn, he is not fit to be boss. The day has come when such a man will not be able to keep workmen in his shop.

Once the boss picked out his men. Now men are able to pick out their boss.

Big wages are not philanthropy. Big wages are plain business rights.

The speculators who are always ready to stir up labor trouble are not interested in high wages. They are usually interested in hindering the man who pays high wages. They want to hurt him, to drive him out of business. The American Workingman will not play that game, once he understands it.

Unrest Is Not Disorder

PEOPLE whose business is to talk and write are sometimes more active with their imaginations than with their eyes; their dramatic instinct sends them off on fancies which do not exist, and they admire the role of prophet more than that of reporter; but men who can see, see straight, and tell exactly what they see—men who are, that is to say, superlatively good reporters of plain facts—are very useful citizens today, and if there were more of them there would be fewer hectic headlines in our papers and fewer feverish flashes in our thoughts of the times.

It is a fact which needs special emphasis just now that there is less actual disorder in the country than there is said to be.

Great outbreaks are heralded which do not occur. Great dislocations of business are threatened which never take place. Great strikes are said to be "going on," whose strength had failed weeks ago and the major part of whose supporters had returned to work.

There is far less disorder than is reported, as the most casual investigation shows. Everybody seems to be talking of this or that outbreak, but it is always somewhere else; and everybody, while he talks, goes on about his work. "Everybody" is said to be off on a strike crusade, and yet a survey of the situation shows that pretty nearly everybody came down to work this morning and intends to keep coming.

The fact is, there is less *disorder* than *unrest*. A vital distinction exists here. Unrest indicates one thing, disorder another. And this is not said in palliation of the situation at all, but only in the interest of strict analysis.

Disorder would mean that our people had somehow lost their heads, that all the important parties to our common American life had developed a sudden fateful stupidity which marked the end of our famous American common sense. Disorder indicates a

229

brain-storm, the utter collapse of intelligent resource, the breakdown of every sense of responsibility, the destruction of all devices developed by the energy and efficiency of our civilization. Disorder simply means the disintegration of the times.

But unrest may mean something far different. It may mean only that our people are sensing a new pressure, glimpsing a new light, are conscious of a new coming time.

Unrest may be a herald, as well as a warning. Unrest may signify the revival of new life in the people. It has all kinds of hopeful significance once it is hopefully viewed and used.

Not that one would intimate for a moment that as long as it is only unrest we see, and not disorder, we need not worry much. That is not the point at all. The very fact that the people of the United States are even feeling the stirrings of unrest as they contemplate their social status is far more important than would be the fact that another people, not so intelligent and well-supplied and sensible, were engaged in widespread disorder.

Now, no more foolish way could be taken with this fact of unrest than to imagine that we shall be doing quite enough to satisfy its immediate causes and allow root causes to remain.

There is a short-sighted prudence among the employing classes of the United States which may be colloquially stated thus: "Let's feed them a sop, not enough to make them greedy for more, just enough to satisfy them, and let us do this after they have had to fight for it so that it may seem to come hard. It will never do to admit that we could have done this for them before, but would not."

Such an attitude can have only one basis—the belief that there is a master-class and a servant-class among us, and that the only way the master-class can keep its mastery is by dealing shrewdly with the servant-class, as ignorant dependents.

Let us be rid at once of that survival of feudalism among us.

Let us get rid at once of the idea that unrest can be thoroughly dealt with by a system of hand-outs, on the theory that the dog never bites while he is eating.

Let us wipe out of American business phraseology such phrases as "keeping them contented," as if they were children, and "three squares a day keeps the Bolshevist away," as if our people were mere animals.

The whole philosophy is degrading to anyone who believes it or who acts upon it. It is not degrading to the American workingman, because he does not agree with it for one instant.

As long as we adhere to the program of piece-meal settlements, granting a concession here and doing a favor there, "for the sake of keeping the working-class quiet," we are simply dealing in postponements, not in settlements. Now, we know what the demands and program of the disorderly elements are—they are unreasonable and destructive in the extreme; and it would make absolutely no difference whether those demands were granted, or whether they were withheld and the destructive program carried out—the result would be exactly the same. To grant a demand which no equitable system can carry is just as fatal as to refuse it and have industry destroyed by violence. Industry would be destroyed either way. There are some things which cannot be done no matter how much we may wish to do them. We may wish to feed 1,000 people, but if there is only one bushel of potatoes it cannot be done. The demand of the disorderly element is practically that everybody be requested to raise fewer potatoes, and yet that everybody be given more potatoes. One end of the program kills the other. It is all unreason and confusion. If everybody does less work and everybody gets more of the product of work, how long can it last? And where will the unproduced and unearned part come from?

But the meanings of unrest must not be confused with this. The unreasonable demands of the disorderly forces are simply the counterpart of the unreasonable attitude of those who believe that a safe and workable system can be arrived at by a master-class handing out favors to a servant-class.

Unrest may mean something far more intelligent, more constructive and more just.

It would surprise many employers of labor to learn that the unrest among their men does not primarily concern money. That is to say, the central thought of the major part of our citizens who are becoming concerned about our social and industrial problems is not "more money at any cost," but "justice."

Certainly justice will mean more money in many places. Certainly no industry can' be said to be justifying itself which survives at the expense of its employes and thrives upon their losses.

But there is this to say: if justice were done and it so happened that justice did not mean more money, there would be a great wave of real, not temporary, contentment sweep over the working world.

If it were shown and proved that wages as they exist everywhere today were strictly just and equitable, forming an unimpeachable balance between producer and consumer, there would be instant satisfaction with the wage scale.

Why? Because what men miss most is not the extra money in their pay envelope, but the sense of justice in their hearts. They want to live in a world that is playing square with them. They want to be at peace with their fellow-men. True, they want prosperity, but they do not want it at the cost of injustice to others.

The hardest burden of poverty is not its deprivation, but its bitter reflection that the other side of poverty is the injustice of successful greed.

So, while the disorderly elements want nothing so much as to ravage the firm's bank account, the true rank and file of the laboring world wants a system of labor and reward that is equitable and just in itself, no matter what its figures may show. It wants a world founded on rectitude. It wants to know that the square deal rules. It wants to know that it is neither being taken advantage of, nor is taking advantage of any other.

It is a phase of the human spirit we are dealing with, and whenever we fail to see that, we run afoul of elements which are most vital to social and industrial stability.

232

Here is where all conferences and committees fail. They meet each other, one to force the other forward and one to force the other back. They are combatants from the start. They talk about dollars. One side tries to get the other side's dollars away from it by disputing that side's ownership of the money; equally disputatious and material-minded they simply shut out any high considerations. And the result is what anyone might have foreseen.

We must get a higher meeting ground. We have got to get together to consider what complete industrial justice is, regardless of which side will be most affected by that justice when it is arrived at. We must keep it high and above all our petty selfishness and ambitions. We must, indeed, have but one ambition —the noble ambition to be one of the creators of industrial justice.

And if we find that justice means adjustment of working conditions, of wages, the admission of workingmen to profit-sharing and to a part in the management as it affects them, then we must consider who will contribute the difference made by changed hours and wages, and we must consider how these changes can safely be put into effect without disturbing the business in its standing.

All this can be arrived at with great friendliness and common sense between employers and employes if they only seek the higher unity and not their own limited interests. And if so be an employer, having been once a workingman himself, sees the need of adjustments and makes them before his men ask him, so much the better—his act means a great increase in confidence and a new feeling that the world still has a square deal left in it.

This is the way to find a settlement that will stand. Not a contract which may be broken, but an agreement of minds and hearts in a new social industrialism which will endure simply because it is founded on conviction and not on limited interest.

Employment Is Greater Than "Employer" or "Employe"

IN THE discussion which goes on about "capital" and "labor" we forget something. We leave out the very thing that it is all about. We talk a great deal about employers, and a great deal about employes, and say practically nothing about the industry which brings them both together. We hear a great deal about the differences between these two groups, but we almost entirely overlook the foundation that is holding both of them up while they dispute. If the business they are arguing about should suddenly fall to pieces and disappear, the argument would be over; both parties would find themselves floundering in the midst of chaos.

So it may be a worth-while contribution to the general subject if we just make room somewhere between "employer" and "employe" for that very important element, Employment.

Let us begin as near the beginning as we can. Everyone—except the hermit of the woods who lives on berries, roots and game, whose business in life begins and ends with himself—lives by serving someone else.

He can dig, or plant, or build, or teach, or lay out plans, or heal, or amuse, or give general help where labor is required. And those who need his services in digging or planting or building or teaching or healing or amusing, or whatever it may be, go to him for that service and he lives by it. That is his business. The more widely known he becomes for what he can do, and the more customary it becomes with the people to call upon him, the more solidly is his business established. That is, the more accurately he can speak of his "trade" as distinct from himself.

That business, that established custom by which people come to him for his services and by which he renders them, becomes his foundation in life, just as the farm becomes the farmer's foundation. His business has a life of its own. It is known by its name. It has a reputation. It can be injured. It can be killed. It is a created entity which is almost human in its response to demands or conditions.

Now, it makes no difference to the principle involved whether that business is a cobbling shop employing only its owner, or a great factory employing 40,000 men. The business is the medium through which the livelihood of its members comes; it is the medium through which their service is extended to the world in exchange for a livelihood from the world; and any disturbance of the medium results inevitably in serious hindrance to the service both ways.

This idea is, of course, a very simple one, and that is the reason why it is so difficult to make clear. The simplest, most obvious facts are hardest to value properly, because they are so easy to undervalue. They are the small bolts and nuts of thought, apparently trivial in themselves, but their loss is important enough to cripple the whole machine.

If there were ten of us living off a farm of 100 acres, the fundamental economic fact for us would be that farm. We should be just plain fools to stand around and argue while the farm went to waste. If we did that, and the farm did go to wrack and ruin, the argument would be over; we simply should have argued ourselves into the lack of anything worth arguing about.

A shop or a business is exactly the same. It is the living of those engaged in it. It is the place where we win our food and raiment and shelter. There may be something wrong with the relations that exist between individuals there; there may be grave differences in the degree of justice with which the distribution of rewards is effected; still it is true that the business is the ground we all depend on, and it is worth a much larger part of our consideration than many seem disposed to give it.

Ruin a business, disorganize it, scatter it abroad, and you will have no further worry about "capital" or "labor"—it will then become a question of saving our economic lives.

Now, the nucleus of a business may be an idea. That is, an inventor or a thoughtful workman works out a new and better way to serve some established human need; the idea commends itself, and people want to avail themselves of it. In this way a single individual may prove, through his idea or discovery, the nucleus of a business.

But the creation of the body and bulk of that business is shared by everyone who has anything to do with it. No manufacturer can say "I" built this business if he has required the help of thousands of men in building it. It is a joint production. Everyone employed in it has contributed something to it. By working and producing they make it possible for the purchasing world to keep coming to that business for the type of service it provides, and thus they help establish a custom, a trade, a habit which supplies them with a livelihood. All this has a certain practical bearing on the discussions which are prevalent today and which sometimes threaten to damage the good points along with the bad.

When two men are in mid-lake in a boat, their common interest, no matter what their personal differences may be, is in the integrity of that boat. They may differ and argue and contend as much as they please regarding what seat each ought to occupy, but if they break the boat or swamp it, the seat question ceases to exist—and possibly the men too.

It will not make much difference how we decide to divide the golden egg, if during the squabble we destroy the goose that lays it.

"What ought the employer to pay?" and "What ought the employe to receive?" are minor questions, the basic question being, "What can the business stand?"

Certainly no business can stand an outgo that exceeds its income. When you pump water out of the well at a faster rate than the water runs in, your well goes dry. And when the well runs dry, those who depend on it go thirsty. And if, perchance, they imagine they can pump one well dry and then jump to some other well, it is only a matter of time before the same shortsighted policy will dry up all the wells.

Just now, when there is such a widespread insistent demand for more justly divided rewards, it must be recognized that there are limits. The business itself sets the limits. You cannot distribute $150,000 out of a business that only brings in $100,000.

Instead, therefore, of men saying that the "employer" ought to do thus-and-so, the expression ought to be changed to, "the business ought to be so stimulated and managed that it can do thus-and-so." Because, *only the business does it.* Certainly the employer cannot do it if the business will not warrant it. But if the business will warrant it and the employer will not do it, there is a way to secure it without endangering the business.

As a rule the business means the livelihood of too many men, to be tampered with. Nothing could be more criminal in the economic realm than the assassination of a business to which large numbers of men have given their labors and to which they have learned to look as their field of usefulness in the world and their source of livelihood. It must be said, however, that this form of assassination has been more frequently practiced by speculative capitalists than by workingmen.

So that in making the adjustments which a new industrial order will require, it will be better if the employer stops looking at the employes as he asks himself, "How little can I get them to take?" and it will be better if the employe takes his eyes off the employer as he asks, "How much can I force him to give?"

It will be infinitely better if both turn their eyes upon the business and ask, "How can this industry be made safe and profitable, so that it will be able to provide a sure and comfortable living for all of us?"

If the two groups would take their eyes and minds off each other and turn them to the industry as the only possible means of obtaining what both of them want, there would be an advantage gained.

First, there would be the advantage of forgetting personalities. It is when we talk about labor and

237

capital that we find class lines appearing, and class prejudices, and class antipathies. The two opposed groups look too much at each other as men, and imagine too many wrong things against each other.

Second, there would be the advantage of both groups converging and centering on one common interest; and there is no question whatever that the solution of our problem will never be the find of any one group, but the creative construction of both groups working together. When we cease to talk about "capital" and "labor," and begin to talk about Industry, then both capital and labor are talking about the same thing—that on which they both equally depend for their living.

Let workmen stop imagining this and that about the boss and let bosses stop imagining this and that about the workmen; let both of them get back to normal thoughts by thinking more of the job.

The job is the place where capital and labor, producer and consumer, financial and industrial and public interests meet on common ground. All that any of them will ever get, they will have to get out of the job.

And it may well be that, thinking less of employer and employe, which are terms of division today, and more of Employment, which is a term of unity, we may reach a good understanding, a fuller justice and a deeper contentment much earlier than we have expected.

Profit and Cost in a
Day's Work

HOW much profit does a workman reap from his
day's labor? How much ought he to reap? Does
a "good living" come under the head of profit, or is
it properly a part of the cost of producing a day's
labor? How far can human energies be measured and
human values standardized in order that the cost of a
day's labor may be standardized?

Questions like these occur in one period or another
of every man's thought about a system of economics
which shall be more solidly based than any which
serves us now.

But a more than academic interest attaches to
these questions, for they are the real, even if unspoken,
basis for much of the irritation and confusion which
exists in the industrial world today.

The workingman is beginning to understand that
he is in business. His raw material is human energy.
His product is a day's work. All other business men
seek a profit above cost of production, why should
not he?

The difficulty thus far has been in making out the
cost sheet. How much does it cost to produce a day's
work?—that is the question for which there seems to
be no satisfactory basic answer.

It is perhaps possible accurately to determine—
albeit with considerable interference with the day's
work itself—how much energy the day's work takes
out of a man. But it is not at all possible accurately
to determine how much it will require to put back
that energy into him against the next day's demands.
Nor is it possible to determine how much of that expended energy you will never be able to put back at
all—because a "sinking fund" for the replacement of
the body and vital strength of a worker has never been
invented.

239

It is possible, however, to consider these latter problems in a lump and provide for them under a form of old-age pensions; but even so, we have not thus attended to the question of profit which each day's labor ought to yield in order to take care of all of life's overhead, all physical losses, and the inevitable deterioration which falls upon all earthly things.

Moreover, there are questions having to do with the pre-productive period, which would have to be solved. Here is the man, let us say, ready to begin his service to society by turning out days' work throughout his life. How much did it cost to rear and educate him to his present age and usefulness? And how can that be figured as part of the cost of the energy he puts forth as he works today? Now, if it were the case of a machine, you would know what to charge. The machine cost a certain sum; it wears out at a given rate; it would cost such-and-such an amount to replace. It is a simple matter to figure the actual cost of the machine and its productive work, and add the profit.

Can we do that with men? Rather, can men do that for themselves, so that selling a day's work they will have as intelligent an idea of the cost of that day's work and the profit it ought to bring as any manufacturer ought to have of his product?

The problem becomes more complicated when you consider the man in all his aspects. For he is more than a workman who spends a certain number of hours at his work in the shop every day.

If he were only himself, the cost of his maintenance and the profit he ought to have would be a simple matter. But he is more than himself. He is a *citizen*, contributing by his cultivation and interest to the welfare of the city. He is probably a *householder*, living under conditions which represent more than mere maintenance, in that they represent the graces of social life. More than that, he is probably a *father* with a more or less numerous progeny, all of whom must subsist and be reared to usefulness on what he is able to earn.

Now, it is obvious that to regard the man alone,

refusing to reckon with the home and the family in the background, is to arrive at a series of facts which are misleading and which alone can never suffice even for a temporary solution of the questions that concern us.

How are you going to figure the contribution of the home to the day's work of the man? You are paying the man for his work, but how much does that work owe to his home? How much to his position as a citizen? How much to his position as the provider of a family? The man does the work in the shop, but his wife does the work of the home, and the shop must pay them both; on what system of figuring is the home going to find its place on the cost sheets of the day's work? It finds its place there already in a sort of haphazard way. If a man cannot support himself, his wife, his children, his habitation, his position in society—why, he doesn't stay at the job, that's all. It isn't a matter of cost and profit to him; it is the matter of a "living."

Is a man's own livelihood the "cost"? And is his ability to have a home and a family the "profit"?

Is the profit on a day's work to be computed on a cash basis only, measured by the amount a man has left over after his own and family's wants are all supplied?

Is the livelihood of five or six persons beside those of the actual worker to be charged up to "profit"?

Or, are all these relationships to be considered strictly under the head of "cost," and the profit to be computed entirely outside of them? That is, after having supported himself and family, clothed them, housed them, educated them, given them the privileges incident to their standard of living, ought there to be provision made for still something more in the way of savings profit, and all properly chargeable to the day's work? These are questions which call for accurate observation and computation.

Perhaps there is no one item connected with our economic life that would surprise us more than a knowledge of just what excess burdens the day's work actually carries.

It carries all the worker's obligations outside the shop; it carries all that is necessary in the way of service and management inside the shop. The day's productive work is the most valuable mine of wealth that has ever been opened.

Certainly it cannot be made to carry less than all the worker's outside obligations. And certainly it ought to be made to take care of the worker's sunset days when labor is no longer possible to him, and should be no longer necessary. And if it is made to do even these, industry will have to be adjusted to a schedule of production, distribution and reward which will stop the leaks toward the pockets of men who do not assist production in any way, and turn all streams for the benefit of those who do. In order to create a system which shall be as independent of the good-will of benevolent employers as of the ill-will of selfish ones, we shall have to find a basis in the actual facts of life itself.

It costs just as much physical strength to turn out a day's work when wheat is $1 a bushel as when wheat is $2.50 a bushel. Eggs may be 12 cents a dozen or 90 cents a dozen—it makes no difference in the units of energy a man uses in a productive day's work.

One would think that the real basis of value would be the cost of transmuting human energy into articles of trade and commerce. But no; that most honest of all human activities is made subject to the speculative shrewdness of men who can produce false shortages of food and other commodities, and thus excite anxiety of demand in society.

It is not in industry that the trouble lies, but in those regions beyond, where men lie in wait to seize the fruits of industry and create false scarcities for the sake of arousing an anxious demand for things which, normally, are and ought to be accessible to all who engage in daily productive pursuits.

We must begin with the land; we must continue with the day's labor; and we must keep so close, so jealously close to both these fundamentals that we shall be suspicious and fearful of all that robs the land of men, and robs labor of its primal importance in material life.

We shall think out, and try out, and establish more enduring economic systems as we go on about our work, than we shall ever be able to do sitting idle with our heads in our hands trying to "think" a new world system out of our brains.

The day's work is the hub around which the whole wheel of earth-life swings. It must be kept central, both in our thinking and our action. Any system that shunts the day's work off to one side as unimportant, is riding to a fall.

Who Is the Producer?

WHO is the Producer? It is really an important question in these days of revised thinking, because there is growing up a new class-conscious aristocracy which calls itself "the producers," and is very exclusive of everyone else. It is, of course, a good sign that emphasis is being placed on production and that a new appreciation has come for the producer; and perhaps it is natural that a kind of class pride should grow up which would limit the right to wear that honorable name; but all this makes it the more necessary that we should be clear in our minds as to who the Producer really is.

The most common description of the Producer would lead us to believe that he is the man from whose hands comes the finished product. We are easily deceived on this point. This man, we say, makes horseshoes. He produces something useful. He is thus a valuable member of society. We can see his work, we can see him perform it, we can see how it serves the immediate needs of the community. Therefore, we have no hesitancy in awarding him the title of Producer.

But behind that man are others whom we do not see. There is the miner who dug out the iron ore. There is the mule-driver who transported the ore to the mine shaft. There is the engineer who hoisted it to the top. There are the men who handled it in the smelter. There are the other men who sailed the ships that carried it to the steel mills. Then in the steel mills it passed through the hands of many men who transformed it into steel; and there were railroad men and truckmen who carried it to the place where material was needed. Finally there was the blacksmith who with his brawny arm and practiced eye shaped it into the article that was needed—a rod, a brace, or a horseshoe.

When you actually trace any article of use through the numerous hands that worked upon it, and then attempt to divide the price of the article among those various men, you not only get an idea of the vast co-operation which production involves, but also how quantity production is the only method by which a low price to the purchaser and an adequate wage to the producer can be maintained.

During this process of tracing, you would also come upon another fact which is often overlooked; you would become aware of a very considerable body of workers whose hands did not directly touch the product at all, but whose whole work was in serving the Producers during the time they were actually engaged in the work of production. We are not now speaking of the various forms of service rendered to the Producers outside the shop, but that service which is rendered them inside the shop.

Take the shop sweepers, for example. They never touch the product of the shop. To the careless eye they are not producing anything at all. They are mere "extras," so to speak. Many would indignantly deny them the title of Producers.

Yet they serve the processes of production in an indispensable way. Sweeping the shop has a direct bearing on the production of the special article which the shop exists to make. For example, an accumulation of waste would hinder production in two ways; first, the waste itself would get in the workers' way; second, to get it out of his way the worker would have to leave his job and go sweeping.

Now, when the sweeper goes through his appointed section of floor space with his broom, he is clearing the way for the worker, he is allowing the worker to continue straight on with his job, unhindered.

Again, the sweeper serves the worker in a still more indirect yet important way: cleanliness of the shop brings sanitary benefits with it, and so the sweeper serves the worker's health, and through it, production, by cutting down lost time due to illness.

Perhaps the most subtle service the sweeper renders is a psychological one. A clean shop has an influence on the men. They become more clean-cut in their own work. Wherever you see a shop cluttered up with a mass of waste, or with material dumped around anywhere in disorderly fashion, you will find that the workmen's minds become cluttered too; they partake of the general disorderliness. Now, the sweeper has worked for weeks and months and has not touched a single process of what we call production, and yet he has served the Producer and aided production.

If the man whom we call the Producer had been compelled to stop and do his own sweeping, he would have drawn the same rate of pay for handling a broom as was given him for the skilled use of a tool. It would have been a waste of skill. The sweeper relieved him of that necessity, and so made it possible to keep the mechanical skill where it was most needed.

And because the sweeper is thus a contributor to production through rendering service to the more direct Producer, it is believed that he is entitled to a wage that recognizes his value. That is why the minimum wage, which always ought to be high enough to support a very creditable standard of living, should include the sweepers also, or any other similar workers whose efforts contribute to the general work of production.

Are we going to deny the name of Producer to those whose services are a part of the immediate producer's services?

That is just what is sometimes done. There is a sort of an aristocracy of skill growing up. There is an exclusiveness which would shut out the contributors to production from the status and rewards of Producers. It is rather strange to see these divisions arise, and to see how the urge of human pride always makes for separateness among men. There are others, of course, beside the sweepers, who serve the immediate Producers of articles of use. The man who plans the work, who makes it possible for the Producer to begin the job at once instead of waiting to lay it out and plan it ahead—he, too, has his part in production.

Then, before any of these came upon the scene at

all, there is the man who had vision enough and faith enough to win the necessary means to start the work going in the first place: the man whose credit or whose idea was good enough to secure capital and machinery and a place to work. Surely it will not be denied that he, too, had his part in Production—that he served Production and the Producer, too.

The difficulty has been in the past very similar to that which confronts us now, namely, a tendency on the part of one group to minimize the importance of the other group, as if that were the only way to secure its own importance.

Our enormous and insistent demand for the finished product has, in these days, given an exaggerated prominence to the man who does the finishing. The last man to handle the article is the first man the public sees, and thus he is the one who is most often given the title of Producer.

The man who "turns it out" is the man whom modern opinion acclaims as the real creator.

And yet it must be clear to all that this man could not "turn it out" unless a whole series of processes had produced it to his hand almost ready to be "turned out."

When all is said and done, it is the organization that produces, and no individual worker. And by "organization" is meant not only the specific shop which makes the specific article, but the whole industrial process, from those which deal with the raw materials of the earth, to those that give the finishing touches which prepare the worked material for the market and for use.

They are all part of the plan. It may be that some of the processes could be shortened up a little; it may be that profiteers push in here and there to collect an unwarranted tax on the completed article as it passes along the channels of commerce; but aside from these, which can easily be remedied, it will be found that the actual shaping of the article occupies a place about midway in the whole process of Production. It is not the whole. It is indispensable, of course; but it is not warranted in assuming a lordly dominance over all the others.

Certainly there is no place in a just and well-regulated world for any labor that does not in some measure contribute to Production. This is not to take a sordid view of life, but only to insist on usefulness in the things which we support. Every man who eats and wears clothes and enjoys creature comforts, does so at the expense of someone else's labor. Now, he ought to yield an adequately useful return for what he receives—that is the principle.

All Are Members of the Consuming Class

A CORRESPONDENT suggests that in classifying society into groups, such as the Producing, the Consuming and the Public groups, or the Capital, the Labor and the Public groups, there should have been added the Government group, thus placing the structure on four solid legs, instead of leaving it the "three-legged stool" of recent popular expression.

The suggestion illustrates the fundamental falsity of dividing society at all, for it is an undivided organism. If we set it off into classes and interests, we do so simply as an aid to our thinking, as children first use blocks to learn arithmetic; we never imply that society is really thus divided; we never imply that life is such a hard and fast matter that every man is shut up into one caste or class.

That is where class-consciousness usually fails as a motive, and that is why the propagandists of a class-conscious strife are doomed to failure—you cannot cage an individual in any one class. Even while you are tagging him, he eludes you and glides into another class, if only for an hour. In a free country like ours, a man usually does—at least he always may—belong to all classes at once, except perhaps artificial and unwholesome classes like that which we call "the leisure class." To belong to the "leisure class" simply means that down in the mine and at the forge and in the shop there are men working for themselves and for idlers whom they never saw; it is to be a sponge, a parasite, a sign of economic disease.

There is one class in which none of us escapes membership, and that is the Consuming class. By the law of nature we are all consumers. It means our very life. Rich or poor, learned or ignorant, it does not matter—every living organism consumes the material of life, and for us this means mostly food for the body and the material necessities of residence on the earth.

Every man, be he the greatest producer ever known, is a consumer the first thing in the morning when he sits down at his breakfast table. Whether he produced what he consumes, or whether someone else produced it, does not matter—sitting at that table and eating, he has joined the Consuming class. The total produce of the world is a little less because he sat there.

And then he goes to his work. He enters the shop and takes up his task, and by that act he has passed into the Producing group. No jolt and no jar attended the transition, no change in his fundamental interests occurred, he is not on one side of the fence while he is eating his breakfast and on the other as he plies his job—he is just a human being trying to support himself and dependents in a world maze.

Membership in the Consuming class is compulsory if life is to go on, but evidently membership in the Producing class is not, for there are some—a very few comparatively—who go on consuming all day long, week in and week out, during a whole lifetime, without ever putting back a single valuable contribution into the general supply. "They are living on their money," we say. But they are not. They are living on the grain which other men raised, the clothing which other men spun, the commodities which other men made—and their "money" is one of the modern fetishes by which they are enabled to do this. Money is always a sign of production, but its *possession* is not.

But returning to the normal man who has no desire to escape his duty, and who is willing to replace by production the stuff which he takes for consumption, what is his relation to these two conditions? The fomenters of labor strife say that he should be a "bull" when it is a question of how much he shall be paid for production, and a "bear" when it is a question of what he shall pay for what he consumes. In other words, make the loaf of bread cost more to bake, but sell it for less because the man who was highly paid for baking it will presently come around the front door and buy it for his family.

This, of course, would be a very favorable arrangement for the baker, if it could be kept up; but unfortunately for that dream, there is an inviolable relation between the cost of consumption and the cost of production; even in the physical body, when repair and replacement cease to equal waste and use, old age comes and death is not far. Decrepitude and collapse come to business from the same cause.

There is, doubtless, a difference in the interests of the individual as Producer and that same individual as Consumer, but the difference merges into the same interest at last, namely, to gain enough as Producer to meet the demands made upon him as Consumer.

Some would-be guides talk as if all this could be easily arranged if the Producer took what he produced and let it go at that. The matter is complicated by another class which comes into existence between the production and the consumption. The producer is not buying of himself as producer, but of someone else who has acquired his product. This gives room for a mixture of motives—to get as much as he can as producer and give as little as he can as consumer.

This double attitude is assisted by the man's belief that he is dealing with two sets of persons whose interests seem opposed to his—his employer, who he thinks is trying to get out of him more labor than the wage is worth; and the merchant or trader, who he thinks is trying to get out of him more money than the article is worth.

The man doesn't see that—banish human greed from the equation—he is dealing only with himself after all, and that if he robs commodities at one end of the process, they rob him at the other; and so equality is established, though in a very unsatisfactory sort of way.

Now, there are advisers who insist that the way out of this condition is for the Producer-Consumer to add to his "class membership" and become Trader, too. For that is all that the abolition of the commercial class could mean. But as very few men could subsist on the commodity which they produce (the commodity usually being only a part in some larger process of production), and would have to stop producing in order to hawk their product in the market and gain the wherewithal to procure a subsistence, the process might end practically in the same place as the present one does—but probably it would end in a much lower degree of efficiency and in a much lower state of general comfort.

In our capacity as workers we are interested in just rates of reward; in our capacity as consumers we are interested in just rates of exchange; in our public capacity we are interested in the general welfare, not of ourselves alone, but of all men.

So, when our correspondent suggests that we add the Government group, it means just this: we add to all our other "class memberships," a new membership which carries power and authority with it.

The Government is not a group of men who control a group of the Public and a group of Producers and a group of Consumers; the Government is the Public, the Producers and the Consumers united to produce a political life which shall be the safeguard of all their rights and their just interests.

Perhaps the time has come for Government to consider taking over the control of economic conduct as well as those other phases of conduct which are indicated in existing laws. Certainly a Government that has power to say what shall be the standard quart or bushel, should also have power to say what shall be the standard day of work and the standard rate of reward.

The world is now moving around in a dazed sort of way simply because some extremely simple questions have not been answered—questions relating to the cost of a day's work to the man who gives it, and the rate of reward he ought to have to put him on an equality with other men who also are rewarded.

There is natural wealth enough, there is human energy enough; one is also persuaded that there could be found enough human good will, if mankind only knew what to do. The race is waiting for someone to show it the simple way out, that all interests may be brought into harmony, and the friction of unjust conflict abolished.

Every Man Needs Elbow Room

WHEN a man deals in theories it is very easy for him to exaggerate, because a world that is spun out of fancy can be more easily rearranged than a world of throbbing, driving life. Men find it easy to rear Utopia in their dreams, and make changes overnight that would dislocate the whole human race if they were decreed in a real world. But when we are dealing with real days and actual conditions we find that our very life is so bound up in the conditions which surround us—as the life of the body inheres in its organs—that sudden and total changes, which are fortunately impossible, would be fatal, if they were possible. The danger of our dream-worlds is that they influence us too greatly in discounting the real world in which we live. On the whole it is not a bad world, as practically everybody will admit. It is not perfect by any means; it will stand much retouching here and there, much adjustment and improvement; but on the whole even the most ordinary mind is able to see that what we have is infinitely better than it might be, infinitely better than some of the systems which are now being proposed by men whose minds would be clearer if they worked for their living.

Every man with red blood in his veins will agree that whatever else we may desire, we do not desire a world that will leave no elbow room for individual initiative and ambition.

No man would wish to place his son in a school where the lad would not be required to meet things that would test his qualities and develop his powers. He would not want his son coddled. He would want him to take boy's luck with the rest of the boys, learn by the friction generated by rubbing against hard tasks and other people's natures. He would want for his son such a discipline as would render him a self-reliant man.

And, when we take time to think of it, that is just

the kind of world we ask for ourselves. We don't want to be supported by government, clothed by legislature, and apportioned our work and reward by commissary; we don't ask to live in houses furnished us by the state, fed on fixed ration, and educated according to certain schedules fixed for the various classes of society.

What the normal man wants is a free field and no favorites, a chance to show what is in him, and take the measure of success and reward that he is able to win. For that is Freedom in the economic sense. Some people talk as if economic freedom meant liberation from the necessity of toil, but as food itself means toil, and as food is a necessity, that view is clearly wrong. Freedom means an opportunity to go out with other men, working with them in co-operation, and alongside them in friendly competition, so that every man shall have the chance to demonstrate his ability.

That is what gives life its zest, and any social program that takes that zest out of life is foredoomed to failure even before it is tried. Indeed, it never will be tried, because the healthy zest of human nature is against it from the beginning.

What we want for our boys is what we ask for ourselves—free opportunity on the field of endeavor, a fair chance to measure powers with other men, and may the best man win!

Now, when we have tried this opportunity for a number of years it is inevitable that we settle into the classifications which our abilities, our use of our opportunities, and our general value to society, fix for us. That is the only classification possible. Each man eventually finds his own place. He finds his own work. He is rewarded according to the contribution he makes to the general welfare.

There is nothing arbitrary about it. It is not done by legislation nor by the pressure of group interests. It is purely natural in its operation. Cotton goes into cloth and iron goes into dredges; there is no discrimination; there is only classification by fitness.

But the contest of life leaves a certain proportion of human beings very low in the economic scale, and this constitutes the largest item in our social problem. This residuum near the bottom has heretofore been waste material to a very large extent. We have been just as wasteful of men as we have of certain materials. For generations we have been throwing away what we called the "waste" of mines and the "rubbish" and "garbage" of cities. But we have now awakened to their value and are making them useful and therefore valuable. In the same way we have been counting certain classes of unskilled individuals as waste. Humanity's scrap-heap has at times been very large. But modern industry has turned all this waste humanity to new and increased usefulness, thus making these classes of men more valuable to themselves and society.

It was not so much a matter of "man's inhumanity to man," as it was society's lack of managerial ability to use the naturally less useful classes, which led to the sad spectacle of "a human scrap-heap." Modern industry went to that scrap-heap and found good useful stuff, and today even the unskilled man can feel that he is playing his part in the making of the world. The man of initiative, ability, and energy has always been able to take care of himself. He has asked no favors and has agitated no new form of society. The problem has always been the other man who must be helped to help himself.

That man is receiving more of the material of self-help today than at any time in human history. He counts for something. He is necessary to the work of the world. Productive processes have been so standardized that his steadiness is as good an asset as genius, and his labor as prime an investment as capital.

And still more will be done for him. He has not only been given a place in the world; he will be given a share in the wealth he helps to create over and above that share which comes to him as wages. He will participate in the "extras"; he will be enabled to count his connection with his job not only on the basis of the day's wage, but of the year's bonus and dividend. All this is made possible not by a soft sentimentalism, but by new methods of production and new genius for

255

management which have given value to the work of these formerly discounted groups of men.

There is a theory that profit-sharing is impracticable because it is not balanced by loss-sharing, that a full partnership between capital and labor would involve a sharing of the risks as well as the benefits. The theory is faulty at several points. Whatever profit a business shows is produced by labor in conjunction with efficient management, and labor is therefore clearly entitled to a share. Moreover, the losses, whether caused by ill-management, depression or other conditions which are still beyond control, are certain to be shared by labor, whether it will or no.

But why expect losses at all? Why should a business which supplies a legitimate need of the people, ever suffer from lack of work at a profitable figure? Eliminate the speculative element, contribute efficient management, give honest labor on an honest product at an honest price, and you have established business on a substantial basis, at the minimum of risk.

Labor and management are partners—if both be efficient, the results are as certain as human affairs can be. Management furnishes the method, labor furnishes the medium; both together spell service; service is the basis of reward; and upon the basis of honest reward, prosperity is built.

With capital making the first move toward fairness and equality, there is bound to be a receptive spirit on the part of labor, and a revision of some of the old prejudices and misconceptions. After all, we are only human—all of us; and a real man can always sense the note of sincerity, or its absence, in another's proffer of friendship.

The sincere desire of the manufacturer to be just to his men and to the public must result in a tide of loyalty rolling in to meet, augment and solidify the new spirit which is coming into industrial relations.

The Need of Social Blueprints

ALMOST anyone you may chance to meet will tell you that "something ought to be done" and will assure you that it must be done very soon. But you will travel a long way before you will meet anyone with a plan that has a single point of practicability.

Many plans, so-called, are not plans at all; they are pleasant pictures of conditions as they may be after all the planning, all the preparatory work and all the constructive labors are done. A plan is not an oil-painting of a complete object; a plan indicates the "how" and the "where" and the "what" of every joist, joint and pillar. You cannot build a house from a charming photograph; you will need a blueprint.

Every thoughtful man has an idea of what ought to be; but what the world is waiting for is a social and economic blueprint.

There is something deadly exact about a blueprint. It is not a speech; it is not a propaganda; it is not a burst of enthusiasm; it is a simple thing of lines and signs which tells you what to do and just where to do it. It speaks of only one quality—orderly work.

Now, this is why good intentions are of so little value to the practical solution of the problems that confront us. Good intentions, of course, are very good—as intentions. And doubtless good intentions must exist in every good plan. But everyone has had enough experience with well-meaning people to know that good intentions are often sterile.

It is very surprising to learn how much of the distrust of people in plans for the advancement of justice in human relations is due to the failure of so many ill-planned and badly managed good intentions. Human history is full of the wreckage of high and noble intentions for social good and human betterment, which failed simply because they had the visionary quality without the creative quality.

And one result of this is the almost universal assumption that whatever is good, generous, just and warmly human, is prevented by those very qualities from being practical. There is an unspoken belief that if a plan is to be practical it must disregard humanity to a greater or less extent. Consideration of others and success for oneself are believed to be incompatible.

Another result is the assumption that "creative work" can only be undertaken in the realm of vision. We speak of "creative artists" in music, painting and the other arts. We thus limit the creative functions to productions that may be hung on gallery walls or played in concert halls, or otherwise displayed where idle and fastidious people gather to admire each other's show of "culture."

But, if a man wants a field for real vital creative work, let him come where he is dealing with higher laws than those of sound, or line or color; let him come where he may deal with the very laws of personality and society. Creative work! We want artists in industrial relationships. We want masters in industrial method, both from the standpoint of the producer and the product. We want those who can mold the political, social, industrial and moral mass into a sound and shapely whole.

We have limited the creative faculty too much and have used it for too trivial ends. We want men who can create the working design for all that is right and good and desirable in our life together here.

Now, it is pretty clear that the creative plan, when it comes, will propose surprisingly little that is new; it will consist largely in a readjustment of the old things.

We shall not outgrow the need to work. Some people are talking as if the "good time coming" is going to eliminate labor altogether. Some people appear to think that the only thing that is wrong with our present system is that people have to work for their living.

Well, we may be sure on one point: work is not what ails the world. The world would be infinitely worse off than it is, both physically and morally, if it were not for work. One of the danger-spots of the present time is that so many men are trying to evade work as if it were a disease. There is a class of men who regard the white collar as a sign of emancipation from work. An idea like that, if true, would soon bring the white collar into disgrace.

There are too many men dickering in real estate and not enough men digging in it.

There are too many agitators, who do not work at all, telling these groups who cannot think for themselves that they are to be commiserated because they have to work.

Think of it! here in America, the one country in the world where it has always been held honorable that a man should work with his hands—in *this* country honest work is sought to be made the badge of servility!

Say what you will, the man who works with his hands has the best of it—other things being equal. And what we all want in this country is that the workingman shall have the best of it all around. This cannot be done by abolishing work, for work cannot be abolished; but it can be done by abolishing those limitations and false practices which have kept from the worker the reward which ought to be his.

Profit-sharing, additional annual bonuses, stock-sharing and dividends, a close and sympathetic interchange of counsel between the production and management parts of the business; or, to state it another way, between the strictly business and the strictly human aspects—these constitute a promising beginning. The human part must serve the business part, else there would be no great center of useful work which would provide the living of all employed there; yet the business part must also serve the human part, else the service which the business can render to human well-being would be cut in half.

The principle which must become clear to the mind of this and the coming generation is that good intentions plus well-thought-out working designs, can be put into practice and can be made to succeed.

There is nothing inherently impossible in plans to increase the well-being of the workingman.

If there has seemed to be, it is only because the world has heretofore thrown all of its thought and energy into selfish schemes for personal profits.

If the world will give as much attention and interest and energy to the making of plans that will profit the other fellow, such plans can be established on just as practical a basis as the others were—with this additional advantage: the latter kind of plan will last longer than the other kind, and will be far more profitable both in human and financial values.

What this generation needs is a deep faith, a profound conviction in the practicability of righteousness, justice and humanity in industry.

If we cannot have these qualities, then we were better off without industry. Indeed, if we cannot get those qualities, the days of industry are numbered. But we can get them. We are getting them.

There will come men whose highest joy will be to diffuse benefits instead of accumulating heaps of personal profits which they will never use. There will come a race of men to whom money will mean only the opportunity to develop still bigger benefits for the men and their families who carry the world on their shoulders.

If selfishness can only be curbed, if the long-range values can only be shown in their desirable lights, if men who are in authority could only see the wisdom of exchanging the low gratifications of mere gain for the finer gratifications of human service—why, then there would be no end to what might be done.

The Good is the only practicable. Anything less than that is not only impracticable in any sense whatsoever, but it is vanishing too.

Party Politics

THE open season for politics is upon us. The voice of the candidate is heard in the land. "Keynotes," which are strangely out of key with the thought and needs of the people, are being piped in various quarters. And the offices of authority and influence, which are soon to be opened for a confirmation or a change of policy, have not the smallest opportunity to go seeking for men to fill them, they are always besieged beforehand by men of all degrees of fitness and unfitness; so that the attaining of an office has come to be a more thrilling political motive than the filling of it.

There is nothing to say against politics as such, but only against its governing motives when these are wrong. The only motive that can keep politics pure is the motive of doing good for one's country and its people.

Originally, politics belonged to the citizens of the state. They inaugurated the issues and they proposed the policies that should be applied. Politics was simply the application of the community mind to the community problem. As such, politics may have been unwise sometimes, but not unclean. A community may not always know what is best to do for itself, but whatever it does is done with good intention. It is contrary to experience to say that the people are the depository of political wisdom; political wisdom exists in small quantities at any time; but it is absolutely true, and it is our duty always to insist upon it, that the people are the depository of political power. Wherever political power is permitted the people in its fullness, there is likely to be fewer errors; and when errors are made there is likely to be a readier and more pliant reversal of them, than where the people are permitted only partial power.

But politics in our day is not so much a popular matter as a professional matter. Instead of being

261

always the exact effect of the whole community's thought upon public questions, it is often only the community choice between two limited programs prepared by professional partisans who themselves have personal aspirations to serve or whose welfare is linked up with the personal aspirations of others.

There was a time when parties represented very accurately the divisions of public conviction upon public questions. It is questionable if they do so now, to as great an extent. In any event, there is a less rigid adherence to party on the part of the people; there is an easy passage back and forth as one party or another seems to represent the popular mind.

This of itself indicates that professional partisanship and not popular influence constitutes the mechanism of politics. Parties come more and more to mean ·the men who are in charge of the partisan machinery, the political corporation, so to speak, of this name or that. They constitute a hierarchy which exists within itself, with very slender sanction from below.

This upper and inner circle is a sort of unofficial supreme court. It passes on issues and policies and candidates. Its purpose is to "sell" itself to a majority of the voting public by setting forth the most attractive candidate or the most alluring promises. When the "party" goes into power, it is really a very few men who go into power. The party is the support this inner circle was able to win at the polls.

It is very easy to see that this view is correct if you will consider how many times and for how long a time the people have had to knock at the door of party councils to induce the "leaders" to consider some issue and some reform which the people deemed pressingly necessary. We have had some experiences along that line that make very curious spectacles indeed.

Imagine a party, supposed to be the channel and outlet of the people's thought, having power enough in its upper councils to refuse to consider the people's thought and insist upon determining within what limits the people shall think and vote. Politics as a partisan profession has always been the barrier and enemy of politics as the natural upflow of the popular mind on public questions. It has frequently occurred that

262

by an apparent agreement between the leaders of both parties, the people who adhere to the parties were narrowly limited as to the matters they could vote upon. Whereas politics in its real sense makes for the fullest expression, in its partisan sense it has been the strong instrument of suppression. The "slate" has been a boundary which the people have been forbidden to pass.

It is apparent, however, that a change is beginning to come. Not that the partisan and professional politician has changed his spots—which even an optimist could not expect—but an alarming aloofness from partisan political authority is being exhibited by the people.

The people plainly have the "leaders" guessing. The "leaders" were never more a close corporation than they now are, but they can no longer count the people as one of their safe assets. The people have developed something more than independence of mind, it even approaches contempt for a class of self-styled leaders.

The people have apparently left the "organization" high and dry, and politics in the ordinary sense fails to get the rise out of them that it used to get.

And yet, anyone who would believe, as a result of this condition, that the people are simply indifferent and will leave the whole question to the party corporations, does not know the American people. They are not indifferent. They are not going to surrender their citizens' rights to anyone. They are going to exercise them, but just how, upon what issue, or for what candidate, has not yet appeared.

The people are interested in wider views than the politicians are ready to entertain.

As a result of our political system, the people have had a very costly experience in recent years. The war gave them a new education in national and international affairs. They are thinking in broader terms than ever before. They are not thinking in terms of one state, or one party, or one nation. They know now that all humanity is interrelated. They know that any prosperity we buy at the cost of adversity to another people is sure to react upon us. They know that we cannot build our little paradise here or any-where else, and remain regardless of the world around. The internationalism of humanity, of liberty, of economic balance, of supply and demand, of service and reward, have all been very plainly observed by our people. And there is no indication that the leaders of the partisan councils have been nearly so observant, or that their education has been broadened by the events through which the world has passed.

It is too late now to talk of nationalism or inter-nationalism. That question was settled when we entered the war.

Something bigger than a "party ticket" is asked by the people this year. Something that carries more assurance than the "party platform" of other years.

"Getting power" or "keeping power" have nothing to do with the vital and fundamental needs of the nation at this time, both in its internal affairs and its international relations. We want a program, American and humanitarian, which the American and humanitarian elements of all parties would be bound to support and put through. Such a program would leave little room for partisan fights, but it would clear the stage for the next step of progress which already has been far too long delayed, and enable us to proceed with the work of reconstruction.

Honest and Dishonest Propaganda

WE HAVE seen a great deal of propaganda during the last five years and have had ample opportunity to appraise its wisdom, sincerity and effective-
ness. The fact that it still continues to be used for
one purpose or another, with an assurance that the
human mind can be wheeled into position and marched
this way or that as the propagandist desires, is beginning to get on the nerves of the people; they are
reaching out beyond the propaganda for the facts, just
as in a lawsuit the jury reaches out beyond the con-
tentions of the lawyers to get at the knowledge which
the witnesses may have.

Like the great financial "drives," this new business of propaganda has become so very obtrusive that
it is compelling a rather critical scrutiny. There was
a time when all you had to do was to start a "drive,"
threaten the non-contributors with an unpopular
stigma, and millions rolled in. But even the "drives"
are falling down. And the simple reason is that you
cannot "drive" people to think any more than you
can "drive" them to give.

Legitimate propaganda during the war period is
very simply described. The nation was agreed that,
being rightly in the war and on the right side, it had
to win. It did not have to be urged to a desire to win.
The desire was there. Propaganda did not create it;
propaganda did not increase it. All that propaganda
did was to tell the people how they could help to win.
It was a distribution of information, not a storm of
argument; it was knowledge and education, not mere
exhortation.

And that is the mark of legitimate propaganda at
all times—the facts. A fact is like granite—it stays.
Winter will not freeze it, summer will not melt it,
rains will not wash it away. Men may neglect it for
a long time. They may stumble over it and curse it

265

many times. But after a while they begin to build
with it. The man with a fact need not worry about
the indifference of the multitudes; let him tie up to
his fact. In due time it will find its place. But he
must be careful that it is a Fact, and not merely a
notion of something he thinks could be made a fact
if he could get enough people to agree with him.
Agreement doesn't make facts. But facts make agreement. People who don't agree with facts get bumped
by them. But it is not your place to do the bumping—
the fact takes care of that.

What kills propaganda is the obvious purpose behind it. One little admixture of self-interest and
your effort is wasted. You cannot preach patriotism
to men for the purpose of getting them to stand still
while you rob them—and get away with that kind of
preaching very long.

You cannot preach the duty of working hard and
producing plentifully, and make that a screen for an
additional profit to yourself.

There has been too much of this kind of psychological crime committed in the world these past few
years—the crime of bringing men to act from the
highest and sincerest motives of self-sacrifice, and
then using that high spirit for the lowest purposes.

We are going to pay the price of that sort of
trifling, for there is nothing that heals so slowly and
hurts so long as wounded faith.

Just now the country is being flooded with propa
ganda designed to improve the state of mind in which
the people find themselves with regard to industrial
and economic questions. This new propaganda contains much truth, a great many things which the people
need to know, and knowing which they would be
saved from some very grave errors of thought and
action.

But for the most part it is propaganda from a class
to a class, and it has a design behind it which arouses
suspicion.

The workingman is not going to take his views of
duty from a man or a class whose privileges or profits
depend on the workingman taking that point of view.

Employers or capitalists or close corporations of

international speculators who think they can mobilize the mind of the common people and issue orders to it, or who think they can hire a few writers and speakers and solve the whole troublesome situation with nicely selected words and phrases, are either very ignorant of human nature or are unbalanced by an exaggerated sense of their own importance and wisdom.

The plain people have stood in line a long time and have been lectured and ordered about. As long as they were persuaded that it was for the good of their country to be thus regimented, they agreed to it. But the wastes and shameless profiteering which accompanied the war have brought them a disgusting sense that in sacrifice as in other things there may be class lines too; one mass may do all the sacrificing, while one class reaps all the gains.

Propaganda issuing from a recognized class whose interests are all bound up in the preservation of the old order of things, is not only a waste of effort, it is a positive irritant to the people to whom it is addressed. They resent it, and there is hot blood in their resentment.

Undoubtedly the employing class possess facts which their employes ought to know in order to construct sound opinions and pass fair judgments; and undoubtedly the employed class possess facts which are equally important to the case and which everyone ought to know.

It is extremely doubtful, however, that either side has all the facts.

And this is where propaganda, even if it were possible for it to be entirely successful, is defective. It is not desirable that one set of ideas be "put over" on a class holding another set of ideas, but that out of both sets of ideas the true, constructive and harmonizing truth may be brought forth.

If you are going to rely on ideas, that is the way you must get them.

But there is something better, more immediately effective than the propaganda of ideas just now, and that is the Act that illustrates the Idea.

The best propaganda an employer can use is to

do right now for his own men what he knows he can and ought to do. We have been waiting too much for "social changes." We might make a start with shop changes. We have been talking too much about the "conflict of the classes." We might make a start toward abolishing classes in our own sphere of influence.

The best propaganda you can ever have is the reputation of being square, humane and thoughtful of others all the time. There are some things you can never *tell* men, nor *persuade* them of by speech or literature. But if the things are there, the men will *know* it—you may be sure of that.

There is a great fever and flutter in certain high financial circles, and much speaking and discussion, about getting in closer touch with the men, introducing the human element, and so on.

It is all very good. But you will have to take it out of speeches and committees—you will have to get it into your own heart first. You have got to *do* something that no one but yourself can do. That is, what you do must be *personal* and it must *cost* you something. It is too late in the day for mere "jollying" and "gladhanding." Men are ready to meet you half way, but it must be something more than a sentiment they meet; it must be the real thing; actual, manifest, worthy.

Society isn't something thrust down upon us by some law; we make it ourselves. Social conditions are not made for us from outside, like the weather; we make them ourselves; they are the net result of the daily relations between man and man. We give them high-sounding names, but this is all they really are.

Every shop can become a center of a new social order simply through the introduction of a new social spirit—a new social spirit evidenced by some *act* which *costs* the management something and which benefits all. That is the only way you can prove your good intentions and win respect for your attitude. Propaganda, bulletins, lectures, everything that can be hired done or made by machine fades into insignificance beside the persuading, compelling power of a right act sincerely done.

Grow Along With the Business

W E WHO have found our place in life and have become matured, are sometimes inclined to forget that the young men who are coming after us are troubled by the same urge and the same questions which troubled us. Every young man who is sensitive and intelligent enough to realize that the life before him must be *made* is almost certain to pass through a period of painful searching before he finds the place which he feels will give him *his* opportunity. He knows he must work, but where? at what? He knows there is a place for him somewhere, but how can he find it?

We are likely to forget this pain of youth. We are likely to forget how earnestly we sought counsel of older folks, and how inadequate and unconvincing the counsel was when we got it. And yet young men, in spite of all their apparent difference from what we were when we were young, are really treading the same paths. The world of affairs has changed a great deal, but man has not.

It is not the intention of this article to give any of the ordinary advice to young men. There are certain things which were true a thousand years ago and will be true a thousand years hence if civilization endures that long, and which everyone knows—knows, that is, as far as *being aware* can constitute knowledge; but there is a knowledge by experience which drives the outer knowledge home and clinches it like a nail. And this experience cannot be provided for another or substituted. The best we can do in that matter is to prevent as far as possible the needless and bitter experiences which come from folly.

But perhaps it would serve a useful purpose if we answered the young man's question as to whether the new industrial conditions of the world have had an effect on his chances to achieve success in a special way; that is, whether the intensive organization of our life has not operated to close up some of the former avenues of advancement.

There is no use whatever in dealing with stale platitudes in such a matter or in giving the young man a general counsel. Certain matters must be admitted at once. There has been a change, but in what does it consist?

It is true, that more young men than ever before make their start in places prepared for them. To the young man with no influence, this looks like a disadvantage at the very outset. But he is exaggerating its importance. For one thing, those boys who drop into nice specially prepared places do not always make good; indeed, a very small percentage of them do. No man of affairs ever had enough sons or relatives to run his business. The men who are in the important places of American business concerns are not the men who began in soft berths; they are the men who showed themselves more capable than those who were born or lifted into those berths.

It may also be admitted that the young man who enters industry today enters a very different system from that in which the young man of 15 or 25 years ago began his career. The system has been tightened up, there is less "play" or friction in it; fewer matters are left to the haphazard will of the individual; the modern worker finds himself part of an organization which *apparently* leaves him little initiative.

Yet, with all this, it is not true that "men are mere machines." It is not true that opportunity has been lost in organization. If the young man will liberate himself from his false ideas of this matter and regard the system for what it is, rather than for what it is not, he will find that what he thought was a barrier is really an aid.

Factory organization is not a device to prevent the expansion of ability, but a device to reduce the waste and losses due to mediocrity. It is not a device to hinder the ambitious, clear-headed man from doing his best, but a device to prevent the don't-care sort of individual from doing his worst. That is to say, when laziness, carelessness, slothfulness and lack-interest are allowed to have their own way, everybody

270

suffers. The factory cannot prosper and therefore cannot pay living wages. When an organization makes it necessary for the don't-care class to do better than they naturally would, it is for their benefit—they are better mentally, physically and financially. Ask yourself how much wages we should be able to pay if we trusted a large don't-care class to their own methods and gait of production. Now, the young man ought to get that idea very firmly in his mind, and he ought to look at the entire question seriously and observe the system itself intelligently to see if this is not just the way it works.

On the other hand, if the factory system which brought mediocrity up to a higher standard, operated also to keep ability down to a lower standard—it would be a very bad system, a very bad system indeed. Even a system, be it ever so perfect, must have able individuals to operate it. No system operates itself.

More brains are needed today than ever before, but perhaps they are not needed in the same place as they once were. It is just like power; formerly every machine was run by foot power; the power was right at the machine. But nowadays we have moved the power back, concentrated it in the power-house; it is no longer necessary to generate it by muscular power at the machine. Thus also we have made it unnecessary for the highest types of mental ability to be engaged in every operation at the factory, and by doing this we have enabled men of very ordinary mental equipment to profit by the plans of men of larger mental ability, and the consequence is that everybody is producing more and enjoying more than ever before.

Everyone who knows anything and "knows that he knows"—this last is very important—begins at the beginning; that is to say, he begins wherever he is fit to begin. Where are you fit to begin? "Well," says a young fellow, "I suppose I would have to begin at the bottom." Good! It is the best place to begin and the easiest place to get away from.

But, remember this, you are not there to stay unless you ought to. It is really your duty to progress in order to make room for the man behind you.

But you must not think that the factory exists for

271

the express purpose of promoting you. As long as you are there, your business is to promote the business of the factory. Then, as it advances, you go with it. Every business that is growing is creating new places for capable men. It cannot help but do so. A settled business that is just holding its own, where someone must die or resign before there can be advancements, is necessarily slow in promotions. But growing businesses are not.

This does not mean that new openings come every day and in groups. Not at all. Ambitious young fellows often wish that chances would occur at a rate which would be simply ruinous. But it is the fellow who can stand the gaff of routine for a long time and still keep himself alive and alert in it, that will be remembered and chosen. It is not sensational brilliance we seek in our business, but sound substantial dependability day after day. Not skyrockets, but men whose sounder qualities can be depended upon.

More young men lose out through impatience than any other cause. Big enterprises of necessity move slowly and cautiously. When you become impatient, you had better lay it away for a year or two. At about the same time that you saw a certain thing ought to be done, and were irritated because it was not done, your superiors saw it too, and began to readjust affairs so that it could be done. That takes time. Don't lose your own chances by jumping out just when your advancement might have been absolutely secured by patient industry. Industry is just doing the same thing time after time with an effort to do it better. The young man with an ambition for his own future ought to take a long look ahead and leave an ample margin of time for things to happen.

Revolutions Not Promoters
of Progress

THE Root problem, after all, is human nature. But to say that is to lay oneself open to the charge of platitude. There is an almost instinctive human dislike of any reminder that it is humanity, and not something outside of humanity, that is responsible for conditions. Even our wise men would rather talk learnedly about the effects of faulty human nature, as we view those effects in society, than about faulty human nature itself. However, there is a very good object to be secured in compelling people to think deeply enough at times to penetrate as far as themselves, as far as their own secret natures, and as far as their individual responsibility for conditions.

We don't want to standardize human nature—we could not if we would. It is the endless variety of individuality that makes society endurable. But what all of us would like to do would be to standardize human moral dependability. We should like to be sure that to a certain essential degree we could absolutely depend on human nature "staying put." We are not sure of that now. We are not sure that we ever shall be sure of it.

We can depend on the ability of certain elements which affect human nature. Man's need of food, sleep, clothing and family life will influence him to a considerable degree; but even in spite of these he will still remain an unknown moral quantity.

When you form blocks of granite into the shape of a house, you are pretty sure that the granite is going to stay. But when you form men into an orderly society, you are not at all sure how long that form of society is going to stay. Unlike material of the house, the material of society changes under your hands. There is no forecasting whether it will turn into adamant or sponge. It is now solid, now fluid, now hot, now cold, now orderly, now exulting in vast

273

Whatever may be the conditions in which we find ourselves at present, this is absolutely true of them; they were caused by people; they are being continued by people; they will change when people change, and not before. We cannot control the weather, nor every plague, but we can control—rather, we could control if we would—our social weather, with its storms, its uncertainty, its destructiveness and its unequal seasons.

One of the strange phenomena of the present is the ascendancy of the destructive type of mind.

The world at large seems to be infatuated with the idea that if something is pulled down, something is thereby built up; if something is destroyed, something is thereby created.

There is in every country a party which believes that if it could destroy the orderly institutions of that country, it would thereby create a new era of social justice.

Every community has a group which believes that if only the channels of orderly justice and decency could be smashed, a new brotherhood of man would rise automatically out of the ruin.

Would-be philosophers preach the doctrine of the necessity of revolution; never was any progress made, they say, except through violent revolutions. But everybody knows that every revolution was a mistake and disgraced or postponed the liberties it sought. The most revolutionary thing in the world is an idea, and a conquering idea does not need to imprison, punish or kill a man to make itself powerful.

In the name of Order, disorder is counselled; in the name of Liberty, the dictatorship of a few idle and non-productive agitators is urged; in the name of Brotherhood, profound and venomous hatred between the classes is fomented. Surely, human nature is the sum of all contradictions!

What every thoughtful man should fear about a possible revolution is not its occurrence, but the course it would take after it was started.

The difficulty about revolutions is the impossibility of controlling them—an impossibility shared even by the men who start revolutions. They get out of hand.

274

They rage like forest-fires. Very often they destroy even those who instigated them.

Revolutions are not orderly, social forces marching to the establishment of a new and better order. They are an outlet of hellish hatreds and unbridled passions, massive thefts, the death of moral and social responsibility, a most horrible debauch of all that is rottenest in human nature.

Humanity does not know of what stuff it is made until the restraint of society is taken off, and the mask is taken off, and human greeds and jealousies and ignorances and passions are given full sway.

The revolutions of which we may read comfortably in the books are not at all the revolutions the people went through. The real thing is the collapse of every element that justifies mankind considering itself as a high animal.

However, it is not alone to the disgruntled man that we must look for these destructionist influences. We are far too prone to talk as if the "Reds" were the only ones engaged in destroying social order and the solidity of social institutions.

Not at all. Any man, rich or poor, in business or in politics, who does anything that undermines men's faith in the essential justice at least of society's intentions, is thereby destroying society as rapidly, as menacingly, as criminally as any "Red" could do it.

What you find at one extreme of society, that you will find at the other. Rich criminals make poor criminals. Lawless millionaires make lawless miners. Lawless statesmen make lawless citizens. It works out inevitably this way.

If you have profiteers in the big brownstone buildings, you will have hold-up men in the streets.

If you have a "to hell with the People" spirit in your higher offices, you are going to have a "to hell with the Government" spirit in the lower sections of your cities—and don't you forget it! What's sauce for the capitalistic gander is sauce for the laboristic

It is not too much to say that the whole impetus of this present plague of lawlessness came from the top. Its whole reason for being comes from what we so wrongly call the "upper classes." These more

275

favored classes were lawless first. And their lawlessness is coming back upon them with redoubled retribution, for the very fact that it is they who are now pleading for law and order is the reason why the plea is laughed at. Yes, law that the people may be kept in order, but no order so strict as that the privileged ones shall have to obey the law!—that is the mocking answer.

When they are trying the criminals of the Great War, they ought not to overlook the profiteers.

The profiteer is the most dangerous of all the "Reds" that have ever appeared on earth. He is more dangerous than kings—for we can get rid of kings. He is even more dangerous than militarists—militarists turn out to be very fallible men when their helmets and gold braid are removed. But the profiteer is always there, playing inside all the lines, making money out of soldiers' deaths and the distress of nations— the dirtiest money that ever found its way into a

The profiteer ought to be charged specifically with (a) defrauding the Government, (b) treason to the Army, (c) giving aid and comfort to the enemy, and (d) fomenting disloyalty in time of war.

It is pretty hard to gainsay the now common argument that a society which harbors the profiteer is itself in need of reform.

The profiteer is one of the excuses—one of the good excuses—which the "Reds" offer for their present attitude. And if the "Reds" would only center their attention there and help us get rid of the profiteers, that would be doing a regenerative and constructive act.

The crimes of the profiteer after the war, the increase of his already too big gains by speculating with the food of the people, certainly point him out as the one influence which more than any other has driven people into enmity toward our present form of society. This is where the destructive spirit was born.

Why would it not be a wise move to attack the destructive spirit at its source? Why not go after those men whose actions destroy the people's faith in the possibility of justice? They ought to be made to pay the penalty, and not society.

The Obstructionist

THE destructionist groups, which have been making so much noise of recent months and causing
the government so much difficulty in dealing with
them, represent a type of individual which we always
have with us. If they are apparently very noisy now
about destroying the more settled and time-proved
institutions, it is only because these institutions happen to be to the fore. When the subject was something else, the attitude was the same.

That is to say, the man whose only remedy for
governmental flaws is to destroy the government, is
the same type of man who goes to breaking dishes on
the floor in a fit of anger. He would rather smash
his pipe than clean it; he would rather strike his son
than counsel him; he would rather damn his opponent
than understand him.

Whenever men of this type are placed up against
any problem which needs intelligence and patience for
its solution, they react at once to their temperamental
cure-all, destruction. They are the kind of men who
rip a collar to pieces because a buttonhole will not
readily open. In a world of their own these men
would not be bothersome, for in a world controlled
by them there would be nothing to destroy. The very
lack of the product of other men's constructive patience
would force them to grub for the means to live; it
would leave them no time for their peculiar disorder
to assert itself. There is mighty little of the destructive element in a state of society which strains
everybody's energies to make both ends meet.

Destructive temperaments are largely the product
of a condition of plenty and leisure. "Men kick when
they wax fat." Destructiveness is a pest which can
live only in cultivated fields. Let it destroy that on
which it lives, and the destructiveness dies too, like a
mania which has sated itself.

The world is large and there is much merit in a

recent suggestion that a fertile island under control of the United States should be set aside for those who apparently abhor government, an island where, without duress or hindrance but with unlimited encouragement, they could work out their own theories to logical conclusions and see with their own eyes the end thereof.

However, it is not the destructionists that society needs to fear today, but another and larger class which we may call The Obstructionists. The absolute destructionists are few and futile. They never really destroy except in the physical sense, they never really change anything; at best they are but the tools of those whose principles are constructive.

But the Obstructionists are many and influential. The friends of destruction form the red-hot center, but there is an outer rim of people who escape the fire but remain within range of the heat—a more numerous group than the others, but very harmful.

One of the differences between the two is this: the destructionist is always conscious of his position and purpose, but a man may be an obstructionist without knowing it. It may show itself in him not so much a temper as a bad habit.

If we could assemble the wastes, the leaks, the costly hindrances against which the world must make headway every day, the sum of them would stagger us. They are all the result of intentional or thoughtless obstructionism.

Take the coal situation: everybody connected with it in any way whatsoever has come in for his criticism, and yet there is an element we never hear about that affects every coal user. The little thieves that rake the coal cars at every stop—how much do they add to the price of coal?

Very considerably. A car is shipped containing so many tons. It arrives containing a less weight. Shortage claims are made and the railroads have to make up the difference. These shortages amount to very large sums of money. Who pays it? Ultimately the coal user. The railroad, to protect itself against the shortages caused by thievery, adds the cost to the price of carrying the coal. The man who uses the coal pays for the average amount of coal the thief takes, in order that he may get the amount of coal he ordered. Probably never a single coal thief ever dreamed that he was an element in the situation at all, but he is. He is an obstructionist.

Little dishonesties, multiplied by twenty-five or thirty million citizens, are a far costlier drain on the country than the large dishonesties of a few powerful rich men. Yet it is more convenient to blame the prominent few than the obscure multitudes.

In fact it is a fetish with the people that everyone may be wrong but them. And it is one of the signs of a true leader of the people that he dares rebuke them, that he does not praise them as all-wise and perfect.

Obstructionism is the real trouble of the country today. The attitude of a large portion of our people seems to be to sag back in the breeching. The only use of a breeching is to hold the wagon back! When the breeching is most in use, the wagon is going down hill! Let this be a word to the wise.

The yard-master down at the freight yards is also a very important factor. If he is still playing the old game of waiting for a bribe before he will move urgently needed cars in or out, he is an obstructionist. One day's delay on a car may mean the loss of 10,000 days of work. A day's delay on material may mean the loss of an important contract. No one can compute the loss which has been forced on the people of the country by incompetency or unwillingness among men who are responsible for the movement of material and cars throughout the land.

But it is the same wherever obstructionism prevails. Even an office boy may have his part in slowing up the business day, or snarling it at some important point. The stenographer may unconsciously disarrange a whole series of transactions. The janitor responsible for the lighting or heating of an office or factory may help the organization press forward into the collar, or assist it to sag back in the breeching.

Someone may say, "Why talk of breeching in a day of gears? Only farmers and horsemen will understand what you mean by breeching."

279

Well, this is the reason: life, after all, is run by man-power. You may dispense with horse-power both in man and beast—for the ordinary use of human energy for purposes that might as well be answered by machinery, is just taking your horse-power out of men's bodies, that is all.

Man-power, not muscular power, but man-power, is still the staple of all achievement.

Men harness themselves to a task. The power they put forth in it is their interest, their efficiency, their hope. When these are present in full force, men press forward into the collar; when these are lacking, men sag back into the breeching, for our jobs are only the harnesses we have put on in order to accomplish something. If we sag back on the job, we hold back the load, we don't deliver the goods.

We have machinery to take the place of man's muscles; we have no machinery to take the place of his willingness and interest. Man is like a pulse, he beats strong and full, or slow and weak, but it is the pulse that determines all matters at last. There is no substitute for men, there is no substitute for human co-operation and industry and willingness to put things through.

We suffer for lack of that man-power which it is peculiarly the gift of man to put forth—the power of self-motivation, the power of going at it and sticking to it and getting it done. Too many of us have become wheelbarrows which must be trundled along. We need to become self-starters, and so move obstructions out of the way, instead of becoming an obstruction ourselves.

Would the Farmers Strike?

PERHAPS you overlooked it in the day's news, because the most important occurrences are not always deemed worthy of emphasis in the newspapers. But the fact that the farmers of the United States have considered the "strike" as a method of solving their own difficulties, and have arrived at the conclusion that they have no moral right to strike, is one of the most significant decisions made in this generation. And the conclusions which the farmers draw from their own attitude and belief are of very great importance to the labor question in general. Everybody at one time or another has asked himself the question, "Suppose the farmers should strike—what then?" Serious men have been appalled by the mere suggestion.

But wiseacres, who apparently do not know what is going on, have put it aside as impossible. "Why, the farmers are not organized," they say. Which shows how little they are informed.

It was at a national meeting of the organized farmers of the United States—The National Grange, the Patrons of Husbandry, the American Farm Bureau Federation, the Cotton States Board and the Association of Farmers' Union Presidents—whose aggregate membership covers the country and whose influence is unimpeachable, that the decision referred to was made. If the farmers had so far forgotten their relation and duty to humanity at large as to put their private or class rights above the Public Right, it would not be impossible for them to start a curtailing movement that would make the wiseacres turn pale.

This national meeting adopted a memorial from which we quote one paragraph:

"What would be the verdict of the people if the farmers of the United States should go on a strike and should refuse to supply the wants and needs of those who are not in a position to produce food and

281

clothing for themselves? The farmers would be con-
demned from one end of the country to the other, and
the fact would be pointed out that the owners and
tillers of the land had no right, either moral or legal,
to bring about such a calamity. If the farmer has no
such right, those who handle his products have no such
right."

That is basically sound—both in economics and
morals. It is especially notable because in the last
sentence it links all industry with farming, and this
is a point that we often forget.

We are accustomed to say that the farmer produces our food. That is a partial statement. He
produces our clothing too. Where do the wool and
the cotton and the leather and the flax come from?
Why, they come from the farm!

Farming produces railroading too. Would 'there
be any railroads without farming? The farmer feeds
the trainmen, and the moving of crops is the basic
reason for the railroads' existence. Farming produces manufacturing too. It may be the coal beneath
the boilers that keeps the factory wheels turning, but it
is the farmer's products that keep the workers going.
Food is the fuel of human effort.

Now, whenever railroad men, or mechanics, or
miners go out on strike, they go out on the food which
the farmer furnishes. The farmer is the commissary
of everything, good and bad. And he has a right to
his word when the very products of his toil are used
to create conditions which make it harder for all the
people to live.

The three great arts are linked together—Agriculture, Transportation, Manufacture. They all serve
each other. But the origin and sustenance of all is
Agriculture.

The farmer feels this more keenly than anyone
else, because he still lives amid conditions that make
for sanity of mind. He lives under the sky, he deals
with the soil, he knows the flawless and beautiful order
of nature's laws; and he sees also that the anarchy
of human society is not constructive but steadily destructive.

Yes, he could strike too. The farmer could strike

hardest of all. Why doesn't he? Because he feels deep and sacredly in the core of his heart that when mere man grows so impudent as to attempt to hold up the God-given processes of nature, it would constitute the last rebellion of mankind on the physical plane. Whether he would say it in just those words or not, this is what the farmer feels. If he struck he would be a traitor to Nature. The shining sun, the falling shower would rebuke him. Seedtime without seed would denounce him, and harvest-time without harvest would curse him.

No, the farmer is not going to trifle with the Powers that are above and around him. He is Priest of the Soil. He would not profane his earthly altar. America should be thankful for the strength of the moral imperative among American farmers! Now, the question is, "Has any other man who handles the fruits of the soil the right to do what the farmer has no right to do?"

Has the miner the right to refuse coal that the wheat may be baked into bread? Has the spinner a right to refuse labor that the cotton and wool may be spun into clothing? Has the railroad man a right to refuse his skill that food and clothing and the means of living might be transported to those who need them? Clearly, if the farmer has no right to withhold, the others have not.

To say these things is to challenge many popular fallacies. Our economic past has been so filled with greed and selfishness and absolute wrongdoing that it is difficult for some to believe that to deny the right to strike is not also to deny the right to high wages, proper working hours and conditions.

Let it be said right here that labor has a right to high wages, a right to proper hours, a right to proper conditions, a right to a share in the profits, a right to a voice in the conduct of industry. These are moral rights; they are inherent. Whether they are acknowledged or not, whether they are granted or not, they still remain rights, because they are fundamentally human rights—they are just, they are good, they are humane, they are practicable, they produce social good and prosperity.

But that these rights entitle anyone—to quote again from the Farmers' memorial—"to starve the people of the cities," in order to force, by the suffering of the innocent, a proper respect for rights on the part of the employing class, is drawing an unwarrantable conclusion.

"How are we going to get our rights without striking?" Here again we run up against one of the snags of our industrial system. If an employer won't do right, how is he to be made to do right?

Well, how would it do to educate the employer to a knowledge of how he could do the right thing and make it pay? And the men can do that, if the employer is not bright enough to see it for himself. (An employer who cannot see these things for himself is not fit to direct his workmen.) Men have been dividing themselves off into classes for the sake of hindering and hurting each other, when they should have endeavored to draw themselves nearer together for the sake of educating each other in different points of view. The employer knows things that the employe doesn't know, and the employe knows things that the employer doesn't know—and all about the same economic conditions too. The sensible, direct way would be, not to begin to try to starve each other out because they don't know the same things, but to come together and share their light, and all get the broader point of view, and go on together in partnership of production and profits.

A strike is war. War is unnecessary. War is an irrecoverable loss to both winner and loser. Let us delay both war and strikes and use the simpler and more effective means of meeting man to man, face to face, as fellow-laborers who desire to find the right basis. For it is only the right basis that can continue. Anything that is not right, whether it temporarily favors the employes or the employers, cannot last—because it is not right.

And anything that is not consistent with our duty to ourselves, our work and the community, is not right.

Who Is Their Boss?

THERE has been an interesting evolution in the questions which the people have put to office-seekers. Years ago we asked candidates what they were seeking office for. This was the consequence of a period of school instruction by which the American boy was taught to admire the fame and glory of public office. Merely to achieve an office and a title was considered to be "success," and naturally men did not scruple as to the methods by which the success was achieved. Their principal occupation after election was to repay at public expense the political trainers who groomed them for the race and counted them in. In the general disgust which has followed this seeking of office for glory's sake, the people are beginning to ask candidates for *what* they were working. The people exalted the standard of Fame Through Service rather than fame through office.

There is now, however, a new question. It doesn't go directly or exclusively to the *motives* a candidate might think he has, but to the *masters* he has. The question to ask of candidates today is not only, "Why do you want this office? What do you think your motives are in seeking it?" but rather, "Who specially wants you to have it? Who is your master? For whom are you working?" The basis of the new question is this: Power goes with office, regardless of the strength or weakness of the incumbent. There are concealed interests whose whole existence depends on such a hold of the higher offices. Indeed, it is the higher offices of our government that are most necessary to the continuance of certain interests and privileges. It is therefore of vital importance to them that they retain their control, and there is no surer way of doing this than by guarding all the approaches to our highest offices so that only a certain kind of men are permitted to arrive there.

The question, "For whom are you working?" is

therefore a most important one for every electorate to ask and every candidate to consider.

But here is the amazing thing—some candidates don't know who it is they are working for! They fancy they are working for themselves. They sometimes believe they are working for the people. But they do not always know who their real masters are. There are lawyers in America who do not know who their ultimate clients are: they know the person with whom they do business, they do not know in whose ultimate interest the business is done.

Likewise there are financial institutions in America and elsewhere which apparently are independent concerns, managed by and in the interests of the men whose names appear as officers and directors. But sometimes even these men do not know *whose* game they are playing. They are but the "fronts" of interests which are never known to the public, and which keep their identity concealed that they may the better play interest against interest.

Strange as it may seem, not every man knows for whom he is working. There are highly placed men in these United States who would get the surprise of their lives if they followed back the clues which would lead them to their real masters.

When a man is in honest business he wants his name to appear at the front of the business. The young man opens a shop or a store and he is proud to have his name in front. He puts out a useful and honestly made product and he is proud to have his name known in connection with it. But the biggest business interests in the world, those who play back and forth with the riches and the destiny of nations, never want their names to be known, nor their organization, nor their power. They break themselves up into numerous corporations in each of which only a trusted agent will appear, while the remainder of the men will apparently be the real masters of the business, and sometimes actually think they are.

That is why it is said that not every man knows who his master is. And it behooves every man to find out; especially those men who commit their lives to the searching test of public service.

This concealed international control of the world flourishes because people do not believe it exists. They don't see how it can exist. They imagine no selfish group could hold together strongly enough to manage the world. But if they knew the special international elements involved they would readily see how possible it is. Some day a world-wide exposure will be made and many things explained which have always puzzled the plain people, and we shall see that much which we have charged up to the "mystery of life" has really been the deliberate effect of a deep-wrought, unified international but private program.

In politics the effect of this control has been to take out the local and human element. That is, candidates are no longer selected for their individual attitude with reference to public problems, but for their relationship to this invisible hierarchy.

Few states select their own senators any longer, save in very exceptional instances. The national group, taking care of its end of the international group's business, knows the kind of man it wants, chooses in each state one of the men it has kept in training, and creates the conditions under which the people elect him. It appears that senators no longer represent their states; they seem to represent "interests" which are interstate and international.

The same is true of almost every office. Representatives to the state legislature are becoming less and less district representatives, and more and more the representatives of state and national "interests" in their districts. Representatives in Congress also tend to become less than formerly the representatives of the people who voted for them, and more the representatives of the interests who groomed them and nominated them. Even governorships are going the same way.

It simply indicates that instead of Government rooting down into the people, it is heading up into an international control that picks out of the midst of the people the men who will serve it.

And some men serve it unconsciously. They do not always know the source of the business that has been thrown their way. They do not always know the

287

source of the interest which is shown in them. They do not always see the vision which others have of their future usability in office. And so they go on, fancying they are being carried on the pleasant crest of cumulative success, when really they are being picked out because their inclinations or obligations may render them useful at some time. It is a wonderful system and its ramifications have no end. Cities are networks, states are networks, nations are networks, and the whole net is drawn by interests who have no nationalistic interests whatever. They are apart from the world, living upon the world, using the world as their counting table. The whole system is founded on self-interest. Everyone allied with it gets something out of it. The little fellows get a little, the big fellows get more. Usually the little fellows get an income and a taste of public honor. The big fellows get the big public honors. It is what the public has within its gift that keeps the system going. The system never sacrifices anything for principle; it has no inspired reformers; seldom are its servants big enough to be called States; the whole system exists to curb and destroy the wisdom and foresight of true statesmen.

Who is master of all these men who want the high offices within your gift? Do you know? Do they know?

Who has chosen them? Who has groomed them? Who is supplying the means by which the bait of their personality is dangled before the public?

Is there any difference in them? Can you see in the lot of them one man who really stands out in all his records and ideas as a free man, untangled by any favors?

That is the mark of distinction. Where all candidates are equally acceptable to the concealed interests, it simply is proof that they own the field.

288

The American Shop

I F YOU ask an employer what kind of a shop he
has, he should be able to make the proud reply,
"An American Shop." If you ask an employe in
what kind of a shop he works, he too should be able
to say, "An American Shop." There are all kinds of
names for shops; there is the closed shop and the
open shop—terms which are redolent of strife and exclusion; there is the piece-work shop and the straight
wage shop; there is the shop that is booming along
all the time because of the quality of its workmanship,
management and output, and there is the shop which
hobbles along like a cripple, hardly able to live; there
is the shop where human principles rule, and the shop
where men are treated as impersonally as if they were
but raw material. But the main difference that exists
between shops is just this: either they measure up to
the American ideal, or they do not.

There are many employers who indulge in great
talk these days about "100 per cent Americanism." It
would be a good thing if they were required to ac-
company their boast by a statement of the profits they
took from the government in the recent war. It would
be found that the percentage of their profits was
equal to or in excess of the percentage of purity they
claim for their Americanism.

The flag that flies above the shop is not the only
index of Americanism a shop can have; the policy that
is practiced inside tells the story. We all reverence
Our Flag as the symbol of a great free people, but
we cannot reverence all the uses to which profiteers
have put it.

America needs the American Shop. It needs it
not only to meet the vast economic problems which
confront us in the production of an adequate quantity
of goods; but also to solve the problems which have
grown out of past injustices on the part of both leadership and labor.

289

It is pretty well conceded, even by the most slow-minded employer, that the question of production cannot be settled until the question of the producer is settled. The principal and controlling factor in all our difficulties is the human element. Indeed, all our difficulties, of whatever nature, are human difficulties: they are the signs of humanity in trouble.

What would be some of the characteristics of a true American Shop? In personnel and policy it would be representative. There is no room for national, racial or religious prejudices in an American Shop. Its purpose is industry, and that ought to open wide its doors to all the industrious. The need of men's labor, and the need of men themselves to labor, is universal. Work is the burden laid on us all and no man shirks it without doing harm to himself and the whole social body. No race is superior, no race is inferior, neither is any individual so superior or inferior as to escape the necessity of work. In the arctics and in the tropics, among civilized and barbarous peoples, the rule of "work to live" is operative, and men are found obeying it. There are no class distinctions in industry. The only nobleman an enlightened estimate can recognize is the citizen who is carrying his own end of the common burden and doing a little more in order that society may be carried along prosperously and harmoniously.

By being representative in policy is meant that the American Shop will be conducted with a view to all the rights and benefits of the men engaged there and that portion of the public which it serves. It is too sadly true that in the past most shops have been conducted with a view to the benefit of one individual, one family or one group of investors. But we have come upon a new vision in industry. We have caught sight of the power of industry to make men as well as the commodities of commerce. When we consider how much of our waking time is spent in working, it is a thousand pities if the time so spent does not contribute to the workman himself, in his moral, social and intellectual life, as well as to his physical needs. Work is sanative; it is educative; it is preservative. It produces results in the man himself as well as in

290

the material that passes under his hand. But, if it only saps the man, if it makes him less a man, if it withdraws him from a sense of belonging to and serving society, there is something wrong. An American Shop will protect the rights of all engaged in it. One of the greatest errors into which commercial greed and selfishness have led us is the acceptance of a policy that no rights are to be granted until it is absolutely impossible to withhold them any longer. This has led to a sense of industrial disturbance which has seriously affected the foundations on which we live at peace with one another. The American Shop will grant rights because they are Rights, in the sound faith that whatever is right is practicable, and if not practicable under the present system, then under a revised system which common sense and justice shall erect.

This simply means that the principles upon which we live together as a nation and out of which we have reared our great free institutions shall operate in industry also. It is the transcription of the Declaration and the Constitution into industrial terms. It is the act of making our political liberty complete by adding thereto economic liberty also.

Our nation has been slowly made, but it had a great advantage in starting right. Little by little it has modified its Constitution, not to change the spirit of it, but to enlarge its application and to render it more effective in achieving its original objects.

And in this way our industrial relations must be remade. We have certain sound foundations now. We believe that labor is what all must engage in for self-development, for social service, and to promote the evolution of humanity. We have no fatuous idea that we shall ever be free of the necessity of work. Baked bread will never grow on trees, nor will Nature ever provide us with homes and schools ready built.

If practices and attitudes have crept in which are not in harmony with the truth that we are all human beings of equal needs, then these will have to be revised and corrected. All of us are fallible. The one and only superman has not come, but we are in a super-stage of society wherein the general level of power and vision is elevated to a degree that a previous age would have considered miraculous. Therefore we are better fitted to work out our problems by ourselves, in the American Way. And what is the American Way? Why, by all of us starting out with the agreement that wisdom is not the exclusive possession of any man or party. All that we have in this country is the outcome of many points of view merged into a workable program. We have all shades of opinion in this country, each of them strongly endorsed and propagated. But the country itself merges all shades into one distinctive American whole.

The American Way is constructive. It grows out of ideas, not out of violence. It works by education, not by disintegration. Nothing permanent is accomplished by forces pulling apart, because in this country everything that is accomplished comes by various opinions pulling together toward a desired end.

There is no difference of opinion in this country as to what we desire our common life to be. All agree on the desired object. The difference comes in the methods of attaining it. But even this difference is educational. Radical and conservative interact upon each other, modify each other, until presently they come together for united achievement. That is the American Way, and the results of it stand.

The American Shop should reflect the Republic in its highest ideals. Liberty, unity and fraternity should be its bond and its method from the front office to the last man at the last machine at the end of the shop—and then out beyond to all the families which the shop serves, and to the public which is the beneficiary of its work and planning.

The Small Town

WE LIVE better in small communities than in
large ones. Individually and in small groups
we are human, but in great masses our human qualities seem overruled. Cities have no souls because
their whole tendency is toward soulless conditions.
In small communities the better qualities of our nature
have a chance; they have a much better chance of
setting the standard; but in large communities it is the
looser standards and the more heartless qualities that
set our fashions and our customs.

Every social ailment from which we suffer today
originates and centers in the great cities. But you
will find the smaller communities living along in uni-
son with the seasons, having neither extreme poverty
nor wealth, and none of the violent plagues of upheaval and unrest which afflict our great populations.
There is something about a city of a million people
which is untamed and threatening, while 30 miles away
are happy and contented villages that read of the
ravings of the city as if it were an unexplainable
phenomenon. A great city is really a helpless mass.
Everything it uses is carried to it. Stop the transport
and the city stops. It lives off the shelves of stores,
but the shelves produce nothing. The city cannot feed,
clothe, warm nor house itself; its industries are dependent on the raw materials brought to them, often
from a thousand miles.

City conditions of work and living are so artificial
that men's instincts sometimes rebel against the un-
naturalness of them. Groups of men soon learn how
to dislocate the city's life and they take a malicious
pleasure in doing it. Designing men know how to
upset a city's sense of security and thus force for
themselves concessions which the rest of the people
have to pay. The city, especially of late years, has
been at the mercy of any one of a dozen groups, all
of which in turn use their dislocating and disturbing

power to compel the other people to satisfy them. The strike of any industry is a strike against the rest of the city. If it be more than a local strike, it is a strike against the rest of the country. All strikes, in their last analysis, are against the people.

If we lived in smaller communities it is conceivable that we should still sometimes rebel against being shut up within four walls all the year round. It is a strain upon our natures to work indoors all the time. There is a part of the year which calls all free men out-of-doors, the time of the year when indeed men must go out-of-doors to labor if food is to be provided for the people.

Now, if we lived in small communities where the human touch would not be lost in the mass; if we had a good and useful manufactory set up beside the nearby stream which would supply us with water power and where we could work during the indoor months; then, when springtime came and the land called to us, we could go.

And we could go in the consciousness that we were not quitting work, nor curtailing production, nor dislocating the economic processes of society, but doing the thing most needful at the time.

The city not only produces conditions which tend to make men reckless of their duty to bear their share of the work of production, but it also makes it impossible for men to give vent to their grievance, whatever it may be, in any way except by idleness. Every protest they make by the strike method is sheer loss. Leaving out of the question the other damage it does in increasing the feeling of uncertainty and undependability, the distress it causes, and its general contribution to the prevailing condition, a strike is sheer economic loss.

If a body of men became dissatisfied with their work in the railway yards or the shop and left their jobs to go out and work in the fields for a while, there would be no economic loss. What they withdrew from transportation or manufacture they would simply contribute to agriculture. Their productive capacities would at least be employed in a useful field, and result in benefit to some one. But as it is now, the strike is

an appeal to idleness and loss as prime weapons in
coercing society. The men just stop. And as a result, a world that is already behind in everything it
needs, is thrust behind thousands and millions of days
of labor more, simply because a few men have learned
and applied their hindering power.

Industrial disturbances, we are learning, are not so
much due to wages or hours or any other tangible
condition, as to "human nature." Just plain human
nature. A workingman in a certain institution com-
plained of his job. He was carefully taken around to
other jobs, some of them less important, some of them
more important than the one which irked him. He
was given a trial on all of them. But still he chafed.
Finally he said, "Well, I guess I won't work at all for
a little while."

Now, all the industrial conferences in the world
could not make a reputation dealing with that case.
None of the usual elements of the labor problem affected that man; it was just "human nature," a sort
of schoolboy carelessness. He had been drawing good
wages and therefore felt that because he had money
in his pocket he had a right to withdraw himself from
production, even though the world was suffering for
lack of the article on which he worked.

Maybe the man was tired. Maybe he wanted a
change. If we were organized in small communities,
with the town manufacturing establishment next door
to the food-producing fields, such a man would have
had his summer work out-of-doors, and he would
have had interest and stamina enough for his indoor
manufacturing work. He would have had, in other
words, a balanced work-ration.

It is useless to say that everybody ought to go on
the farm and stay there, for if everybody did that,
farming would soon decline as a satisfactory occupation. It is just as useless for everyone to flock to the
manufacturing towns, for if the farms be deserted, of
what use are manufactures? A city cannot live on
its own manufactures.

But when a reciprocity exists between farming
and manufacture, the manufacturer giving the farmer
what he needs to be a good farmer, and the farmer

and other producers of raw materials giving the manufacturer what he needs to be a good manufacturer;
and then when Transportation comes in to act as the
messenger between Manufacture and Agriculture, we
have a system that is stable and sound because it is
built on service and employs these three principal arts.
If we lived in smaller communities where the tension
of living were not so high, and where the products
of the fields and gardens could be had without the
interference of so many profiteers, there would be
less unrest.

Many of our problems, at least the fiery edge of
many of our problems, may be analyzed down to
"nerves." But "nerves" are very real none-the-less.
Only when the condition is largely "nerves" it would
help us if we were to recognize that fact, and not
charge the condition to some other cause that is not
responsible.

There is no reason why life should be lived at such
a nervous tension. Moreover, money is not a cure
for "nerves." The cure is in a saner way of living,
under more natural conditions. Economy of production will probably always mean large groups of men
working together. But that need not preclude them
working in close proximity to the open fields where
they may be in touch with the most basic industry,
the production of food.

When we begin to use the water power of the
smaller streams and establish our workshops through
the country districts, we shall then see men working
and living under natural conditions, with an annual
opportunity for out-of-door work; we shall see the
necessity of transporting coal done away with and
manufacturing villages free of smoke; and we shall
also see men healed of their restlessness which always
causes and seldom cures their trouble.

Man's Laws and Nature's Law

WE ARE told that 60,000 laws were made in this country last year. This seems to be quite a number for one people to bear. But probably the most of them were improvements on old rules, and a considerable proportion of them were probably called into being by the new conditions that have arisen. Most of our so-called laws are only rules which we lay down to facilitate action, like the rules of the road which are based on a knowledge of the acts which most often cause trouble. By establishing such rules we promote safety and ease of progress, we give every man a very definite idea of his rights, we provide a standard by which he may know what to expect from others.

It has become quite fashionable, rather it was a few years ago, to make sport of the laws. Unequal and incomplete laws which lent themselves to the jugglery of lawyers and the evasion of the powers that prey, became the butt of popular ridicule. Sometimes, too, the action of the agencies appointed to administer the law gave rise to the opinion that there was one law for the rich and another for the poor. Or, if not that, then so many more laws into which the rich man could wriggle because he could pay for it, that finally he could tangle justice in its own web and go free.

There are three kinds of laws, and their intention is, each in its degree, to save us from the next higher one, if only we let it.

At the bottom of the ladder is *man-made law*. It is a human product. It is subject to all the fallacies and faults which inhere in human efforts. There probably never was an absolutely perfect human statute.

Still, to confess that does not indicate that human law is worthless. Human law is an attempt to crystallize the fruits of our experience into rules by which others may benefit by our experience without having to pay the price that we had to pay. Men found that certain ways of doing things wrought hardship, injustice and danger. They found that certain lines of conduct terminated in certain conditions. They found that if the community pursued a certain course with reference to social relations or material possessions, certain distressful results ensued. So, instead of running the risk of everybody upsetting the order of life while he was learning by his own mistakes, the community simply made rules in which its experience was embodied and which saved it from a continual suffering of the same kinds of disappointment and pain.

Now, if men do not heed man-made laws, if they escape the first barrier which society itself has reared across false paths, then there is another barrier—they will come in conflict with *economic law*.

Economic law is that law which is written in the nature of *things*. Not in the nature of the human soul and mind, but only in *things*. We know very little about it as yet. If we knew very much we could write our knowledge down in man-made laws and so prevent society tumbling headlong every little while over some economic law which will doubtless seem very clear and simple once we discover what it is. Many learned men have composed books on political economy, and many other learned men have composed other books on the same subject to show that the former books were wrong.

This law isn't written in books at all; if it were, we should all know it. It is written in things, and as a matter of fact the world has been too busy getting the things to pay much attention to the law of them. Fundamental in that law is the system of the earth, the seasons. Without sowing, no reaping. Wild sowing, little reaping. Without work, little product. We have compressed part of the law into a saying that "you cannot get something for nothing." That appears to be one certain rule of economic law. You might evade and befool man-made law, but economic law operates infallibly. But it isn't limitedly personal in its operation. Sometimes a few powerful men violate the law by idle and unproductive speculation, and then a great number of people who did not violate

298

it at all are made to suffer. That is where man-made
law will come in again when we know economic law:
we shall prevent by law any man doing things the
consequences of which will be adverse to people who
are innocent of wrongdoing.

If you take it more limitedly still, we may say
that a young man may disobey and positively deride
his father's advice that he ought to be industrious.
Well, he may be able to escape his father's law, but
if he isn't industrious the economic law will get him,
and it is a great deal harder to deal with.

There is still a higher law which gets all without
exception—it is *the moral law.* You *may* violate man-
made law, and no one be the wiser and, apparently,
no one the worse. You may violate economic law
and still be carried through by the momentum of society's economic soundness. But the moral law you
can never evade. *You cannot even break it!*

That may seem extremely odd, and perhaps untrue. You may say, "The moral law says, 'Thou shalt
not lie.' Very well, I here and now deliberately utter
a lie. Have I not broken that moral law which you
say cannot be broken?"

No, you have not. The law stands there in its
eternal integrity. You have not broken it, but you
have broken something in yourself against it. In conflict with the moral law all that we can break is ourselves. If we steal, we break some bulwark of self-
respect within us—inevitably break it. If we lie, we
break some tissue of integrity within us. If we deceive our fellow men, we break down the subtle something that advertises us as trustworthy to those about
us. If we are always motivated by narrow selfishness,
we ground the living current which connects us in
social sympathy with our fellows.

Every virtue we practice is a battery filling us with
power, for there is power in straightforwardness. It
gives power to the eye, the voice, and to the subtle
effluence of personal influence. And everything that
is not virtuous, but indirect, unclean and shifty, takes
power from the eye and confidence from the voice and
steadiness from the purpose; the electric substances

299

which flow from an ill-lived life advertise its low estate.

Many men have escaped man-made law, they have escaped economic law—so far, at least (nobody need be too cocksure about this, for the end of the test has not come), but no man ever lived without receiving sentence in himself upon every violation of the moral law. It gets us all, for sentence or reward. High or low, none escape. It is godlike in its impartial operation. It cannot be postponed, nor fought to a higher court, nor bribed. No one else can take the sentence for us—the law is there, and no man ever so much as shook it a hair's breadth. It has the final word, and its word is final.

Now, with these things in view, ought not our regard to increase for the purpose of man-made law? Man-made law is an attempt to prevent men going so far as to become liable to the penalties of the higher laws. Eventually the transgressor in every field will be dealt with by some law. Some transgressions are so great that they are dealt with by all three laws at once. But it is safe to say that if all had regard to the experience of society as boiled down into our written statutes, there would be far fewer candidates for the higher and harder degrees of discipline and retribution. Man-made law is really the expression of wiser ones' desire that those who come after should not pay too high a price to learn what might be learned by the experience of others.

The Fact Shortage

THE question of spending money in politics is like the question of earning money in business, it is a matter of honesty. Money may be dishonestly spent just as it may be dishonestly acquired, and a great deal of it is being dishonestly spent all the time, even outside politics. All waste is dishonest, especially the waste of that into which another's labor has entered, or that out of which a good use might be obtained. Thus all appeal to the extravagant tastes of the people is also dishonest, the tempting of buyers with gewgaws that merely "get the money" and never give it equivalent in use. Everything that wastes material, debases taste, encourages a flashy, thoughtless, spendthrift habit, is dishonest.

Now, spending money in politics is partly a matter of taste, partly of conscience, partly of law. Ordinary personal modesty ought to prevent a man spending his own money to gain a prefermeht for himself. A good colonel would not think of buying promotion to the rank of general; he would desire to win that rank by the method of merit. A lawyer would not be fit for the bench who would consider buying his way there; as a lawyer he would get more satisfaction out of the honor by having it bestowed upon him through the unbiased judgment of others as to his worthiness. Honors that do not confer Honor are of all things the emptiest; they are like hired cheers or subsidized tears, abhorrent to the normal man.

Yet money is made to be spent and there was probably never a time in the world, especially in this nation, when so many men were anxious to get into the spending orgy. Men have a sort of blind faith that if they throw enough dollars into the machine of destiny it will come out just what they desire—a presidency, world church unity, complete Americanization, or whatever it may be.

By all means let money be spent by those who have money to spare, but let the spending contribute to the general wealth of the people, let it meet some actual need, let it go to accomplish something more than further glutting the mails with political propaganda, or serving selfish purposes.

If all the money thus far spent on the Presidential campaign by candidates who will never see more than the exterior of the White House had been used to meet the great Fact Shortage from which the country suffers, the benefit to the country would have been greater than if all the aspirants landed in office.

This is a suggestion which may be worth considering by men who are wondering what to do with their money. Granting that a number of men who can never be President, nor hold any other office commensurate with their dignity, are truly desirous of serving the Nation, this suggestion is offered for their candid consideration—Why not spend some money in *relieving the people from the Shortage of Facts?* It is positively startling to discover how little reliable knowledge is to be had on any of the real problems that confront us—not the speculative problems dealing with untried forms of social life, and new propositions of industrial adjustment, but the concrete problems having to do with wheat, sugar, coal, houses, and the like.

Sugar is scarce. Sugar is high. Is it scarce only in the retail store, or in the world? Is it high because it is really scarce, or because its flow is being held back to boost prices and thus bring more profit to speculators? Do you know?

Opinions are useless. Guesses solve nothing. Denunciation does no good. The one thing that is worth a thousand opinions and guesses and would accomplish the work of the most terrific denunciations is the Fact About Sugar.

The fact is obtainable. Some people say, "The Government ought to get that fact." Perhaps so, but whatever the Government has done or omitted to do, it is certain that the demonstrated, unchallengeable Fact has not been given to the people. There is no one really "informed" on the question; everybody seems to walk in a haze, as if men had as little control over the work of their own hands as over the weather. The sun shines or it rains; sugar goes up or down—people regard both with the same sort of helplessness to change them. Now, sugar is not a principle. It is not a theory. It is not a mystery. It is grown, refined and distributed. It is absolutely possible to know whether it was grown. It is absolutely possible to know whether it was refined. It is absolutely possible to know where it is now, why it is kept there, and what and who determines the price. These are not deep scientific problems; they are not mysteries nor veiled philosophy. They are Facts which can be found out. For an amount less than some candidates have expended in their campaign propaganda, they could be brought to light—and the man who would spend his money that way for the unselfish purpose of giving the people some bedrock facts to work upon, would recommend himself for a position of service to the people much more than any speech-making or self-advertising campaign could ever do.

Perhaps the time has come when we shall demand of candidates preliminary specimens of the work they would do if elected, the thoroughness and persistence they would bring to the big questions.

Does anyone know how much coal is being mined, or whether next winter's needs will be met?

Does any one know what the wheat acreage is for this year, and whether in event of the promised crop shortage, as some say, the unsold portion of last year's crop will still prove sufficient, as others say? There are two sets of statements made upon that question—which is the true one? or is the truth somewhere between them? It would not be impossible to find out. It would cost money, but not as much as some campaigns are costing.

From one point of view it is a splendid advantage for the country to have fifteen or twenty men who openly admit their ability and desire to be President. It is splendid that so many men are willing to serve the entire nation. And the incident of their failure to win nomination or election is not sufficient reason for laying aside so laudable a desire. Let them go on and serve—let them get to work, spending their money, using their executive ability and proving their separation from the exploiting class, by meeting the present Shortage of Facts.

It would be a genuine benefit to the nation if, in addition to the candidate showing before the nominations a piece of work of presidential size and importance, the defeated candidate after the elections should go ahead and demonstrate some of the services he had it in mind to render had he been elected.

National service is not restricted to men in office. It would perhaps not be too much to say that much of the valuable service rendered the nation, aside from purely executive decision, has been rendered by men out of office. There is a sense in which a man out of office is freer to get at the truth than the man in office. It should not be so, but often it is. If there is anything being "put over" on the American people today in the matter of clothing, food, fuel and special necessaries of life, it is being done under cover of darkness, and the darkness is nothing but lack of knowledge which is a lack of Facts. The only light that is needed to drive conspirators against the people into oblivion is the light of Facts. Merely to have the thing *known*, to have the method *exposed*, to have the *Fact itself exploited* is to accomplish what courts and investigations and threats could hardly do.

If there is any conspiracy against the easy access of the people to procurable necessaries of life today, that conspiracy proceeds under cover of such phrases as "scarcity," "increased costs," "the war," and so on, which mean little or nothing, mere words that serve as "blinds." If there is no scarcity, if the charges are increased out of all proportion to the increase in costs, if the condition is not due to the war but to the manipulation which profiteers learned from the war, Facts will explode the whole delusion.

The exploiters of the people fear the Facts, which is one more reason why the aspirant to office should show he is not in fear of the exploiters by showing the Facts, which service would also prove him to be free of the charge of exploiting. The Fact is worth money. Facts would put the public in control of the situation. The main shortage is a shortage, not so much of necessities, but of Facts.

Should Married Women Work?

THE question of women in the work of the world comes up to claim attention every little while, even though it had a year or two of rest during the war. It has been a very persistent question, and although its first character was industrial, its significance is now becoming social. In earlier and freer forms of society there was never any question about women working; they simply worked because the work was there to do. Sometimes it was work which we now class as men's work, but with a different meaning, for in a former period all work was directly connected with the production of food or the simpler necessities of life, while nowadays we refer to "work" more as a means of getting money. Anyway, the women who were the mothers and grandmothers of the present mature generation were not troubled by the question— they solved it before any one thought to ask it; they worked.

Women appeared in industry at a later period, that is, women working for money at labor disconnected from their homes. There was objection to this, first by the people themselves who fancied it was somewhat beneath women's dignity to work for wages at anything but housework or nursing; and then the later objection from organized labor that women were in danger of usurping men's places, or effecting a general reduction in wages. These fears were genuine at the time, and illustrate how little the accuracy with which some tendencies are forecast. The tendency has been for women to go up to men's scales of wages, as indeed they should where they are producing work of equal value. Even the labor unions, some branches of which very stubbornly resisted the entrance of women into certain trades, have opened their doors for membership on equal terms to women.

Nowadays there is seldom a question raised as to the propriety of women supporting themselves by paid labor. In even the wealthy families the idea of rearing a daughter in idleness is rapidly dying out, although there is always, of course, the consideration of a choice of labor.

In fact, it may be regarded as settled, and no question at all, that the girls of the family may renounce a life of idleness and become self-supporting, or contributors to the support of the home, without being even the slightest the less womanly for it, as some of the forefathers thought they were. The self-supporting type of young woman has added a new strain to American femininity, a strain of wholesome self-reliance, clear-eyed vision of the facts of life, and a general sanity of reaction. She has not been made masculine; rather, the sounder qualities of womanliness have been brought out in her. The so-called "new woman" really represents womanhood released from artificial effeminacy.

But now comes a new angle to the question. Ordinarily upon her marriage a woman stopped working for wages. Her sphere thenceforth became the home, not that she worked less, but her husband became the bread-winner while she became the home-maker. To assume the work of keeping a house is not exactly a retirement from work, as every woman knows.

This was a division of labor which seemed in harmony with the fitness of things, and which we are convinced will remain the normal condition in spite of instances or periods of aberration.

We appear to be in one of those periods now, and hence arises in many quarters the question, Should Married Women Work? Employers are frequently asked for their views upon it. Social workers are very outspoken upon it. More than that, thousands of the very women involved in the matter are wondering whether they are really the pioneers of a new era or whether they are merely the signs of a period in which many standards are temporarily disturbed. It seems pretty true to say that however numerous may be the present day instances of married women working, they are not the pioneers of a new condition of things in which it will be thought right and proper that all married women should work outside the home for wages.

Certain factors are irremovably opposed to such a practice becoming established. There is the idea of Home, for one. A Home is a place inhabited, not an apartment to which two working people come tired from their labor, to rest from a day's work. A Home is a place inhabited by the spirit of home-making which spirit somehow requires the pretty constant bodily presence of the home-maker, who is supremely the woman.

Then there is the idea of Family. Certainly the intrusion of even one child breaks up the plan of the wife going out to work. And, not to repeat the counsel which has been given on this subject from the earliest times, who can separate between the idea of Home and Family?

There are, of course, exceptional circumstances, but as a rule, where the man of the house is able-bodied, he should be the sole representative of the family in the industrial world, at least until his children grow up. He should make the living and his wife should make the home.

It is unpleasant to relate that while some married women are forced to work for their living, there are far too many who work merely to gratify those extravagant tastes which a normal family income cannot support.

To say it plainly, the great majority of married women who work do so in order to buy fancy clothes. And not the clothes that they need, not necessary decency and tastefulness of covering, but extravagance of decoration. It is not to keep the home together that they work, but to maintain an outside appearance entirely out of keeping with the kind and quality of their home. It is amazing to see the peacocks that emerge from commonplace cottages, and to see the ridiculous excess of finery which can only be accounted for by an excess income represented by the wife at work. Is there anything more pitiful, more disregardful of the real dignity and beauty of life than that a woman should choose menial labor through the day in order that, though tired, she may shine in cheap imitation silks and plumes an hour or two at night?

People sometimes argue that if these married women work, they at least contribute to production. It is a question whether they do or not. Indeed, it is very doubtful that they do. For, whatever their labor may contribute, the use they make of their wages is to encourage a number of nonessential industries that cater to cheap tastes, and thus they destroy by their money what they create with their labor.

There are doubtless cases, heroic cases, where the married woman goes out to labor to gain some substantial benefit for the home which otherwise would not be had. There is no danger of these cases ever being confused with the others. Little more is needed than a glance at the face of a wife who works to see whether her reasons are high and serious, or whether they are selfish and trivial.

These serious ones who know all that they are leaving, and who are really the victims of a situation instead of the exploiters of a situation—these are the ones to whom everyone would listen if they should give their own hearts' thought about the advisability of married women working. There is no doubt as to what they would say.

As a broad rule, a great deal can safely be sacrificed to preserve the spirit of Home. There are many impressively dressed women whose homes are not impressive. The best setting any woman ever had is her own home.

The cost of living is not so high as the cost of pretending to live better than one really can. The cost of anything real is not quite so high, in comparison with the values possessed, as is the cost of pretense. Least of all should any sacrifice of substantial values, such as the Home atmosphere, be made for mere pretense.

The Story of Jones

THE story is told of a man named Jones who, with others, was shipwrecked. They were hoping to be saved by main strength at the pumps, keeping the hulk afloat. To stimulate their energies, they began to ask one another what they were pumping for, and one by one each man named the dearest object in his life. One man was pumping that his aged mother might not be deprived of her only son; another, that his wife might not be a widow; another, that his children might not be left fatherless. At last the question came around to Jones—"What are you pumping for, Jones?" And Jones replied, "I'm pumping for Jones."

In a way Jones was right, and in a way he was wrong. Every stroke of his arm at the pump was for others as well as himself. Every gallon of water he ejected from the leaky hulk bought an added chance of life for his companions as well as himself. Every strain of his muscle which he thought was solely for Jones, was for Smith and White and the rest. He could not keep his part of the deck afloat without helping to keep the whole ship afloat.

They all came safely ashore, but the man who saved least was Jones.

A man may work as selfishly as he pleases; he may rule out of his mind all thought or intention or desire to do something for someone else, but he will find in the end that Nature has tricked him; he has not been permitted to live for himself alone; his very works of selfishness have been made to serve others: he has only deluded himself, robbed himself of the higher and more satisfactory rewards which come from including the good of others in one's own good.

Suppose a man should deliberately set out to be absolutely selfish, the benefactor of none and the beneficiary of all. He could not do it. There is no possible system upon which he could organize his life in total selfishness. He could not keep a cow, without serving the cow by milking her. He could not raise enough grain for his own need without serving the seed in its life destiny and opening the very soil of the earth herself to a fuller expression and value. He could not breathe without delighting the cells of his lungs and making his very blood glad. A man who would be absolutely selfish would have no outlet but to lie down and die, even then Nature would outwit him, for she would take the very materials of his body and distribute them in one form or another to the plant world.

Everyone knows, however, that there are selfish men in the world—that is, men who are selfish in their intention. They don't mean to help anyone else. They would not go out of their way to advance another's good. They may even flatter themselves that they are going through life on the narrow gauge line of "Every man for himself, and the devil take the hindmost." But they are simply the dupes of a fallacy. The baker may bake bread and have no other motive than his own profit. Yet others are fed by his bread, but he is not himself fed by the sense of having helped his fellow men. The farmer may till his land with no thought in his mind but the money profit of it; the thronging cities are supplied just the same even though the farmer has been cheated out of a finer harvest than can be cut with a scythe. The surgeon may go home hugging his fee, but he has saved a home from disruption by the saving of a threatened life. A manufacturer may invent and administer and expand his business, with no other conscious object than to amass a great fortune, but he is providing jobs for workmen; he is really working for his workmen, although he does not realize it. He would get a double profit if he only knew that secret.

We cannot do anything which brings us the right to live, without extending some service which helps others to live. Narrow people may think that they can, but wise old Nature lets them play with the idea even while it is being disproved.

There was a man in a Michigan village who always voted against public improvements, especially against adequate fire protection. The time came when he constructed some valuable buildings which held an inflammable stock. Then he demanded of the village, that as his enterprise redounded to the commercial importance of that place, fire protection ought to be provided for it. He wanted it only for himself, but in order to give it to him, it had to be given to all the residents. But that man did not have in his own heart the satisfaction of knowing he had made every other villager's home safer.

A man may be selfishly concerned for the protection of his own children from disease, but he cannot quiet that concern without providing for town sanitation, pure water, healthful school buildings and public health rules—and when he achieves these for the protection of his own children, he will discover that he has given them to every other child in the community.

Pumping is the weariest work in the world when it is done for Jones alone; and if it is for Jones alone, the time will come at the shriveled end of his life when he will wonder if it was worth the effort. The things we seek for ourselves alone dry up and lose their flavor sooner than any others. In 999 cases out of a thousand—yes, in all but one case out of a million, the person who is "tired of life" is not tired of life at all, but tired of living solely for himself.

The action of life upon us, if we have the least wisdom to react to it, is to draw us out of ourselves into a sense of human unity. Here is a big, crude, selfish hulk of a boy. His motto is "Get." There is something almost barbarous in his self-centeredness. Human society is as yet an unborn idea with him. Mankind, if he visualizes it to his mind at all, is but a collection of beings who possess something which he must get for himself by hook or crook. He is an initial product of nature, the raw material of humanity, a man in the rough.

Then Nature wakens him to love a girl, a girl who attracts him—perhaps he does not define it—by her unselfishness, by her regard for the rights and feelings and interests of others. Ah! he is no longer the self-centered cub that he was; he finds himself thinking day and night of some one else, and planning ways to please her. Nature has divided him into two, enlarged and amplified him, widened the bounds of his humanity.

But even that love may be tinged with the desire to possess, so when he has won the girl, Nature sends him a babe. He is now divided by three. Perhaps in time he may be divided by four or five. He is no longer working for himself, he is working for a family. He sees other men through his own experiences and gradually widens his sympathies and insight—his sense of humanity-at-large.

That is the strange arithmetic of nature; it multiplies by division. It is the good which we cut in two and share with another that doubles in value and brings good to us. A man cannot be unselfish without serving himself best. "He that loseth his life shall find it."

The young man meets this problem at the very threshold of his active life. What work shall he choose? What shall his life motto be? What shall be the reward he seeks?

He will find at the very outset that the work which promises him most is that which serves most people. If he sets out to serve himself, he will be his own paymaster, and he will be restricted to payment in the worthless coin of his own selfish spirit.

It is just there that selfishness loses. Gain it ever so much, it misses the very element which gives value to gain. Some gains are very bitter; they are like heaped-up ashes; they are flavorless and colorless before they are well in hand. They have not the stamp of social approval on them, and lacking that stamp they are counterfeit and worthless.

Jones saved his carcass. He lost his character. Thereafter it little mattered what he gained or lost until he had retrieved that first imperishable wealth.

What It Costs for War

IT COSTS money to run the United States, but not
so much money as the people pay for that purpose.
. . . . If a politician should say that you would pass·it
over with the thought that he was only charging his
political opponents with extravagance. But that is
not the nature of the statement made on this page. It
has nothing to do with politics, nothing to do with
politicians, nothing to do with any propaganda whatever. On the basis of figures prepared in a department
of the Government of the United States—a discussion
of which appears elsewhere in this issue—the statement is made that more money—much more money—
is paid by the people than is needed actually to run
the United States Government.

How much more? About fourteen times as much.
That is to say, if you take the budget for the fiscal
year which ended May 1, 1920—the whole sum being
$5,868,005,706—you may leave the billion figures stand
($5,000,000,000), and then if you will divide the mil-
lion figures, the $868,005,706 which follow that big
"5," you will still have more than is actually spent in
the real work of government. You haven't diminished
the billions at all, you have scarcely cut the millions
in two, and yet the billions and half of the millions
represent the amount that is not necessary for the
conductive, civilized functions of government.

Some people are dazed when they see figures. This
is a form of blindness which permits the political and
economic sharpers to get the better of them. The
people would do well in their own interests if they
would become accustomed to figures. Just set down
on a piece of paper the sum, $5,868,005,706. And
then beneath it set down the sum $406,384,443. The
smaller sum represents all that is spent on the real
work of government. Do a little work in subtraction
and you will find that the difference is $5,461,621,263
—and this is the amount which we spend annually for

313

what we call government and is not government at all. What do we mean by Government? Well, we mean the public business of the nation. There is Congress, the legislative body; we must have it and it costs money, but its cost is hardly a drop in the bucket compared with the cost of other national responsibilities. Then there are the President, the White House with its domestic and official staff, the Federal courts and officers and penal institutions—sometimes distinguished by the terms executive and judicial departments. And then there are the various administrative departments organized for the purpose of managing the multitude of interests which every nation has— law enforcement, foreign relations, the coinage, customs, public lands, relations between the states of the Union. There is also the expense incident to the District of Columbia as a special bit of territory assigned to the use of the Federal Government.

Now all this, from President down to United States Marshall, costs only $181,087,225. These are the primary functions of government. Compare their cost with the total.

The Post Office, Land Office, Panama Canal and other public departments are not included because they are self-sustaining; the work which they do and the service which they render bring in enough money to pay their expenses. Instead of living by taxes they live by fees for the service rendered, as when you give two cents to have your letter carried.

Besides these there are necessary works, including the improvement of rivers and harbors, the construction of public buildings, the reclamation of waste lands, the establishment and maintenance of national parks, which every prosperous nation desires to see carried forward, and these cost the sum of $168,203,557.

Not to daze anyone with more figures, look now at a comparatively smaller amount, namely, $57,093,- 661. It is the smallest amount yet used. And what is it for? It is for all the research, development and educational work which the government is doing. The Department of Agriculture (and remember that our farm products are worth more than 25 Billions annually); our Bureau of Mines (and we produce each year metals and minerals valued at Six Billions) ; our highly useful Bureau of Standards which keeps us straight with regard to the real values and uses of the more than 12 billions of dollars' worth of raw materials that enter into our manufactured products every year; our Bureau of Fisheries; our government research into problems of health, housing, fuel, gasoline and every big pressing problem that vitally relates to the life of the people—all this real work of advancement and human benefit is supported to the extent of $57,093,661. Just look at it as a matter of percentages. Cast your eye again upon that first big total—$5,868,-005,706. Now the sum spent on the official functions of government, from the President to the most obscure Federal clerk, represents a little more than three per cent of that sum. The public works of the government, represented in rivers, harbors, national parks and Federal buildings, account for another three per cent; while research, education and development is supported by the munificent proportion of one per cent!

There you have seven per cent of your government expenditures accounted for, or seven cents of your government dollar.

Where does the other 93 per cent go? Where does $5,461,621,263 out of the sum of $5,868,005,706 go? Out of Five Billion some odd dollars, how does it come that only the "some odd" dollars go for straight government expenses? Where does the Five Billion go?

Listen! These are figures prepared in a government department at Washington. They are not the figures of any propagandist. You can get the figures for yourself if you want them. And the figures will show you this—

That 93 per cent of the expenditures of the United States Government are because of, and in the interest of, War!

The bills of our national housekeeping read this way: Peace, seven per cent; War, 93 per cent.

"Oh," says someone, "the war figures are so high because we have just finished a war."

No! Recent and previous war expenses comprise ·

67.8 per cent, and the annual upkeep of army and navy represent the other 25 per cent. We are paying for wars—all the wars—the United States ever fought. That is, we are not paying for them, for we are not able; we are only paying *interest* on them. The Public Debt is very largely the debt incurred by war. But no one ever speaks of paying the Public Debt. All that the country can do is to pay *interest* on it.

There is no doubt that protection is one of the functions of government, just as much as legislation or administration is. But try to realize the proportion which this item of protection has assumed—93 per cent! It would be worth it, if it were necessary. But is it necessary in a civilized world?—or can it be called a civilized world in which such a tax on safety is necessary? If every family were compelled to spend 93 per cent of its income to save itself from violence, living on the other seven per cent, could that family be said to be living in a civilized community?

Someone is benefiting by that 93 per cent. Some influence has been brought to bear everywhere to cause this great and continuous outpouring of wealth, generation after generation, in a single direction to continue. The nations have been tricked into a situation which the nations themselves could break up—which the people themselves *would* break up—if the enormity of the fact were only made clear.

Perhaps if our government should spend more than seven per cent on the civilizing and constructive functions, these might in time bring so much enlightenment and prosperity as to crowd out the other. There is a strong movement afoot in that direction, and it may be the movement which is going to show up war from another effective angle and perhaps indicate those whose interest is to foment war.

Paying for Greed's Mistakes

SOONER or later we pay for the follies of our
past. A great deal of the cry about our transportation difficulties is due to our past sins in this
respect. This is not always understood: people are
led to believe that something suddenly has gone wrong.
Nothing of the kind has happened. The mistaken
and foolish things we did years ago are just overtaking
us and collecting their due. At the beginning of railway transportation in the United States, the people
had to be taught its use, just as they had to be taught
the use of the telephone. Also, the new railroads had
to make business in order to keep themselves solvent.
And because railway financing began in one of the
rottenest periods of our business history, a number
of practices were established as precedents which have
influenced railway work more or less ever since.

One of the first things to be done was to throttle
all other methods of transportation. There was the
beginning of a splendid canal system in this country
and a great movement for canalization was in the
height of its enthusiastic strength, when the railroad
companies bought out the canal companies and let the
canals fill up and choke with weeds and refuse. All
over the eastern and in parts of the middle western
states are the remains of this network of internal
waterways. They are being restored now as rapidly
as possible; they are being linked together; various
commissions, public and private, have seen the vision
of a complete system of waterways serving all parts
of the country, and, thanks to their efforts and persistence and faith, progress is being made.

That was one folly which the advent of railway
transportation forced upon the country.

But there was another. This was the system of
making the haul as long as possible. Anyone, who is
familiar with the exposures which resulted in the formation of the Interstate Commerce Commission, knows

317

what is meant by this. There was a period when rail transport was not regarded as the servant of the traveling, manufacturing and commercial publics, but when it regarded itself as a Moloch to be served by all these. Business was treated as if it existed for the benefit of the railways.

During this period of folly, it was not good railroading to get goods from their shipping point to their destination by the most direct line possible, but to keep them on the road as long as possible, send them around the longest way, give as many connecting lines as possible a piece of the profit, and let the public stand the resulting loss of time and money. That was once counted good railroading. It has not entirely passed out of practice today.

One of the great changes in our economic life to which this railroad policy contributed was the centralization of certain activities, not because centralization was necessary, nor because it contributed more to the well-being of the people, but because, among other things, it made double business for the railroads.

Take those two staples, meat and grain, for example. If you look at the maps which the packing houses put out, and see where the cattle are drawn from; and then if you consider that the cattle, when converted into food, are hauled again by the same railways right back to the place where they came from, you will get some sidelight on the transportation problem and the price of meat.

Take also the matter of grain. Every reader of advertisements knows where the great flour mills of the country are located. And they probably know also that where the great mills are located is not representative at all of the sections where all the grain of the United States is raised. There are staggering quantities of grain, thousands of trainloads, hauled uselessly long distances, and then in the form of flour hauled back again long distances to the states and sections where the grain was raised—a burdening of the railroads which is of no benefit to the communities where the grain originated, nor to any one else except the monopolistic mills and the railroads. The railroads can always do a big business without helping the business of the country at all; they can always be engaged in just such useless hauling. On meat and grain and perhaps on cotton, too, the transportation burden could be cut in half, yes, reduced by more than half, by the preparation of the product for use before it is shipped at all. If a coal community mined coal in Pennsylvania, and then sent it by railway to Michigan or Wisconsin to be screened, and then hauled back again to Pennsylvania for use, it would not be much sillier than the hauling of Texas beef alive to Chicago, there to be killed, and then shipped back dead to Texas; or the hauling of Kansas grain to Minnesota, there to be ground in the mills and hauled back again as flour.

It is good business for the railroads, but it is bad business for business. One angle of the transportation problem to which too few men are paying any attention is this useless hauling away and hauling back of material which should be hauled only once. If the problem were tackled from the point of ridding the railroads of their useless hauls, we might discover that we are in better shape than we think to take care of the legitimate transportation business of the country.

In commodities like coal it is necessary that it be hauled from where it is to where it is needed. The same is true of the raw materials of industry—they must be hauled from the place where nature has stored them to the place where there are people ready to work them. And as these raw materials are not often found assembled in one section, a considerable amount of transportation to a central assembling place is necessary. The coal comes from one section, the copper from another, the iron from another, the wood from another—they must all be brought together.

But wherever it is possible a policy of centralization ought to be adopted. We need instead of mammoth flour mills at one corner of the country, a multitude of smaller mills distributed through all the sections where grain is grown. Wherever it is possible, the section that produces the raw material ought to produce also the finished product. Grain should be ground to flour where it is grown. A hog-growing country should not export hogs, but pork, hams and

319

bacon. The cotton mills ought to be near the cotton fields.

This is not a revolutionary idea. In a sense, it is a reactionary one. It does not suggest anything new; it suggests something that is very old. This is the way the country did things before we fell into the habit of carting everything around a few thousand miles and adding the cartage to the consumer's bill.

This idea is not advanced solely for its relation to the transportation problem—although it would bring inestimable relief there—but also for its effect on our life generally. *Our communities ought to be more complete in themselves.* They ought not to be unnec-essarily dependent on railway transportation. Out of what they produce they should supply their own needs and ship the surplus. And how can they do this unless they have the means of taking their raw materials, like grain and cattle, and changing them intó finished products? If private enterprise does not yield these means, the co-operation of farmers can. The chief injustice sustained by the farmer today is that, being the greatest producer, he is prevented from be-ing also the greatest merchandiser, because he is com-pelled to sell to those who put his products into mer-chantable form. If he could change his grain into flour, his cattle into beef and his hogs into hams and bacon, not only would he receive the fuller profit of his product, but he would render his near-by communi-ties more independent of railway exigencies, and thereby improve the transportation system by reliev-ing it of the burden of his unfinished product.

The thing is not only reasonable and practicable, but it is becoming absolutely necessary. More than that, it is done in many places. But it will not register its full effect on the transportation situation and upon the cost of living until it is done more widely and in more kinds of materials.

Administration Versus Government

IT WOULD be a beneficial act if someone could get it noised among the people that there is to be no change in the *Government* of the United States this year or next, but only a change in its *administration*. One would almost be led to think, by some of the statements that are being issued and some of the promises that are being made, that a most revolutionary change is coming and that the country is to swing off on a path entirely new and untried before.

The Old Ship of State is going to run as usual, but there will be a new First Mate. And he will not be able to upset the winds, nor reverse the ocean currents, nor change the position of the stars—the best he can do will be to make things shipshape and steer a safe course.

The Government is not going to change, but only some of the chief men on duty there.

The Government of the United States is an established institution; it might be just as well to have that understood. The Government, in its personnel, is not the United States by any means; it is only a committee of citizens, so to speak, who have been selected to look after the public affairs of the citizens of the United States.

The affairs which they shall handle and the manner in which they shall handle them are all set forth in the Constitution of the United States. While we are about it, it might be just as well if it were very clearly known that underneath the Government of the United States is the Constitution of the United States, and underneath the Constitution is the great mass of 105 million Americans.

The Constitution of the United States is written on paper. It was written a long time ago. The original copy is kept under lock and key at Washington. But even if that copy were destroyed, the Constitution would not be lost, because it is written upon the heart and mind of the people who compose our nation.

The Constitution was not handed down from heaven and no one has ever said it was a complete and perfect instrument, although there is none nearer perfect in the world. It has this in its favor, however, that under its provisions there has developed on this continent a type of national life of which none need be ashamed, for which none need be apologetic.

This paper is a social contract to which you and 105,000,000 other persons agree for the purpose of regulating our lives together. We agree on our rights, we agree on our duties, we write our agreement down, we appoint men with certain powers to become custodians of the agreement to see that its terms are observed and to perform other duties with reference to all of us; and there you have the Government, based on the Constitution.

Several times in the more than fourteen decades since the Constitution was first written, it has been changed, not, however, to undo anything it had done, but to do something it did not foresee. That is, the details of the Constitution have been somewhat enlarged; the spirit of it has not been changed.

Within the Constitution itself are described the methods by which it may be amended. It is one of the marks of the nobility of this document that it has, as it were, an open side looking toward progress. Its makers did not regard it as a fence, but as a foundation.

So, whenever anyone feels that there is a defect that goes deeper than government administration he is free to suggest an amendment of the Constitution, and if he can get a sufficient number of states to agree, the amendment will be made.

But there are certain changes advocated today which never could be made because to do so would be to destroy the principle of the Constitution itself. It goes without saying that if anyone should propose an amendment which would destroy a man's right in what his labor has produced, and if such an amendment should be made, something more would be done than merely to add another article to the Constitution. The very spirit of the instrument would be wounded and killed.

There are some things which could never become constitutional though you wrote them into the Constitution a thousand times and confirmed them by the thousand ratifications of all the states. The reason is that they are not in the constitution of *justice*.

So, while the people are indeed supreme over the written Constitution, the spiritual constitution is supreme over them. The French Revolutionists wrote constitutions too—every drunken writer among them tossed off a constitution. Where are they? All vanished. Why? Because they were not in harmony with the constitution of the universe. The power of the Constitution is not dependent on any Government, but on its inherent rightness and practicability. The power of the Government, however, is entirely dependent on the Constitution, and because that parchment says certain things about elections, the administration of the Government is this year being put before the people for a new selection.

The administration of government is so vitally connected with the people's welfare that it is amazing to see how really little initiative interest they take in the selection of the administrators.

No one will deny the statement that there is more interest being shown in the Government today by the would-be administrators than by the people in whose interest the Government is to be administered.

There are, of course, several reasons for that. One is that the people know that whichever old party is appointed by the people's vote to the administration of the Government, the difference will not be noticeable. But perhaps the strongest reason is that the desire of the would-be administrators to get into the office is greater than the desire of the people to put any of them in. That is to say, the election now approaching is like many another in that respect: those who are seeking office have made up their mind as to what they want, with far more decision and ardor

323

than the people have made up their mind as to whom they want.

The people are caught between two currents. One current drives heavily in favor of the idea of government as an aid to the people in all their interests. "The Government can do it," is the keynote. This is true—however much it may be overdone, it is true. Why should it not be true that the people acting collectively—that is, through the Government—should not be able to accomplish whatever they wish?

Well, then, this faith in the Government is built up. And then another current sets in—an administration is put into office which, through incompetency or dishonesty, absolutely disappoints the expectation of the people. Then follows that sinister propaganda which spreads distrust of all government and suspicion of all administrations.

This nation is founded on the Constitution, and the Constitution provides for the government, but if the Administration fails to administer the Government for the people for whom it was set up by the Constitution, then it is serving the dark forces which work to undermine all confidence in the idea of government.

The people should be aroused to the truth that, if the Administration does not serve them, it is not the fault of government, and that if they wish the Government to serve them they must themselves make the choice of those who administer it.

Election time—good old Constitution-protected election time—puts the whole matter directly into the people's hands. Conventions have nothing to do with it. Parties have nothing to do with it. The people may have it all their own way, to put in whom they will.

Loyalty Has Two Sides

IT MAY be useful, for a change, to commence a discussion of Loyalty in Industry at the point of the Loyalty of the Employer. There is always enough being said about the need of loyalty in the employes, and indeed that is a most important point. But the other is important too. Loyalty, to be fruitful and enduring, must issue from opposite sides. Loyalty on the part of employes must be met by loyalty on the part of the employer. Perhaps, in these times, it is the part of the employer to be first to demonstrate loyalty.

What are we to be loyal to? If we can settle that question, or even throw a little light upon it, it might do much to help us think straight.

What is it that brings employer and employe together in the first place? In modern industry they first meet as strangers. Sometimes, so far as personal acquaintance goes, they remain strangers. Yet it is not long before they get a pretty definite idea of each other. The idea may be wrong, but it is definite. The employe may have a wrong mind-picture of his employer's intentions, because of the harshness and injustice of superintendents or foremen. It is one of the biggest problems on the human side of management to prevent the employer's real ideas for the good of his men from losing all their vitality by the time they have filtered down through the subordinates of the organization.

On the other hand, the employer may have a wrong mind-picture of the employes, because of the actions and utterances of a noisy and obstructive minority. Whatever may be said about "collective bargaining," so-called, and other related matters, one objection is that there is too little "collectiveness" about it. A spokesman who does not work in the shop, who does not work in any shop, whose sole ambition perhaps is never again to have to work in a shop, is usually the

325

"bargainer," and it is from what he says or does that many employers draw their opinion of the men in the shop.

This, of course, is wrong, and it leads to many misrepresentations and misunderstandings which could be adjusted in a minute if the two parties actually knew each other and the conditions under which each of them have to work. No thoughtful man will deny for a moment that there are too many "go-betweens" who are really "keep-aparts"; they increase the distance between the two interested parties.

Here is a man, perhaps a wage-earner, who gets a mechanical idea which he develops and in which he sees possibilities of great usefulness. He cannot put it on the market alone—no man can do much alone— and so he calls in men to help him, and he pays them. If he is a success, his force increases, and with it his own managerial problems increase, until he is so busy, and the men in the shop are so busy and numerous, that personal contact largely ceases. Those who knew him when his office problems were so light that he could lend a hand in the shop are usually loyal to him personally. They know him; they know him to be one with them in his ideas and experience and sympathies.

But after while the business itself grows so large as to supplant the personality of the man. In a big business the employer is just like the employe—he is partly lost in the mass. Together they have created a great productive organization which sends out articles which the world buys because they are useful, and which bring in money which provides a livelihood for everyone engaged there. The business itself becomes the big thing.

There is something humanly sacred about a big business which provides a living for hundreds and thousands of families. When one looks about at the babies that are coming into the world and carefully tended, at the boys and girls who are being sent to school and educated, at the young working men who, on the strength of their jobs, are being married and setting up for themselves, at the thousands of homes that are being paid for in installments out of the earnings of the men—when one looks at a great productive organization that is enabling all these things to be done by those who are engaged in it and for their families, one feels it to be like murder, a terrible crime, to attempt or to risk anything that would jeopardize in the least degree a business on which so many depend.

The employer is a man like any of his employes, subject to all the limitations of humanity. The only thing that justifies him in holding his job is that he can fill it. If he can steer the business straight, if his men can trust him to run his end of the work properly and without endangering their settled condition in life, then he is filling his place just like anyone else. Otherwise he is no more fit for his position than a schoolboy would be on an important job of pattern making. The employer is judged by his ability, just as everyone else should be.

He may be but a name to the men—a name on a signboard. But there is the business—it is more than a name. It produces the living of everyone in it, and a living is a pretty tangible thing. The business is a reality. It does things. It is a going concern. The evidence of its fitness is that the pay envelopes keep coming.

Why not begin loyalty there? If the shop is keeping your family, educating your children, buying your home, providing you with a reasonable certainty of employment and a money return that you can do things on, you are entitled to regard it as something which is definitely connected with your interest: its welfare *is* yours.

As to personal loyalty, only the independent employer can be loyal to his men. The other kind of employer may want to be, but the influences above him on which he depends often prevent him. The independent employer, who does not have to bow to capitalists above him, can prevent anything being done that will decrease the return which his men draw from the business. He can, indeed, freely devote himself to devising ways and means by which they shall be enabled to draw more. Not only may he feel this to be a duty which he owes to his men, but he takes a pride in it. High wages are the result of two elements: the industry of the men, first. But this industry can be nullified by bad management. So the second element is good management, and it is here that the employer's pride may come to him. When he adds good management to his men's industry, and this enables a great return to be made all round, the business as a human concern is a success. There is a great distinction between a manufactured article being a success, and the organization that manufactures it being a success. The one is a mechanical problem; the other is a human problem.

The forces which are aiming to undermine American industry—and some of these forces have a very high capitalistic origin, don't forget that!—aim first for the breakdown of loyalty of any character whatsoever. They want it to break down.

It is a truth which every American workman ought to know that 95 per cent of the agitation which they see around them does not grow up out of the working people, but it comes down through hired agitators from the would-be capitalistic rulers who want to use the workmen themselves to break down the very industries on which the workmen depend, in order that then the workmen may be thrown on their tender mercies.

You are not hitting the capitalist when you hit industry; you are hitting the workman. Industry, independent industry, is the only foe the capitalist fears. Employers and employes have a common interest against the speculative capitalists. These international capitalists know that if they can split employer and employe apart, and so break up industry, they can control the field. And the pity of it is that so many employers and employes are blindly playing the game of their common enemy.

A man is loyal to the house that shelters him. He doesn't see what is to be gained by knocking it down. The same kind of loyalty to the industries that provide for us will block the game which the hired destructionists are playing.

What Shall Prevent War?

THERE will be a "next war" just as certainly as
tomorrow will be a new day, if there is a more
deliberate organization for it than there is against it.
It is not a question of what the people "want"; it is
a question of what they Will. It can be safely said
that the people seldom "want" war; but just as seldom
do they Will peace. In 1914 when those who saw
the stupidity of war in this age went out into the arena
and tried to stop it, they found that there were no
tools to work with. The world had been systematically
organized for war; there were no instruments, no
weapons prepared for a peace offensive. Just as truly
as there can be no war without preparation, so there
can be no peace without preparation. Preparedness
is a necessary condition; it is just a question of what
we are to prepare for.

A small well-organized minority in favor of war
is more than a match for a large, unorganized majority which is sentimentally inclined toward peace.
The world is ruled by organized minorities. In Russia there are 180,000,000 people; yet 600,000 Bol-
sheviks rule them.

It is not so despicable as it once was considered to
be interested in world peace. Previous to 1914 the
person who was interested in the peace of the world
was regarded as an amiable faddist; he would have
been counted more virile had his diversion been poker.

But the past six years has shown the world what
war is, and now everybody professes to believe that
it is unspeakably cruel and stupid. The most amazing
confessions have been made by those who were formerly the most ardent militarists as to the uselessness
of it all. It is true that soldiers exhibited super-human
courage and devotion; it is true that nations proved
almost miraculous capacity for sacrifice; the human
contribution lavished upon war was most glorious in
its pure unselfishness; but the men who promised most

329

for the achievements of the war are confessing one ‘
by one that they were mistaken.

The criticism of war is not of the qualities which
are contributed to it—life, love, loyalty and every sacrifice—but that war, having these immeasurable riches
to work with, could do so little with them.

If any constructive program of humanity could
command a tenth, a hundredth part of the human
values that war can command, this world could be
completely transformed in little time.

The "next war" is being planned when the last
one ceases; that is, men whose principal business is
to fight make preparations for doing it again. It may
not be that they desire it, but they fail to see in human nature any direct "set" against it.

In one of the countries a force of 5,000 military,
naval and air experts is already at work on plans.
This does not mean that they intend to provoke war;
they are merely getting ready. It is pretty certain
that the old formality of a declaration of war is a
thing of the past. The next war will not be "declared."
There will be no exchange of notes and a sparring for
time. In the older days it was military etiquette to
permit the enemy to fire first. After many years this
was abandoned, but out of respect for the public
opinion of nations a "declaration of war" was made
in formal fashion. We all remember how those dec-
larations were made in 1914, and how our own declaration was made after an all-night session of Congress.

The next war will sweep down like a tropical storm,
unannounced by any trumpet of thunder or herald
of lightning. That is being planned by those who are
studying the future.

It is certain that if war is permitted again to deluge
the earth—and to *permit* it, all we have to do is to
fail to prevent it—the tactics of the Great War will
be as out-of-date as if it had been fought in ancient
times. War will be less an affair of men and more
an affair of machines. The individual soldier with
his rifle is almost a thing of the past. Even battle-
fields, vast armies confronting each other in the same
territory, belong to outworn methods. Invisible gases,

330

the suffocation of whole cities without noise, silent horrors of every kind, stealthy assaults by very few men armed with most potent powers, will be the new order. The forces of nature will be used more and more to supplant the muscular force of soldiers. Ray warfare is already the theme of military study and experiment on a large scale. Light rays and heat rays are being trained to become allies of Mars. The old heroic manner of man fighting man will be largely done away; warfare will become world murder, with nature as accomplice—if nothing happens to prevent.

Germ warfare had already made its appearance before the recent war closed its main phase, but it was still in a crude stage. Wells were poisoned, cholera and typhus germs were let loose, women who carried disease were early recognized as capable of great usefulness against an enemy. But all this was very crude.

Things were done which the common people of very few of the nations would have approved. No nation, no government ever felt it safe during the recent war to take its people into its confidence even on matters that the enemy knew full well. All through the war and even today the only people who do not know the whole truth about the war—not the diplomatic or political truth, but the truth about the actual conduct of the fighting itself—are the people who stood the brunt of it all.

The people don't know the truth about war contracts, about war profits, about the connection of government employes with private business, about the "inside" group that really ran things—the people don't know any of the truth, and no government has ever dared to let them know.

There are people making money out of war today. Millions are being minted out of blood and suffering this very minute. There is enough war tinder lying about to kindle the whole fire again—if nothing prevents.

What is there to prevent? Nothing, except the people's Will. But they must exert that Will.

You do not have to speculate about what the people will do: you are one of them—judge by yourself. Ten chances to one you yourself are thinking this moment that it is a waste of time to talk about war and peace. "The war is over," you say, and let it drop at that. But is War over? That is the question. Is War over?

War is not over. It never will be over until peace actually is more than a sentiment and becomes a program.

Nothing but the Will to Peace of the people can put an end to war. Nothing but that. You may have everything else, but if you lack that, War is still possible.

The world had a Peace Palace at The Hague; it did not have the Will to Peace in the people; therefore war came. Suppose we have a League of Nations, a World Court, a Parliament of Man. We ought to have it. We have the opportunity of getting it now. But, without the Will to Peace, without a strong *set* toward peace as an ideal, a League of Nations would be of as little consequence as was the Belgian treaty.

Paper can only hold ink. But the Will of the People for Peace can hold back every warlike force in the world.

This is not an academic question. But no doubt it is so regarded. It begins to seem as if peace will have to make as hard a fight as if there had been no Great War at all.

One point is important just now: the world this moment is doing more for war preparedness than for peace preparedness. Does that concern you now? If not, it will later.

The County Fair

THERE is one American institution not provided for in the Constitution of the United States which could command the votes of all of us if it required them—and that institution is the County Fair. At this season of the year it begins to emerge in a gorgeous array of colored lithographs, with promises of "better, bigger, best" liberally sprinkled over them, and adorned with scenes of grain field and pasture land. The very air, as autumn comes on, is redolent of the soil and the harvest.

Town and Country meet at the County Fair, or State Fair, in a manner and under auspices that cannot be equaled. And anyone who has observed the efforts—the deliberate efforts—made of recent years to divide Town and Country and provoke antagonism between them, knows how necessary such a meeting is.

It is natural that the Country should be interested in the Fair, because the Fair is first and foremost an exhibition of Farming skill and progress. Men in the same business like to compare results, and that is how the idea of a Fair began. In Fair-Time the year's work is mostly done; its results are fairly apparent, and it is possible to pass a verdict on it all. Choice grains, fruits, vegetables; the choice of flock and herd and dairy—these are brought together for the judgment of the farming community. The domestic side of farming is represented too—choice quiltings, embroideries, and the handiwork of the women of the farm.

If you go to any one of the little one-day Fairs held in the mountains of Vermont you will see this institution in its pristine simplicity—a Fair where there is nothing to sell, but where the choice of the hills has been turned out to show. There is nothing elaborate about it, but everything you see has come from the hills. The exhibits are not large, but behind each of them is the home-farm, and you can read

333

everywhere, in the legible writing of life, whatever the hardships or whatever the successes have been. There are Fairs and Fairs, and many famous ones, but it is in the little Fairs of the Eastern United States, where families still come behind ox-teams, and where a crate of chickens brought for exhibition gains free admittance for the whole family, that you see the Fair as it was in the beginning.

But Fair-Time is money-time on the Farm, and therefore was added a commercial element by which the Farmer and the Manufacturer were brought in touch with each other. That is to say, the Fair became hospitable and widened its borders so that the Town could come in and exhibit its year's progress too. And so it comes that when we have wandered up and down the long rows of well-washed sheep, and have listened to the pleasant laughter of the children where the little pigs delight them, and have emerged from the noisy shed where the chickens are displayed, and have passed in admiration past the big box stalls where glossy horses nuzzle the caressing hands of passers-by, and have breathed the aroma of the fruit exhibit and observed the clever manner in which the grain display has been arranged—we are drawn away toward the clatter of the threshing machine, the ditch digger, the farm tractor, and other impressive exhibits which warn each succeeding Fair crowd that the day when the Farmer had to work like his horse is past, and the day when the Farmer may become an engineer is here.

The old single-beam plow, the old windmill, the old method of harvesting by hand, all the old ways which broke men's backs and burdened women's hearts —they look very pleasant in pictures and they were very romantic in fiction; but they were often cruelly hard on flesh and blood. We shall never be able to thank the old-time farmer for his devotion and his toil.

But that day is passing, it is passing before our eyes. Farming in the old style is rapidly fading into a picturesque memory. The benefits of modern invention and standardized manufacture are being heaped upon the Farmer with a plenitude which makes up for its too long delay. This does not mean that work is going to be removed from the Farm. Work cannot be removed from any life that is productive. But Power-Farming does mean this—*Drudgery is going to be removed from the Farm.* Power-Farming is simply *taking the burden off flesh and blood and putting it on steel.*

Farming, of course, has advanced. Time was when men dug with their fingers the hole where the seed was planted, and pulled the crop by hand. There was an era of Hand-Farming.

Then came the time of Tool-Farming. The plow supplanted the spade; the disk took the hoe's place, and the harrow the rake's. The drill lifted the seed-bag off the farmer's shoulder. The threshing machine put the flail into the discard. The mower retired the scythe and grain cradle. No one can deny that Tool-Farming made great strides.

But it was still the Farmer whose muscle and nerve made the tools go. The Farmer does not need new tools so much as he needs Power to make the tools go. And thus we are in the opening years of the Era of Power-Farming. The motor car has wrought a revolution in modern Farm Life not because it was a vehicle, but because it had Power.

That is what the noise of machinery on the Fair Ground means. It means that Power-Farming is coming in. Power-Farming is using motors instead of men's muscles, machine speed instead of the drooping gait of the tired man or horse. Power-Farming is the magic of modern mechanics whereby the element of Drudgery is extracted from Work.

So Town and Country meet at the Fair, the one to see the fruits of the fields, the other to see the fruits of the factories. Both serve each other. The trouble is that they do not serve each other more directly. There are too many interests squeezing in between them. There is too big a tax or toll exacted on the exchange between them.

It would be a good thing if we could add a third section to our Fairs—a section where large groups of city people could meet with large groups of country people, discuss their problems together, and make

335

trade arrangements direct. Suppose 100 families living on Block 9, Smith avenue, should say to Farmer Johnson, "We want you to be our farmer. We, 100 families, will guarantee you a straight direct sale for all your produce." What would be the result? Farmer Johnson would get more from those people than from the men with whom he now deals, and he could sell to the city people for less than they have to pay now. Both would make money, and neither would be at the mercy of artificially created market conditions. Only a "bad year," that is, an act of Nature, could affect the arrangement.

Frank judges would probably say that of the two classes who meet at the Fair, the farmer has the better of it. He may look toward the Town and sometimes envy the things which City Folk have and he has not. But something must be allowed for illusion. Things are not always what they seem. City Folk have many, many things that are not desirable at all, and, strangely enough, these are usually the very things which give glamour to the city. The city has nothing worth while that the Country has not, or cannot have if it will. It is too bad that the City shines so gloriously from afar in the eyes of the young people of the Farm. If they could only see the City as it really is, they would thank the good fortune that brought them to. birth on a Farm. Many and many a boy and girl learns this bitterly.

So we are all going to the Fair. Old and young, rich and poor, the city rube and the farmer, all are going to the Fair. And you will notice one very significant thing: the fruits, the grains, the fowl, the cattle which are produced where Power-Farming is practiced, are just as flavorous, just as nutritious, just as "country"—in short, just as natural as Nature herself; only, they are more plentiful, and the Power-Farming family will look much more natural, because now they have more leisure for self-development, more time to grow, more money to aid their happiness.

The Old Ways Were Good

ONE of the American poets has a line which runs somewhat like this—"All of good the past hath had, remains to make our own time glad." He probably had his own special thought about that fact when he wrote the words, and being a poet it is quite likely that some aspects of the truth, or illustrations of it, did not occur to him. But the heart of any great utterance, the quality that makes it live, is its element of truth. And many a truth is uttered, the full meaning of which is not comprehended by him to whom it is given to utter it. There is a prophetic element in truth—the future keeps fulfilling it.

If you begin even at so common a point as house furnishing, the poet's line still holds good. There was something about the old-fashioned furniture that not only satisfied the demand of utility but also satisfied the eye. The old chairs were not only strong and comfortable, but because they were that they were graceful also. They were pleasant to look upon as well as rest upon. They became "old-fashioned" in the eyes of a succeeding generation, and were displaced by strange designs which were often neither useful nor ornamental. But now, do you notice, they are coming back, the old-fashioned rocking chairs, the old-fashioned straight chairs, the old-fashioned sofas and the old-fashioned tables. And for no other reason than that they satisfy better than the new fashioned ones.

This is perhaps more generally noticeable in the return of fireplaces. It was once the fashion to board up the fireplaces in old-fashioned homes and "paper" over the space. Stoves were all the style. Stoves, of course, are useful, but people like to see the fire. Children love to see "eyes of fire" shining through the sliding front doors of the kitchen cookstove. Adults like the sight of fire in the old-fashioned "self-feeder," now rechristened the "base-burner."

337

But none of these satisfy like the free leaping flames of the fireplace, and it is becoming quite the custom in many parts to build even the smaller homes with fireplaces. Our contact with fire is about the only natural contact we can keep in our city life. Fire is elemental. Fire is common to the earth beneath and the stars and sun above. We feel united again to the natural order in the presence of domestic fire. Simply to look at it—how it draws our gaze, how it fascinates us into dreams and visions!

There is a passage in the Bible which says all this in a few words: "I am warm; I have *seen* the fire." The very sight of fire, domestic fire, is comfortable both to the spirit and the body. The fireplace is coming back because it is one of the good things of the past which the present is not willing to let disappear.

It is so with wheels. In the earlier days everyone, or nearly every family, had its own conveyance. It was so much a necessity, a family necessity, that no one thought of it as a luxury. Animals were cheap, conveyances were easily constructed.

Then with the invention of steam transportation and the growth of cities, individual conveyances began to decrease in number, so much so that in England the term "gigman," or a man who owned a gig, was descriptive of aristocracy. Until a few years ago everyone, except a comparative few in the whole population, traveled by train or street car. And although the railway did a great deal toward diminishing the greater distances, it tended to increase the lesser distances. The intercommunication of the community was decreased. People could not so easily get about their immediate environment. It became difficult even to cross the space of a city. Wheels for local conveyance became fewer and fewer.

But once more the world is on wheels, and it will never get off them again. Individual and family transportation is not only a nation-wide but a world-wide fact. Instead of there being less wheels under personal direction in the future, there will be more and better ones. What the past found good and necessary, the present is finding good and necessary, and it will be the same in the future.

So, you could go through the whole round of daily living and find the old things coming back. We are even going back to the use of water power to a greater extent than ever our forbears did. It may be that we shall some time find many of the old-time domestic arts return to the household. What an influence for good it would have on trade at large if the households of the land learned again what constitutes good quality in clothing and food. We are being clothed with shoddy because we do not know how to identify good quality in the goods we buy. Our mothers could run their fingers over a piece of cloth and tell to the thread what constituted it. They were good buyers because they knew material qualities. But since the household arts have disappeared, we are at the mercy of the adulterator in foods and fabrics and other manufactured materials. Who knows but that the spinning wheel may yet return alongside the fireplace, the old settle, and the family conveyance? Who knows but that the family bake oven will return also? One thing is quite clear, if there were more of the art of baking bread in the land, the price of bread would more nearly conform to the price of wheat than it does now. But this phase of return to the old ways awaits a period of invention which will put at the disposal of the housewife the same improvements which have come to pass in other fields. We may yet see contrivances appear which will make the household more a self-sustaining community than it now is. Contrivances that shall separate the work from the drudgery will revolutionize the work of housekeeping, as they have done in other fields.

One former practice ought to come back at once, and that is the good old-fashioned habit of providing for the winter. All-the-year-round industrialism has had a tendency to make us an improvident folk in this regard. The fervor of the old-time Thanksgiving arose from the fact that men could see their winter provisions ahead of them. They had a feeling of snugness and security. The woodpiles were ample, the cellar was stored with the substantial necessities of life. There was no dread of the ordinary preventable lacks of supply.

It would seem that this practice is well worth restoring and preserving. It is an undeniable fact that
although we live in cities, although we have largely
left the agricultural field, we are still affected by the
seasons, just as it is true that although we have practically abolished night from our cities, we are still affected by the night. Civilization has not abolished
winter in the least, only a few of its physical dis-
comforts.

We should be approaching the winter in a better
frame of mind if we could think of all the families of
the country as well provided against their winter
needs. If we could feel today, in looking abroad on
our country and the world, that like the bees and the
squirrels, the families of the earth had kept winter
in mind all through the allurements to summer extravagance, and had fortified themselves against the
slackness and needs of winter, it would generate a
spirit of thankfulness which would be entirely purged
of selfishness and would itself constitute a hymn of
happiness.

The old ways were not so foolish after all. They
met the old necessities, and the old necessities are with
us yet. Life is a business to be managed, and a great
many people are "poor managers." This is not because they cannot be anything else, but simply because they have not grasped the idea that life is to
be *managed*. The home is a little corporation in itself
and needs something of the wise foresight, the wise
repression of unprofitable impulses which keep other
institutions solvent and afloat.

The old industry, the old thrift, the old preference
of the necessary rather than the unnecessary, will help
bring back something of the old material security.

It Is Imperfect—But It Works

IF YOU take our present social system and set it down as a diagram on paper, as the various reformers do with their social schemes, you will discover a curious thing—you will discover that the present system of society is utterly impossible, it will not work. Yet it does work! As you diagram it, it would seem to contradict itself at every step, it would seem to be the most unbalanced and ill-jointed and incoherent entity that anyone could conceive. Yet here it is, and it answers certain ends.

On the other hand, if you take Bolshevism or any of the other various forms of socialism, and put them upon paper in diagram form, you will apparently have before you the perfect scheme of a perfect society, and you may be easily convinced that it will work. It seems plain that it must work. Thousands of people, viewing the diagram, are thoroughly persuaded that it cannot help but work. Nothing remains to do but start it! Yet, the curious and disillusioning fact is that it does *not* work.

That is one of the strangest discoveries we can make: the utterly impossible thing goes; the apparently perfect thing fails. Make a diagram of social and economic life in the United States, and you would be ready to say, "Impossible!" Make a diagram of Bolshevist social theory, and you would probably be ready to say, "How practical, perfect and desirable!" Yet life in the United States goes on securely, while Russia, except to a few grafters, is a nearer approach to hell than was ever witnessed on this planet. Any Bolshevist who has had a full taste of Bolshevism as it is, will tell you so.

So many things are clumsy, stupid and imperfect; and so many offered substitutes are clever, logical and alluring, that it grows to be a wonder why the imperfect thing lasts and why the apparently perfect thing does not take its place.

The reason seems to be a deep-set instinct of humanity that paper-plans may be all right on paper, but society is an organism, society is a process, a life, a growth, which cannot be laid out on a blueprint, any more than a soul can be diagramed. ·

There is little chance of an intelligent people running wild with the fundamental processes of economic life. Most men know they cannot get something for nothing. Most men feel, even if they do not know, that money is not wealth. The ordinary theories which promise everything to everybody, and demand nothing from, anybody, are promptly denied by the instincts of the ordinary man, even when his mind does not form reasons against them. He *knows* that they are wrong, and that is enough.

But that does not dispose of the other fact that the present order, always clumsy, often stupid, and in many ways imperfect, can work along as well as it does. Admitting that it is not a perfect order by any means, it still has this advantage over the others—it works. To be sure, this is a fact in its favor, but it is not a fact which cannot be true of any other order. Doubtless this order will merge by degrees into another, and the new one will work also, not so much by reason of what it is, but by reason of what men will bring into it.

The reason why Bolshevism did not work, and cannot work, is not economic at all. It doesn't matter whether industry is privately managed or socially controlled; it doesn't matter whether you call the workers' share "wages" or "dividends"; it doesn't matter whether you regimentalize the people as to food and clothing or shelter, or whether you allow them to eat what they like, wear what they like and live where they like. These are mere matters of detail. The incapacity of the Bolshevik leaders is indicated by the fuss they made over such details.

No, the reason for Bolshevism's failure is its deliberate ignoring of common morality and human nature. Human nature is addicted to moral revolts, but it never respects a system that depends upon the moral revolt being constant. There are conditions under which every man will steal, but not even the confirmed

342

thief respects the system that drives everyone to thievery. Bolshevism has exacted the greatest sacrifice ever demanded of a people—the sacrifice of their essential morality and the sacrifice of their former freedom. It was a great price, a price worthy of a great return. But there will be no return. Why?

There is no truth and sincerity, therefore there can be no mental or moral strength. These things go together. Bolshevism does not know it. You may change social methods as much as you please; as long as the earth gives her yield, and as long as men are sincere, a satisfactory form of life will be possible. The trouble with perfect social diagrams is that they assume the control of men who are destitute of the moral sense, and who have no conception of the depths and heights of common human nature.

That is the explanation of the operation of our own social system as at present constituted. Wrong? —of course it is wrong, at a thousand points! Clumsy? of course it is clumsy; reminiscent of the Dark Ages at a hundred points! By all right and reason it ought to break down. Why doesn't it? Because it is instinct with certain economic and moral fundamentals. That is the reason.

The economic fundamental is, of course, labor. Labor is the human element which makes the faithful seasons of the earth useful to men. It is men's labor that makes the harvest what it is. That is the economic fundamental; every one of us is working with material which we did not and could not create, but which was presented to us by nature.

The moral fundamental is, of course, men's rights in their labor. This is variously stated. It is sometimes called "the right of property." It is sometimes masked in the command, "Thou shalt not steal." It is the other man's rights in his property that makes stealing the crime that it is. When a man has earned his bread, he has rights in that bread. If another steals it, he steals more than bread; he makes an invasion of sacred human rights.

Now, there is just enough of the presence of these two fundamentals to enable society to continue after a fashion and to yield the fruits of life to an increasing number of people. The majority of people work. Of course there are some who do not, but they have been so small a minority that they do not affect the whole. Property rights are acknowledged to a large extent. Not to the full, perhaps, but sufficiently to keep the social scheme intact and working.

"Not to the full," has just been said, but surely nearer the full than to total denial of rights. The scale will show that progress has been made more than half way, at the very least; yes, very much more than half way; and, what is better, moving toward the "full" all the time. You know, all there is to divide is what we altogether create. What we together create is distributed, that is, pretty well divided already; if it were not there would be no commerce. The contention seems to be as to whether the rewards have been divided. And regardless of differing attitudes as to this, the fact remains that here too the scale is rising toward the "full."

So that is what keeps our society afloat. Clumsy as it seems when put on paper, it has that saving essence within it—an essence compounded of industry and morality. You cannot build society without morality any more than you can build a span of broken planks. Indeed, what represents tensile strength in the social world is just this thing we call morality—no society is stronger than its moral conceptions, and when you seek the caliber of a society's moral conceptions you look at the security of the rights of property among them—the rights of the individual in himself and in the products of his labor.

A New Year

IT IS a New Year, but there will be an astonishing number of old things about it. Its newness is undeniable, but its familiar lines are unmistakable. One would find it not an easy task to separate the newness from the oldness during the year. Yet the Year itself is new. Every experience that shall befall us during its 52 weeks, will also be new. It may be familiar, known, but still it will be new. Life is made up of a repetition of similar experiences, with now and then an unfamiliar one to stand out as a landmark.

It is a new cycle of time. A new breath, as it were, woven in the Loom, raw material of which to make what we will. That—the time cycle—at least so far as we are concerned, is new.

But it is raw material. The fully made-up year is the finished product. What it may be like we have just had the opportunity to see. A made-up year has just passed out of the Time-factory, to take its place among the other 1919 years of this era.

It is not a particularly flattering product, the year we have just finished. Stand it up, turn it around, and examine it, and it doesn't stand scrutiny very well. It appears to be decidedly amateurish and very much botched. In no single particular is it standardized. There are spots here and there upon it which would seem to indicate that moments came to the makers when they really had an idea of making something— but then they seem to have resumed their aimless puttering again.

No; as we look at the year upon which history has just affixed the label "1920" we are not willing that it should serve as a sample year. It isn't good enough.

The reason is, of course, simple to understand. The human race has not been very long in the business of Year-Making. There are only 1920 credited to the production record of the Christian Era, and that is a comparatively small number.

345

"But after making 1920 years, a perfect year ought to be turned out now and then," might appear to be a natural objection.
That brings us to the "labor turnover." The same people have not been engaged in making the entire 1920 years. There is an immense turnover of humanity every generation. People appear on earth, pass a few careless apprentice years, and then seriously try—some of them—to do a man's work upon the making of the Years. But hardly have they learned the rudiments when a new shift comes, new and unaccustomed hands take up the work. The years run on, they come out precisely at the end of December on schedule time, but they do not show on their human side the marks of unity and mastery.

The year is after all but a small bit in the mosaic of the Age, and perhaps we shall be better able to judge it from a perspective which enables us to see the whole pattern; but even so, we are right in feeling that the whole mosaic of the age would be better, if each bit were better made.

Inevitably, next December, we shall have to deliver to the Builder of the Age another year, and it is natural to wonder what it may turn out to be.

What have we *new* about the year? Very little, except the time. That has never been used before, will never be used again.

But the old things that troop along into the New Year are very numerous. It is almost like the same old family moving into a new house; very little is changed after all.

It is the same old Earth, for one thing. And that is a genuine benefit. We know what the Earth will do. We know what we can absolutely depend on it to do. That is a great saving of time, for, if this year the human race had to begin all over again and by careful and costly experiment find out the powers of the Earth, the year would be almost empty.

But we know that the soil will radiate the sun's warmth in spring, that moisture and heat will create chemical conditions out of which man's food will come; we know that the earth will produce lumber and ores and material for clothing. We have learned

346

all that. It is no longer a question of anxious uncertainty. Take up a handful of soil; in it are the elements of food, clothing, shelter for all mankind.

Then, we bring into the New Year the same old necessity of getting busy in order to set the soil doing for us the things we need. And it is remarkable, when you begin to put the soil to work, how many men you have to put to work too. If it is the era of "the man with the hoe," somebody has to make the hoe. And then somebody must take part of the product of the hoe's work to the man who helped make the hoe; and before you know it you have started the Great Sisterhood of Arts in motion—Agriculture, Manufacture, Transportation.

It may be a better Agriculture—exchanging the hoe for a tractor; it may be a better Manufacture—exchanging the burden from men to machines; it may be a better Transportation—leaving the hand-drawn or ox-drawn cart for the motor vehicle on land or in air; but in spite of improvements it is the same raising, making and carrying of what we need. It is work in its primary and essential forms.

We are also taking with us into the New Year the old-fashioned rule that what a man earns is his own, and no one has the right to take it unjustly from him. It is a very good rule; without the stability it offers, society would be as impossible as agriculture would be if there were no certainty about the order of the seasons or the operations of nature. Many men try to change this rule; they want what another man has earned, and they want to take it in the name of "society." But people who have learned this fundamental wisdom and justice of the relation between personal and property rights, never unlearn it.

It would be very hopeful, however, if we could get some new things for the New Year. We begin work on 1921 under strange conditions. The Earth is just what it always was. Human needs, which are the mainspring of all activity, are just what they always were. Material and men, the essential components of civilization, are both here in abundance, and yet there is a stoppage of activity.

Why? Because, apparently, something has hap-

347

pened to—what? To the soil? No. To men? No. To material resources? No. But something has happened to that quantity known as Money. They are making it "less" in the country, "contracting the currency," they call it. They are trying to make money more nearly measure up with the gold. Why? Because "they" have decreed that Gold is the basis of Money.

There is not enough gold to go around. Even as a measure of wealth, there is not enough gold to equal in figures the actual wealth. There is not enough gold in existence to pay the interest on the war debts accumulated by the nations during the last few centuries. To make business wait on gold is like making the passenger traffic of a main line dependent on the facilities of a local branch with one small train a day. If gold did the work it might be as acceptable as anything else; but it doesn't.

It would be a splendid thing if in 1921 some financier, whose business is making prosperity instead of making money, should show us the way to avoid having business tied up for money, when all the elements of business are here. Financiers have been very skillful in devising schemes which draw all the money to New York; now for a financier who shall devise a scheme to keep the money in the local communities where it is needed! As long as we must have money, let us have it under a system where it helps instead of hinders, where it keeps men in their jobs instead of letting them out. Such a plan would make 1921 a great year. It would help the millions who are not financiers, but who are always under the pressure of our present financial system.

How It Will Be Solved

W HEN men grew tired of waiting for the wind to blow, they invented something that would take its place. For sails they substituted steam engines. For windmills they substituted force pumps. There was no objection to the wind, but there was objection to waiting for it. Men wanted something they could start themselves. They could light a fire in the steam engine and make things go. They could work the pump handle and keep water flowing. They could start things.

That is really the mark of human progress, when men can start things going, without waiting for the usual natural currents to create a movement. Some men can think; that is, they can start their mind working, they can determine when and on what problem their mind shall go to work, quite regardless of mood or liking. But other men can only receive thoughts; they are recipients, not projectors. Their minds are open stretches over which plays now cloud, now sun; they take what impressions they receive; their minds are sensitive plates, not creative dynamos.

There has been a certain amount of control achieved in the material world, but until the same degree of control is achieved in the economic and social world, we can hardly be said to have made progress.

Men no longer wait for the wind to blow, but they "wait for business to start up again."

Men no longer depend on the wind-driven pump, but they still wait for "things to take a turn."

That is, in everything but mechanical power we are still in the primitive age of our fathers. We are still dependent on the whim of the wind. If it blows, we go; if it is calm, we stand still. We speak about "business" with something of the same tone of the inevitable that we use when speaking about the weather. Panics come like rainstorms, depression like cloudy days, prosperity like "a bright spell," for all that human beings can do with regard to controlling these things.

The question is constantly becoming more and more pressing as to the amount of control that mankind can exercise over these matters.

As a matter of fact, the heart of the problem is just in that point. It is a human cause, whether you designate it ignorance or selfishness or what not—it is human. If it be mostly ignorance, the cure is in knowledge. If it be mostly selfishness, the cure is in social-mindedness.

But the one point to be clear about is that the cause is in humanity and not in outer Nature. If the Earth had at any time failed, the basis of human society would have been wrecked beyond repair. But there have been seed time and harvest continuously, and though there have been local crop failures, never has a failure occurred that would have prevented the whole world being satisfied if transportation conditions had been equal to the need. The Earth has always yielded enough to feed the people on it; the Earth goes on doing it year by year. Even with Central China and Eastern Europe starving, there is still enough food on the earth to feed the entire human race.

Now, we may use very high-sounding names to describe the activities which engage us during this life, but the one term which describes them all is "getting a living." And a living means food, clothing, shelter. Food means agriculture; clothing means manufacture; all three mean transportation. The basis of all is the Earth; it has never failed.

And yet it cannot be denied that as long as mankind regards its economic welfare as the effect of natural forces, now blowing toward prosperity and now toward depression, there is sufficient appearance of uncontrollable fate to give color to the supposition. If things are let alone to go down to zero, they do come back; and if things are left to rage along in a riot of prosperity with no thought of the future, they do come to a fall. There is just enough to justify man's lazy supposition that "if it's to be, it's to be" and nothing that he can do can change the result.

There are economic laws, but who knows what they are? The bankers don't know. The men who would frame the laws so that a gold dollar would mean much more than a man's labor don't know. Nobody whose interest is merely himself, whose sense of prosperity ends with his own position or business, can possibly know what economic laws are. And that accounts for the various rules set up for finance and industry—wholly artificial rules—which pass as "laws," but which break down with sufficient frequency to prove that they are not even good guesses.

The basis of all economic reasoning is the Earth and its products. If these are present, you have the beginning. The process then becomes a simple use of what is on hand in order that it may reproduce itself in the necessities of life. To make the yield of the Earth, in all its forms, large enough and dependable enough to serve as the basis for real life, the life which is more than eating and sleeping, is the highest service of any economic system.

Now, just there is probably where the sprout of the next development is to be looked for. We can make things—why, the problem of production is one of the most brilliant instances of human ingenuity. We can make any number of different sort of things by the millions. The material side of our life is splendidly provided for. There are enough processes and improvements now pigeonholed and awaiting application, to bring the physical side of life to almost millennial completeness.

Then what's the trouble? Principally this: if we had advanced to a type of life which was not mainly material (although, of course, it would necessarily rest on a material basis), then our interest would naturally center there, and our only interest in the underlying material and economic processes would be to see that they worked right.

Just now, we are wrapped up in the things we are doing without being particularly concerned about the reasons why we do them. Our whole competitive system, our whole creative expression, all the play of our faculties are confined to one of the lower chambers of life, which is the chamber of material production

351

and its by-products of success and the going standard of wealth. And it is regarded by some very short-sighted people as being to their interest that the present system never shall be perfect because it would interfere with the narrow scope of rivalry which is now afforded. It is perfectly plain why the outlook upon a standardized economic world should fill some people with dismay because of its dullness.

No need as yet to fear the dullness of a world which is in perfect economic adjustment, for mankind will never consent to perfect adjustment until he finds in a higher sphere the same outlet he now finds in the lower sphere. There was a time when part of man's business was to make fires, and keep making fires; making fires was a career to him. Then came the time when higher interests claimed him, and he wanted a fire that would burn of itself without bothering him. Finally he put his fire downstairs in a furnace where he could not even see it and where it need not trouble him more than once a day. Lately he has been putting it farther away still, in a central power house where it doesn't bother him at all. And it is all the time becoming a more perfect fire. He has grown. He now wants only the products of the fire. He does not want imperfections in his fire to distract attention from his higher interests.

Just so with mankind; it will wholly solve the economic problem when it gets an interest higher than the economic problem. Any kind of life mankind may live needs bread. Therefore, in order to prevent the question of bread breaking into his higher interest, he will come to the point where he will agree that the whole bread question ought to be placed on a standard base.

Lining Up on Your Own Side

WE ARE on the very threshold of a new age. The dates are unimportant, for in the advance of the plan of the ages it is not the sharp-cut dates, but periods of time, that are important. Old things pass away in a fading-out process; new things gradually dawn. Only on looking backward do the people usually realize that "a great thing took place back there." Surprisingly few of the real turning points of the world come amid signs and wonders and people standing in awe of what is passing. In the minds of most, the War was *the* cataclysm, because it was noisy; but something greater than the War, though much less clamorous, is in passage now.

It is neither for man to help or hinder, but hold himself ready to do what is right, whatever may be the circumstances. When the age begins to turn, we are too late to stop it, for the causes thereof were set in motion long ago and are now invincible. Nor can we help the new age be born, because we are but creatures of months, and the new age is generations in process of formation. We can but will the Right, not for our particular race but religion or nationality, but the Universal Right, which harms none, and in which each finds its own fulfilment.

One of the principal human duties that devolve during periods of change is *the duty of conscious allegiance*. What do you, *as* a personality and *in* your personality, stand for? And are you standing for it by standing with others who are standing for it? These are questions which are pressing home from many directions today. The bugles of Time are blowing "Assembly" and men are dividing themselves, each according to the moral note within.

It is not a question of allegiance to opinions or programs or philosophies; it is a question of allegiance to moralities. A man may be hopelessly wrong in all his opinions, but if he is morally right, he is of the

353

stuff of the continuing order of life. On the other hand a man may be perfectly correct in his opinions and knowledge, and yet everything he does may collapse and die because of moral anemia. In this time of change it is not a question of having the correct economic theory, it is a question of being loyal to the Right. Immoral or unmoral men never yet constructed an enduring social structure, nor enforced a single beneficial social change.

This coming to conscious allegiance is not always a pleasant experience. Especially in this day when everybody is obsessed more or less with the idea of wanting to be a "good fellow," and when the flabby philosophy of "Boost" has reduced us to spongy masses of saccharine sweetness.

Men have been taught to put even their moral convictions in the background, indeed to possess no obstructive moral convictions, in order that a false show of fellowship may be made.

This fellowship has now fallen apart. It was based on nothing enduring. It had no meaning except a desire to escape the penalty for being "different," which so many people fear.

It is a time now when conscious allegiance costs something, for it will mean division, and the very first division must be between those who will be loyal to moral conviction and those who will not. And this, quite apart from the consideration of persons or majorities.

The country has had considerable experience lately in the lining up of majorities on questions like Peace and Temperance, and because the majority of the people always believe, as a matter of principle, in Peace and Temperance, it has been made to appear that moral allegiance is always just that easy. It is not. The line-up, impressive as it was, has brought us neither Peace nor Temperance; and no such easy, popular line-up ever will.

The majority of the people are naturally straddlers. They are not in the world to pioneer but to be as happy as possible. If pioneering in a cause brings discomfort, they would rather not. If Truth and Error meet in combat before their gaze, they would rather wait and see which proves the stronger. They may have a lazy faith that Truth at last will win, but it may not be the time as yet, and they do not wish to lend a premature support.

And yet majorities are essential, not to the truth, but to the acknowledgment of the truth; and minorities are essential to the fructifying of majorities. The majority is the sodden dough, the minority the yeast; it is the yeast that changes the character of the dough to something better. Majorities are the position to be taken, as it were, and sometimes Truth takes it, and sometimes Error.

The natural tendency to straddling inheres in most people, and the exceptions to this tendency are not always praiseworthy. There are those who are merely contrary, because they like it; others are contrary because moral allegiance compels them. The majority wants to know if this thing cannot be amicably settled.

No! It cannot be settled. There are some opposites in the world that shall never be reconciled. There are some programs that shall never be harmonized. There are some wars which must continue until one side is exterminated. And that is what frightens some people. They want to be happy; they want to live and let live; they do not want to be bothered. They want leave to enjoy the world as it is, and if there are those who would improve the world, let them do so, but not in a way that interferes with the present schedule.

It is not hard or hardened men that the world needs, but men of moral hardiness who possess spiritual backbones. Men to whom the palliatory "perhaps" comes too easily, who are so impressed with the idea of "relativity" that they seek refuge in a near-vacuum, are men who are lacking in moral gristle. An Idea may be very valuable to them, but they are of no value to the Idea. And the world advances only as Ideas gather believing men about them.

It is a time of taking sides. There is a growing pressure to that end. Whether men desire it or not, the time is rapidly approaching when they will be counted on one side or another. In this country, at least, it may be expected that the majority will finally line up on the right side, but it will be an impressed majority—impressed by the force without in alliance with the still small voice within.

To take sides is not to exhibit prejudice. That is where many people mistake. The men who are freest from any taint of prejudice are those who have taken sides with their convictions, and stand there as sentinels and defenders.

If you want to know where the prejudice in the world lurks, look where there is no taking of sides, where everybody is trying to pretend that there is nothing to take sides about. That is where you will find most of the world's prejudice.

A man who has taken sides is thereby freed from prejudice. His step is open, frank, straightforward. His energies are free to flow naturally. But a man who fears to take a side finds prejudice grow within him like a cancer; it grows from the irritation of an unexpected antagonism in conflict with an unexpressed allegiance. It is suppression.

However, the movement has set in, and will be complete before the old era completely passes and the new begins. Everyone will have to take his own side. It is not too early now for everyone to begin to ponder on which side he really belongs, and whether, morally belonging to that side, he has the moral hardihood to give that side what belongs to it.

Change Is Not Always Progress

STRONG efforts have been made to fasten upon the public mind the belief that newness and change spell progress. A state of mind has been generated in which the mere statement, "Oh, that is the way they did it years ago," is considered sufficient to condemn anything. A fever of newness has been everywhere confused with the spirit of progress.

For many years the learned men who were supposed to know more than anyone else about social tendencies, were of the opinion that there were mysterious seasons and wind currents in human life, and that these accounted for almost everything, but that these seasons were as unalterable and these wind currents as uncontrollable as those of the natural world.

This idea has largely passed away. Most of the manifestations which we see in human life today have been started and promoted by people who know exactly what they want and how to get it. Many of the so-called "social tendencies" are just as much invented and controlled by human wills as is the organization of a grocery store or an oil stock company.

Last year men wore hats of a certain color, a certain shape, a certain material. One year the tone is brown, the next year green. One year the material is velours, the next year felt. One year a slouchy, rakish form is affected, the next year a shape at once free and neat.

Why green hats last year? Was it just an unexplainable fancy of the public that it wanted the color green to predominate that year? Of course not. The public had nothing to say until the hats came on the market. And those who placed the hats on the market had determined a year before what the people should wear. It was a promotion scheme. If you are in the right circles it is possible for you to get a pretty

357

accurate idea of what the crowds on our streets will look like for several years in the future. These are matters of engineering, not of free taste and tendency. The reasons, of course, are commercial. Hats are no better than they ever were; materially they are not as good, except when special prices are paid. The purpose is that a man shall buy several hats a year—four or five. It is not planned that any of them shall last over the year. In case, however, the *quality* does outlast the year, the *style* is changed, and that, of course, with people who are easily influenced, puts a perfectly good hat out of commission.

So that the basis of more than one line of business, involving vast quantities of material and human energy, is built not upon the durability of that material and the serviceability of that labor, but only upon the decree of some interested parties that this is "old" and that is "new."

Next to the fiction that gold is wealth, this fiction of "style" is one of the most potent devices for robbing the public purse. Both fictions originated with and are propagated by the same groups and for the same purposes.

These remarks are only illustrative of what now follows: There is just as deliberate a plan to flood the popular mind with changed ideas, and thus bring it into a condition where it will not think anything that is not "new," and where it can easily be led away from any truth that may perchance be labelled "old."

This course is most successful among those who do not think—and whether these are a majority or a minority is left to the reader's own observation and judgment.

The effect, however, is harmful, and in time will prove ruinous. The jack-in-the-box thinker is not impressive simply because his utterance belongs to today instead of yesterday. Everything we have is yesterday's, even to the bread we eat—which is literally last year's; and even to the political ideals we share—which are literally last century's, and earlier. We are not such "smart folks" as we think we are. The world today is full of the sound of crashing failures built on fresh, upstart theories. The trouble with

358

us today is that we have been unfaithful to the White Man's traditions and privileges. We have permitted a corrupt orientalism to overspread us, sapping our courage and demoralizing our ideals. There has always been a *White Man's Code,* and we have failed to follow it. It is natural for those outside the White Man's tradition to invent their destructive devices and ideas, but it is unnatural for the White Man to fall an easy victim to them.

Capital and labor are apart today, in spite of the natural tendency of the White Man's Code to bring them together, because an oriental idea has been thrust in between them for the poisoning of both.

The White Man's Code has always been to "do things"; the accomplishment of useful results is his highest satisfaction. For that reason the White Man has been throughout history pre-eminently the Doer. But an orientalism has crept in under cover of a social discovery, which has proved progressively destructive of everything it has touched—the professions, management and industries.

Industrial leaders have been poisoned to the extent that some of them look on their industries as "money makers," instead of plow-makers, or chair-makers, or clothing-makers. That is the new code: "Get the money." If you can get the money quicker by destroying the business, then destroy the business!

Professional life has also been infected with the same idea. Lawyers once had clients and doctors patients: now they have "customers." It is a sad drop, but it is precisely the condition desired by the orientalists who are busy injecting "new ideas" into the public mind today.

In industry, the man who still takes pride in his day's work, who really looks for satisfaction in the labor of his hands, is rated by his fellows as a "boob." He is a "back number." Even the American boy coming into life no longer believes that merit counts for anything; he is inoculated by the oriental virus which causes him to pull back, remain sullen and stupid, and give as little as he can.

At Ellis Island where formerly the immigrant used to come with shining eyes and hopeful heart, what

359

do we now see? A horde of people who have been systematically educated beforehand in the thought that the United States is "a capitalistic country," not to be enjoyed but to be destroyed; and the very first literature put into their hands on American soil conveys the same idea. We read a great many touching stories in fiction papers about the hopefulness and longing of the immigrant. The immigrants we have been getting for several years have no hopes nor dreams: they have a *program*.

All of these things come from the same source—a subtle orientalism that is breaking down the rugged directness of the White Man's Code.

We ought to go back to it. The type that made this country is still here, but its backbone needs stiffening. It needs to hear the call of its own race. It needs to seal its ears against the false cry of "Peace, Peace, when there is no peace." That which we used to recite in the village school—*"Eternal Vigilance Is the Price of Liberty,"* is more than a saying, it is a Truth; and its truth is being proved now, when Liberty is slipping away because of our lack of vigilance, not only, but our *impatience with anything that requires vigilance.*

The White Man's Code has three main points: Square Dealing; Fear of God and Absolute Fearlessness of Man; Unrelenting Vigilance.

These three points, if practiced today, would cleanse our country of every lurking foe. And the practice of the last point would keep it clean.

In Bondage to a Reputation

IT IS not with the distinction between reputation and character that this page deals today, although that distinction may well be kept in mind during its perusal. Reputation is what people think a man is; character is what he really is. Usually reputation and character go along hand in hand; what people think a man is, he is very likely to be; but not always. There are just a sufficient number of differences between men's reputations and characters, to make a sweeping statement impossible, except to emphasize the distinction.

One distinction not often thought of is this: the people make a man's reputation; the man himself makes his character. Reputation is repute. Repute is just what the people think over and over again; a repetition of thought, a multiplication of opinion. It is clear, then, that reputation is something the people give to a man. He himself, of course, must be sufficiently active or interesting or important to give the initial impulse to their thought; but, after all, it is their thought that paints his public portrait.

The public makes mistakes. It must have its devils and its angels, and its devils must be very bad, even as its angels must be very good. The hankering of the public after a good man to believe in is very pathetic. Being too wise to have anything to do with God, they set up a statesman, a philanthropist, a public benefactor of any kind, and then they begin to weave about him a romantic robe of dreams until he becomes a cross between Santa Claus and Gabriel.

No man is ever so good as the public wants its good idols to be; and no man is ever so bad as the public wants its bad idols to be. The reason is that the *public* gives repute, and not the man himself.

Reputation is, of course, an important point, but it is not of first importance. A man who is always careful of his reputation usually has not much to spare.

Reputations are such partial things anyway. Here is a man who has a reputation for ready wit. Another, during some retentive period of his mental life, stored up much knowledge of the sort which quickly turns to attic lumber—he has a reputation for learn-ing. Another, because of some act performed in a moment of indignation, gets the reputation of being quick-tempered or courageous. Another, a normal man, not self-centered, but living free in mind and body, does for a friend, without thinking of it, an act involving danger to himself, but effecting the other's salvation. He awakes to find himself a hero. There is nothing funnier than finding oneself a hero. One has read of heroes, admired them, dreamed one's boy-ish dreams of emulating them, but we supposed that heroism was something very grand to feel. We thought the hero felt heroic, felt as heroic indeed as the hero looked upon the stage. But he doesn't. The hero discovers for himself the immense difference between reputation and the inner sense thereof.

It is only part of the man that is involved in the reputation, good or bad. G. K. C. has a reputation as a writer; but he is more than that. M. J. P. has the reputation of being a good mender of boots, pro-fessionally a cobbler; but he is more than that. Rep-utations are such partial things.

But it is only when reputations become something to trade upon that they begin to bind men.

There are some men who regard their reputations as assets, who ought to regard them as liabilities, and they are "good" reputations, too, in the moral sense. It is a mistake to think that it is the "bad" reputation that is always the liability. Not at all. Good repu-tations sometimes hang like millstones around a man's neck; they are, in reality, the millstones on which his epitaph is already carved. A man has a reputation for cautiousness. Well, cautiousness is only a partial virtue. Sometimes a man ought to be cautious, and sometimes greatly daring. Sometimes he ought to walk across the street and sometimes he ought to run. To commit himself to follow either course all the time would be equal to a prison sentence.

Other men have a reputation for what is called

"common sense." Common sense is; as the term implies, the common possession of common people. It is very valuable. The majority of people are actuated by common sense. They are conservative. The majority *must* be *conservative.* That is the majority's *business*—to have and to hold, to protect and conserve the good of the past. If it were not for the conservative we should have nothing at all. He is the brother who stays at home and keeps the family farm in shape while his other brother roams afield, sometimes as a prodigal. In the end, all radicals come home to the conservatives; that is where conservatives justify themselves.

But, see what a hindrance a reputation for common sense may become. A man says to himself, "I have always been known as a man of common sense. I have always done what most people do, with an element of protective caution thrown in. People do business with me because they know I am 'safe and sane.' Yet, here I have a vision which I know is safe with a higher safety and sane with a higher sanity than any of my neighbors know, and I am moved to follow this vision—but if I do, bang goes my reputation for common sense!"

In such an instance, a reputation is the death warrant of a man's growth. He is not *living up* to his real self; he is *living down* to the self that he was twenty or thirty years ago. He is simply refusing to outgrow the features of the portrait called "reputation" which public opinion has sculptured in the gallery of public imagination. For that is all public opinion is, and that is all fame is, and that is all reputation is, just public imagination.

Too many men are afraid of being fools. It is granted, of course, that public opinion is a powerful police influence for those who need it. Perhaps it may be true that the majority of men need the restraint of public opinion. In this class of cases, public opinion keeps a man better than he would otherwise be—if not better morally, at least better as far as his social desirability is concerned. But doubtless there are cases, and many men feel the truth of it, where reputation keeps a man from being as good and as useful as he might be, because in service he would be led into the "unusual, don't you know."

Well, it is not a bad thing to be a fool for righteousness' sake. The best of it is that such fools usually live long enough to prove that they were not fools, or the work they have begun lives long enough to prove they were not foolish; and so the fool for righteousness' sake is revenged on Reputation after all.

Heaven help the man who has been poisoned by regularity! Not that belonging to the regulars, and being regular in everything from agriculture to religion is an evil thing—not at all. If a man deliberately chooses and selects a place among the "regulars" for the good he can do them, very good. The regulars need their servants and prophets, too. Many men are justified in saying, "I cannot do that, because it would injure the influence which I now possess in this special channel of work." There are men who, for the sake of moral usefulness among men, must make deliberate sacrifice of certain otherwise desirable things, and to these rightfully belongs their meed of honor.

This is not the class of men to be warned. These are not victims of regularity; they are missionaries to it. Others, however, who believe that the present form of regularity is the eternal pattern, who are in nervous fear of being so regular that they succeed only in being stupid, to them there might be given a stimulus to forego the bugaboo Reputation, and let their native decent impulses expand to fill the pattern they were meant to fill.

Depression, First Step
Back to Normalcy

TIMES of piping prosperity are often bad for business. Strange as it may sound, this statement will appear very plain and true upon a little consideration. We may say what we please about the business conditions which have hit the country during the last two months, but the real damage was done when everybody said that everything was lovely and the goose hung high.

By the same token, this period of depression through which we have been going has been good for business. The best thing that could have happened—it did not happen too soon. Business is on a better basis today than it was three months ago; it will be on a better basis next month than it would have been had not a halt been called.

These are simple ideas, but they are worth turning over.

You can see the good effects of poor business by just looking at the stores, the corner stores, and the big downtown concerns. It was not long ago that the ordinary frugal buyer was somewhat in contempt. Clerks caught the contagion of the profiteers, and it was "Buy it or leave it" almost wherever you went. The morale of salespeople slumped at a terrific rate, and that is a pretty serious thing for business.

Not so very long ago the coal merchant sat in his office with the air of a king dispensing favors. His attitude in many cases was, "I don't know whether I will sell you or not—I'll think it over." It was bad for him and for his customers. When any business man in any line of business becomes independent of the public, or even thinks he is, it is a calamity for his business.

In some industries all that has remained for salesmen and managers to do during the last few years has been to take orders and deposits, and adopt the air of, "We may let you have it in about six months—if you deposit enough now." Orders came without effort. Customers were doing all the clamoring and worrying. Whereas once it was the customer who favored the merchant by dealing with him, conditions changed until it was the merchant who favored the customer by selling to him.

Now all that is bad for business. Monopoly is bad for business. Profiteering is bad for business. The lack of necessity to hustle is bad for business. Business is never so good and sound and healthy as when, like a chicken, it must do a certain amount of scratching for what it gets.

Things were coming too easily. There was a letdown of the principle that an honest relation ought to obtain between values and prices. The public no longer had to be "catered to." There was even a "public-be-damned" attitude in many places.

It was intensely bad for business, all that kind of prosperity.

But there has come a change. The era of rampant prosperity so-called died down. The reckoning-up time came. Customers no longer besieged the doors. Indeed, customers have a memory, and they remembered that in the heyday of trade they were treated rather cavalierly. Many merchants are discovering today that he was a wise man who was just as anxious to serve and please his customers when trade was brisk, as he is now when trade is a little slower.

The best point of all is that this period of slackness is showing up the damage which false prosperity did to business ethics and efficiency. A good business is one that can sail along comfortably in the face of adverse gales. Since 1914 almost any fool could do business. There was more business to be done than there were business devices with which to do it.

It will be generally conceded that the period of so-called prosperity had a very deleterious effect on salesmanship. Salesmanship is more than taking orders, but that is about all it has amounted to during the last six or seven years.

When the rush of prosperity began to dwindle and then to cease, and it became necessary to pull in the collar rather than hold back in the breeching, then was the test. It was found in many cases that salesmanship had softened. The easy-chair and order-taking habit had demoralized it. It could not stand for the rough, hard work of going out and being refused, and being refused again.

So, it has been a blessing for business, all round, this period of depression; it has shown up the flabby spots. It has disclosed those people who were content comfortably to watch the wheels go round, but were not very handy in getting out and making the wheels go round.

We were getting to a place where no one cared about costs except the consumer—and he didn't count. Not only did no one make a move toward reduction of costs, they actually dreaded to think of the time when it would have to come. Business lay abed, like a boy who hates to get up and go into the cold barn to do the chores. Business was soft with too much good living.

Nothing has happened in our history to render out of date the business philosophy of Benjamin Franklin. Poor Richard's Almanac is still the best business compendium. The old American virtues of thrift and industry have no successors or substitutes. Business success is still a matter of making friends by *service*, and not a case of cornering necessitous people in such a way that they will have to come to you.

Free trade still exists in the local sense. Trade will always remain free regardless of monopoly or combine. Trade gravitates toward the man who has the desire and the will to please and serve those who need what he can give. When a man gets bigger than his business, when he begins to think that he has got things coming his way, and therefore may relax, he is in a bad state.

Every successful business is troubled with that sort of disease—complete satisfaction and relaxation. It should be ruthlessly exterminated. If this disease strikes the principal leader of the business, he should retire or be removed as quickly as anyone else would be. That kind of success is very bad for business.

Young men have been asking for a number of years

whether there was any possible chance for them to start for themselves in a world which is apparently so completely organized. Sometimes the answers were encouraging, sometimes not.

But now they can see for themselves. It is any man's game now who will play it according to the old-time rule of "value received." A business man is a servant, and when he gets too rich, or too high and mighty for that, then something happens, and some one else gets a chance. And that is occurring on a large scale now. Business is weeding out the over-ripe ones.

Thus it comes, reasonably enough, that a period of bad business is really a good thing for business, because it drives business back to its sounder fundamentals of honor in negotiations, quality in merchandise, and willingness in service.

It is a splendid lesson for the younger group of business men. They will keep their heads better during the next rise of commercial prosperity. They will be taught to trust more confidently in those principles of business which are as indispensable in brisk times as in slow times.

And, on the whole, it has been an easy lesson. It might have been much more severe. It will have been worth all it cost to all classes of society, if only we have sense enough to remember it.

We have been influenced too much by the grab-bag philosophy. We are making careers, and that is incompatible with the practice of "getting while the getting is good." Such getting is not good for long.

Flattery Used as Bribery

A MONG the dishonest ways of getting along is the
practice of working on the self-esteem of men by
praising them to such a point that they feel inclined
to favor you. Some crooks chloroform their victims to
rob them; others just suffocate their good judgment
with praise. The first method has at least the virtue
of directness; the second, even at its best, is suspiciously
on the other side of frankness.

We have developed in this country a habit which
must be modified by honesty, and that is the habit of
back-slapping and indiscriminate boosting, the glad
hand and the oily compliment. These never did go
down with men of hard horse sense, but they had a
considerable and pernicious influence on young men,
because young men naturally thought that this was the
standard way to do things.

Now, this is a situation which more mature business
men have observed with something of impatience and
something of misgiving. It must not be assumed, however, that they regretted to see a more human tone come
in business relations. Nor must it be assumed that they
protest because their ideal of a business man is one who
is strong as steel and just as cold, who cannot be bent,
nor even melted except in the hottest fires.

There is just the danger, that returning from the
orgy of back-slapping and artificial good-fellowship
which has marked the last few years—the era in which
the "smooth" person "got by"—we shall revert to the
opposite extreme of coldness and brutality. Not at all.
Extremes are always to be avoided. But whatever the
attitude, *sincerity* is desirable about all things. And
it is just the lack of *sincerity* which made so much of
this praise-mongering to be nauseating to plain men.

There are two great barriers to the free intercourse
of minds, to absolute transparency of conduct, and they
are, first, a designing attitude toward another; and
second, that which the designing attitude breeds, namely,

suspicion in the mind of the man against whom the design is laid. They are both unwholesome mentally, and disruptive socially. They constitute the major part of the silent warfare of life.

Now, all men like praise. If a man says he doesn't, he should examine himself again. He may not like to be praised to his face. He may be irritated by the fawning form in which praise is offered him. He may be angered by his knowledge that the offered praise is insincere and has an ulterior motive. He may be sickened by the hollowness of it. A man who had done something very well was once pained by the praise he received. He said, "They all praised me for the wrong thing." They had not considered his work enough to see the real point in it. And what he wanted was not the sticky sweetness of personal compliments, but discriminating and appreciative consideration of his work.

All men like their good work to be praised—but that is quite a different thing. There is something normal and wholesome about friends being able to meet frankly in consideration of a piece of work.

So, if a man says he dislikes praise, he must define what he means. When a man is able to praise his own work to himself, to behold the work of his hand and take pleasure in it, he is taking praise, just as much as if he eagerly drank in compliments spoken by another.

Now, the evil of life consists in all these wholesome and pleasurable sensibilities being misused to selfish ends. No matter what department of human nature you look into, the evil you see comes from selfish misuse. And so men have brought in evil through the gate of praise.

If you see that a man's weakness is flattery, and you take advantage of that to manipulate his judgment and his will, you are following, precisely the same tactics as the man who sees another's purse conveniently exposed, and takes it.

If you see that a man is built of such malleable material that a friendly, complimentary advance disarms him and lays him open to your power, and you deliberately thus disarm him for the accomplishment of your design, whatever it may be, good or bad, you

370

are working along a dangerous line; you are exalting yourself to a place which no human being is entitled to assume toward another for reasons of profit. It is a serious thing to descend to this kind of strategy or trickery even for the best purposes.

No one takes these tactics without sacrificing a great deal of sincerity. And besides, they are not necessary. There is nothing that this sort of strategy can accomplish, that frankness, honesty of purpose and even blunt truthfulness of statement cannot better accomplish. The straight open way is healthier for the mind of the man who is making the advance, and it cements a better relation with the man who is being advanced upon.

Now, inasmuch as there are still in the world many hold-overs from the last régime, who still trust in the strategy of the tongue, it is just as well that young men, especially young business men, should be on their guard. Instinctively, the majority of them are. There is something inside the normal human being—a sort of spiritual submarine detector—which warns of the approach of hollow words. Many lies are told: very few lies get across. Many deceptions are planned; comparatively few succeed. The interior detector sounds an alarm in most people. They are protected.

But there is among young men a native kindness which prevents them revealing the impostor to himself. When it is said that very few lies get across, that is true; but the liar does not know it; people whose detector warns them do not always tell him what they think. They sometimes act as if they believed the lie—and so, insincerity creeps in from the other side, too.

The young business man will more fully trust the older man who does not flatter him and who does not follow his flattery with presumptions on the young man's favor. Thousands of people are that way: they pay a compliment, and they believe that constitutes an admission ticket to special privileges. Deny them the privilege, and they go away saying quite opposite things about the person they hoped to "work." It is the meanest kind of cadging, this passing of compliments, and then waiting until the complimented man is so committed by the reception of the praises that he cannot say "no" without embarrassment. That is the meanest

371

kind of trickery. But young men who have been tricked that way soon learn the technique of it and are on their guard.

A certain delicacy of character would teach the self-seeking person that it is a vast presumption to offer praise to anyone, and the only consideration that can justify it is its sincerity and unselfishness. Otherwise, it is a profanation of one of the finest forms of human relationship.

If a young man in business is wise he will pay less attention to those who flatter his self-esteem, and more to those who stir his energies. A good, well-balanced critic who is looking to the success of the work and not to the feelings of the men who may be at the head of it, is the best kind of friend for a young business man to have. And if the young business man is keen he will see that such a one's interest and attention is the most real, yet the most delicate form of friendship and praise. It is strong. It is based on frankness. *AND* it will be there though failure and unfavorable criticism overwhelm the project.

Divide between your flatterers and your friends, and you already have a chart by which to sail.

Inflated Prosperity the Real "Bad Times"

ONE of the common habits people fall into is to explain everything by the term "business." We explain depression by saying that "business is bad." We explain far-reaching changes by saying that "business is undergoing a readjustment." We look hopefully toward the time "when business will pick up again."

The mistake is rather childlike, as if we should declare that the thermometer governs the weather. To be sure, the thermometer is "down" when it is cold, and "up" when it is warm, but the thermometer is acted upon by other forces; it does not act upon them.

Business is a barometer. It registers various conditions. But it is not the master-force in the world. It is a sign of life and creative activity; more than that, it is the sign that for the moment the interaction of all the social elements has reached a degree of harmony sufficient to give all men the happiness of being busy and the satisfaction of being supplied. So, when it happens that business is "down," like the thermometer, it does no good to put it "up" by artificial means. The thing to do is to change the general condition, whatever it may be, and business will reflect the result as surely as the mercury rises with the first mild days of spring.

Many other adjustments must occur before we get the "business adjustment" which people believe is the one thing necessary.

And these adjustments are now in process. That is a point we ought to bear in mind: *these adjustments are now going on.*

People often say "things are at a standstill." No, they are not. If we could see the whole economic process, not merely the one point where it makes contact with us as individuals in our jobs, we should see that nothing is at a standstill, but that everything is moving and changing—even now, when everything seems to be dull.

· What we call "hard times" are economically the beginning of "good times." That is, a period of depression is not the tail end of the old era; it is the introductory period of a new era. Now, that idea is worth getting, for it shows us as by a light just how foolish we mortals are in the matters which most vitally affect us in our economic interests.

We think that this business slump is the end of the old period; *it is really the beginning of the new.* If we had been wise we would have recognized that the feverish prosperity of last spring and the preceding winter were the real "bad times" of which we should have been afraid. Wise men told the people that, but did anyone heed? Only a few. That feverish, flashy prosperity during which money was spent in fast and furious manner, and everybody was independent and felt that he could walk out of his job any time he wanted; that complete let-down of all common sense in expenditures and manufacture and labor—that comprised our hard times! But we did not know it.

That period had to end. That was the ruinous period. All the damage was done then. And when it did end, then readjustment immediately began. The slow-down and stoppage was the first sign of healthy recovery from the fever of irresponsible folly. The slow-down was not the disease; it was the convalescence. We were sick, sick during what we thought was the heyday of our economic golden age; so sick, that in our delirium we mistook dangerous economic conditions for "prosperity."

Whatever disaster may be falling now is not a consequence of present conditions, but of former conditions. From this time forward, indeed from the time the fever left us, the general economic condition has been on the mend.

When people are able to see that the time to be fearful is in times of irresponsible prosperity, in the drunken revel of profiteering—then, we may hope for the prevention of periods of what we call "hard times." The only way you can eliminate the periods of convalescence is by eliminating the periods of illness. And

374

the only way to eliminate economic illness is not to confuse it with economic convalescence, as the people have done for a century.

The whole matter is so intertwined that you cannot speak of it under such terms as "money," business," "credit," or the like. These only represent a special angle of the general whole. The crucial readjustments that take place at times like this are not fiscal at all, but human. The whole secret of economic recovery is stated in human, and not banking terms.

When a crowded excursion ship is lurching too heavily on one side, threatening to capsize, what is the remedy? Readjustment of the burden. If all the people have rushed to the port side, have half of them return to the starboard side. This equalizes the burden. It is evenly distributed, and thus more easily carried.

Something like that has happened to the economic ship. Too many people crowded over to one side. The City constitutes but a small part of the world. The Manufactory constitutes only one part of the work of the world. Yet everybody wanted to crowd into the City, and to enter the Factory. And the result was that an artificial congestion arose, and we called the fever of that congestion by the delusive name of "prosperity." All sorts of unnatural things came out of it. Unnatural ideals of life. Unnatural exaggeration of the value of money. Uhnatural disproportion between qualities of materials and the price asked for them. Unnatural notions of what constituted "a good standard of living." Unnatural waste of materials in cheap and gaudy "luxuries," which were only toys. The whole condition was unhealthy in the extreme, but because there was a hectic flush upon its features, men thought it was the color of "economic health." It was the consuming fever of economic dissipation.

You see, therefore, what line some of the readjustments had to take. People had to do a lot of readjusting themselves. What is the meaning of the "For Rent" signs in our cities and the deflation of the rent profiteers' balloons? Simply this: people are readjusting the inequality of the population between country and city. Thousands of people are going back to the real country, which lies outside the cities.

375

The people who are now going back to the country are an advance guard. The time is coming when, if industry needs them, it will go to the country and get them, erecting pleasant little workshops beside the local streams, and begin industry anew under natural conditions. It is natural for people to like industry, to want to work in industrial institutions; but it is unnatural that a million people should have to be packed in the narrow area of the City in order to gratify that desire.

We must not think, therefore, that those who are leaving the cities are the defeated ones. Not at all. Heaven forbid that our standard of success should ever be in the present type of city life! Those who are going back are the vanguard of a new movement which will continue until a proper adjustment has been reached.

So, all these wholesome things are occurring now. The whole situation is mending fast. No one will doubt that the people are in a much more wholesome frame of mind than they were a year ago. And there can be no prosperity without this sound state of mind on the part of the people. The first essential of prosperity has therefore come back already: the fever has left the public mind.

Choosing and Being Chosen

MOST of the wisdom of the world was in the copy books. The lines we used to write over and over again, the homely old maxims on which we practiced to obtain legibility of our p's and q's, were the essence of human wisdom. They were the first-aid packages which the philosophers made to assist men who might need help out in the midst of the field of life. Most of the books that have been written since the copy books are only commentaries thereon; they say with more and harder words what we used to read in our first lessons.

It isn't learning, it is wisdom or plain sense that helps one through. Any man can learn all that he needs to know. No one ever learns more than he wants to know. We never learn anything unless we want to. Sometimes you will find a man with what appears to be a lot of useless learning, and you discover that he accumulated it not because of his interest in its special departments, but because he thought that acquaintance with a multitude of subjects added to his prestige. He accumulated knowledge as he accumulated neckties or golf sticks.

The whole secret of a successful life is to find out what it is your destiny to do, and then do it.

Now, that idea has several sides. When we speak of what we "do" we usually mean what it is we "do" for a living. "What are you going to do when you are a man?" we sometimes ask the children; it means at what occupation are they to be engaged.

Well, we all have to work. But most of us have something else to "do" as well. If all that a man has to "do" in the world is the mechanical operations he performs during working hours, then it would follow that if machinery should be invented to perform that operation for him, he would have nothing to "do." One of the really useful figures of his time used to say that his work was of quite a different character than appeared to observers; the observers thought he was a cobbler; but he said he mended shoes only to pay the expenses of his proper work.

We toil because we have to square our debt with the earth—we have to pay for the wealth she lends us in every material thing we use. But what do we do with the life that we thus buy? That is the true form of the question as to what we "do."

But there is something besides our toil—there is also our work. Our toil is what we have to do to bear our part of the work of production in which mankind is engaged, and the fruits of which are essential to our well-being. That is our toil. But our Work is that which we would do all the time if we, could. Happy is the man whose toil and work are one. There are many, however, not so happily situated.

Most of us are doing two things: that by which the body is kept alive, and that by which the higher part of our nature lives. We go to the job to pay expenses, and then we indulge ourselves in what we like to do, and maybe were meant to do.

That is the secret of all the "amateurs" in the United States. Amateurs are not always what we think they are. They are often more intelligent and skillful than the professionals. We shall have to change our ideas of the meaning of amateur; formerly it meant those who knew very little and were unskillful; those who had a liking for an art or a science, but merely dabbled. That idea will have to go in favor of the truer one, that the "amateur" differs from the professional only in this, that the professional gets his living by it and the amateur does not. In some respects the amateur is better off, for he has two fields—that by which he pays expenses, and that in which he finds expression.

It is amazing to find how many people in the United States have evolved financial systems. Here, there, everywhere are men who have occupied their spare hours with the great subject of money. Farmers, store-keepers, mechanics, country editors, could collectively roll up a mass of research and speculative literature on this subject that would literally swamp the received authorities in the region of finance.

All this has a meaning. It means that the people

are being prepared for something in the money realm. When you find receptive minds in all classes of society being moved by the same master note, you may be sure something is coming. All this mass of thought by plain people is the prophetic soil whence shall come the one whose mind can gather up all the fruitage of the others and bring the epochal change to pass.

In truth there are no discoveries. Nothing is ever entrusted to one man alone. We know now that no one man invented printing; the idea was seeking incarnation and found its way into life through several men at about the same time. Columbus was not the only discoverer of America: other men's thoughts had been set this way. Destiny takes precaution that no purpose shall fail through the unfaithfulness of one man; and so the new truth is entrusted to several. It is this which leads to so many bickerings in the matter of discoveries; it is hard to prove who was "first"; the idea was abroad "in the air," and it came through to the minds that were receptive, that were keyed to its quality.

Now, when you look at this from another side it is a mighty encouraging thing. Some day there may come to you the duty to do a disagreeable task, to take up a cause which will yield you no reward, which will at first envelop you in misunderstanding and abuse, which will make you look like a fool before men. You will shrink from it naturally, yet if you are the person selected for the task, some way it will make itself known to you as a serious proposition regardless of your likes and dislikes.

The appointed task may be less to your likes than you expected. A man's real work is not always what *he would have chosen* to do. A man's real work is what *he is chosen* to do. There is all the difference between *choosing* and *being chosen*. Sometimes our choices are our destruction.

But when you are sure of what you have to do— and unselfish sincerity, simple willingness to do what is right are the only compasses by which you can be sure—then you may also be sure of this: *you are not the only one.*

Others have been notified and called out, too. But maybe not to initiate the work. Maybe just to form the silent background, the receptive soil for the effects which your work will bring about. No man ever stands alone in any cause, if it is a righteous cause. When he calls, his voice will be heard and answered. He will be made aware by a thousand means that what he trembled before as a stern, forbidding task, is really the silent interest of many people.

There is a great deal of nonsense spoken about "the lonely heights." They are not lonely, though they may be silent. The loneliness comes when a man settles within himself whether he is to be a mere form, following a conventional routine, or whether he is to listen and obey the voice of changeful life. It is lonely for him while he is deciding. If he decides to do what duty bids him, then he is no longer lonely; he comes at once into the fellowship of all liberated souls. The only liberated souls are those dedicated to perpetuate obedience.

Most of us will never get fame. In a way this is to be regretted, for if we could get it we should know how well-off we are without it. Most of us will never shine as the captain-leader of great movements; but the real success and achievement of life is to be one of the foot soldiers of those great silent movements which, like the motion of the sea, keep humanity from stagnation

Can You Stand Friction?

PITY the poor fellow who is so soft and flabby that he must always have "an atmosphere of good feeling" around him before he can do his work. There are such men. They produce with a sort of hothouse fervor while they are being coddled, but the moment the atmosphere chills and becomes critical they become perfectly helpless. And in the end, unless they obtain enough mental and moral hardiness to lift them out of their soft reliance on "feeling," they are failures. Not only are they business failures; they are character failures also; it is as if their bones never attained a sufficient degree of hardness to enable them to stand on their own feet.

There is altogether too much reliance on good feeling in our business organizations. People have too great a liking for working with the people they like. In the end it spoils a good many valuable qualities.

Don't misunderstand; when the term "good feeling" is used, it means that habit of making our personal likes and dislikes on purely affinitive and emotional grounds, the sole standard of judgment.

Suppose you don't like that man. Is that anything against him? It may be something against you. What has your like or dislike to do with the facts, anyway? If you are a man of common sense you must know that there is many a man whom you dislike, whom you must admit is better than yourself.

When you were a lazy young fellow you probably disliked the boss who tried to keep you busy. When you were a careless, wasteful young sport, you probably disliked the wise old head who took you aside and told you how many kinds of a fool you were. When you got into business and settled into a rut, you probably disliked the progressive fellow who came along with some live-wire competition and make you get out and hustle again.

But what do these dislikes show? Simply what *you*

were. That ought to be enough to make you careful to remember that your dislike always tells more about you than it does about the other fellow. Your dislike may be wrong about the other fellow; it is perfectly unmistakable in what it says concerning you.

Now, if you are one of those easy-going people who prefer to have a certain type of persons around you—just that type and no other—it is a sign of which you ought to take notice. There is a dangerous psychology in having only agreeable people around you; it is too much like a man reclining on cushions all the time. Some men like to have around them women who "understand" them, and men who agree with them, and friends who will always defer to them, and a public that will always say "Bravo" no matter what is done.

The worst of it is, a man can have just these things if he wants them. But they leave him without gristle and marrowbone in the end.

You can have far too much harmony, especially in business. You can go too far in picking men because they harmonize with you in your nature. You can have so much harmony that there will not be any of the thrust and counter-thrust which means life, any of the competition or friction which means effort and progress.

It is one thing for an organization to be working harmoniously toward one object, but it is another thing for an organization to work harmoniously with each individual unit of itself.

Some organizations use up so much energy and time maintaining a feeling of harmony in themselves that they have no force left to work toward the object for which the organization was created.

The organization is secondary to the object. The only harmonious organization that is worth anything is an organization which is all bent on the one main purpose—not to get along *with* itself, but to get along *toward* the objective. A common purpose, honestly believed in, sincerely desired—that is the great harmonizing principle.

Now, if John Smith does not like James Jones, what does that matter? The main question is, does James Jones know his business? Can he advance this program toward its objective? Away with personalities! This trivial, unexplainable temper which turns to likes on one hand and to dislikes on the other; this apparently unreasonable and irresponsible influence of attraction and repulsion—these are stray mental phenomena ,which may have reasons and meanings in some spheres of our being, but the man who allows such feelings to be the sole judge of men and the sole determinant of his comfort in working with men, is certainly laying out trouble for himself.

The whole matter of harmony has been over-emphasized. Not only over-emphasized but wrongly based. Everybody has the idea that harmony means the various units of the organization getting along well with each other, after the manner of guests at a party. But that is not the basis of the harmony that achieves: the only basis for effective organizational harmony is a common belief in a common cause.

A certain amount of friction is a good thing everywhere—not antagonism, for that is waste; not jealousy, for that is infantile stupidity; not a selfish and unprincipled cutting under of another fellow—but frank, open understanding that on this job at least we stand for what we are and nothing more.

Everybody knows of businesses where fellows are being "held up" through friendship. The staff thinks that So-and-So is a good fellow, or the boss likes him, or he maintains a sort of position because he "is easy to get along with." But what about the business? For everybody thus being held up, someone is doing the holding up, and the business is burdened to hold up both of them.

An organization can be so perfectly "harmonious" that it has lost the power and the courage to prune itself of its own dead limbs.

An organization can be so perfectly "harmonious" that its only salvation depends on someone coming in and making it work with people it "doesn't like," and making it do work that it "doesn't like"—in short, making it amount to something by doing what it doesn't like.

Don't do all the things you like to do; and do most of the things you don't like to do; and then you will become a character strong enough to step out and accomplish things with men whom you don't like and who possibly don't like you.

The young man, especially the young business man, had better put this "like" stuff away from him entirely; it is as enervating as lolling among cushions all day. The wise manager will get most of his work done through men whom he doesn't like and who may not like him; all that is necessary is for him to know and respect their ability and dependability.

Men who know will agree with this: there is a stronger bond between men who respect each other for their strong qualities, than there is among men who "like" each other for their merely amiable qualities.

How would you measure a man's value? You reply, "By what he is worth." Not by what you think of him, that is, not by how you react to his personality in liking or dislike? "No." Very well. If that is the rule you follow, you will not be likely to do an injustice to your fellow-man by misjudging him, nor to do an injustice to yourself by fortifying the always human tendency to unreasonable prejudices.

If you feel yourself getting soft and ineffectual, get out where there will be no sympathy, no understanding, no admiration, but just plain challenge to do what is in you. That will brace you up.

If You're Settled
You're Sagging

THE pull of gravitation upon us is mostly felt in the desire to find some routine that will almost run itself, to organize a business that will operate itself automatically and for an indefinite period, to strike a single comfortable rut and to keep it. This is the downpull which men ought to resist, especially in these changeful times when the future is offering itself to foresight, and will be the servant of those who are able to detach themselves from the familiar and adventure with the new.

In the horse age we used to see this tendency represented in animals who were accustomed to a certain daily round. The doctor went to certain houses, and his horse became accustomed to stop there, and would always turn in whether reined in or not. The milkman went his round, and his horse behaved as if displeased if any change was made in the daily program.

Men fall into the same half-alive habit. Seldom does the cobbler take up with the new-fangled way of soleing shoes, and seldom does the artisan willingly take up with new methods in his trade. Habit conduces to a certain inertia, and any disturbance of it affects the mind like a trouble. It will be recalled that when a study was made of shop methods, so that the workman might be taught to produce with less useless motion and fatigue, it was most opposed by the workmen themselves. Though they suspected that it was simply a game to get more out of them, what most irked them was that it interfered with the well-worn grooves in which they moved.

There are business men who are going down with their businesses because they like the old way so well they cannot bring themselves to give it up. One sees them all about—men who do not know that yesterday is past, and who woke up this morning with their last year's ideas. It could almost be written down as a prescription that when a man begins to think that he has at last found his method, he had better begin a most searching examination of himself to see whether some part of his brain has not gone to sleep. There is a subtle danger in a man thinking that he is "fixed" for life. It indicates that the next jolt of the wheel of progress is going to fling him off.

The only business that has a promise of security is the business whose manager has hardihood enough to change it, even though he may love it ever so much, when his common sense tells him that a change is coming. It is a hard thing to do, but the hard things are usually the right things to do, and a man is better for following his vision instead of his "likes."

And what makes it hard?. It will not be hard for the man who comes to do it for the first time—why is it hard for the other? Because he has softened down into the old methods; he has allowed them to mold him, instead of himself molding them; he has become a creature of his method, instead of its controller.

The past has a strong hold on us through its detail. We cannot break with the past, but we can scrape off the clinging seaweed of its details. We can break down the whimpering laziness of mind which resents the intrusion of new methods. We can acknowledge each day as a new day and not a mere repetition of yesterday.

Life is not a "battle" except with our own tendency to sag under the downpull of the habit of "getting settled." If to petrify is success, all one has to do is to humor the lazy side of the mind; but if to grow is success, then one must wake up anew every morning and keep awake all day. Great businesses become but the ghost of a name because some one thought they could be managed just as they were always managed, and though the management may have been most excellent in its day, its excellence consisted in its alertness to its day, and not in slavish following of its yesterdays. It is not likely there will ever

386

be many really new things to do, but it is certain that
most of the old works will be performed in a new way,
Fundamentally, agriculture will always mean producing foodstuffs and clothstuffs from the field; transportation will always mean conveying materials by
wheel across the surface of the earth or by bottoms
across the surface of the waters; manufacture will
always mean armies of men working raw materials
into articles of use.

Everything we now point to boastfully as evidences
of our progress consists simply in doing some old
work in a new way. Most of that progress consists
in getting light from filaments instead of tallow, getting wheel-movements from fire instead of ox-muscle.
Most of the history of material progress can be written as a story of the successive ways by which wheels
have been made go round. There is nothing new except in the way it is done.

Society is always in danger from two classes, those
who fear change, and those who crave it. The first
class tends toward decay, the second toward destruction. Change is not to be sought for itself alone, but
in following to best advantage the obvious beckoning
of the times.

There is always something outside ourselves that
gives the signal; a motion of advance that comes over
the earth like the coming of spring, and those that
are alive respond to it; those who prefer to continue
their hibernation in the old methods, fall out of step
with the advance. They remain comfortable enough,
no doubt, but they no longer count.

It pays a man always to have ideas in advance of
what he is doing; that is the only valuable capital.

Changes are coming in every field, and the ·cause
of the jagged interval between two periods is men's
hesitancy to give up the old and plunge into the new.
The old leaves fall to make room for the new. The
old methods are suddenly found to be inadequate because new combinations are arriving. The sleepy side
of our minds complains that we are being shaken out
of our old life; the vividly alive side of· our minds
would show us, if we would permit it, that we are only
being shaken into our new life.

It is not given to every generation to pass through a period of change. Life ran placidly for our forefathers for long stretches at a time, and in the older countries a certain method of life became so fixed that it left century-long traces on city and countryside. But in these latter days the intervals of change become shorter and shorter. The pace is quickening. Period follows period out of all reckoning with the old calendars. We have seen an almost complete revolution in the past 15 years, and now we are on the eve of another; and as soon as that will have come, another will be visible on the horizon. The world is moving with breathlessly eager haste to some new position, and we cannot stop it. We can only stop ourselves from following along.

Life is not a location, but a journey. Even the man who most feels himself "settled" is not settled, he is probably sagging back. Everything is in flux, and was meant to be. Life flows, and is not in the same stretch of country for very long. Even the solar universe, we are told, is flying along like a flock of shining birds always occupying a new position in space. We may live at the same number of the street, but it is never the same man who lives there.

These facts may be resented or welcomed: the man who acknowledges them in a practical way in the form his service takes will always find himself in service; the others will be retired. Finding it hard to give up an incrusted method is a sign of a hardening of the mind which, like the hardening of the arteries, is not to be neglected.

When Not to Borrow Money

THE time for a business man to borrow money, if ever, is when he does not need it. This is a rule whose observance would prevent a great deal of trouble and, what is more, would turn out a better disciplined class of business men.

A business is one entity which must stand on its own feet. There is a great deal of talk about the soullessness of business and about the ruthlessness with which big concerns take their own wherever they are able, but just the same, if business were superintended by sentiment and managed by dreamers, there would be no business.

It is the unconscious compliment which people pay to business, that they always are ready to believe that business can help them, but who ever saw the public run to the aid of a sinking business? Why? Because there is an unconscious belief that the business that cannot stand on its own feet is not worth bothering about. And it is true. That is the whole austerity and severity of business; there is no monastic rule more austere; there is no military discipline more severe; that business is justifiable only as it serves, and that it is permanent only as long as it can stand by right and not by favor.

A business concern is a living body, though not nearly so perfect as the human body. If the business entity were as united and as responsive as the human body, the progress that we are making now would seem nothing in comparison with the progress we should then make. In the human body, the executive functions located in the office up in the head are able to convey their orders directly to the hands, feet, eyes or mouth. Normally, orders are precisely obeyed. But in business it often happens that the executive ideas could not be recognized by the time they have passed half-way down the shop.

Now, because business is like a living body, it is

capable of derangement, sickness. We make a great mistake when we think that business becomes sick only from without. The real illness to fear is not "depressed trade" (that is an outer condition), but deranged functions, an internal malady.

Take the tree. In times of "good business," so to speak, it clothes itself luxuriantly with leaves; it pumps streams of sap from the nourishing earth; all its leaf-factories are kept going, in the daytime gathering the necessities of life and growth, in the hours of darkness absorbing them. Then come "bad times," so to speak: autumn storm, winter cold. The tree easily and naturally adjusts itself to the change. It detaches its leaves. It slows down. But it does not "fail." It does not "borrow." It simply trims itself to the situation; it does not even freeze up. When the life processes begin to flow full again, the tree is there ready to receive them. It stands on its own feet. If it did not, it would die. Indeed, the failure to do that is all that constitutes dying.

Now, the internal ailments of business are the ones that require most attention. "Business" in the sense of trading with the people is largely a matter of filling a want of the people. If you make what they need, and sell it at such a price as will make possession a help and not a hardship, then you will do business as long as there is business to do. People buy what helps them just as naturally as they drink water.

But your process of making the article will require your constant care. Machinery wears out and needs to be restored. Men grow uppish or lazy or careless, and that is a situation that must be remedied, too. A business is men and machines united in the production of a commodity, and both the men and the machines need repairs and replacements. It is a fact which every business man should realize that sometimes it is the men "higher up" who need this treatment most and get it least.

When a business becomes congested with bad methods; when a business becomes ill through lack of attention to one or more of its functions; when executives sit comfortably back in their chairs as if the plans they have inaugurated are going to keep them

going forever; when business becomes a mere planta-
tion on which to live, and not a big work which one
has to do—then look out for trouble.

You will wake up some fine morning and find yourself doing more business than you have ever done
before—and getting less out of it. Keep on, and you
will begin to feel the pinch. It is then that you show
what is in you; it is the last examination to determine
whether you are entitled to the degree of Business Man.

In such a situation you can borrow money. And
you can do it, oh, so easily. People will crowd it on
you. It is the most subtle temptation the young business man has.

Or in such a situation you can take off your coat,
plunge into the business and see what ails its internal
workings. Go through it like a surgeon. Remove dangerous growths, cut off wastes, purge away accumulated customs which hinder, put your business on the
operating table and give it a chance for its life.

If you borrow money, you are simply borrowing,
stimulus to whatever it may be that is wrong. You
are feeding the disease. Is a man more wise with
borrowed money than he is with his own? Not as a
usual thing. To borrow under such conditions is to
mortgage a declining property.

*The time for a business man to borrow money, if
ever, is when he does not need it.* That is, when he
does not need it as a substitute for some things he
ought himself to do. If a man's business is in excellent
condition and in need of expansion which the business
can take care of, that is another matter. But if a
business is in need of money through mismanagement
or a disorder of the internal functions, then the thing
to do is to get after the business and correct the trouble
from the inside, not poultice it by loans from the outside.

Money is only another tool in business, anyway.
It is just a part of the machinery. You might as well
borrow -100,000 lathes as $100,000, if the trouble is
inside your business. More lathes won't cure it; neither will more money. Only heavier doses of brains
and thought and wise courage can do it. A business
that misuses what it has, will continue to misuse what

391

it can get; the point is, cure the misuse. Then, when
that is done, the business will begin to make its own
money, as a repaired human body begins to make sufficient pure blood.

Borrowing may easily become an excuse for boring
into the cause of the trouble.

Borrowing may easily become a sop for laziness
and pride. Some business men are too lazy to get
into overalls and go down to see what is the matter.
Or they are too proud to permit the thought that anything they have originated could go wrong. But the
laws of business are like the laws of gravity, and
the man who opposes them feels their power.

Borrowing for expansion is one thing; borrowing
to make up for waste and mismanagement is quite
another. You don't want money for the latter, for
the primary reason that money cannot do the job.
Waste is corrected by economy; mismanagement is
corrected by brains and application; and neither of
these correctives can be confused with money. Indeed,
money under certain circumstances is the worst enemy
of these desirable qualities. And many a business man
thanks his stars for the pinch which showed him that
his best capital was in his own brains and not in bank
loans.

Borrowing under certain circumstances is just like
the drunkard taking another drink to cure the effect
of the last one. It doesn't do what it is expected to do.
It simply increases the difficulty. It is the capstan
of the young business man's education when he sees
that the tightening up of the loose places in his business is much more profitable than any amount of capital at 7 per cent.

Tariff—Taxes—Transportation

GOVERNMENT never will be efficient through and through because that is not what Government exists for. But in its tasks, in the various things it undertakes to do as specific services for the people, it should be a model of efficiency. After all is said and done, Government is a business organization, and something more. In so far as it is the culmination of national purpose and aspiration, it is as foolish to require efficiency of a Government as of a poem. That is not the sphere of governmental efficiency. But if it is a matter of digging a canal, of surveying a road, of delivering a letter—if it is anything like the things men undertake in individual or lesser corporate capacity, then we have a right to expect of the Government a perfect performance.

These services, however, are but a part of the work of Government. They lie on the factory side of Government, so to speak, and should be organized under efficient superintendents who are held responsible for results. But there is a great region of policy and progress where efficiency,, by the very nature of the case, cannot be maintained, but where wisdom is indispensable. Efficiency consists in doing in the best possible way anything which we already know how to do. But in the field of government there are some things which we have yet to learn how to do. We are still in the experimental stage.

Tariff is one of these experimental matters. Think of the many minds that have devoted themselves to this problem, of the party battles that have been waged over it, of the artificial prosperities and the needless distresses that have cursed whole populations as the tariff pendulum swung this way or that.

It would be most uncharitable to say that none of this effort to reach the basic principle of tariff has been honest; doubtless most of it has been; and doubtless the tariff idea rests largely on the confidence that

393

a tariff is justified because it is serviceable to the people.

Perhaps there never will be a perfect tariff adjustment until the world itself is perfected, and then there will be no need of tariffs. It is because of the inequalities of the nations and the imperfection of the earthly federation that these walls are wanted. Formerly they walled each city apart from the rest; now they only wall each country.

It is all imperfect, of course, and tariffs are but a part of the general imperfection. We can perhaps tolerate them better for knowing that they are an effect more than a cause. Certainly the tendency of the times is toward less tariff restriction rather than more.

There was once a hope held by a party that the tariff problem could be solved on the principle of "tariff for revenue only," but if that rule were literally applied now, we probably should have the highest tariff wall in our history.

Tariff has always been relied on as a tax producer, and as a side line it served the industrial party—the greedy and short-sighted financial party—as a monopoly-maker. It is right to protect American industries when this does not mean protecting and coddling the greedy inefficiency of individual Americans. This country does not protect the individual that way; why should it protect a group of individuals formed into a corporation? If it is an American industry, it can meet the world. If it cannot meet the world, it should not be artificially sustained to represent American industry.

Taxation is another problem still in the experimental room of government. There never was an ideal tax because there never has been an ideal expenditure of taxes. There has never been a perfect basis of taxation because we have no basis of value. Many plans have been suggested to meet this lack. The single-taxer would make land the basis; others would take a certain percentage of the income. We try both after a fashion, and instead of people feeling that the tax is their contribution to the cost of the benefits they enjoy under their Government, they oftener feel that

394

it is a burden. The very word has come to have an ugly sound.

The present administration must raise taxes, and of recent months most of the tax-producing sources - have dried up. What happens then? What does the Government do then? Maybe the Government will go into production to earn its own money. We have 100,000,000 people here who never stop eating, who continue to wear clothes—it is a pretty good market and ought always to keep business pretty brisk, if there were not some kink in the money machinery which the Government says it controls.

It is easy to say, "Lower taxes." But to stop taxes altogether might mean to lower our Flag. How would you like a 50 per cent reduction in all your taxes? Well, that could easily happen, and still give the Government 40 per cent more than it is now receiving for the purposes of government, if we were not so dumbly tied up with a system that takes oceans of gold every year for the upkeep of our man-killing machinery.

If the tax system were even 50 per cent perfect; if people had a view of the course of their tax monies which should be half as clear as their view of the influence of their ballots—that is, if the people knew their government, or if the facts of government were such as would make the government desirous of having the people know them, then the payment of taxes would become a pleasant ceremonial, like unfurling the Flag or firing off firecrackers on the Fourth of July. Taxes provide the method by which people enter most closely into the work of Government, yet nobody knows it. Fundamentally there is a wrong, wrong principle.

Then there is Transportation—that also is still an experiment. Nothing is more arresting than the service breakdown of the railways five years ago under increasing business, and their fiscal breakdown now under increasing income. When more business breaks a business, and more income renders it poorer, there's something deeper than mere mismanagement, there is something fundamentally wrong.

Of course, fiscally, our railroads are paying for multitudes of dead horses. Gamblers first controlled our railroads, robbed them till there was no-more gamble in them, and left it to honest management to pay the IOU's. Railroads developed artificially because their gambling controllers strangled the railroad's side partner, the canal—the canal, which, had it been left alone to perform its functions, would have assisted the railroad to grow on a more natural basis. But, no, the gamblers filled the canals with rubbish, and today the railroads are breaking down for lack of waterways to help them.

Our railroads are striking illustrations of the retribution which overtakes even a national and international business which is victimized by speculation. By being regarded as mere financial devices, railroads were cheated of the mechanical development which today would have enabled them to meet the changed conditions. Worse than being inefficient, worse than being near bankruptcy, our railroads are not admirable even in the railroad sense. They are equipped wrongly and operated wrongly and they never will be efficient and they never will be profitable again until they have been changed from the bottom. You can't run railroads from a speculator's office.

There, then, are three problems, all of them touching our times pretty vitally—Tariff, Taxes, Transportation. Each of them a field for dreams that come true.

Illusions Are Not Faith

M ANY a man thinks he has lost faith when he has lost only his illusions. It is one of the penalties we pay for not making proper distinctions between values. The power of illusion is so great, that when the illusion vanishes we think that the bottom has fallen out of reality; the truth is that only the mists have been dispelled. The mists sometimes give illusions of flowery meadows beyond; when they lift we see a hard road.

Illusions can be lost, but faith cannot. A good deal of credulity can be turned into skepticism, but faith cannot. A man may lose many things, but he cannot lose anything that he once possessed as part of his very self; and faith is such a part.

It is perhaps impossible correctly to see illusions until they have vanished, because they fill so large a part of the foreground of our minds while we have them. They are like the dreams of youth which are very real while they last, and even after they pass leave fragrant vestiges behind, but which in the clearer light of reality we see to have been wrongly placed. They were beautiful, but they were not true; at least they were not *yet* true. They may have been foregleams, as when a sunny day foretells the Spring but is succeeded by weeks of raw and changeable weather.

Illusions are numerous and take their color from the man himself. Perhaps the most common of them all relate to ourselves and society. There is a comfortable feeling which most of us possess at some time in our lives and which is based on the supposition that all men are good and unselfish. This feeling seems to be confirmed during youth, for as a rule the world does not show its hard side to young people. A great defect in ordinary education is the teaching that everyone is all right, when later experience, if it be normal, cannot but show that everyone is not all right. There is a sort of education which tends to make us soft and overdeveloped on the conciliatory side, so pathetically anxious for harmony that we are afraid to stand up for the truth which comes like a divisive sword and cuts men into parties.

Society is suffering a reaction from that attitude now, because of the weakness in ordinary thinking which leads the ordinary mortal, for a time at least, to say to himself, "Everybody is for himself alone; I will therefore be for myself alone, and the devil take the rest."

There are people who in their reaction turn to a deeper dye of the thing which they thought was not there and have found to be there; their reaction is not toward the actual condition as a real condition but incomplete, and then goes still further toward the condition that ought to exist. That is, men disappointed in their illusions as to human society often turn defensive and predatory, instead of constructive.

That is the cause of what is called "class consciousness" today—a predatory attitude toward a class to which one conceives he does not belong. It is seen at its most fateful development in Russia, and its existence is a warning to all men.

There is enough good in society to preserve it for all social purposes, but it is not of the ice cream party ·or missionary kind. It doesn't go out in large and generous waves, but it is there, waiting to greet its own kind when it comes along. But some men's bitterness upon the loss of their illusions is so strong that they miss the very thing for which their natures are searching. In the great social upheaval in Russia, there is a terrible lack of idealism. As one who has been through it says, the idealists become rapacious hypocrites as soon as they come into power. No political or social philosophy can be blamed for this; it is simply human nature.

Illusions are fine things to keep us afloat until we find our feet, and the best thing that can be said of them is that they trend mostly in the right direction. If they were not mainly tinged with the right color, they would not last long as illusions. Uncomfortable illusions depart sooner than any other, for truth drives them out; if truth is kindlier to our comfortable illusions, it may be because these are more akin to truth itself. However, illusion is at best a mirage, while faith has something solid about it—it is perhaps the solidest thing in the world. All faith at last is one faith, though the expressions of it may vary.

People do not commonly think of faith as solid and substantial; they regard it as an airy fairy nothing, colored balloons which one sends up for one's own amusement. This is because they have confused faith with something else.

Faith is know-so more than hope-so. Faith may begin as a conscious preference; it ends as an ironclad proof. The man who has faith *knows*. There may be still much work to be done on the drawing board or in the experimental room to make his faith articulate, but nevertheless he knows just as assuredly as if the thing were the commonplace of everyday agreement.

Faith is a higher grade of intelligence and is accessible even to those whose brains do not move easily in routine methods, who do not manufacture their thoughts according to the rules made and established by the professionals.

The rule ought to be, the less illusion the more faith, because illusion may be balmy, but faith is dynamic. Illusions are sedative, faith is stimulative. A man rests on his illusions, he climbs on his faith. Illusions grow less and less as life goes on; faith grows more and more. Illusions are many, faith is one.

Faith is the material out of which all the things that are yet to be are made. It is an invisible and plastic substance capable of taking upon itself the reality of visible form. Not only is it substance, but it is force as well. It probably does not create anything that already does not exist, but it has power to bring the invisible things into the visible plane where all men may use them. Faith is the matter out of which new pattern things are made, and after they appear, then commonplace men may make the same things out of wood or laws or systems, or whatever it may be.

We talk about having faith in ourselves. Well,

if we know what that means, it is true; but too often it means only a stimulated self-confidence, the assumption and presumption of a "front." But plainly and simply, faith must be in ourselves, because there we make the only contact with reality that we can make. It is faith in ourselves as having become at last a useful part of the whole, that the term really signifies.

We sometimes talk about faith and sight as if they were opposed; they are the same thing. The only man who walks by sight is the man who walks by faith, for he is the only man who can see. Nobody sees anything until faith has brought it within the sphere of vision.

Faith is the sixth sense that completes all the others and it shows itself chiefly in loyalty to Duty, for Duty sums up all the creative work we do. Our career is our duty, and our duty is our contribution to life. Creative work is not a fine and pleasant frenzy; it is often doing what we would not choose to do, for we are chosen oftener than we choose. A man plodding along at what he knows to be his duty is an agent of the universe, in his right place. Not only is he doing something, but something is being done for him. Faith works changes both in the agent and the objective. It is the creative medium, without any limit that has been found.

What Makes Immigration
a "Problem?"

THE immigration question has come to the front
again and gives another illustration of the difficulty of deciding national policies with rigid mathe-
matical precision. The fact that this question occurs
is proof that something is wrong; the fact that no
offered solution can be considered as final is proof
that we have not yet found the principle that should
govern us.

Two points are fixed, of which it will be very hard
to dispose. One is our national tradition as a place
of refuge for all people. It will be impossible to cause
the people of the United States to turn their faces like
flint against the populations of the Old World who
wish to come to us. We have stood before the world
as the open door for all who would begin their lives
again in a condition of liberty; we have never refused
sanctuary to the person fleeing from persecution.

The other point has already been made: our national attitude is the first; the plight of the alien is
the second; they merge together. To close our doors
is not a national act alone, it reacts upon human beings
elsewhere. And that we shall ever be loath to do.

That is to say, perhaps, that we are incurable sen-
timentalists on this question. We may admit this, even
while we keep a shrewd eye on those who diligently
play upon our sentimentality for their own purposes.

We may admit most of what the spokesmen tell us,
too—the spokesmen who are more interested in other
races than they are in America. We may admit, for
instance, that this country was made by immigrants.
So it was. The pioneers were immigrants. They
came to a wilderness and made it blossom. They came
to a bleak and stormy coast and filled it with commerce.
It is impossible to honor them too much.

We ought to be frank enough, however, to see that

not all modern immigrants are of pioneer quality. It is one thing to come to a country to help make it, and quite another thing to come to a country as to a ripe tree to pick it. *There was no immigration problem in the United States so long as immigrants came to help make the country.* The country knew its friends, felt the impulse of new life with every shipload of those who came seeking a place to bestow their best. But as soon as the type of immigration changed to include people who came to pluck the country of its good things, immediately the body of the nation felt its vitality decreasing, as with some slow insidious disease, and presently we knew that we had an immigration problem.

The pioneers came on their own initiative. A very large proportion of those who come now, are brought; they are transported as literally as an army is; they do not form that surging forward of the free and independent portions of other peoples which characterized our former immigration tidal waves. No country can have too much of the pioneer spirit, too much of that loyalty which contributes to the upbuilding of its institutions.

But what have we been getting in this country, particularly of late? What have we been importing besides immigrants? The immigration of destructive ideas has been enormous, too. It is easier to deal with immigrants, in whatever condition of physical, mental or financial decrepitude they may come to us, than with the false ideas which so many of them bring. That is one of the conditions that make the immigration question: we are importing something else besides people and the danger of disease; we are importing dangerous and false ideas—dangerous because false.

Now America is on the right road, or she is on the wrong road. The United States stands for personal liberty within the limits prescribed by the public good, and for equality before the law, or it does not. Our Constitution is the charter of a proper kind of national life, or it is not. We must take one side or the other on these matters, and we must classify men according to the side they choose. If they are of the opinion that the United States ought to be changed into something else, let them be so classified. They, however, cannot be considered as citizens contributing to the upbuilding of this country. If there is a class of people who come to us saying, "We are the apostles of a new era; your way of doing things is wrong; your whole system must be changed," we are entitled to say in reply, "That many of our ways are imperfect, we have long known; we are trying to perfect them; tell us how it is that a light has shone on you with reference to American problems that has never shone on us; show us what you have behind you in achievement and then we shall consider your fitness to become our rulers."

And, for the most part, we find that these people have no constructive record at all, and have nothing within or upon them that recommends them to us as the friends of the American spirit. They may propagate the idea that Americans think them dangerous only because they are dangerous to certain practices by which some Americans practice: they are wrong; we think them dangerous because they run contrary to the spirit of America.

The immigration problem is not only a question of numbers. The country is not in danger of being overpopulated. There are still great areas of land waiting for people. It is not the number of the newcomers that constitutes the problem, but their unwillingness to begin as pioneers, with the land, and their unwillingness to become American in the American sense.

This, of course, is due to several causes. And before the immigration question can be tackled satisfactorily, a number of things must be done.

The custom of hawking about Europe for immigrants who have least to leave should be prohibited. We are getting now those classes which their home governments are gladdest to get rid of. Indeed, their home governments are so glad to be rid of them that they facilitate their progress hither.

The custom of certain societies in the United States of assisting thousands of immigrants to evade the law by providing them with the amount of money required should be stopped. The same fold of bills brings any number of immigrants into the country, thus destroying the virtue of the law which makes possession of a certain sum an indication of certain desirable qualities. The custom of immigrants settling in the cities should be so regulated as practically to be stopped. What immigration is doing for us now is simply extending the slums of our large cities until they threaten to taint every part of every community. The United States should assume the right which other governments have assumed and say to the immigrants, "You may go here and settle where you will, but you may not go there." President Taft once said he wished that Russian Jew immigrants would go elsewhere than to the cities. "The more we spread them out in the West the better I like it," he said. "I have tried to help it along so we could help them directly on to the plains of Texas."

This custom of city settlement is encouraged, it is believed, merely to give power to racial rulers which set themselves up in every large city. Settled on the land, the immigrant would more readily imbibe American ideas and would be less amenable to the leaders' plans, and thus a leadership built upon so-called "racial solidarity," but really upon ignorance of American ways, would fall. This type of leadership is a very grave danger in this country, and it is the cause of some very disquieting manifestations in our national life.

More stringent rules of citizenship should be made. The immigrant should be more stringently required to look forward toward citizenship as an important part of his career, and the standard of the requirements of citizenship should be much higher and more strictly applied. It should not be more difficult to acquire membership in a lodge than it is to acquire membership in the citizenship of the United States of America. We have been far too negligent.

The Three Foundation Arts

NO MAN is more dangerous, in war or in peace, than the man who tries to stop the processes by which the legitimate needs of the people are supplied. When a man attempts that in time of war, he is dealt with as a traitor. His character does not change when he carries on his work in time of peace, although his punishment does. The reasons which move him to act at one time are precisely the same as at another. He wishes to aid some cause by breaking down the established character of the people's lives.

Everyone remembers what was thought during the war of men who tried to induce the farmers to raise less food, the shop workers to complete less work, the railwaymen to invent unnecessary delays.

Now, suppose there is today a return of that same program, is it to be regarded as any more desirable now than it was then? If a thing is good and right to do, is there ever any justification for a conspiracy to stop doing it? Yet there is considerable propaganda at work today to make men quit doing the right things for society. The farmer is urged to raise no more than he needs; the shopman is urged to do no more than he must; the transport man is encouraged to let society go hang.

And this propaganda is having a certain amount of effect. To understand it, however, you must not too hastily condemn it. It is not enough to say that the program is wrong in every way in which it is possible to be wrong. We must understand why men are persuaded to such a wrong program. Men do not enter wholesale into a conspiracy to do wrong. Americans do not undertake to injure society for the fun or malice of it. They have been persuaded that it is a means to a good end—a harsh means, perhaps, but to be condoned for the sake of what it has in view.

That is the point. Take the farmer's case, for example. Many farmers are saying now that they will not raise any more this season then they need—little more, anyway. The farmer is, in many cases, sore in his mind. Things have gone badly with him—not in failure of the crops, nor in the enmity of the elements, nor yet in the loss of public esteem for his profession— but in a money way. He has as much of the wealth of the earth as he ever had, much more in fact, but it has not meant so much in money. Farming has ceased to be only a matter of making the earth perform her yearly miracle; it has been hooked up with banking; and, of course, the taint of money exerts a disturbing influence.

Wheat will make as much bread as before, but it will not make as much money.

Now, men have been busy telling the farmer that if he will forbid the earth to yield as much food this year, if he will exercise a prohibition over the beneficent forces of nature, prices will go up next year.

Doubtless they will, and with them will go up the cry of the people because of a scarcity of food.

The farmers are persuaded to do this as a protest against the banking and financial system that juggled their prices downward. That is to say, farming has been advised to annex the evils of the financial system in order to get even. It is a clear case of two wrongs being counseled in order to make a right.

The farmers do not deliberately say, "We'll make food scarce in the cities." They say, "We'll do something to check this game the masters of the money market have been playing on us." Yet the latter means the former. And even then, it does not mean that the game will be won. Instead of food there will be prices, and nothing was ever sustained on prices alone.

Now, having this understanding of what the farmers are taught will result from their action, let us see how the whole case stands.

Society is like a city. There are some functions which, in a city, can never stop without disaster: they are the primal functions, for the benefit of which people gather together in cities of similar communities. They are such things as water, light, police and fire protection.

Now, these things must be supplied, regardless. If the city is wild or drunk, still the firemen and policemen must stand guard, and the water station must keep pumping. If the city government is inefficient and the revenues of the city wasted, still policemen must pace their beats and fire stations must keep the watch alert. There are some duties which, if deserted, destroy the last chance of betterment and reform.

In the great national community, in the great world community, there are certain primary functions without which modern life is simply impossible, and even primitive life is impossible.

These are Agriculture, Manufacture and Transportation, the three great arts. Community life is impossible without them. They hold the world together. Raising things, making things and carrying things are as primitive as human need and yet as modern as anything can be. Yet we cannot get beyond them. They are of the essence of physical life. They are to the world what water, light and fire protection are to the city—indispensable. When they cease, community life is no longer possible.

Now, the truth is this: things get very much out of shape in this present world under the present system, but the hope we have of a betterment of matters is that certain things are going to stand firm. The basis for a better state of things is here, if someone does not destroy the basis. As long as the foundations stand sure, a better building is always possible. Destroy the foundation, and no building at all is possible.

The great delusion today is to make the Men of the Foundation feel that they may trifle with the part they have been given by Destiny to play in the social process. They are being told that they are the victims, when as a matter of fact they are the world's chief hope, socially and economically. If they stand firm, they will help bring about the order that is desired; if they go fooling with the fundamentals committed to their care, no one knows what will happen.

Now, we have the main timbers for the new order, whatever it may be and whenever it may come. These main timbers are the men and means to *grow* things, to *make* things and to *carry* things. These will be the hold-overs, so to speak, or a better figure still, they are the bridges all set to see us across without disaster. As long as Agriculture, Manufacture and Transportation go on, the world can carry any economic or social change.

But, if this bridge is destroyed, who knows what will come? And if it is destroyed, it will only have to be rebuilt again, and of the same men and means, and for the same purposes—growing food, making utensils, carrying goods.

It seems that if the men engaged in the three arts were only able to see the part they play, that they are really the great natural elements which prevent the old order from being as bad as it might be, and are absolutely indispensable to the new order, they would regard their responsibility more highly than the propagandists wish them to do.

The best service any man can now do to bring about a better state of things is to be absolutely loyal to the thing he is doing in the Three Principal Arts. Speculators may have to stop, but not farmers. Money-makers may have to quit, but not plow-makers. These necessary things tide over any break, and are already the substance of the newer time.

Anyone laboring in the Three Principal Arts today has a hand in remaking the world for his children. Anyone curtailing them is holding back society.

A Few Remarks on Education

E VERY little while the old question is brought up again—"Does Education Educate?"—and we have more or less entertaining demonstrations of the ignorance of college students, the illiteracy of the reading public, numerous diverting tests of knowledge, and debates concerning the difference between wisdom and learning.

It is one of our favorite sports, this habit of getting fun out of the question of knowledge: we make fun of men who never went to college, because they did not go; and we make fun of men who went to college, because going did apparently so little for them.

There never was and probably never will be a system devised that will put brains into men's heads, and until such a system appears we must expect to find in men the same differences that have always marked them, whether with books or without them, in or out of college.

Take a group of wholly illiterate men, men who cannot read a date on the calendar, who cannot write their own names, and you will find a difference in brain power among them. Equally illiterate, one man will exhibit more native intelligence; he has brains even if he has little book knowledge; he has foresight, insight, initiative; he knows what he knows, and, therefore, possesses confidence and a sense of mastery.

Passing that group through college would probably not change the comparative brain values; one would still be brighter than the others. The average of ability might be raised, but there would be no essential enlargement of native brain power.

Just as there are some stones that will not take a polish, so there are minds that cannot be standardized so far as knowledge and the ability to use it is concerned.

An able man is a man who can do things, and his ability to do things is dependent on what he has in him, and what he has in him depends on what he started with and what he has done to increase and discipline it. An educated man is not one whose memory is trained to carry a few dates in history, but one whose mind can accomplish things. A man who cannot think is not an educated man, however many college degrees he may have acquired. Thinking is the hardest work any one can do, which is probably the reason we have so few thinkers.

There are two extremes to be avoided; one is the attitude of contempt toward education, the other is the tragic snobbery of assuming that marching through an educational system is a sure cure for ignorance and mediocrity. One benefit that education can confer on a man is to give him an equal start with his fellows. Sometimes even that is not an advantage, but in the main and for the general run of human beings, perhaps it is. You cannot learn in any school what the world is going to do next year, but you can learn some of the things which the world has tried to do in former years, and where it failed, and why it succeeded.

If education consisted in warning the young student of some of the exploded false theories on which men have tried to build, so that he may be saved the loss of time in finding this out by bitter experience, its good would be unquestioned. One sees a great deal along this line among the amateur inventors of the day. Inventors, by the way, are not made by education, but if they have enough education to save them from puttering away over the mistakes that have been conclusively proved to be mistakes, it saves them time. There are men at work today on theories fundamentally wrong, but they do not know that other men have followed that road and have had to come back. An education which consisted of signposts indicating the failures and the fallacies of the past, doubtlessly would be very useful. If education had as its objective the putting of the student in possession of the world up-to-date, so that leaving the school he could start in step

410

with humanity, it would be a great service. But whether this is the objective, it may be better to let educators themselves decide.

It is not education and it is not learning to be in possession of the theories of a lot of professors who do not know and never will know. Speculation is very interesting, and sometimes profitable, but it is not education. To be learned in science today is merely to be aware of a hundred theories that have not been proved. And not to know what those theories are is to be "uneducated," "ignorant," and so forth. But neither the man who knows these theories nor the man who does not know them, really *knows* anything. If knowledge of guesses is learning, then one may become learned by the simple expedient of making his own guesses, and by the same token he can dub the rest of the world "ignorant" because it does not know what his guesses are.

But the best that education can do for a man is to put him in possession of his powers, give him control of the tools with which destiny has endowed him, and teach him how to think. The college renders its best service as an intellectual gymnasium, in which mental muscle is developed and the student strengthened to do what he can.

To say, however, that mental gymnastics can only be had in college is not true, as every educator knows. A man's real education begins after he has left school, as any university graduate will tell you. True education is gained through the discipline of life.

The trouble is not with the schools altogether (though their one-sidedness in filling the field with books and leaving no place for the training of eye and ear and hand is recognized), but with the public illusion that schools can do for a young man what he must do for himself. If young men come out of college uneducated it is their own fault, and the same would be true if it were a canning factory they came out of, or a boiler shop, or anywhere else. Any place, any work offers an opportunity for education, but it is something

411

the recipient takes, it is not something that can be handed to him.

Here is a farmer boy working in the greatest school that ever existed, walking all day long on the greatest textbook ever written. If he could master the secrets of one acre, or even one square foot of land, he would be a learned man. There are more things to be learned on one farmstead than in Harvard, Yale and Princeton put together; though it sometimes occurs that the young man doesn't know this until he has gone through school first.

ᵎ We are a nation of casual readers. We read to escape thinking. Reading has become a dope habit with us. Learning has become a thing of accent and of facts. It is "learning" to have read the latest novel, but not to know that it's a silly, trivial thing. It is "learning" to have looked into this or that book-suffocated man's speculation, but not to know that he would be a wiser man and have more wholesome blood coursing through his brain if he would take a hammer or an ax and get out where he could sense life. Booksickness is the modern ailment. There's more wisdom in the shop where men deal with real materials and real persons every day.

What can you do to help and heal the world?—that is the educational test. If a man can hold up his own end, he counts for one. If he can help ten or a hundred or a thousand other men hold up their ends, he counts for more. He may be quite rusty on many things that inhabit the realm of print, but he is a learned man just the same. When a man is master of his own sphere, whatever it may be, he has won his degree—he has entered the realm of wisdom.

Common Life Is Standard
and Best

THE time is here when many young people are leaving school and casting about for clues by which they may settle the question of their careers; they want to know what they are going to do, what niche they will fill, what name people will know them by as to trade, service and success. It is a trying period. It is astounding sometimes how little can be done to help. The very anxiety of the search seems to be a stage through which the developing life must come.

There is probably not so much nonsense to be got rid of by the person leaving school nowadays, as there formerly was. Years ago no school was believed to have done its duty which did not send out every pupil filled with the idea that some day he (and now it would be also she) might become President. As the United States has required only 29 Presidents in the 145 years of its national existence, there has been a rather alarming waste of raw material.

The majority of people are blessed by being destined to the very best kind of life there is, the life of a plain person upon whom all the liberties descend and who with others of his kind constitute the ruling class of the world. They will not be President, nor Congressman, nor town councilman, nor even secretary of their lodge; they will just be folks.

It is very easy to state this another way. It may be said that "they are doomed to mediocrity." It may be said that "they are destined to live the colorless life of the common man." It may be said, "They are sentenced to a proletarian life."

These phrases are the scum that rose to the surface of those old false teachings that success consisted in getting the place that was accessible to only a few in a generation. Failing that, then life was "doomed" to be common. Utter rant and nonsense!

The very word "proletariat" is an insult, and if the majority of the people knew what it meant they would repudiate it and cast off the propagandists that foisted the name upon them. Proletariat means that class that is good for nothing but to raise children for the state —the lowest, most vulgar and useless type of human beings.

Yet whole bodies of well-read and highly useful American citizens are induced to parade around calling themselves the Proletariat, and reading about themselves as Proletarians. The man who calls himself a Proletarian, and knows what the word means, ought to be ashamed to look his wife and family in the face.

There are no such people as common people, in the sense that makes all the others uncommon. We are all common, or we are all uncommon, however you choose to look at it. The king is common, once you get to know him. The Presidential office is not a common office, but the President is common. Ask him, and he will tell you that he never felt himself to be anything but common. That is to say, people on the same plane of character are common possessors of pretty much the same qualities; they are citizens of the same commonwealth.

To say that the king is common and that the President is common, is, however, not quite the whole truth; for these statements are made sometimes to soothe those who are in rebellion against being themselves. The major half of the truth is that no man is common; individuality, personality, the moral dignity of a human being as a creation of the infinite mind, these are the most uncommon things we can think about. No man is common. But in the compass of that fact, all men are common. They have a common uncommonness by virtue of their being human beings. Their commons is the universe.

Now, the book that the majority reads is said to be the best book. The food that the majority eats is held to be the most natural and nourishing food. The mode of life which the majority pursues is held to be the most satisfactory mode. The life that the majority leads may be called the standard, the normal of life. Very well; that standard, normal life is the same life we call common, and which some poor pitiable people regard as a life of failure. Life itself is at once the common and the uncommon thing. The richest and most successful person is the one who has the most life; and life is within; it is within and from within; there is no favoritism, no "pull" at the source of life.

Now that is what is meant when the false guides say "the majority are doomed to live the life of the masses," and that also is what is meant when others say, "the majority are going to live the standard, normal human life." That life is common to all. It is the life which everybody must live in order to live at all; the life of labor and food, of day and night, of home and family, of body and soul—the same life which the President must live in his White House and the pioneer in his prairie home. It is the same life. It ought to be a relief to know in advance that it is to be ours.

Life is divided into two main periods—the period when we take in and the period when we give out. Youth is the receptive period, and although that period does not end, there comes to keep company with it an expressive period when the individual makes his or her contribution to the general life. He does more than that, however; in his work he also makes a contribution to himself. The sum of earth life is the making of character. It is inevitable.

We make character whether we want to or not. We make it whether we are conscious of it or not. We make it wherever we are and by whatever we do. There is no special location or no special occupation which is more favorable to character-making than is another location or occupation. There is no station in life that is favorable to the production of a finer type of character than is any other station.

The more and better character that is made, the more the outer world is changed to conform to it. The money question, the industrial question, the political question, the social question—all these wait for the settlement of the character question.

The reason that high office is so powerless to bring about reforms, the reason that titles and prerogatives are helpless in making a clean sweep of injustices, is just this—no office or authority gets any further than the character that creates and fills it. Character is the great authority. Given character, office can be dispensed with. Presidents and kings and magnates of all degrees are but the servants of great characters. And great characters are independent of riches or power. They *are* rich and they *have* power, and are therefore invincible in whatever right things they undertake.

We have rather successful inventions, successful businesses, successful policies, but not enough successful *men*. The success of a man is to become a Man in the character and power that make him, stripped and alone, a Man. And this is all within his own control; no outer circumstance can control that, but he can use that to control outer circumstance.

No one should be content with poverty, because if it is poverty instead of the clean, hard type of bareness which constitutes the voluntary "doing without" of camp life, it is degrading. If a man is poor, it should only be by his own choice. Many men have been poor by their own choice, and therefore they escaped the depression of *poverty*. In the perfect society, most people will choose to live on the plane of the average man of today—it is more comfortable, more human, more conducive to peace. The state to which the majority of society has attained today, with such corrections of the money and governmental system as will prevent dishonest tampering, is, with certain changes, approximately the state that will prevail when society becomes what it ought to be. Why not? What better base is there for the development of character?

Discouraging People From Thinking

THERE is a false theory which dates from ancient times that the way to prevent social or political disruption is to prevent the people from thinking. Keep their minds off fundamental problems and everything will go along without disturbance. Sometimes this was done by free circuses and free distribution of food, as in ancient Rome. Sometimes it was done by bringing on a war when the population seemed to be growing restless. Sometimes it is achieved by bringing upon the stage a leader with a Roosevelt personality who captures the imagination of the people and gives an appearance of rushing hither and thither on an endless series of hopeful quests.

In these days, the same doctrine is preached with reference to unemployment—keep the people employed, because if you do not, they will begin to think, and thinking is not a good sign.

It is doubtless true that unemployment is unnecessary, or would be unnecessary if our affairs were managed by plain common sense. There is always enough to do and always enough people willing to do it, but there is always also that little-understood matter of money which usurps so big a position in the question. Unemployment is everybody's fault, and not the fault of a class only, as the false teaching of the day asserts. The class propaganda is merely a postponement of the sense of general responsibility which all the people must feel before substantial and enduring progress can be made.

As to the dangers of the people thinking, there are several points to observe. Thought, of course, is the most powerful dynamite in the world. Thought has achieved whatever we see. Wrong thought has achieved

all the wrong we see. It is not thought that is dangerous, but its temper and direction.

It is perhaps true that one of the root causes of our
troubles today is that there is too little public thought.
More people are reading than ever before—as witness
the enormous editions of incendiary literature which
the radical organizations circulate—but what they read
stirs up something besides thought. It stirs up passion,
resentment, hatred, the latent destructive faculties, and
puts the man into fierce vibration, but this is not stir-
ring up thought. Thought has quite another tone and
result.

What little thought may be mixed in these manifestations of the destructive passions is thereby contamin-
ated, prostituted and neutralized. Men cannot think
under such conditions. The real problem is not how to
prevent the people thinking and asking questions, but
how to make it possible for them to think under right
conditions.

During the period of stress and unemployment
which is now happily past, many people did a great
deal of so-called thinking. That is, they brooded and
they made vows and they gave vent to great denunciations. It was not purposeful thinking. How could it be?
When a man is in a corner, how can he be expected to
be philosophical? Unless, of course, he is an extraordinary man; and if he were that, the chances are he
would not be in a corner.

Our best social thinking is not done in periods of
stress and enforced idleness. Indeed, you can measure
the difference between real thinking and brooding, by
measuring the difference between leisure and idleness.
Leisure is necessary to thought, but idleness seems to
be the enemy of thought. Leisure is a breathing
period in a situation in which the man feels secure;
idleness is a brooding period in a situation in which the
bottom has apparently dropped out of the man's security. If the lay-off last winter could have been employed as leisure, if men had been so well provided for
that they could have looked upon the lay-off as a welcome vacation, the mental results would have been
beneficial to the country. As it was, the idleness was

418

not leisure, and the psychological recovery is just as necessary as the economic recovery.

The farmer is a good illustration of this. No one can deny that the farmer has been very hard hit and that his problem is the problem of every one of us. Until we regard the farmer's problem as our own, we are neglecting a bulwark of our economic security and our social solidarity. We hear in other countries of "Soldiers' and Workmen's Committees"; what we need in this country is a better understanding and a closer relation between workmen and farmers.

During the slack season of the winter, when the farmer himself was shut out of his fields by winter, he did a great deal of brooding. He had enough to brood about, too. And he expressed himself quite fully. His leisure was robbed of its value because of the change that had come in his economic standing, and his thoughts veered likewise. He said, among other things, that he would not raise a bushel more grain this year than he needed for himself and family! He was through being the football of the profiteers! He would show them that they could not do as they liked with him!

It was a serious threat. Aside from the economic phase of it, there was something ominous in the priests of the soil threatening to prevent the forces of nature doing their seasonal work.

But what has occurred? The sun of spring began to shine and the spring rains came down, and the farmer went forth to his fields. He began to work. Work began to heal him. It is safe to guess that what the farmers think by the end of the season, by the time of harvest, will be more constructive than what they thought during the winter.

If the people only would think, and if conditions could be maintained which would enable them to think constructively, few problems would remain unsolved. Prosperity is the best time to think, for then you have the elements which are desirable to be maintained, and which the thoughtlessness of the people is sometimes a very large element in destroying.

Why is it that public thinking, under conditions of prosperity, is more valuable to the public interest than the so-called thinking which is done under economic stress? The answer is clear. First, the man is free to think without bias or resentment. There is no sense of personal wrong resting upon him, no feeling of bitterness twisting all his views into one channel. Second, the elements which are fundamental are present before him—the fact of work and its necessity; the fact of home and its security; the fact of society and the great dependence it has on ordered industry. Third, a general view into all grades of life which ease of mind permits him and which stress of mind often shuts out: he can consider his children and their education; morals and their sanction; literature, science, politics—all the things which are shut out and undervalued when mental stress forces the mind into merely class questions.

Now, with none of these things present, but with himself forced down to the animal plane of finding something to eat, plainly the man is not in a position to do all-round thinking. And it is all-round thinking that is going to save the people from lopsided mistakes. Our education cannot be too general, our acquaintance with the grades of life too wide, for in the breadth of our view comes the correction of our tendencies to narrowness.

Therefore, the agitators of destruction know exactly what they are doing when they choose the times of depression for their propaganda. Would that the children of light were as wise to choose the times of prosperity for the cultivation of sound, unbiased and constructive thinking upon the matters pertaining to our common life!

Anyone who preaches that the people must be prevented from thinking is as dangerous to society as are those who spend immeasurable zeal in their efforts to make society think wrongly. It is when all the people think, normally and wholesomely, that the world will become what it might be.

Getting Rid of Fear and Failure

THE only communism that ever helped men, and that ever will help men, is the communism of thought and understanding. Our modern life has taken a direction which makes it necessary for people to become acquainted all over again. We form our conclusions of persons and classes apart from them and, as a result, the world is dealing with dummy figures which never existed, and with types of men who are few and unimportant.

There was a time when people knew one another more intimately than they do now, and that time is still present in other countries. People knew one another in America when they were more dependent on one another. When neighborliness consisted in a community of understanding, sympathy and helpfulness, when neighborliness was a duty such as "keeping up an appearance" is now regarded, there was a widespread social knowledge, gained by contact, which is now only imperfectly gained from other sources.

Then the industrial era opened; the amount of money handled by each family increased; the things that people used to do for one another, were hired done, or done within the family; in a word, people became more independent of one another, and thus drifted apart. Neighborhoods, on the surface at least, are not what our forbears remembered them to be, nor even what they were in our youthful years. Indeed, there are no "neighborhoods" in the larger cities; there are just "localities."

Perhaps it is not as bad as this; it only appears as bad. From time to time there comes news of a revival of the old neighborly spirit. Trouble comes to a family that has lately moved in and whom no one knows, and presently the neighborhood spirit—sleeping, but apparently not dead—discloses itself again in those old and homely acts which, while they often have

small power to heal the circumstance, have ne.·rthe-
less a very potent power to soothe sore hearts.

Try as we may to relegate all this to the realm of
useless sentimentality, the fact remains that there is
mysterious power in just the compassion of men for
one another in their difficulties. There is not enough
of it, and the reason is that we have made ourselves
believe that material sufficiency makes us independent
of all men. Not so. As a matter of fact, no one is so
constantly dependent on other men as he whose interests and responsibilities are great.

But if experience teaches us anything it is this, that
there is no readjustment without its compensation. The
only constant and reliable fact is change. Life is a
river whose sources are hidden, whose ultimate sea is
not in view, and no work of man is quite so vain as
that which seeks to fix life in a certain form for all
the future. Create the form you dote on; establish it
by revolution or the people's suffrage; yet as soon as
it is established, the law of change begins to eat it
away, and in a generation men reared under your form
will be sadly saying, "Things are not what they used
to be."

And if we have been dislodged out of our reliance
on the neighborhood, it has all been a profitable thing;
by it we have been thrown back into more reliance
upon ourselves.

After all, the successful man is the man who has
no fear of himself. The true man of the world is the
man who feels that as long as the earth turns round
and the seasons come he is in his proper home, with
all needful things awaiting his command.

If there is one element of darkness which one
would banish from the earth sooner than any other, it
is this element of fear. Fear is the offspring of a reliance placed on something outside—on a foreman's
good will, perhaps, on a shop's prosperity, on a market's steadiness. That is just another way of saying
that fear is the portion of the man who acknowledges
his career to be in the keeping of earthly circumstance.
Fear is the result of the body assuming ascendancy
over the soul. It is the fruit of the mind that ac-

knowledges itself to be a bond-slave. Many men fear every undertaking, and when you analyze the sources of their fear you will find that it is nothing but the memory of their own previous failures. Men are like colts; if they are permitted to fail too often, it becomes a habit with them. Colts, however, fail because they are overloaded; men, because they do not "adjust their efforts to obstacles"—which was Napoleon's rule.

This habit of failure is purely mental and is the mother of fear, and like any other bad habit, it carries a great deal of blameworthiness with it. Men fail—everybody fails—experiment and the getting of expertness can be achieved by no other means than by items of failure; but to let failure in details or in experiment fix the habit and the fear of failure on the mind is not only tragic but positively sinful.

This habit gets itself fixed on men because they lack vision; that is, they start out to do something that reaches from A to Z of a certain matter. Now, at A they fail, at B they stumble, and at C they meet what seems to be an insuperable difficulty, and then they throw the whole task down—beaten! They have not even given themselves a chance to fail; they have not given their vision a chance to be proved or disproved; they have simply been beaten by the natural difficulties that attend every kind of effort.

It is a very serious thought that more men are beaten than fail. It was not wisdom they needed, nor money, nor brilliance, nor "pull," but just plain gristle, plain bone. This rude, simple, primitive power which we call "stick-to-it-iveness" is the uncrowned king of the world of endeavor.

People are utterly wrong in their slant upon things. They see the successes that men have made and somehow they appear to be easy. But that is a world away from the fact. It is a failure that is easy. Success is always hard. A man can fail in ease; he can succeed only by paying all that he is and has. It is this which makes success so pitiable a thing if it be in lines that are not useful and uplifting to the people.

Men ought to learn not to keep putting their trust

into what they deem untrustworthy. If a man is in constant fear of the industrial situation he ought to change his life so as not to be dependent on it. There is always the land, and fewer people on the land now than there ever was before.

If a man lives in fear of an employer's favor changing toward him, he ought to extricate himself from dependence on any employer. He can become his own boss. It may be that he will be a poorer boss than the one he leaves, and that his returns will be much less, but at least he will have rid himself of the shadow of his pet fear, and that is worth a great deal in money and position.

Better still, is for the man to come up through himself and exceed himself by getting rid of his fears in the midst of the circumstances where his daily lot is cast. Become a freeman in the place where you first surrendered your freedom. Win your battle where you lost it. And you will come to see that, although there was much outside of you that was not just right, there was more inside of you that was wrong. Thus you will learn that the wrong inside of you spoils even the right that is outside of you.

A man is still the superior being of the earth. Whatever happens, he is still a man. It may rain tomorrow—he is still a man. Business may slacken tomorrow—he is still a man. He goes through the changes of circumstances, as he goes through the variations of the temperature—still a man. If he can only get this thought reborn in him, it opens new wells of water and new mines of wealth in his own being. There is no security outside of himself. There is no wealth outside of himself. The elimination of fear is the bringing in of security and supply.

The Exodus From the Cities

I T IS human nature to want to sit down contented,
to get everything so nicely arranged that it will go
without tending; but everyone knows that that is not
the way life goes. There is a difference of tempo, a
difference of purpose, a difference of method between
human nature and life. Human nature would seem
to be the sleepy pupil, and the forces of life the stern
teacher who prods the pupil and keeps him doing what
he would rather not do. Which, of course, is the highest education, the best discipline—the power to do
what we would rather not do.

Every now and again something comes along to jar
us loose, and start us going again. The conditions we
thought were settled turn out not to be settled at all.
The method we thought was established turns out to
be the most temporary of expedients. Life steps in
and orders us to move on.

The thermometer is one of the staffs of authority
which life wields over us. You will find within a certain belt around the world all the progress that is contained within the world, and the secret of that belt's
prosperity, progress, morality and superiority is revealed to us by the thermometer. The thermometer is
mightier than the sword. Those races whom destiny
has not set within that earth-belt need not be fought
with swords; the thermometer fights them and keeps
them in their place. The People of the Four Seasons
are four times set upon every year by the forces of
nature; they have the sternness of winter, the promise
of spring, the rich fruitfulness of summer and the
beauty of autumn in their make-up. They are not
suffered to loll upon the earth as others are. The gad
of destiny is always whisking their flanks.

Take the gentler upset which the coming of the
present season brings to our ways of thinking. "Spring
fever," so-called, and summer discontent are not mere

425

individual restlessnesses, they are comparable to the tremor which sometimes runs through the earth; they indicate that new settlements, new bases are being sought for. What we overlook too often is the fact that our desires are our prophets, foretelling what is to be. Millions of people at this season of the year are becoming sensible, often in a dull, dumb, unconscious way, of the difference between the way we have organized our life and the way in which nature has organized the world.

People go out under the trees and beside broad waters; they endure dust and heat and crowding and the plaints of children, to seek a place where they may lie on a shaded hill and idly watch the cloud-fleets sail the sky. They get a new sense of the expanse and freedom of the world. Their minds range where there are no walls, no bounds, no close schedule of limitations.

Say what you will, this contact with nature, though it be but for a day, is more than a pleasure, more than a vacation from work; it is a jolt. People are made sensible of a jar between what is and what might be. Reflective people do not even enjoy the time of their vacation as they ought to, because it comes so clear to their minds that something is wrong. They may be inclined to think that it is merely their freedom from their usual work that causes this uneasiness, their freedom to think once more—but that is not always the case. The Voice of Nature is saying to them, "Up, for this is not your rest, you must march on!"

It is not that the city is hot; the country is hot too. It is not that the city means daily toil; there is daily toil in the country too. But somehow, at this season of the year, when the men of the cities come into the temples of the groves, and see miles of meadows and the sweep of rivers, they are torn between two feelings —first, that the cities have their disadvantages; second, that the cities have their advantages too.

One thing you may set down as true is that the cities are doomed. Not immediately, but perhaps much sooner than even the most adventurous are willing to believe. There is no city now existing that would be

426

rebuilt as it is, if it were destroyed; which fact is in itself a confession of our real estimate of our cities.

There is a strange new movement afoot, which is well to attend a little. Never was there such an influx of people from the country into the cities; never was there such an exodus of people from the cities into the country. The two go on together. The people who don't know the cities are flocking in, as many as can. The people who do know the cities are flocking out, as many as can.

Now it means this: the city has had a part to play in the civilization of the world, and that part is now being played with accelerated speed. All our cities have changed their inhabitants the last few years. More and more people have been passed through them to gain what they have to give. When the full part is played, and it is being played out fast, cities will pass off the stage. To this many lines of indication agree.

So, the unrest we are beginning to feel, and which we increasingly feel at this season, is prophetic. Men are going to live nearer the source of things, not walled away like exiles from the very sun by which they live, and from the very soil that gives them bread.

The city had a place to fill, a work to do. Doubtless the country places would not have approximated their present livableness had it not been for the cities. By crowding together, men have learned some secrets. They would never have learned them alone in country life. Why, even the fresh air method of treating tuberculosis is a city discovery. Sanitation, lighting, social organization, all these are products of men's experience with each other in the city.

That is to say, practically all the improvements that have been made in country life have originated in the city and have passed on to bless the country. In that we may see the city's place in the world—it was a gathering place in which men might work out those necessary devices of successful living which, when transplanted into the country, would make the desert blossom as the rose and, what is better, make the gray waste of life a colorful thing.

People who are getting out of the cities now are

taking the best of the cities with them—those discoveries and inventions which make life safe and pleasant, and which unburden men of loads that are better borne by iron and steel.

It is not the advantages of cities that are doomed, but the disadvantages—the congestion, the inequality which reigns even in the matter of air and sunlight and ground space. And yet, the world has known for many centuries that air and sunlight and ground space were not of themselves the infallible sources of happiness and success, for without certain improvements even country life becomes an insupportable drudgery and an unrelieved loneliness. The advantages of the country are natural; the advantages of the city are human; when both are fused, as they are being fused, the cities lose in large degree their justification for existence. When they bring their best to the country, their work is done.

Cities, in the sense of central assembling places for manufacture and commerce, may continue to exist; but people will live outside them. Wherever people can carry with them the advantages which the city has produced, they move out of the city. And that is the natural, necessary movement; for you cannot carry the country into the city, it cannot be done; or if it could be done, the city would be destroyed in the process. But you can carry the city into the country, without destroying the country, but even improving it.

So while it is clear that cities are to pass, let us not regard them as a sad blunder; they were a school for the race. They taught us something. They filled their place and did their work of education. But an end comes to every phase of education, and it seems clear that an end is coming to this also.

Use Is Better Than Economy

IT IS rather a strange arrangement of nature that only the most precious values can be wasted. You can waste time, you can waste labor, you can waste material—and that is about all. You cannot waste money. You can misuse money, but you cannot waste it; it is still somewhere. You can waste your own opportunity to use it for benefit, but that is all. Which would seem to put money in at least the second class.

Time, energy and material are worth more than money, because they cannot be purchased by money. Not one hour of yesterday, nor one hour of today can be bought back. Not one ounce of energy can be bought back. Material wasted, is wasted beyond recovery. These things are in the front rank of values. They are the precious elements out of which all wealth is made.

It is worth noting that these precious values are not of human creation. We have done a great deal with our human intelligence and energy, we have accomplished much by the manipulation of natural material and forces, but the severely modifying fact remains that ourselves and all we have worked with, and the very intelligence we have worked by, were not our own creation. So, while mankind may be pleased, and even thankful, it ill becomes it to be boastful.

All our values were given us. Mind-values, power-values, material-values were all here. And we, the human race, have simply been cutting our eye-teeth on some of the elementary problems. The tree makes apples, mankind makes engines and philosophies—the tree cannot boast itself to be very original and powerful; it does what it was given power to do.

But mankind always has promise of being permitted to do still greater things. If trees bore different and finer apples every succeeding year, we should say, "Well, there is progress in the apple kingdom, and some day those apple trees are going to develop into beings of wonderful powers." But we don't see that. We see, however, mankind putting out different and better fruits age by age, and even helping the tree bear better apples, and the bush better berries; and therefore we say, "Well, there will come a time when this wonderfully endowed and protected race of beings will work in some finer material than steel, and by some finer force than electricity or gasoline explosions. Its present progress has every sign of being only preparation."

The waste which we practice upon the original store of wealth is always repairing itself. That is to say, the time we waste is wasted for us, not for Time —somewhere the unused hours and days return to original source where there are neither days nor hours, nor yet Time, but endless duration. Hours and days are doled out to us as small coin to see how we will use them.

It is the same everywhere. Wasted material is replaced; the earth never ceases making what we need and is prepared to fill future needs of which we have not now the slightest fore-knowledge. If men waste energy, it is lost to them as individuals—the great reservoir of energy on which all life draws is not exhausted.

Therefore the great word of life is Use.

Some would say Economy. Not so. The word economy represents a half-idea born of fear. Its history is something like this: the great and tragic fact of waste is brought home to the mind by some circumstance, usually of a most materialistic kind; or there comes a violent reaction against extravagance—for even nature rebels against our unwise courses (which is the reason why so many people break down from "overwork," which is not overwork at all); and as a sudden revulsion against it all, the mind catches hold of the idea of "economy." It flies from a greater evil to a lesser one; it does not make the full journey from error to truth.

Economy is the rule of half-alive minds. There can be no doubt that it is better than waste, neither can there be any doubt that it is not as good as Use.

People who pride themselves on their economy sometimes bristle when it is attacked, as if one of the virtues had been denounced. It is principally in the interests of the economizers that this attitude is taken. For if there is anything more pitiable on earth than a poor, pinched mind spending the rich days and months pinching at a few pieces of metal, or paring the outer necessities of life to the very quick—if there is anything more pitiable, where is it?

Obviously, a practice that so pinches the mind is a wrong one. We all know economical people who seem to be niggardly even about the amount of air they breathe and the amount of appreciation they will allow themselves to give anything. They are all shriveled up.

Indeed, economy is waste: it is waste of the juices of life, the sap of living. For there are two kinds of waste: that of the prodigal who throws his substance away in riotous living, and that of the sluggard who allows his substance to rot from non-use. In the precious things of life the strict·economizer is in danger of being classed with the sluggard.

The beauty of the principle of Use is that it obtains all the advantages of economy and at the same time gives healthy expression to all the instincts of which wastefulness is the diseased symptom. Most people's extravagance is a reaction from severe suppression of expenditure. Most people's economy is a reaction from extravagance.

Under the principle of Use the expansive experience of expenditure is obtained, as well as the self-control and economic discipline of "economizing."

Everything was given us to use. There is no evil from which we suffer that did not come about through misuse. There is no function which human beings can fulfill that is not good. But we have all about us the spectacle of whole nations having to make laws against things, not bad fundamentally, but bad in their misuse. The worst possible sin we can commit against the things of our common life is to misuse them. "Misuse" is the wider term. We like to say "waste," but waste is only one phase of misuse. All waste is misuse; all misuse is waste.

It is possible even to overemphasize the savings habit. It is proper and desirable that everyone have a margin; it is really wasteful not to have one, if you can have one. But it can be overdone.

We teach children to save their money. As an attempt to counteract thoughtless and selfish expenditure, it has its value; but it is not positive; it doesn't lead the child out into safe and useful avenues of self-expression or self-expenditure.

To teach a child to invest is better. Most men are saving a few dollars who, if they would invest those few dollars, first in themselves, and then in some useful work, would find it easier to save because they would have more to save.

Young men ought to be investing instead of saving. They ought to be investing in themselves to increase their creative value; after they have brought themselves to their peak of usefulness, then will be time enough to think of laying aside, as a fixed policy, a certain substantial share of income.

You are not "saving" when you are preventing yourself from becoming more productive. You are really taking out of your ultimate capital; you are reducing yourself in value as one of nature's investments.

The principle of Use is the main guide-post. Use is positive, active, life-giving. Use is alive. Use adds to the sum of good. Start out on that principle. You will have just as much materially, but you will have a great deal more mentally and spiritually. Investment is the prerequisite of returns. Investment is in the old-fashioned term, "putting out to use."

Interest Robbery in Bonus Loan

THE word "bonus" is frequently heard these days in connection with the men who fought for our country in the Great War. And wherever it is heard, there will be found two opinions upon it. Perhaps everybody, those who are for it and those who are against it, feels that at best it is a makeshift, that the granting of a bonus will not do much for the soldier after all, and that it will constitute no *permanent* good for him. The principal element is the spiritual: to refuse the bonus is felt to be ingratitude, and this is to be avoided as an evil spirit. But at the same time no one will be found to say that to grant the bonus, a mere $10 or $15 for every month of service, is an adequate show of gratitude. It doesn't discharge the debt. Heaven help us if we measure our gratitude to our soldiers by the amount of any bonus.

So there are the two points: the bonus pays nothing. It is a small and temporary aid to men who may be in need of ready money by reason of unemployment, but who would prefer a return of their rightful work in the world to anything else we could do for them.

The American Soldier, the boy who left shop and store and office and school, taking a year or two out of his life to settle the military question overseas, should not be placed in a false light in all this discussion. He is not asking for charity. He would not take charity. He should not be used in argument or plea as if he were asking or expecting charity.

But he has a right to expect that after having done what we asked him to do, we shall give him the opportunity to regain the place he left, and shall leave nothing wanting in our effort to restore him to the same degree of competence which he had before.

That is one of the really black blots on our whole war organization. We had a splendid organization for the handling of copper, for example. We had many men ready to leap in and offer their services where it was a matter of rounding up war supplies. Our war government, with its price fixers and its general manipulators of "understandings" here and there, was certainly an amazing institution. But when it came to cleaning up the ruck and riot of war, there wasn't one to help. They had all resigned. There is no profit in teaching a blind soldier a trade. There is no profit in helping to salvage the human wreckage of the war. There is no profit in taking the armless and the legless and the shell-shocked and helping to restore them again. And so our famous "war government" is not on the job. It is out looking for other worlds to conquer. And about the only thing we hear is complaints about the mistakes and lacks of the restorative program, and urges for the bonus.

The soldier has a right to complain, although to his credit be it said that he is not complaining for himself so much as for his wounded "buddy" who isn't getting the chance he ought to have. And he also has a right to reflect that the so-called "bonus" is a mighty little thing after all.

In one state where it is proposed to pay the soldiers a bonus, no soldier will receive more than $300, yet the state will expend about $30,000,000 in paying the amounts, and an additional $54,000,000 for interest on the bonds which it had to issue in order to raise the bonus money. There is the matter of $150 to $300 for the soldier, and a matter of $54,000,000 for the money-lenders. Indeed, whatever bonus the soldier gets, he will pay for over and over again in his taxes.

Now, if the people of that state should go down into their pockets and by a self-imposed assessment of about $10 a head, raise a fund to present to their soldiers as a special gift to tide them over a tough time, there would be something tremendously human and moving about that. But the trouble is that bonuses have not even that much sentiment. They are first politics, then they are debts, and the only people who really benefit are the money-lenders. They get their "bonus" regularly for 30 years afterward.

If a bonus, no matter how small it was, came as a

wreath of victory; if it were really the conscious act of. the people in showing their appreciation, that would be quite another thing. But all it amounts to nowadays is the sale of interest-bearing bonds.

If a state really wants to do something for the soldiers, *why does it not give them the interest?* If the state would arrange to give the soldiers the *interest* on the projected bonus loans, the soldiers would get nearly *twice as much,* and the state would save the entire principal.

To give its soldiers $30,000,000 the state in question is going to give the money-lenders $54,000,000; a total of $84,000,000 in all to finance the giving away of $30,000,000. If the state would give its soldiers the interest, $54,000,000, it would save the principal, or $30,000,000. And the soldiers would get nearly twice as much.

If a state can pay interest to the banks, it can pay interest to the men it ought to help.

Now the soldier himself does not regard our system as a very good one, when it works out that way. He is not impressed with the wisdom of a system that mortgages a state for 30 years in a great sum, and still doesn't do much for the soldier.

If the bonus really set the soldier up for life, if it established him in his place as a professional man, commercial man, mechanic or farmer, if the bonus settled anything at all, it might be worth any state's effort to do it.

But what does a scrawny $150 to $300 do for a man? It is totally inadequate as a testimonial of the state's gratitude; it is totally inadequate to the establishment of the soldier in his place in the world.

When you give a soldier $300 and a banker $540 interest for the privilege, it would seem much wiser as well as much kinder to give the soldier the $540 interest and save the $300, thus costing the state only $240 when measured by the other plan. And, if the state wanted to go as far as it goes under the bond plan, let the soldier have the $300 and the $540 too, $840, and let the state pay both interest and principal to herself.

The best bonus that can be given the soldier is a

,place to work where he can snap his finger at bonuses, and a state to live in where the money-lenders have not the deciding voice about everything.

Money is the least valuable of all the commodities, yet it brings the highest price; and though we have the manufacture of it in our own hands as a nation, yet it is the scarcest of all the things we make. The controllers of money were able to smooth the way for the soldier when they wanted him to fight; they seem strangely helpless to smooth the way for him now that he only wants to work.

There is doubtless a duty and a debt to those who, in response to our call, suffered loss, of whatever kind the loss may be. Certainly there is an element of fairness in the consideration that the man who stayed at home and had a year or two advantage over the man who went, should not thus put the soldier at a disadvantage. The breaks of war were many; they must be repaired where possible; many of the breaks can never be repaired. But can it be done in this slip-shod, half-hearted borrowing which profits nobody but the lender? If a state desires to give its soldiers $30,000,000, let it tax its people for that amount, instead of taxing its people for $84,000,000 in order to expend $30,000,000. The soldier himself would be of that opinion.

On Being Fit for the
New Era

I T HAS become common and almost boresome to say
that we are on the threshold of a new era. It ought
to be one of the most startling announcements that anyone could make or hear. But it has always been true
that great changes have come over the human race,
never to be noticed until, a century after, some observ-
ing soul has said, "That was a great period back there
one hundred years ago." We understand gunshots and
wars and industrial failures and depression, but the
real changes of which these are the passing signs, go
mostly over our heads.

The trouble is we don't realize that the "new era" is
going to mean something to us—something different
than we have supposed. We think everything is going
to be lovely and that the world is to be humored along
in its old ways.

In short, when it is said that we are entering a new
era it is accepted as meaning that now, at last, things
are going to be very nearly what we lazily wanted them
to be.

We have been using the phrase for comfort, when
really it is challenge.

If it were said that tomorrow we are to wake up on
another continent to make our lives over again, it would
not be regarded as a very soothing sort of statement.
We should find it hard to lie back in our chairs and
say, "Well, times are going to be all right again." The
knowledge that we were to begin anew, under unknown
conditions, would keep us awake and alert.

You remember how it was when you went to school.
It was great to be promoted, but the "next grade" was
never viewed with ease of mind. That "next grade"
loomed up before you with its unknown tests and tasks,
and your mind was set to grapple with something
bigger than you had yet encountered.

437

Well, something like that should be our feeling when we contemplate the fact that we are entering upon a "new era." It is the next grade. We are not going back to retravel familiar ground, we are entering upon a new continent with new tests and new tasks. The past is past in a double sense now; not only is the Time that made it, gone; but the temper and principles out of which it was built are gone too.

All the mature generations of today have grown up in the era of their own fathers. There were improvements upon their fathers' times, of course, but the general period was the same. Sires and sons were in the same "grade," so to speak, one nearer the beginning of the "term," the other nearer the end. The sons have now come to the end of the "term." The road ahead is untraveled. The conditions to be passed are new.

Just why this comes about as it does, no one knows. It would be useless to guess. Something has been switched off, and something else has been switched on. The time that was, is not; the time that is to be, begins. One course of lessons has been finished, the doors of the next "grade" open.

There seems to be a difference, however. In school, there is an examination. The standard you maintain in your examination determines your fitness to leave the lower grade. In the present change that is reversed; examinations will determine whether we are fit to enter the higher grade—the new era. It is quite possible that in matters of character a man stays on the lower plane until he is ready to enter the higher plane; but when the new era is fully arrived there will not be vestiges ot the old era left—all the people will be New Era People who have shown themselves fit to be promoted. The others will have vanished as worn-out and unprogressive races have always vanished.

You see, therefore, that it is more than ah eloquent flourish of words to say that "we are on the threshold of a new era." It is as startling to the individual as was the announcement of the new conscription law in 1917. The question for every individual is, What will it mean to me? Am I fit to be one of the New Era People?

438

Am I going to pass the examination requirements into the new time? The test is going to be made all down the line, but it is going to begin at what we call the "top." There will always be leaders. Even in anarchic Russia they have leaders—very hard leaders, too. Leaders are necessary and have a special part to play and bear an extra degree of responsibility. We say leaders are at the "top," presumably because they ought to be found at the head of the column. And that is where the testing and weeding out is to commence.

It is in process now. We are not speaking of something that will begin next year; we are speaking of what has silently overshadowed the world for several years. It is a Day of Judgment for the leaders of the old era. If they cannot pass their examinations, if their faces are not toward the future, if their hearts are not more devoted to righteousness than to the preservation of some old and respected iniquity, they fail. They disappear. New leaders take their places.

Look where you will—in railroading, in banking, in manufacturing, in commerce, in teaching or preaching, in making newspapers, in farming—everywhere the New Era is crowding in and is crowding out those who are against its coming. It is not merely a matter of new and better ways of doing things, but a new and better spirit and purpose in doing them. There have been New Era People in the world for some time, but they have been rated as "fools"; now their day is come.

This is news worth while for the young fellow. It is genuine news. He has been hearing for a long time past that opportunity was pretty well sewed up. Indeed, certain labor leaders have written and preached that no one has any right to expect to improve his condition in the world, that "the laboring class" constituted an iron-bound caste out of which it was practically impossible for anyone to break.

Of course, no one ever breaks out of "the laboring class" unless he turns gambler or some other sort of financial criminal. Honest men stay in "the laboring class" all their lives. But this is what the false

439

teachers mean: that a man need not hope to rise to his own level of ambition and ability in the laboring class, and that is false. This is the New Era, and New Era People are in demand to fill the places of old era leaders who failed in their examinations; and the present time is the most glorious period to be young and ambitious. There wasn't much chance during the last years of the old era, that is why it closed so quickly. But it is morning again and a new day is full of opportunity.

The only "hold overs" from the old era are the qualities which gave it its worth. They are the old-fashioned virtues of honesty, industry and courage. They are just as necessary now as in the first year after the Independence of the United States or the first year after the Civil War. In fact, they are never out of date. Many people seem to think that the New Era is merely another chance for them to work their old games, cheating the laws of value, the laws of work, and every other good law. Not at all. The old era died of these old games, and died in discreditable circumstances, too.

Rewards will not be less but greater in the New Era. New Era People are going to produce as much or more, but they are going to have a larger share in it, they will live broader lives. The world is going to continue practical—always practical—even more practical than before, because the world was not practical while it tried to break the laws of value, and work, and justice. Some people had the notion that in the New Era we were to sit down under the trees and spin beautiful theories. No; we are going to spin beautiful realities on the loom of more and better work.

Much Nonsense in Titles

RECENTLY a financier made a speech in which he said a few plain things about the effect of titles in business. He was of the opinion that it was being very much overdone. / He thought he observed harmful effects on industrial and business organizations by this method of decoration, and he seemed to feel that something ought to be done about it.

It is a refreshing sign of the times that a business man could be found who had the courage to stand up at a banquet and talk about so simple a matter. It is refreshing because it shows a willingness to climb down from the pedestal and look at the machinery of business as it actually works.

We are all going back to work—even the men in the front office. Business has made a discovery, it has rediscovered work. The magic of money has been exploded and the invincible power of work is again becoming appreciated.

Business men have believed for too long a period that you could do anything by "financing" it. The most frequent item of business news that has marked the past five years has related to hundreds upon hundreds of concerns that have been "refinanced." The process of "refinancing" is simply the game of sending good money after bad. In the majority of cases the need of "refinancing" has arisen through bad management, and the effect of "refinancing" is simply to pay the poor managers to keep up their bad management a little longer. It is merely the postponement of the day of judgment which is overtaking, and must overtake, all concerns that have not played fair with the law of Use and Service.

This makeshift of "refinancing" is, of course, a device of the speculative financiers. Their money is no good to them unless they can connect it up with a place where real work is being done, and they cannot connect it up with a place where real work is being done unless, somehow, that place is poorly managed. Thus, the speculative financiers delude themselves that they are putting their money out to "use." They are not; they are putting it out to waste, and the end of the transaction is usually a·sad experience.

That, indeed, is one of the elements in the present condition of affairs which has troubled the country, but from which there is now a promise that we shall emerge.

Take the railroads, for example. Theirs has been one long story of dependence on money before everything else. True, the railroads are a great national institution. True also, there have been men of vision connected with their development. But the major part of railroad history has had to do with stock markets and games of exploitation.

Today far too many railroads are run, not from the offices of practical men, but from banking offices, and the principles of procedure, the whole outlook, is financial—not transportational, but financial.

There has been a breakdown of railroading generally, in this the greatest railroad country in the world, simply because more attention has been paid to railroads as factors in the stock market than as servants of the people. Outworn ideas have been retained, development has been practically stopped, railroad men with vision have not been free to grow—the dead hand of finance has been heavy on every department.

As a result—what? Why, it is thought that perhaps One Billion Dollars, or thereabout, will solve the difficulty. Let this be understood—One Billion Dollars will only make the difficulty One Billion Dollars worse. The purpose of the billion is simply to continue the present methods ¯of railroad management, and it is because of the present methods that we have any railroad difficulties at all.

This is not new. Every business man who thinks, knows it. But it is hard to get out of the ruts.

Going back to dependence on Work and not on Money will make a big difference everywhere, and one of the effects will be the displacement of titles by real jobs. Titles are too often the dress uniform that should be laid aside for field uniform.

442

A foreign observer, in a recent book, has written that in America we are very strong on titles. Everybody seems to be a president of something. There is a story of a President of the United States sojourning in the country and calling up the village post office on the phone. "This is the President," said he. "President of what?" inquired the boy at the other end. In his village there were plenty of presidents, from the town government to the ladies' aid society.

Most men can swing a job, but they are floored by a title. The effect of a title is very peculiar. It has been used too much as a sign of emancipation from work. It is almost equivalent to a sign—"This man has nothing to do but regard himself as important and all others as inferior." Not only has it been injurious to the wearers, but it has had its effect on others as well. There is perhaps no greater single source of personal dissatisfaction among men than the fact that the title-bearers are not always the real leaders. Everybody acknowledges a real leader, a man who is fit to plan and command; but there are mountains of evidence everywhere that the real leaders are not always the titlebearers. And when you do find a real leader who bears a title, you will have to inquire of some one else what his title is. He doesn't boast it.

It has been greatly overdone and business has suffered from it. One of its specially bad effects is such a division of responsibility as amounts to a removal of responsibility altogether. Where responsibility is broken up into many small bits and divided between many departments, each department under its own titular head, who in turn is surrounded by a group bearing their nice sub-titles, it will be difficult to find anyone who really feels responsible.

Everyone knows what "passing the buck" means, and the game must have originated in industrial organizations where the departments simply shove responsibility along.

The health of every organization depends on every member of it, whatever his place, feeling that everything that happens to come to his notice relating to the welfare of the business, is up to him. Railroads have gone to the devil under the eyes of departments that say, "Oh, that doesn't come under our department"—some other department 100 miles away has that in charge, and the interests of the road go to rot and ruin while each department tries to keep within its own narrow limits.

There was formerly a lot of advice given to officials not to hide behind their titles. The very necessity of the advice showed a condition that needed more than advice to correct it. And the correction is just this—abolish the titles. A few may be legally necessary; a few may be useful in directing the public where to do certain kinds of business with the concern, but for the rest the best rule is to get rid of them.

As a matter of fact, the record of business just now is such as to detract very much from the value of titles. No one would boast of being president of a bankrupt bank. Well, business has not been so skillfully steered as to leave much margin for pride in the steersmen. The right to bear titles is to be won all over again; the field is open; past honors are withered; the contest is on anew.

The men who bear titles now and are worth anything are forgetting their titles and are down in the foundations of their business looking for the weak spots. They are back again in the places from which they rose trying to reconstruct from the bottom up. They are leaders in the reconstruction. And when a man is in that work, he doesn't need titles. His work decks him with honors.

Developing Talent in a Small Community

WHEN the passing of city life is discussed, and the rediscovery of the small town is affirmed, one of the commonest questions to arise is this: "What are your small towns going to do for the advantages of the city—the theater and entertainments, for example?" That is the form in which the question usually comes, with an anxiety about the "theater and entertainments."

The question assumes two conditions: First, that a majority of city people attend the theater and other entertainments to such an extent that these institutions have become a necessary element in their lives; and, second, that the theater and entertainments normally fulfill the human desire and need for recreation. Neither of these assumptions is true.

It may be found to be just a question whether the theater is as popular—in point of attendance compared with the population—as it was 50 years ago. The totals are larger, but it may be doubtful that the proportions are. We are not half so theater-mad as some people suppose. The proportion of regular attendants, people who haunt the theater, who are always looking over the list of shows for "a place to go tonight," is not very great. In a certain city where it was assumed that the theater was carrying everything before it and that church attendance was a contemptible little quantity in comparison, it was found that the church with one day a week excelled in drawing power all the legitimate theaters of that city with seven nights a week and two matinees. Leaving the modern theater would not be such a terrible loss, as tens of thousands who have moved to the small town can testify.

And as to the "entertainment" values of the modern commercialized amusement enterprise, the bored audiences of any large city bear eloquently silent wit-

ness. The fresh, blithe wholesomeness which repro-
duces the childishness of human life is lacking. Real
entertainment is lacking and would be undoubtedly
considered as amateurish, so depraved has the public
taste become through bedroom farces and bathroom
dramas. Those who are inoculated with the sordid
sensuousness of the stage would undoubtedly miss that
kind of thing in the small town, just as the drug addict,
locked in a sanitarium, would miss his favorite poison.

However, that still leaves the question where it
was: what are the small towns to do for recreation,
for the indulgence of the play spirit? The play spirit
is a part of life. Its misdirection leads to harm. In
youth especially it is a safeguard, in maturity and
age a recreative force. Temperaments differ, but taken
by and large the human race *will* play.

There are, however, no profits in mere playing.
That is the reason amusements became commercialized.
Instead of play, there arose the spectacle. People
ceased to play, and watched players. Football is a
husky game, but of the thousands of "fans" who shout
for football, how many take the risks of it? The same
is true of baseball; it is called "sport" to sit on the
bleachers and boo or boost. We are mere spectators;
other men do the so-called "playing," and because we
are merely spectators their playing is not Play at all,
but work. There is no community of entertainment
and enjoyment, there is no participation.

In the small town of the future there will be a
Little Theater, and the play instinct of the people
will work itself out through themselves, not by wage
earners called "actors" or "players." There will be
many actors and players, of course, but they will not
be under the commercial domination which every sincerely devoted actor and player feels today. The great
geniuses in the dramatic world will still have their
vogue—or, to state it more accurately, their vogue will
return, because in these sad days dramatic genius is
not necessary. The art of play will be like the art
of music, imported into the community for daily consumption, and not retained in the concert hall as dramatic art is retained in the modern theater. The thea-

ter as a servant of life is being tided over these destructive times by the Little Theater which is springing up in small communities, where the people are developing themselves.

The commercial monopoly of this natural phase of life is being broken. And why not? If, when a writer completes a story, we may all have a copy of it to read in our own homes; why may we not also have the play of the playwright, interpreted in our own community by our own people in our own way? The question has been answered. The flow of people back to the country places is bringing with it these new possibilities. And the benefit is double: the country is being lifted out of the crude and inexpressive practices into which its play exercise degenerated for the lack of inspiration—*and*—the people from the city are being benefited by the wholesome restraint which comes from amusements which have their rise and issue in the same community.

That is a point well worth remembering: when the community shall provide its own recreation and entertainment out of its own resources and by means of its own people, indecency will simply automatically disappear. Why? Well, consider what constitutes the present situation: a theater audience gathers, a few hundreds from a city of half a million or a million people, an audience of strangers. The shield of anonymity protects them all. Young women are there, but they reflect that no one knows them. The people on the stage are from another city, strangers, too. The condition is ideal for putting across anything which common shame would otherwise prevent.

Now, in the home town, with the home folks in the chairs and home folks on the stage, it would simply be impossible—there is not enough brazenness in human nature to permit home folks to enact bedroom farces before home folks, or to revel on the stage in matter that would not be permitted within a thousand miles of any home-town parlor.

That will be one of the effects of a return to the small town, and a necessity of drawing upon the community's creative powers to supply the normal need for entertainment.

447

Of course, the principle extends further. Reference has been made to amusements only because it was involved in the question which has been asked. But the principle applies to every element of community life. City living has made us entirely too dependent. City dwellers will soon lose the art of building fires. Most of the other domestic arts are "lost arts" already. And the art of providing entertainment or amusement for ourselves was about to disappear.

The ideal community is self-sustaining to a greater extent than any community now is. If near flowing water, every community should be self-sustaining in matters of power, heating and lighting. Every community in the midst of an agricultural district should be self-sustaining in the matter of food. The grain grown near by should be milled near by, a sufficient supply reserved and the surplus sent to the great centers of consumption. Each community should be constructed out of materials near at hand, and thus preserve unity with its basic soil. And each community should derive from the wellsprings of its own life those finer inspirations and recreative activities which put a bloom and a flavor upon life. ꞁ It is all contained in that principle known as "self-development." The reward of self-development should be self-sustenance, with the community as well as with the individual.

Parties Are Born, Not Made

POLITICAL parties are like poets, born, not made.
And yet political parties have been found to be
so useful to certain purposes and interests that numerous attempts have been made to manufacture them for
occasion. A political party is a publicity organization,
a semi-legislative organization, often a coercive organization which can render more service to special interests than it can sometimes render to the public.

The people, of course, who are living mostly in the
nursery atmosphere with regard to these things, imagine that a political party is a fellowship of conviction
upon certain principles. That is what it ought to be;
and it is the belief that the political party is just that,
which keeps it going. But the party is other than
that. It would take almost psychic eyes to see just
what the so-called political organizations consist in,
what holds them together, where their ramifications
run, and what type of mind it is that finds congenial
the atmosphere of the "organization." Perhaps it is
the least moral organization in the world, outside the
realm· of those which are distinctively subversive.

And yet, such is the irony of things, this lower
network of organization forms the basis for much
good work. All men who are interested in politics
are not on the inside of the "organization," not at all.
The real motive power of politics, so far as the motion
of the people's mind is concerned, is in the "idea,"
the "issue," the genuine proposals of government policy
and legislative action. But these seldom have their
source in the "organization." They are imported from
the people. All that the "organization," or the "party"
does (the "party" not being the whole number of adherents, but the hierarchy of leaders) ·is to sort out
the possible issues and select the group which they
think will "sell" at the election. Any other set of
issues—even quite opposite issues—would do just· as

449

well if they would "sell." The main object is to keep
the "organization" in offices. The party never gets the
offices; only the "organization" does that. As a whole,
our offices are manned by the prettiest lot of political
gamesters that any country ever saw.

So, there we have the genesis of two evils. One
evil is the existence of a party which has neither political nor moral principle, but which lives for the thing
called "power," using as its steps to power such "issues"
as appeal to popular approval; the other evil is the view
of certain apostles of moral or political principles that
a political organization can be whisked into existence
by publicity agent methods, to serve the purpose of a
certain candidate or a certain principle for a single
election only. So, on the one hand we have the politicians whose object is office, poking around among
possible "issues," ignoring the ones which would require moral courage to espouse, and choosing the ones
that seem ready to ripen in a campaign; and on the
other hand, we have the possessors of progressive
ideas looking for a party to "put them across."

It is a situation which speaks indisputably of the
sorry collapse which has overtaken political effort in
this country.

The "third party" demonstrations have been a sign
of the same condition. The only third parties that ever
had a reasonable and sincere motive and purpose were
never permitted to attain party maturity, because the
older parties took their issues and rode to power upon
them. An illustration of this may be seen in the adop-
tion of the Prohibition Party's most distinctive plank
by both the older parties.

Lately our "third parties" have been launched either
for the purpose of putting a candidate across (which
must be the final judgment on Mr. Roosevelt's effort)
or for the purpose of cementing the radical elements
of political disorder and giving them the respectable
appearance of political organization. Both were vivid
commentaries on the truth that political parties are
born, not made. When the genuine Third Party comes,
it will not be a Third Party at all, but the First Party,
relegating both old parties to secondary status. It

will be a national party, summoning New Era Men from all the old parties, and from no party at all, to do the work which others have neglected.

We do not need a "third party" in the United States, we need a party that is first for Americanism, by which we mean the principle that the fulfillment of life consists in the largest liberation of the creative and constructive forces in nature and in humanity for the service and prosperity of all. Americanism is communistic only in that it stands for a community benefit, instead of an exclusive personal benefit, proceeding from all industrial, financial and political activity. The Old Era was individualistic in its objective. The New Era will remain necessarily individualistic in its method, but will enwrap the whole community in its objective. Communism fails just because it is not communism, because it is individualism of a type that defeats the benefits of individuals, and so cheats also the community of its benefits. We are individuals in action and communists in responsibility.

The division between modern parties is not political, nor philosophical, nor moral any longer, but purely sentimental. All of the old subjects of division are now subjects of scientific examination and adjustment. Locally, politics has come to be a preference of individuals for office: one group wishes to place this man, another wishes to place the other man. A sufficient number of experienced electioneers finds this kind of politics a sport, to give it zest. But, as for the profound political convictions which marked the birth and the vigorous years of the Democratic and Republican parties, they simply don't exist.

The two great parties are being used—that is, the "organization" of them is being used more and more as bulwarks against the changes which must inevitably overtake the stupidities and injustices which have become fastened in our national life. Every old slogan which warns the people against progress as something dangerous finds its hearty echo in the political "organization." The "organization" knows nothing about finance, administration, international relations—literally nothing about anything that affects the heart of our

451

national life—but it is always ready with the cries which sustain the old order of things.

That is where the two old parties are in the greatest danger: they have anchored to an era that is even now growing dim in the distance: unless they cut the cable, they will disappear with it.

And it is just here that we mark the fatal distinction between party and people. The people do not comprise the party. Parties are merely bidders for the people's suffrage. When parties disappear the people remain. This is the logic of third parties. The old parties simply die off the limb like leaves that have ceased to nourish themselves with the life of the tree that bore them. The people grow and keep growing. If parties lag behind, as parties now are lagging behind, a new party is inevitable—not to put a chosen candidate across, not to stampede the people for a new "interest," but as an expression of the life of the people. Parties are the people's political clothing; when the coat grows too small it is discarded.

Milton Keynes UK
Ingram Content Group UK Ltd.
UKHW022116060923
428148UK00006B/361